The Qualified Student

The development of the diploma from universities, and business and engineering colleges, and the universal clamor for the creation of educational certificates in all fields make for the formation of a privileged stratum in bureaus and in offices. Such certificates support their holders' claims for intermarriages with notable families (in business offices people naturally hope for preferment with regard to the chief's daughter), claims to be admitted into the circles that adhere to "codes of honor," claims for a "respectable" remuneration rather than remuneration for work done, claims for assured advancement and old-age insurance, and, above all, claims to monopolize socially and economically advantageous positions. When we hear from all sides the demand for an introduction of regular curricula and special examinations, the reason behind it is, of course, not a suddenly awakened "thirst for education" but the desire for restricting the supply for these positions and their monopolization by the owners of educational certificates.

MAX WEBER

THE QUALIFIED STUDENT

A HISTORY OF SELECTIVE COLLEGE ADMISSION IN AMERICA

Harold S. Wechsler

A WILEY-INTERSCIENCE PUBLICATION

JOHN WILEY & SONS, New York · London · Sydney · Toronto

Library of Congress Cataloging in Publication Data:

Wechsler, Harold S   1946-
  The qualified student.

  "A Wiley-Interscience publication."
  Bibliography: p.
  Includes index.
    1. Universities and colleges—United States—
Admission. I. Title.

LB2351.W36   378.1'05'60973   76–47692
ISBN 0–471–92441–5

Printed in the United States of America

10 9 8 7 6 5 4 3 2 1

For Mom, Dad, and Robert

PREFACE

This book is concerned with methods of student selection to institutions of higher education in the United States. More generally, it discusses the way that college and university reformers employed those methods to inject higher education into the mainstream of American life by regulating access to an increased number of desirable social perquisites.

Far from being simply another area of university policy, admissions is strongly identified with the most important missions of an institution. We all implicitly know that admission to a "good" college considerably improves one's life chances. Often a B.A. from certain colleges opens doors to jobs that would otherwise remain closed. College education is a prerequisite, often legally sanctioned, for access to many professions, including medicine and law. Very often, "contacts" are made in college—contacts that, even if they do not immediately translate into jobs or status, may have an important effect on a career at some future stage. Often, the selection of a marriage partner, with all that can imply about one's future, is made from among one's classmates, or from students at nearby institutions.

As American society became more "credentialized," that is, as the Bachelor of Arts became a prerequisite for an increasing proportion of jobs, the competition for admission to college intensified, and a larger proportion of the population recognized the importance of obtaining a college education. In turn, during this century, many people measured the strength and influence of an institution of higher education by the quality of the student body it attracted and selected. Of course, the research, the community service, and even the entertainment functions of higher education are important determinants of prestige, yet without its selective function, the American university would have developed along far different lines.

The change in 1870 at the University of Michigan from a passive admissions policy (in which each college waited for students to present themselves for examination by the faculty on each campus) to an active policy (in which university faculty members inspected feeder high schools and waived entrance examinations for graduates of schools that passed muster) proved an important turning point in the history of American higher education. Whether completely intended or not (and the evidence shows that it was not completely intended), this change set a precedent for the positive use of admissions policies to facilitate the selection of students destined to play a leadership role in twentieth century America. The need for such measures arose because of the inability of traditional leadership strata to produce enough progeny to fill all the elite positions created by the new industrial order. An impersonal selective mechanism had to be established, and higher education reformers nominated the educational system to perform this function.

At first university reformers ascribed the task of selection to the high schools, and directed their efforts at removing all "artificial" obstacles heretofore imposed by the colleges upon the proper performance of this task. Especially important for this purpose were the movement to gain uniformity among the entrance requirements of each college, and the movement to liberalize the list of subjects acceptable as college preparatory subjects. These efforts had largely succeeded by 1910. At the University of Michigan and throughout the Midwest, the certificate system served as an important mechanism for achieving these purposes. In return for the privilege of inspecting and accrediting (and thereby indirectly supervising) neighboring secondary schools, the universities employing the system granted accredited schools the privilege of certifying their graduates as having completed the college's stated entrance requirements and therefore as eligible for admission. Such certificates would be automatically accepted in lieu of the traditional oral or written entrance examinations in required subjects. The old entrance examinations placed the candidate for admission in the presence of the president and faculty for an exceedingly short period of time—too short to make an intelligent decision. They also placed the college in the position of having to sit on its hands and wait for the students to appear, not a terribly aggressive tactic for institutions that aspired to considerable growth.

Implementation of the certificate system at the University of Michigan and its subsequent development constitute the first subjects explored in this book. At Michigan the system evolved in response to both internal and external needs. Some hoped that it would promote emulation of the German educational system, in which students completed all preparatory work (including the work called "collegiate" in America) in the gymnasium (secondary school), thus permitting the universities to offer advanced instruction exclusively. Others feared that the recent establishment in Michigan of several denominational colleges each with its own preparatory department (in reality, its own secondary school) threatened the University's ability to attract the small number of college bound youth in that state. Given the success of these colleges, the fear of a "godless" university instilled by the state's clergy, general opposition to public higher education from political conservatives, and the absence of a preparatory department on the Michigan campus, the University's faculty and administrative officers viewed the certificate system as necessary to encourage the growth of public secondary education which in turn would insure a constant supply of students to the budding university.

Adoption of the certificate system did not pose an inherent threat to the largely classical curriculum dominant at most colleges in the late nineteenth century. Reformers soon discovered, however, that the plan could be employed to exert considerable leverage toward bringing about the demise of that curriculum, which many saw as a deterrent to college attendance for many potential students. Colleges and universities accepting certificates found themselves vulnerable to complaints that most of their feeder high schools could not offer all the classical preparation the colleges required and also offer courses in other subjects to students not intending to go to college. By 1900, most colleges significantly expanded their list of acceptable entrance subjects to include many disciplines in the latter category. And, engulfed on one side by a liberalized secondary curriculum and on the other by advocates of disciplines just gaining a foothold on the campus (especially the social sciences and the modern languages), collegiate defenders of the classics succumbed fairly rapidly to the new order.

A few important Eastern colleges, however, did not adopt the certificate system. Not that they lacked for reformers—quite the contrary, two of them, Columbia and Harvard, had for presidents prominent men of that breed. But Presidents Barnard, Low, and Butler of Columbia and President Eliot of Harvard could not always convince a faculty called to their posts during a simpler time to go along with every proposal, and it became necessary to employ more complex means to achieve their ends.

Nicholas Murray Butler's role in this reform movement proved critical. His cumulative writings provided an entire blueprint for the development of the university as a central social institution. Perhaps above all others, Butler recognized the importance of college admissions policies for attainment of social goals. He perceived that under the certificate system teachers in constant contact with students for several years could steer toward college not merely the best prepared students but also those who might some day become political, economic, and social leaders. Although the certificate system was never implemented at Columbia, he proved more successful in reforming other aspects of the admissions process, such as securing uniform entrance requirements and establishing a system of uniform entrance examinations under the aegis of the College Entrance Examination Board.

Butler believed that once carefully selected students enrolled in their respective colleges and universities they would not only have to learn the elements of a profession, but also, as the scientist Michael Pupin wrote, "how to play the game," that is, how to come by the personal qualities that average citizens looked for (or at least ought to look for) in their leaders. Coming from diverse backgrounds, these students could not be assumed to have acquired the latter at home; it was up to the colleges to smooth out the rough edges. Butler's emphasis on a combined course of study, in which a student could obtain both a college and a professional degree in a reduced time period, demonstrates his belief in the importance of both kinds of training.

By the second decade of the twentieth century, much had been accomplished toward facilitating the selective function of education. But evidence began to accumulate which indicated that the reformers had gone too far. Where the certificate system was dominant, the high schools certified many students with inadequate academic training. In large measure this practice arose from the need of the high school to accommodate the vocational education movement then in vogue—a movement that required deep commitments of resources and personnel, and that relegated the college preparatory function of the high school to a subordinate position.

In the Eastern urban areas, the same problem arose for quite different reasons. Butler had always assumed that in guiding students toward and away from college, the secondary school would take social as well as academic criteria into account. If a student did not have the personality characteristics of a leader, elite education would be wasted on him or her. But it became increasingly apparent that the public secondary schools of the East were sending on too many students without the capacity to develop leadership traits. Specifically, Butler lamented that at his own Columbia too many eastern European Jewish students—either immigrants themselves, or the children of immigrants—had been admitted to the undergraduate college.

It became necessary for both academic and social reasons for the universities to effect a not-so-graceful withdrawal from their previous liberal admissions policies. After World War I, institutions like Columbia began to scrutinize with care all applicants for admission, and effected major changes in their admission procedures to enable them to take into account social as well as academic criteria. Columbia, soon to be followed by other colleges, announced that it would limit its enrollment to a fraction of those meeting the stated entrance requirements and reserved for itself the final decision as to which students it would accept. In conscious recognition that its policy implied full assumption of the selection function, Columbia announced its new plan as one of selective admission.

Other colleges followed suit. But the lesson learned by the undergraduate colleges of the University of Chicago demonstrated the weakness of a policy of selective admissions. For an admissions policy to be selective, it needed a large applicant pool from which to choose. Where, as in the case of Chicago, enrollments always could have been better, institutions wishing to depict themselves as selective often had to follow a rather tortuous path.

In the public, Midwestern universities, where academic rather than social objections to students led to retrenchment, the goal of newly implemented policies became selection of students with the ability to succeed in college, rather than selection of those with the proper preparation. In some states where the legislature did not permit restrictions on admission of students, large proportions of each entering class would be flunked out at the end of the first semester or year. And yet at the same time a countervailing trend began to emerge. Higher education, advocates of this position argued, could no longer be restricted to an elite; in a democracy a considerable proportion of the citizenry should have the opportunity to avail themselves of advanced schooling. Among the notable landmarks in the furtherance of this position were the opening of the General College at the University of Minnesota in 1930, the Report of the President's Commission on Higher Education in 1948, and the Open Admissions controversy at the City University of New York in 1969.

Implicit in much of this book is an underlying social and ethical question: How legitimate was and is higher education's regulation of social mobility? Public concern over their practices became inevitable once the colleges and universities became social regulators at least between some classes and increasingly between all classes (for that is the logical outcome of universal higher education). In the future, this concern will increase. The challenging of college and professional schools' admissions policies in the courts, and their regulation by the Department of Health, Education, and Welfare, has just begun to augment similar concerns present in legislative halls for several decades. The evidence strongly indicates that in the past colleges and universities at times misused the authority they possessed. And yet, there is a legitimate area of discretion for institutions of higher education in making admissions decisions. Perhaps an examination of the past history of the tension between the university's sphere of authority and the public interest will explain the restraints that each side must impose on itself in the future.

Since the greater part of it consists of four major case studies, this book is open to the charge that instead of being a history of selective admissions, it is a selective history of admissions. The University of Michigan, Columbia University, the University of Chicago, and the City University of New York are not a cross-section of American higher education. These institutions were chosen for study because of the significant innovations that occurred at each of them. These institutions were pacesetters; they did not adopt a new policy simply because some other college down the road had already adopted it. Certainly, careful scrutiny of the admissions policies of other institutions will produce variations on the themes developed here; indeed, the discussion of the University of Chicago demonstrates this. The history of American higher education has not yet been fully written, much less rewritten by the current generation of historians. I hope that studies such as this will inspire further investigation of this subject area.

The emphasis on Columbia University is explained not only by the intrinsic importance of the story, but also by the lack of a recent, comprehensive history of the University or of a full-length biography of its most important president, Nicholas Murray Butler. This book is not designed to fill either gap; however, the text does supply necessary detail that should have been supplied by other sources. The controversy over the Jews and Columbia is infamous. The information provided here will confirm many suspicions and convictions of earlier generations of critics. However, the chapter on the Jews must be read in the context of the entire book. The chapter is not intended to be an exposé; it is an integral part of the history of selective admissions. It should also be mentioned that most of the materials on which that chapter is based are located in the Columbia University files and that the current Columbia administration unhesitatingly provided me with unrestricted access to that information. The Columbia of the 1970s is by no means the Columbia of the 1920s.

Some topics were regrettably omitted from this study because they deserve extensive treatment by themselves. Two such topics are the history of the admission of women to American colleges and universities, and the use of scholarships to influence the composition of the student body. Other topics, such as athletics and admission to college, the admission of alumni children, and the use of influence to secure college admission are important but secondary to the points I wish to make here. I hope that they too will receive the investigation they deserve.

HAROLD S. WECHSLER

The University of Chicago
Chicago, Illinois
August 1976

ACKNOWLEDGMENTS

During the course of manuscript preparation, every author contracts numerous debts that can be acknowledged, but never fully repaid. Not all these debts are intellectual; sometimes a word of encouragement proves as necessary as learning of an unknown source.

Foremost, this book owes its existence to the encouragement and stimulation of Professor Walter Metzger of Columbia University, who supervised the dissertation version submitted to Columbia's Department of History. His help went far beyond what a doctoral candidate could justifiably expect, and whatever merit this book has derives from an effort to meet his expectations.

I greatly profited from the many hours Paul Ritterband spent discussing the contents of this book. His own important research in the sociology of education helped me to place my research in a wider context.

The members of my dissertation defense committee, Lawrence Cremin, Frederick Kerschner, Douglas Sloan, and W. Max Wise, Chairman, offered many significant comments and suggestions.

Several years ago, Professor Lee Benson remarked to me that perhaps the most important part of a graduate education was the opportunity to share ideas with graduate student friends with cognate interests. The help of three such friends was invaluable for this study. David Hammack helped me construct initial formulations of my research problem. His suggestion that I give careful attention to Nicholas Murray Butler's role in higher education reform proved a major turning point in my research. Paula Fass helped clarify many hazy concepts; her own research on student life during the 1920s was of great benefit. Deborah Moore provided me with a detailed critique of the entire manuscript. Almost every page has been improved as a result of her comments.

Deborah and John Gardner, Susan and Brian Greenberg and Lucy Stein-
itz provided many important insights and, equally important, were good
morale boosters at trying times.

Jenna Joselit read the entire manuscript and offered excellent criticism.
Sheila Gordon, Elinor Grumet, David Hoeveler, Steven Ney, James Rosenb-
aum, and Marcia Synnott read and commented on parts of the manuscript.

The archivists at a number of universities and libraries were uniformly
helpful. These libraries included the American Jewish Historical Society, the
University of Chicago Library's Special Collection Department, the Columbia University Files, the Columbia University Libraries' Manuscripts and
Archives Division and its Columbiana division, the University of Illinois Archives, the Michigan Historical Collections, the New York Public Library's
Manuscripts Room, and the New York State Education Department
Library's Manuscripts and Historial Division. The Offices of the Secretary
and the Chancellor of the City University of New York were most cooperative, and T. Edward Hollander and Robert Birnbaum gave me access to the
important collection of documents they had accumulated pertaining to the
Open Admissions controversy. Kenneth Scheffel and Mary Jo Pugh of the
Michigan Historical Collections were of special help. I am greatly indebted
to Marion Jemmott, Helen Burke, Sarah Vos and Joann Williams, and their
staff for their infinite patience with my requests for guidance through the still
largely unexplored Columbia University files.

Many friends and colleagues have been on the receiving end of long dis-
courses on the evolution of contemporary admissions policies. Among those
whose patience, intelligent questions, and comments merit public acknow-
ledgment are Gerald and Peggy Benison, Shirley Blackman, Elizabeth De-
marest, Roger Dixon, Denis DuBois, Eunice Eckstein, Dorotea Furth, Diet-
rich Goldschmidt, Rebecca Greene, Peter Hall, Laurie Hammack, William
Heinbach, Diane Hoeveler, Joanne and Gordon Klein, Sandy and Ira Kra-
kow, Judith and Kenneth Kramer, Barry Mednick, Rena Miller, MacDon-
ald Moore, Moira O'Malley, Eileen, Marvin and Rochelle Pollock, Weslie
Resnick, Steven Schlossman, Bonnie and Joel Schwartz, Dewey Seeto, Nina
Serafino, Charles and Betty Stephenson, Barbara Stolz, Charles R. Trava-
glianti, Rosemarie Vaccaro, John Van de Graff, Pei Wang, Richard Whittemore, and Christina Zawisza.

Muriel Bennett and Dolores Ford expertly typed the final draft of the
manuscript.

My research was supported in part by a Herbert H. Lehman Fellowship
and by a Woodrow Wilson Dissertation Fellowship. I made extensive manuscript revisions and tried out my ideas before a group of stimulating colleagues as a Postdoctoral Fellow at the Institute for Social and Policy Studies,
Yale University. The Association of Professors of Higher Education awarded

the 1975 Dissertation of the Year Prize to the thesis on which this book is based, and I am indebted to Professors Fred Harcleroad and Mary Corcoran, 1974–1975 and 1975–1976 presidents of the Association respectively, Professor Lewis Mayhew, chairman of the Prize Committee, and to Allen Jossey-Bass, J. B. Hefferlin, and G. Kerry Smith of Jossey-Bass, Inc., Publishers, for their many courtesies.

Eric and Christine Valentine, Peter Peirce, Walter Maytham, and Karen Nelson provided strong personal support as well as excellent professional advice throughout the production process.

Finally, I owe my greatest personal debt to my family—to my parents and my brother—for many things, but especially for believing in me and this project. It is to them that this book is dedicated with love.

Contents

The Qualified Student

PART

1

PREREQUISITES

CHAPTER

1

Admission to College and University

The Committee on Admissions of the college, after careful consideration of your application, regrets to inform you that it cannot offer you a place in our entering class next fall. . . . This year the number of qualified applicants far exceeded the number of places available in the Freshman Class, and it was inevitable that many students who were qualified for admission could not be accepted.

A typical rejection letter

The rejection letter is symbolic of higher education's important role in contemporary society. The competition for higher education and the certification it brings is so keen that, as the letter implies, this college can be highly selective about whom it admits. Admissions officers and committees continually make decisions about the kinds of men and women who will occupy key positions in American society years hence.

Many modern rejection letters further imply that educational qualification is only one of several criteria employed in determining the composition of each entering class. Age, sex, geographic origin, race, religion, family background, personality, and participation in extracurricular activities are other criteria that have been or are considered relevant in determining the success of an application.

The mechanism of selective admission, in which admissions officers employ both academic and nonacademic criteria, evolved only after World War I.

3

Throughout the nineteenth century and into the twentieth most American colleges admitted students on the basis of straightforward, published entrance requirements.[1] All students who could demonstrate acceptable mastery of the requirements were admitted; those who just missed were admitted conditionally; those who fell far short were sent home.[2] Students in this last category did not even receive the courtesy of a rejection letter; instead the names of admitted and rejected students were often posted on the college's main door after all applicants completed their entrance examinations.

This book discusses how the modern rejection letter came to be written. The story begins at a time when most colleges were not at all selective in choosing their student bodies.

ADMISSION TO THE OLD TIME COLLEGE

Thirty or forty years ago historians who examined the development of American higher education during the first half of the nineteenth century emphasized its gradual response to the pressures of an egalitarian society and its eventual triumph over the legacy of aristocratic eighteenth century institutions. They examined modifications of an admittedly stale and prescribed undergraduate curriculum suggested by innovators such as Thomas Jefferson at the University of Virginia, Philip Lindsley at the University of Nashville, Eliphalet Nott at Union College, Henry Tappan at the University of Michigan, George Ticknor at Harvard College, and Francis Wayland of Brown University. Applauding advances such as the introduction of scientific courses parallel to the dominant classical course, these historians painted an essentially optimistic picture of increased congruence between college and society.[3]

Revisionist scholarship during the 1950s and 1960s seriously challenged this approach. Historians such as Richard Hofstadter emphasized the increased dominance of educational conservatives and argued that the typical old time college had in fact retrogressed from its eighteenth century predecessors. Its faults, Hofstadter said, did not result from its concentration on the classics per se, "for just such a curriculum had long contributed enormously to the rearing of the best minds in Western society." According to Hofstadter, the real problem was "that it trained no good classicists, that it reduced the study of classics to grammar and linguistics, that it usually failed to convey the spirit of the cultures of antiquity, that it often failed, indeed, even to teach very much Latin." Even more fundamentally, its problems stemmed not from the curriculum but from the instructional method. The recitation system, in which students memorized a text or translation while the instructor merely checked on the correctness of the student's verbal regurgitation, "dulled the minds of students and blunted the edge of faculty scholarship; and such well-educated students as the colleges turned out were usually triumphs of the human spirit over bad methods." [4]

Most recently, a third generation of historians has again reexamined the old time college and pronounced still another, but less clear-cut verdict. In examining data concerning student characteristics at several nineteenth century New England colleges, David F. Allmendinger, Jr. suggests that they may not have been the drab, isolated places previous historians thought they were. Many students mixed freely with members of the surrounding community, and the colleges themselves were closely integrated into their communities' cultural and economic existence. In addition, Allmendinger attributes to these colleges important social functions—they provided an important alternative for socially mobile students who wanted neither to move west nor to remain on the farm. [5]

On several significant aspects of these colleges, however, representatives of the various historical schools can hardly disagree. First, the typical old time college was small. Richard Hofstadter commented that as late as 1839 Randolph-Macon's 98 students typified the enrollment of the average American college, while Kenyon and Waterville (later Colby), each with their 55 students, constituted the modal college. Dartmouth College's 321 students made it the second largest American college, after Harvard. [6]

Next, the majority of these colleges had a strong religious ethos. In the mid-nineteenth century frequent evangelical revivals and town boosterism led to the rapid multiplication of institutions calling themselves colleges. Such schools did not intend to foster the growth of intellect; rather, they assured parents of a proximate institution that would inculcate a "safe" version of Christian dogma. A number of states established state universities, which sectarian interests denounced as "Godless" while they simultaneously attempted to control them. [7] The typical eighteenth century college had been established on the principle of toleration, that is, "nondiscrimination against students and professors of various Protestant denominations [along with] preferment for the denomination of the college founders, that is, those who had founded and sponsored the college and who, more often than not, constituted a majority on the college's governing board." [8] During the nineteenth century such institutions were gradually replaced by colleges that either supported the teachings of a single denomination or (eventually) espoused a secular rationale.

Third, most colleges were locally oriented. They served a constituency within a small radius and opportunities for college preparation were limited. Typically, a student studied for college either under a private instructor's tutelage (a local minister or a graduate of the college might volunteer his services), or at a local academy. Such academies probably provided the "secondary" education for most of those nineteenth century Americans who obtained it. The quality and scope of their offerings varied widely. Some offered education little more advanced than that found at the neighboring common (primary) schools; others offered education more advanced than that of nearby "colleges." Many gave professional and vocational courses, areas largely ignored by the colleges. Only a minority attempted to adjust their curricula to achieve articulation (linkages) with other educational institutions. However, this minority, along with the preparatory departments operated by many colleges, prepared many if not most of those who did attend the nineteenth century college.[9] As the century progressed, public high schools assumed a greater share of the college preparatory function.[10]

The preparatory agent, whatever its form, "fitted" the student for the specific requirements of a local institution, thereby ignoring the difference in entrance requirements existing among most colleges at this time. If a student did not pass the exams of the college for which he had prepared, he could try again at some later date, request his tutor or academy to prepare him for the college of his second choice, seek out another instructor, or give up.

An example of this process may be found in the preparation of Horace Mann, the educational reformer, for admission to Brown early in the nineteenth century. For the youthful Mann, nearby Brown appeared to be a desirable alternative to the prospect of continued back-breaking farm life in his home town of Franklin, Massachusetts. Being alienated from his local minister who usually prepared Franklin boys for Brown's entrance examinations, Mann attempted to master the required Greek and Latin classics on his own. After a year, he enlisted the help of an itinerant schoolmaster who coached him on the Latin sources and on the Greek Testament. The Reverend William Williams, a Baptist preacher in a neighboring town, instructed Mann in mathematics. Mann was one of dozens of boys Williams helped prepare for admission to his alma mater.[11]

Many colleges, especially those not blessed with neighboring preparatory agencies, established their own in the form of college preparatory departments. Such departments sometimes aroused faculty resentment on the grounds that they had been recruited to offer college level instruction. Their persistence can be attributed to their fulfillment of an important need. Proximity did not imply articulation; an academy may not have had the resources to prepare a small number of students for a nearby college, and may in fact have viewed itself as that college's competitor. From the colleges' point of view, it did not make sense to permit outside institutions to prepare students and thus to receive those students' precious tuition dollars. Although most colleges phased out their preparatory departments by the end of the century, the need for tuition dollars had a continued effect on the mastery levels set for entrance.

Tuition was, in fact, the fourth and last important characteristic of the old time college. Tuition formed a large proportion of the college's income, since private endowments and public appropriations usually proved highly inadequate. Because the incremental cost of educating an additional student was low relative to the fixed costs (salaries, building maintenance, etc.), the student body's size had a direct bearing on the college's financial solvency. Colleges competed with one another as well as with some academies for the students who wished advanced education. Thus, college presidents and boards of trustees determined tuition rates by balancing financial needs with the need to attract potential students away from competitors. Similarly, they determined the mastery level for college admission by balancing these needs with a desire to maintain a certain quality of education.[12] To most nineteenth century college presidents, these comprised the main factors that seemed relevant to an admissions policy.

Just before the start of the fall semester, the prospective freshman of a typical old time college appeared at a stated time in the office of the college president. He would be questioned by the president and perhaps by some faculty members on his previous studies in Greek, Latin, and mathematics. The decision to admit a student with or without conditions or to reject him entirely was determined by the quality of his answers, the college's financial picture, and not infrequently on the kindliness of a faculty member. Again Horace Mann's example is instructive. In the fall of his twentieth year, Mann presented himself for examination before Brown's president, Asa Messer. Messer, says Mann's biographer Jonathan Messerli, "examined him on the Greek Testament, attempting to be helpful, choosing selections which Mann had most recently reviewed." This completed, two faculty members joined them and requested Mann to translate selections from Vergil and Cicero. Finally Mann translated an English paragraph into correct Latin prose. After presenting letters attesting to his good moral character, Mann left the room. The young man's impressive performance on the examinations and Brown's unusual need for students in the aftermath of the War of 1812 prompted Messer to admit Mann to sophomore standing.[13]

One wonders whether these entrance examinations proved more or less traumatic than those given to late nineteenth century applicants. Gradually, as the colleges required additional subjects for admission, more and more of them switched to written entrance examinations. These may have been somewhat less formidable to the student than the battery of oral proficiency tests they replaced, but the relative impersonality of the newer system may very well have worked against many candidates, and the increase in required subjects meant that the ordeal was spread out over several days. Whatever their relative traumas, all nineteenth century college aspirants probably could have thought of many ways in which they would have rather spent their time.

The twentieth century practices of limiting enrollment to a fraction of the academically qualified candidates and of rejecting some students with superior academic qualifications in favor of others with more desirable nonacademic attributes were inconceivable to the old time college president. Such luxuries were reserved for the modern college and university.

HIGHER EDUCATION IN A CHANGING SOCIETY

Many commentators have noted that most communities experience a major disruption in the course of their modernization. Although the terminology and even the definitions of the "before" and "after" stages vary (Tonnies's Gemeinschaft and Gesellschaft, Cooley's primary and secondary groups, Sorokin's familistic and contractual relationships, and Weber's traditional and rational societies), they all identify impersonal, rational, and formal relationships, as opposed to personal, nonrational, and affective relationships as characteristic of modern society.[14] That is, the emergence of society from community occurs when the simple relationships that traditionally dominated both public and private spheres of action and that rendered the boundaries of those spheres amorphous are supplemented by other complex relationships necessary for effective social action in rational, bureaucratic settings.

In late nineteenth century America, Robert Wiebe argues, the old American social fabric based on relatively autonomous "island communities" was replaced by an industrial urban order that transcended individual localities.[15] Business consolidations may be viewed as both a symbol and a cause of this change. Horizontal (merger of competing firms performing the same function) and vertical (merger of firms performing complementary functions) combinations created national industries that required centralized authority for centralized decision-making.[16] Emphasis shifted from the actual attainment of any specific result to the establishment of procedures for routine attainment of desired results. This emphasis on means rather than on ends prompted, as Fritz Machlup says, "A quite remarkable increase in the division of labor between pure 'brain work' and largely physical performance." [17] Machlup discerned this change in the political as well as the economic sphere; it has also occurred in other social institutions including the church, the military, and even sports.

The process of centralization and bureaucratization of decision-making placed a premium on the growth of knowledge, leading in the late nineteenth century to increased status for the professions (including the academic profession). Walter Metzger succinctly describes the function of the professions; they "ease the problems caused by the relentless growth of knowledge." As a set of interrelated propositions, he suggests

that as the amount of knowledge increases, so too does the relative amount of igno-
rance, for each man can know only a decreasing fraction of what can be known: that
knowledge, as it grows more specialized, also tends to grow more potent, more capable
of being used for ill or good; that, as a consequence there comes into being not a mass
society but a lay society—a society, that is, in which each is potentially at the mercy
of someone more thoroughly in the know; that these mutual dependencies grow more
dangerous as knowledge, which had once been held by holy men, kin and neighbors,
passes into the hands of strangers, and as the customary means of assuring its benign
uses—parental love, communal sanctions, religious discipline—tend increasingly not
to work.[18]

Contemporaries who realized that American society required greater technical expertise lamented that although this nation was well endowed with
educational institutions, few contributed to the development of new knowledge or to the ethics of its guardianship. The growth of graduate divisions at
some colleges and the establishment of new institutions emphasizing postbac-
calaureate instruction (the opening of Johns Hopkins in 1876 being most
noteworthy) was encouraging; nevertheless the incorporation of the professional school into the nascent university structure proved decisive. Noting the
high degree of professional self-consciousness existing at many universities
even before the beginning of this century, Robert Wiebe commented, "By
1900 they [the universities] held an unquestioned power to legitimize, for no
new profession felt complete—or scientific—without its distinct academic
curriculum; they provided centers for philosophizing and propagandizing;
and they inculcated apprentices with the proper values and goals."[19]

Complementing the growth in knowledge production was a corresponding
growth in knowledge dissemination. Of course, in a sense this had been the
traditional function of the college, but whereas the purpose of instruction in
the past had been the disciplining of the mind, now the knowledge imparted
was itself valuable. Whereas an instructor at an old time college usually
taught adolescents more interested in outwitting their teacher than in learning from him, a professor at, say, the University of Wisconsin in 1905 often
had many audiences ready to hear his message: government officials, business
managers, trade and professional associations, students, and the lay public.[20]
By placing primary responsibility for the generation, dissemination, and ethical use of knowledge at the university, Americans hoped to assure that general research would be undertaken in all important subject areas and that the
personnel and resources would be available for the application of general
knowledge to the specific problems that constantly arose.

It should not, however, be inferred that late nineteenth century institutions
of higher education grew simply in *response* to social demands. Quite the
contrary: often university officials made the most optimistic predictions about

the role of the university in modern society, and many, legitimizing their initiatives by citing "social demands," offered bold proposals for their institutions. Certainly, the gradual nineteenth century shift from clerical to lay control of university and college governing bodies gives superficial credence to a "passive responsiveness" interpretation. A trustee or other benefactor (here defined as a representative of "Society") might have endowed a chair on the condition that he be permitted to choose the general subject matter to be covered and on occasion the particular professor. Trustees could have allocated a disproportionate amount of resources to divisions in which research and instruction generated an obvious and immediate payoff.[21] On the other hand, some university presidents might have defined a need and sought out donors. The best university presidents understood that their institution had to support, yet stand apart from, the larger society; that it had to perform both an instrumental and a critical function. Early in the twentieth century, Thorstein Veblen criticized America's captains of erudition for succumbing to the demands of the financial and industrial order. In reality, the process was far more complex; presidents sometimes shielded faculty members from trustees and others who would not have tolerated some of their undertakings, had they known of them. Sometimes, an institution's trustees performed a similar function vis-à-vis a state legislature.[22]

It was consistent with society's continuous demand for knowledge that a university president was concerned not only with the quality of knowledge production and dissemination at any given time, but also with the perpetuation of that quality. Further, several "strong men of the academic revolution" realized that as Americans began to accept expertise as a legitimate basis of authority they would look to their institutions of higher education to produce such leaders.[23] Presidents saw student recruitment as a vital step in the performance of these functions, and nowhere was the university's activist orientation better displayed than in this area.

STUDENT RECRUITMENT, ADMISSIONS POLICIES, AND ENTRANCE REQUIREMENTS

A continuous output from America's universities required continuous inputs, most especially of students. But before enrollments could be significantly increased, an initial expansion of plant was usually necessary, and that proved impossible as long as higher education remained largely dependent on tuition fees. Beginning after the Civil War, presidents of public colleges lobbied in their state capitals for ongoing financial aid to replace the sporadic grants they had previously received. Private benefactors, especially those who had amassed considerable fortunes as a result of industrialization, offered large endowments.

curriculum best prepared all students, including those who wished to continue with their professional studies.[27] Reformers' attacks on entrance requirements were viewed as part of a general attack on the classical curriculum. If Greek and Latin were abolished as required courses for entrance, instruction in these subjects would have to commence on the elementary level—precisely what the classicists did not want. They forecasted that removal of Greek and Latin entrance requirements would lead to abolition of required college level work in those subjects, and that as a result, the college would fail in its mission to instill the habit of discipline in its students.

In the last third of the nineteenth century, the University of Michigan undertook a series of reforms that related to most of these themes and that culminated in their ultimate synthesis at Columbia University. We first turn to the implementation of the certificate system at Michigan, which marks higher education's transition from passive to active student recruitment and, by extension, from passive to active participation in the work of modern society.

NOTES TO CHAPTER 1
ADMISSION TO COLLEGE AND UNIVERSITY

1. Most catalogues stipulated that applicants must be of good moral character, but few were ever excluded under this provision.

2. Students admitted on condition were expected to make up their deficiencies during their freshman year.

3. See R. Freeman Butts, *The College Charts Its Course: Historical Conceptions and Current Proposals* (New York, McGraw-Hill, 1939). For useful anthologies of reformers' writings, see Theodore Rawson Crane, ed., *The Colleges and The Public, 1787–1862* (New York, Bureau of Publications, Teachers College, 1963), and Richard Hofstadter and Wilson Smith, eds., *American Higher Education: A Documentary History* vol. 1 (Chicago and London, University of Chicago Press, 1961), parts III and IV.

4. Richard Hofstadter, *Academic Freedom in the Age of the College* (New York and London, Columbia University Press, 1961 [1955]), pp. 228–229. See also Frederick Rudolph, *The American College and University: A History* (New York, Vintage Books, 1962), pp. 86–109. When the student reached his senior year, this routine was finally broken by instruction, almost always offered by the college president, in "moral and intellectual philosophy." The development of proper character traits, especially piety, and the inculcation of discipline being the primary purposes of the college, this course attempted to reconcile traditional Christian dogma with knowledge generated by secular scholarship since the scientific revolution and the Enlightenment (see Rudolph, *The American College,* pp. 140–141).

5. See David F. Allmendinger, Jr., *Paupers and Scholars: The Transformation of Student Life in Nineteenth-Century New England* (New York, St. Martin's Press, 1975) and David B. Potts, "Students and the Social History of American Higher Education," *History of Education Quarterly* (Fall, 1975), 15:317–327. The college's extracurriculum made college life more bearable (see Rudolph, *The American College,* pp. 136–155).

6. Hofstadter, *Academic Freedom,* p. 222.

7. The classic work on the establishment of colleges in these years is Donald G. Tewksbury, *The Founding of American Colleges and Universities Before the Civil War* (New York, Teachers College, 1932). Natalie A. Naylor, "The Ante-Bellum College Movement: A Reappraisal of Tewksbury's Founding of American Colleges and Universities," *History of Education Quarterly* (Fall, 1973), 13:261–274, contains some important qualifications. David B. Potts, "American Colleges in the Nineteenth Century: From Localism to Denominationalism," *History of Education Quarterly* (Winter, 1971), 11:369–373, argues that collegiate affiliations with specific denominations were weaker in the early part of the century than in the latter. See also Theodore R. Crane, "To Build an American University," in Crane, *The Colleges*, pp. 1–33, and Rudolph, *The American College*, pp. 68–85.

8. Jurgen Herbst, "The Eighteenth Century Origins of the Split Between Private and Public Higher Education in the United States," *History of Education Quarterly* (Fall, 1975), 15:274.

9. On academies see Theodore Sizer, *The Age of the Academies* (New York, Bureau of Publications, Teachers College, 1964).

10. On the early high school see Michael B. Katz, *The Irony of Early School Reform: Educational Innovation in Mid-Nineteenth Century Massachusetts* (Boston, Beacon Press, 1968), part I.

11. Jonathan Messerli, *Horace Mann: A Biography* (New York, Knopf, 1972), pp. 26–27.

12. See Rudolph, *The American College*, pp. 177–200.

13. Messerli, *Horace Mann*, pp. 30–31.

14. See John C. McKinney, in collaboration with Charles P. Loomis, "The Application of Gemeinschaft and Gesellschaft as Related to Other Typologies," in Ferdinand Tonnies, *Community and Society (Gemeinschaft and Gesellschaft)*, Charles P. Loomis, trans. and ed. (New York, Harper Torchbooks, 1963), pp. 12–23.

15. Robert H. Wiebe, *The Search for Order: 1877–1920* (New York, Hill and Wang, 1967).

16. See Alfred D. Chandler, Jr., "The Beginnings of 'Big Business' in American Industry," *Business History Review* (Spring, 1959), 33:1–30, and his *Strategy and Structure: Chapters in the History of the Industrial Enterprise* (Cambridge, MIT Press, 1962).

17. Fritz Machlup, *The Production and Distribution of Knowledge in the United States* (Princeton, Princeton University Press, 1962), p. 6.

18. Walter P. Metzger, "What Is a Profession?" in Program of General and Continuing Education in the Humanities, Columbia University, *Seminar Reports* (September 18, 1975), vol. 3, no. 1, pp. 8–9.

19. Wiebe, *The Search*, p. 121.

20. See Lincoln Steffens, "Sending a State to College," *American Magazine* (February, 1909) 68:350–363; Charles McCarthy, *The Wisconsin Idea* (New York, Macmillan, 1912), and Laurence R. Veysey, *The Emergence of the American University* (Chicago and London, University of Chicago Press, 1965), pp. 107–109.

21. Thorstein Veblen, *The Higher Learning in America: A Memorandum on the Conduct of Universities by Businessmen* (New York, Sagamore Press 1957 [1918]).

22. Walter P. Metzger, *Academic Freedom in the Age of the University* (New York and London, Columbia University Press, 1961 [1955]), pp. 177–193.

23. The phrase in quotation marks is the title of David F. Allmendinger, Jr.'s review essay, "Strong Men of the Academic Revolution," *History of Education Quarterly* (Winter, 1973), 13:415–425.

24. On the common school and nineteenth century educational reform see Lawrence A. Cremin, *The American Common School: An Historic Conception* (New York, Bureau of Publications, Teachers College, 1951); Messerli, *Horace Mann*; and David B. Tyack, *The One Best System:*

A History of American Urban Education (Cambridge, Harvard University Press, 1974). See also R. Freeman Butts, "Public Education and Political Community," *History of Education Quarterly* (Summer, 1974), 14:165–183. His bibliography is useful.

25. See "The Morrill Act, 1862," in Hofstadter and Smith, *American Higher Education*, 2:568–569.

26. Charles W. Eliot, "The Gap Between the Elementary Schools and the Colleges," *National Educational Association Journal of Proceedings and Addresses*, 1890:522–533.

27. For the most articulate statement of this position, see "The Yale Report of 1828" in Hofstadter and Smith, *American Higher Education* 1:275–291.

CHAPTER

2

Systems and Students:
The University of Michigan
and Certificates

Historians of American higher education have frequently noted that most of our major nineteenth century institutions chose pastoral settings removed as far as practical from urban centers. Thus Urbana, not Chicago, became the location for the University of Illinois; Columbia, not St. Louis, for the University of Missouri; Berkeley, not San Francisco, for the University of California; Madison, not Milwaukee, for the University of Wisconsin; and Ann Arbor, not Detroit, for the University of Michigan. This aversion to urban settings may have resulted from a generalized distaste for American cities by American intellectuals.[1] But since most nineteenth century American intellectuals did not have college affiliations, the more probable reason was the desire of presidents and trustees to protect their young charges from the supposed and real evils of city life, and perhaps also from the acquisition of too many "alien" ideas.

Although campus insularity could not ward off the outside world indefinitely, it could hinder a university's attempts to reach beyond its pastoral setting. The University of Michigan experienced considerable ferment over questions relating to student admission in the years after the Civil War. The

16

public was preoccupied with the University's policy of refusing to admit women. Politicians and the press maintained a chorus of criticism until in 1870 the faculty reluctantly voted to reverse its policy. Nevertheless, resistance persisted in several quarters after the policy change.[2]

The debates in 1869 and 1870 over the admission of women and over selection of a permanent president, as well as controversies over the University's religious orientation and its finances, obscured the University's adoption of an initiative designed to improve its relations with the state's other public educational institutions. In 1870, the University waived the traditional entrance examinations for students from accredited (that is, inspected) high schools. Principals at such high schools could issue certificates that attested to a student's completion of the University's entrance requirements. Students bearing such certificates were automatically admitted to the freshman class. In effectively placing authority for selection of its student body in the state's public high schools, Michigan's authorities took a calculated risk. They decided that the possibility of abuse was outweighed by the opportunity to obtain a central role for the institution in the state's educational development, the elevation of academic standards, as well as a constant (and even a growing) supply of students. As the system gradually proved its worth, other colleges instituted similar programs. Ultimately, admission by certificate became the most popular method of college admission in the United States.[3] And in the long run it prompted others with even greater consciousness of the importance of education's selective function to give serious attention to the mechanics of college entrance.

THE SETTING:
EARLY HISTORY OF THE UNIVERSITY

That such an innovation should have taken place at Michigan is not surprising in light of the University's earlier history. Michigan was established as part of a comprehensive scheme for public education adopted by the Michigan Legislature soon after the state's admission to the Union in 1837. Superintendent of Public Instruction John D. Pierce and Isaac Crary, who wrote the education article in the Michigan constitution, employed the Prussian educational model which emphasized state responsibility for education at all levels of instruction. A Board of Regents of the University was appointed in the spring of 1837. In the fall of 1841, the University offered collegiate level instruction for the first time. For the next decade, it functioned without a president. Instead the Regents issued administrative directives and the faculty annually elected a "presiding officer" from among its own membership. The state Constitution of 1850 finally provided for a President of the University who would attend meetings of the Board of Regents and who would act as the University's chief executive officer.

After a lengthy search and not without opposition, the Regents elected Henry Philip Tappan the University's first president in 1852. A noted philosopher, Tappan established new university departments including the Law School and the Department of Civil Engineering. His most important contribution consisted of his ability to give the fledgling university purpose and direction. Tappan shared Superintendent Pierce's vision of an integrated system of public education, and believed this could best be accomplished by an initial emphasis on higher education and the subsequent strengthening of the lower levels as the University's influence spread. Tappan devoted much energy to building up the educative and research functions of the University. He solicited funds for the construction of an astronomical observatory, increased the library and museum collections, and appointed scholars of note to fill faculty vacancies.[4]

For both academic and religious reasons, the Regents ousted Tappan from the presidency in 1863. His successor, Reverend Erastus O. Haven, spent six unhappy years in office. During his tenure he managed to secure regular state funding for the University, but eventually the continued controversy over Tappan's removal, and the debates over the admission of women and over denominationalism at the University took their toll. When in 1869 Haven was offered the presidency of the newly founded Northwestern University he quickly accepted. Michigan's student body grew at a constant but slow pace during the sixties, but Haven's preoccupation with other matters and his lack of pedagogical vision forestalled curricular innovations.[5] Haven's two successors, Acting President Henry Simmons Frieze and President James Burrill Angell, resumed the expansion of the educative function with renewed vigor.

FRIEZE AND THE GERMAN INFLUENCE

Henry S. Frieze served as acting president during the interregnum between Haven and Angell from 1870 through 1871.[6] He used this opportunity to secure consideration and adoption of his plan for admission of students on certificate. Born in 1817 and raised in Rhode Island, Frieze was graduated from Francis Wayland's Brown and subsequently taught Latin there. Ironically, one of his students was James Burrill Angell. He then accepted a position at Michigan where he remained for the rest of his life. Angell subsequently wrote that exposure to Wayland, a prominent early reformer of higher education, had not sufficed to enlist the Latin scholar to the cause of reform. Frieze's discussions with Tappan at Michigan and his trip to Germany in 1854, which permitted firsthand observation of German educational practices, proved persuasive.[7]

Specifically, Frieze became convinced of the practicality of a state supported educational system in which coordination would be obtained by the supervision of the lower levels by the higher ones. He further noted that German teachers were appointed by a collegium composed mostly of educators from the higher levels who were in turn appointed by the duke of a state or by his ministers. The collegium visited each school four times a year and determined the curriculum to be taught and the textbooks to be used. Finally, the schools' moral influence impressed Frieze. He concluded that education rather than the church would prove decisive for the maintenance of social order.[8]

Actually, Frieze had not perceived all the complexities of the German educational system. Three kinds of secondary schools coexisted in Germany: the gymnasium, which offered a classical course to the upper social classes; the realschule; and the volksschule, both of which offered a more modern curriculum to those of lower social standing. German educators were not optimistic about the ability of education to become the basis for moral authority. Those associated with the gymnasia feared that their rivals, the realschulen with their philosophy of educational moderism, were the most dangerous enemies of both religion and authority.

After 1834, German universities accepted without examination students granted the Abitur by the gymnasia. This practice became the model for the American certificate system. But serious differences existed between these two programs. In Germany, the state awarded the Abitur through the gymnasia to those passing examinations offered by the Minister of Culture. In effect, by accepting the Abitur as a certificate of admission, the universities permitted their entrance requirements and standards to be determined by the state.[9] In Michigan and in most other states, the University inspected the high schools, prescribed specific entrance requirements, and awarded certificate privileges. Issuance of a certificate by a high school did not imply passage of a formal series of state-sponsored examinations at the end of the secondary course.[10] College authorities registered objections when state Departments of Education were empowered to grant certificate privileges to secondary schools, as happened in Indiana in 1873.

In Germany, acceptance of the Abitur for university admission helped perpetuate the privileges of certain classes. When it became a requirement for admission, only those who could gain acceptance to the gymnasium could hope to secure any higher education. Frieze had no intention of establishing in Michigan an educational system stratified along social or economic lines. In fact, both he and President Angell favored universal public secondary education.[11] However both were generally impressed with the high level of instruction offered by the German university, a level thought possible because the gymnasia assumed all responsibility for preparatory work. The two presidents believed that by selective adaptation of certain features of the German system, beginning instruction could be relegated to the high schools, permitting the University to commence instruction on a more advanced level. They also believed that the certificate system could *widen* educational opportunity in the state—the opposite of the German experience.

CERTIFICATION AND ENROLLMENTS

In 1870, the Michigan faculty unanimously adopted the certificate system of admission despite lack of any American precedent and despite lack of understanding of the German example by most of the faculty. This unanimity cannot be explained by a general desire to become a Germanic university. Nor was it the belief held by some like Frieze that the moral authority previously lodged in the church might be transferred to education. For the faculty majority, the certificate system had the potential for solving a basic problem faced by most American colleges in the nineteenth century—the need to maintain and if possible to increase enrollments.

Agitation for a reliable source of students remained relatively low during the 1850s, but it intensified during and after the Civil War. Although there was room for more, the University's student population grew from 72 students in 1849–1850 to 430 students in 1858–1859. Then the rate of increase began to decline and finally so did the enrollment level. Infighting between Tappan, the Regents, and the faculty shortened the vision of even the most farsighted advocates of growth.[12] With the removal of both Tappan and the Regents hostile to him in 1863, the faculty under Haven began to consider the problem of student enrollment.

Lack of a preparatory department that could offer the precise instruction desired by faculty members for those aspiring to enter the University made the problem more critical at Michigan than at neighboring state universities. During the pre-Tappan years, the University supported a series of branch schools throughout the state. These branches, the brainchild of Superintendent Pierce, were authorized by the Board of Regents in 1837, and the first branch opened in Pontiac soon after. Pierce envisioned that each branch would offer three courses, including a college preparatory curriculum. The branches remained in constant financial difficulty—so much so that in 1846 the Regents withdrew their financial support and asked the communities in which the branches were located to bear the burden. Most localities proved unable to do this and the branches began to fail. President Tappan, interestingly, nailed the last nail in their coffins when he remarked in his inaugural address that the branches did not fit in with his conception of the true nature of the university. He said this despite the obvious parallel between the branches and the German gymnasia. However, Tappan had plans for the University itself and may have feared that additional outlays for the branches would have come at the expense of growth in more important directions.[13]

There is no evidence that the Michigan faculty seriously considered establishment of a preparatory department at any time after Tappan's inauguration. Although such departments were recognized as serving an important purpose wherever no alternative agency for college preparation existed, by the 1860s and 1870s embarkation upon such a course would have seemed regressive to the faculty and to sister institutions. The University of Minnesota, for example, had offered preparatory instruction when it opened in 1867, but gradually delegated it to lower educational levels as they proved capable of assuming the burden. The University's long-range goal included entrusting some collegiate level instruction to the high schools. Henry Folwell, Minnesota's President, announced:

It is an intended effect of the plan of organization then, to build up in every city and large village, at least, of the State, an institution of quasi-collegiate rank, officered by teachers of high culture, which shall retain the youths of their respective neighborhoods,—that is, those of them who are put on a course of higher education, under the wholesome discipline of a well conducted school, til they are ready for University work and University life. All this time, the youth are living at home, where they ought to be.[14]

Acting President Frieze shared this goal. He wrote that the University could perform its proper mission if university and local authorities cooperated so that the public high schools would elevate and increase their courses of study, if those courses were properly arranged, and if a connected and progressive system could evolve from them. Frieze said that conditions within the state favored the growth of such a system.[15]

After the collapse of the branches in the late 1840s, several communities supported union schools, offering secondary education. Their growth after the Civil War led Frieze to urge University sponsorship for them in the hope that they would fill the gap between the common schools and the University. He thought that establishment of a certificate system involving these schools would facilitate the emergence of a statewide system of public secondary education that would identify, prepare, and certify for University admission students of high academic caliber.[16] He consciously excluded private and denominational schools from his plans since these institutions and the sectarian groups that sponsored them comprised the core of opposition of University growth.

COMPETITION OF PRIVATE
AND DENOMINATIONAL SCHOOLS

Public secondary education was widely opposed during the third quarter of the nineteenth century. Many questioned the need for secondary and college education for even the most difficult jobs. Charles E. Stuart, a former United

States Senator from Michigan and a plaintiff in the Kalamazoo case (in which expenditure of state funds for secondary education was found constitutional), wrote that a thorough English (grammar school) education was sufficient for the performance of all jobs from constable to President of the United States and for management of any business in the country, no matter how large. He argued that too much money was already being spent for public education, a service that private institutions could perform better and cheaper.[17]

To those concerned with the preservation of moral and religious traditions, public secondary education posed a formidable threat. Many thought that the major challenges to a child's faith came during the secondary school years. Elementary education was concerned with drill in basic skills; there was little chance that heretical notions could be accidentally learned. Because a child began to "think" during his secondary school years, prudence dictated that he or she be kept at home and sent to a school where his or her creed would be reinforced, not questioned. Popular thought was ambivalent about the "safety" of the University. Many thought it "Godless" and would only send their children to denominational colleges. Others believed that by the college years the child's beliefs were sufficiently formed to withstand attacks that might emerge in the university environment. In any case, those desiring certain types of instruction, especially scientific instruction, had little choice.[18]

University of Michigan authorities never considered their institution's mission to be hostile to religion in general or to any denomination in particular. During its early history the University's Board of Regents contained members of each of the state's major denominations. The hope was that a heterogeneous Board would serve as a guarantee against both secularism and narrow sectarianism and assure the support of all religious denominations.[19] Similarly, during the University's first two decades faculty appointments were expected to reflect a balance between the major factions.[20]

Because the University had been established before the appearance of any "safe" denominational colleges, it was carefully scrutinized for any evidence of "Godlessness." In 1869 a controversy arose when President Haven, a Methodist, preached a sermon at a Unitarian church. One newspaper puzzled over Haven's motives, stating that the President had never before been tinctured with Unitarianism and that any possible beneficial effect he may have had on "outsiders" was far outweighed by the loss of Christian influence over those placed in his care as head of a great university.[21] In 1873, when a local newspaper publisher, Stephen B. McCracken, charged the University with sectarianism, the institution's successful defense raised suspicions that its brand of nonsectarianism might be equivalent to heresy or atheism.[22]

Eventually each denomination established its own college, each with a preparatory department, and most showed signs of growth after the Civil War, especially in those preparatory departments. Kalamazoo College, opened by the Baptists in 1855, experienced an increase in preparatory department enrollment from 38 students in 1864–1865 to 175 in 1870–1871. Albion College, founded by the Methodists, experienced fluctuating enrollment after the Civil War, but its student body was never inconsiderable. In 1866, for example, 49 students were enrolled in the college course, 234 in the preparatory department, and 51 in music and art.[23] The college that the Presbyterians attempted to establish at Marshall during the late 1830s soon closed for financial and other reasons. Later they lent some support to "undenominational" Olivet College. Hillsdale College, opened by the Freewill Baptists in 1855, had consistently high enrollments and by the 1880s was the state's largest denominational college. Adrian College, founded by the Wesleyan Methodists in 1845, had its growth curtailed by financial troubles and sectarian strife.[24]

As each new college opened, the sponsoring denomination began to view the University as a competitor instead of as an institution over which influence must be exerted. University authorities were convinced by the rise of such institutions of the impracticality of depending on private and denominational preparatory schools for students. Parents who desired sectarian education for their children could now obtain it on the college level. If such children were sent to the preparatory department of a denominational college, admission to the college department would be accomplished in due course.

Frieze and others at Michigan hoped to influence public secondary education in the same way that the denominational colleges influenced their preparatory departments. Just as the curriculum of the denominational college's preparatory department led directly into the work of the college, the curriculum of the public high school would lead directly into the work of the University. He asked the state Legislature to support the high schools, arguing that if secondary education were left exclusively to local initiative the result would be unstable and unequal instruction.[25]

Frieze also asked Michigan's faculty to support the certificate system as a device for insuring the responsiveness of the secondary schools to University initiatives. In exchange for a waiver of entrance examinations, the University would be assured that students in accredited high schools all over the state prepared for University work, rather than for denominational education. Academic excellence would be maintained by annual inspection of all high schools granted certificate privileges. In the long run the system could be hoped to elevate the standard of University instruction, perhaps to a level comparable to that offered by the best European universities, by permitting the University gradually to require more advanced work for high school certification. All understood that the denominational colleges would attempt to recruit students from the public high schools. One schoolmaster informed President Angell that people in his area subjected the University to considerable criticism for irreligious tendencies and that eight Christian seniors were weighing the advantages of a University education against pressures exerted on them to attend denominational colleges. University authorities believed that the certificate system would give their institution a decisive advantage in the competition for such students.[26]

"The courage of most college faculties or corporations wavers when a considerable number of applicants for entrance are about to be cut off by a new rule," said incoming President Angell as the faculty embarked on stiffer University entrance requirements in 1871. If the University were ever to become more than "a gymnasium, scarcely of the first rank," it was necessary to insure for the benefit of a nervous faculty a visible source of students. The certificate system was intended to facilitate entrance to the University, at the same time permitting "earnest and judicious efforts to push the work of the preparatory schools to a higher and higher plane."[27]

CERTIFICATION IMPLEMENTED:
THE EARLY YEARS

The certificate system was formally implemented at Michigan upon recommendation of a faculty committee charged with determining "if some system cannot be devised by which the high schools of the state can be brought into connection with the University."[28] The introduction of this formal statement into the University catalogue in 1871 marked its actual beginning:

Special Notice to Preparatory Schools: Whenever the Faculty shall be satisfied that the preparatory course in any school is conducted by a sufficient number of competent instructors, and has been brought up fully to the foregoing requirements, the diploma of such schools, certifying that the holder has completed the preparatory course and sustained the examination in the same, shall entitle the candidate to be admitted to the University without further examination.[29]

Michigan continued to offer the traditional entrance examinations despite the adoption of the new policy. They were necessary so as not to deny access to students from nonaccredited high schools and from out of state, and also to students from certified high schools who either did not meet the University's entrance requirements (in which case they could be admitted conditionally) or who did not receive the recommendation of their principal. For the remainder of the century, a significant but decreasing number of applicants continued to be admitted by taking these examinations. By the early twentieth century, most Michigan high schools had been accredited by the University, and many more out of state schools were accredited under a regional cooperative agreement. But traditional entrance examinations remained, at Michigan as at most other colleges employing the certificate system, as an alternate though increasingly unused method of admission.

School inspections were annually conducted upon request of the high school to determine if the college preparatory program met the University's published entrance requirements. In the plan's first year of operation, University committees visited Adrian, Ann Arbor, Detroit, Flint, Jackson, and Kalamazoo High Schools, all public schools located in the southern part of the state. The entire faculty discussed the committee reports and in each case granted the high school the right to have its students admitted on presentation of the appropriate certificate. Until the early 1890s the high schools underwrote the expenses of the visiting committees.

Despite favorable faculty opinion about the change in admission procedure, students initially expressed hostility. Calling the scheme "A Dangerous Experiment," the student editors of the *Michigan Chronicle* objected that the scheme seemed unfair. Good students coming from high schools not certified by the University would still have to take and pass entrance examinations, while inferior students from certified high schools would be admitted simply upon presentation of the proper credential. Second, the students feared a decline in the academic caliber of the Michigan student body. They believed that many students would be admitted on certificate who, if examined, would not have been admitted. The students feared that local pressure would force principals to certify students not worthy of University admission. Last, the students objected that many candidates for admission in past years were admitted on condition in one or more subjects and that admission by certificate would obscure any deficiencies a student may have had.[30]

A "teacher" replied to the editorial in the next issue. He argued that the system would serve to improve secondary education throughout the state by inducing competition for a place on the University's "approved" list. The correspondent contended that the inspection system would insure against deficiencies in preparation and that if any unprepared students were admitted they could easily be sifted out during their first year at college. The embarrassment this would cause a high school would induce it to become more conservative in the issuance of certificates.[31] The exchange reflected the basic positions of the two constituencies. Students, who resided at the University for only a short time, worried that the value of their college diploma might diminish as a result of the new policy. The faculty, more concerned with the long-term welfare of the University, accepted short-term risks to obtain a constant supply of students while elevating the University's level of instruction and hence the status of their profession.

Five years later, the students' enthusiasm had not increased. They believed that a visiting committee could not make a thorough inspection in a day or two and therefore that the University had no way of determining the criteria upon which teachers and principals would judge the fitness of a student to enter the University. They also charged that without entrance examinations teachers and students had become more lax in their preparation. They viewed the University as compounding the sin by making additional demands on the secondary schools—demands that led the schools to emphasize quantity of preparation at the expense of quality.[32]

Frieze had anticipated such charges at the time of the system's inception. He explained that the system gave the University a pretext to visit the high schools in order to inspire them and elevate their character. The high schools could never be elevated without a certificate system, since the University faculty was too easy on admitting students conditionally. This encouraged students to enter the University rather than to remain in high school to complete their preparation. "The best preparatory teachers," Frieze wrote, "are really more strict than the Faculty of the University."[33]

President Angell's description of the system's workings in the late 1870s indicates that he viewed any early problems as having been remedied by that date. According to Angell, when the University's inspectors arrived at the high school, they requested the staff to continue with its normal routine.[34] After a while the inspectors might ask students to recite or to answer questions so as to determine the extent of their preparation. They would also observe the teachers to determine their competence. The school's curriculum was carefully scrutinized to assure its conformance with the University's entrance requirements. After the general inspection, confidential conferences were held with the local school board. Here, deficiencies in the teaching staff, the curriculum, or the method of certification were discussed. These meetings served primarily to provide principals with guidelines for certifying students to the University. They also provided the inspectors with an opportunity to size up the principal.

Inspections took place on one or two days and the inspection team usually consisted of two professors, one in charge of languages, the other in charge of mathematics and the sciences. Angell himself occasionally served as an inspector. In the early days, most faculty members shared the work of inspection; later, certain individuals served regularly. By the end of the century the University appointed a permanent inspector.

During the system's first years, some asked whether the inspectors really examined students preparing for admission to the University or examined the high school itself. Early official statements were ambivalent. Before the system's adoption, Frieze wrote that faculty members should annually visit the state's high schools and award certificates to students successful in administered examinations.[35] The certificate system in practice was broader in scope. According to Angell, when a relatively small school was inspected the work of each senior preparing for college could be scrutinized and the recommendation for certification was based more or less on the inspectors' evaluation of those students. In such cases the certificate system differed little from traditional entrance examinations since the same professors would have probably examined the same students at the University the following fall. Angell commented that a student in a small, unknown high school might actually find himself questioned more closely than he would have been if examined at the University.

When the faculty inspected a larger high school, with perhaps forty or fifty students preparing for college, each student could not be separately examined and the decision on certification was based on the school's general conditions. As time passed, more schools fell into the second category. Where the conditions were well-known, as in the case of some larger high schools in counties contiguous to the University, the annual inspection became more of a recruitment effort than a formal evaluation. At the same time the inspectors, by gauging the work done in these better "feeder" schools, derived a standard to be applied to other schools. They could also determine how well the high schools adjusted to the changes in entrance requirements imposed by the University.

On completion of a visit, the inspectors reported their findings to the entire faculty. They usually accepted their committee's report, but this did not always bode well for the inspected school. Angell insisted that no school was granted certificate privileges on the basis of its reputation, but only after careful yearly inspection and approval of current conditions.

Michigan authorities believed that most principals used the certificate privilege cautiously since they feared removal from the accredited list in retaliation for poor performance of previously certified students. Public secondary schoolmen fighting for their institutions' legitimacy considered the prestige of certificate privileges of considerable importance. Angell suspected that some principals exercised too much caution, since noncertified students from accredited high schools were admitted when they passed the regular entrance examinations. The principal's recommendation based on several years of daily observation was held to have greater significance than an examiner's opinion based on a few moments' exposure during the frenzied conditions of examination week. Angell rebutted the charge that the University had abandoned responsibility for its own admissions by pointing to the thoroughness of the inspection system. Finally, he cited as evidence of the system's popularity among secondary schoolmen the invitations issued to inspectors by high schools with no chance of obtaining certificate privileges to discuss existing deficiencies.[36]

In 1880, the University issued a report that compared the grades received during the freshman year by students admitted to the University's College of

Literature, Science and the Arts on certificate with those of students admitted by passing the regular entrance examinations.[37] The widely circulated document showed that students who entered on diploma generally fared better in college than did those who entered on examination.[38] By 1880, the University had granted certificate privileges to sixteen schools. Table 2.1 summarizes the changes in proportion of students admitted by certificate and by examination.

The shift to the certificate system lead neither to a massive influx of new students nor to an immediate end of Michigan's entrance examinations. It mainly assured a constant supply of students—an assurance not possible under the old system. During the plan's first decade the number of students admitted by certificate varied only slightly (from 50 to 62 between 1873 and 1880) while the number by examination varied from 42½ to 75. Admission by certificate accounted for less than half of all admittances during the years under consideration, but did account for an increasing proportion of enrollments in the latter years. The number of students who would have come to the University if the system had not been in effect cannot be estimated. Perhaps most students might have taken and passed the University's entrance examinations. On the other hand, it is conceivable that the personal contact that the certificate system fostered may have actually led to increased

Table 2.1. **Number of Students Admitted by Certificate and by Examination to the University of Michigan, College of Literature, Science and the Arts, 1871–1880.**

Year	Students Admitted by Certificate	Students Admitted by Examinations	Total Students
1871–72	35	116	151
1872–73	34 ½	74 ½	109
1873–74	56 ½	53	109 ½
1874–75	62	42 ½	104 ½
1875–76	52	45	97
1876–77	50	63	113
1877–78	61	48	109
1878–79	57 ½	75	132 ½
1879–80	61	57 ½	118 ½
Total	469 ½	574 ½	1044

SOURCE.   University of Michigan, *The President's Report to the Board of Regents for the year ending June 30, 1880* (Ann Arbor, published by the University, 1880), p. 28.

NOTE.   Fractions in the table occurred when an odd number of students left college at the end of the first semester or when an odd number of students, not present in the first semester, began their studies in the second.

attendance. The total number of freshmen declined significantly after implementation of the plan. Lowest enrollments were reached in the mid-1870s, during a period of economic depression and after significant increases in the University's entrance requirements.

Other statistics showed that freshmen admitted on certificate during the plan's first decade passsed a greater percentage of their courses and elected slightly more hours of work than did their classmates admitted on examination, that a smaller percentage of certificate students dropped out of college in their first year, and that the number of "bad" failures was slightly larger for such students.[39] All high schools granted certificate privileges were located within the state, and during the plan's early years about half of all certificate students came from Ann Arbor High School, which had assumed the role of a quasi-preparatory institution. Students admitted to the University with conditions were often assigned to classes there to make up their deficiencies.[40]

Although the statistics the University provided went far to silence the certificate system's critics, we can ask why certified students did not do even better.[41] Such students supposedly were the cream of those high schools with a curriculum and level of instruction approved by the University. Certified students were not a cross-section of all students entering the University in a given year; they were above average and superior performance in college should have been expected. The certificate system did provide a constant source of students while permitting the University to divest itself of elementary instruction by shifting it to the high schools, but it had a negligible effect on entering class quality.[42]

CERTIFICATION IMPLEMENTED:
SUBSEQUENT PROBLEMS

Despite a generally optimistic outlook on the certificate system, some faculty grumbling persisted. Some high schools that received inspection committees and received certificate privileges sent few or no students to the University. The Union City High School, for example, had twelve graduates one year, one in the classical course and eleven in the English program. The school's principal doubted whether any would enter the University the following fall. "I suppose I should confess," he wrote, "that we wish our school on the accepted list rather because of the additional value this gives to the diploma than because any pupils are likely to enter the University."[43]

At faculty meetings, members expressed misgivings over the time involved in sending out visiting committees. Some complained that the disruption of faculty routine was incommensurate with the meager returns. Few students ever came from the northern half of the Lower Penninsula and even fewer made the trip from the Upper Penninsula. Nor did enrollment grow fast enough to please at least part of the faculty. Some professors in growing departments hoped to recruit students to their disciplines from widened enrollments to justify increased University expenditures on their departments.

The University responded to such agitation by agreeing to administer its traditional entrance examinations at distant points. An initial experiment took place in 1881 when the University conducted examinations in San Francisco, Chicago, Cincinnati, and St. Louis. Five students passed these exams. Given the short notice available to candidates, this number afforded the faculty and local alumni great satisfaction.[44] Soon out-of-state secondary schools began to request certificate privileges. This placed the faculty at something of an impass. Regular inspection of such schools would be too burdensome, but to certify these schools without inspection would have left the University open to charges that it granted certificate privileges to out-of-state students on more liberal terms than it did to local applicants. The faculty committee that studied the problem saw only two possible courses: either out-of-state students should be admitted by entrance examination only or all schools should be admitted to the certified list without inspection.

The committee, which reported in the spring of 1883, recommended the latter alternative. Arguing that the diploma system had improved the relations between the University and the secondary schools, and that it had increased enrollment levels, the committee concluded that "the acceptance of students without examination, if properly guarded, would work no embarrassment within the state and would open the way for admission of considerable numbers from without the state who now seek inferior advantages elsewhere." The committee specifically recommended that the entire responsibility for certification rest with the principal or superintendent. All secondary schools with "a regular and thorough course of preparation for College" would be granted certificate privileges, but only those students who completed the University's specific entrance requirements could be certified. Anyone admitted by certificate would be considered on probation for the first semester, and those who did not perform well would be dropped.

Unwilling to forego inspections, the Michigan faculty rejected the report. Its importance lies in the willingness expressed by three highly respected faculty members to eliminate what had previously been considered the most important element of the certificate system, largely because of potential faculty inconvenience and because of a desired enrollment increase.[45]

A slightly reconstituted committee found a way around the dilemma. It reasoned that annual inspection of schools within Michigan had become too burdensome because the number applying for privileges had become large and the distance of some from Ann Arbor was considerable. It recommended that, following inspection, certificate privileges be granted for a three-year period as long as no major changes in course offerings or in faculty were made.[46] Approval for out-of-state schools would not require faculty visitation.

Instead, the faculty conferred on the president authority to accredit any school offering a course that would adequately prepare a student for any of Michigan's programs. Where faculty visitation proved impractical, "the Faculty may designate other persons to constitute the committee of inspection under their direction." The faculty often designated as inspectors alumni who taught at other colleges not far away from the high school under consideration, school administrators, or other prominent alumni. The faculty report, adopted in 1884, formed the basis for Michigan's method of admissions for many years.[47]

Some high school officals viewed adoption of the three-year rule as a mistake. "It will lead to slipshod and fustian work," commented the superintendent of the East Saginaw schools.[48] Others welcomed the change since inspections disrupted the work of their schools and since local school boards frequently objected to the expenses of annual inspection. Not only did some officials see little need for reinspection as long as a district's schools remained under the same management, they viewed annual inspection as a risk since different inspectors might apply different standards and come up with different recommendations.[49] The more remote schools, which sent few graduates to the University and which absorbed the highest expenses, faced considerable pressure to forego the largely intangible benefits of the certificate system. The University partially alleviated this problem when it permitted inspection of out-of-state high schools by nonfaculty, and went even further in 1891 by announcing it would assume the costs of all future inspection committees.[50]

The three-year rule led to some tightening of standards by inspection teams. Weaker schools that managed to gain certificate privileges on a year-to-year basis found the going tougher when the inspection teams granted their imprimaturs for longer periods. La Porte High School felt the sting of faculty reprimand and objected vigorously.[51] So did Charlotte High School, which was asked to assume the burden of another inspection committee before its old privileges had expired. Its principal objected that the school faced intense pressure from denominational schools and warned that "to sever our connection with the University at this time will be to strike a blow at higher culture from which this school will not recover in years."[52] Subsequently the school had its accreditation renewed. Visitations proceeded without additional format changes until the twentieth century. Inspection committees submitted their reports in writing during these years and many reports have survived.[53]

CERTIFICATION AND ENTRANCE REQUIREMENTS

Throughout the 1870s, the University of Michigan continuously raised its entrance requirements, usually after consultation with the high schools, by increasing both the required number of entrance subjects and the required number of topics in each subject. As newer disciplines appeared in the college curriculum, faculty members representing them desired the student to be exposed to preparatory work in that discipline. They hoped that inclusion on the list of entrance requirements would not only add legitimacy to the new discipline but also provide new recruits.

In 1882, President Angell reported that, largely as a result of improved relations with secondary schools accredited by the University, high school graduates entering Michigan had completed almost a year of studies in addition to the work required of their counterparts ten years earlier. During that period, he regularly consulted with accredited schools about proposed entrance requirement changes. When a consensus had been reached, he made recommendations to the University faculty. University authorities assumed that if the better high schools could meet the new requirements, other schools would eventually conform. In 1875, for example, Angell asked the high schools whether German should be substituted for French as an entrance requirement, whether rhetoric and English literature should be substituted for geology for students interested in the sciences, and whether botany should be added to the list of entrance requirements.[54] The high schools absorbed additional work imposed upon them by increasing the length of the school day and by adding an additional year to the curriculum. The inclusion of some courses did not prove burdensome since the high schools offered courses in addition to those required for admission to the University. Sometimes these courses could be readily adopted to meet the University's stated requirements.

It soon became apparent that additional courses could not be prescribed indefinitely, and maneuvering for a place on the list of required entrance subjects intensified. In 1881 faculty members representing the "newer" disciplines, especially the sciences, urged the faculty to consider a scheme calling for redistribution of required entrance subjects so as to provide students with early exposure to their fields of interest. The proposed plan slightly reduced the number of required courses, and redistributed the subjects required in favor of the newer disciplines at the cost of required language instruction. Deliberations became deadlocked when Greek, French, and science instructors proposed additional requirements. The faculty decided to give up the scheme when it determined that these additions would obviate the intended reforms.[55]

As time passed, the University found that the leverage it could exert through the certificate system had declined. Some schools ceased to apply for certification because conflicting local pressures on the curriculum were accorded a higher priority. Superintendent Payne of the Adrian schools wrote Angell that few parents in his district seemed inclined to permit their children to take a preparatory course. Although strong efforts had been made to interest students in the University, experience showed that most desired a course that terminated with high school. In gearing all energies toward this end, the high school could no longer conform to the University's entrance requirements.[56] This tension between education for college and education for "life" went largely unresolved for another generation. When it was finally resolved, the terms did not favor the colleges. At a time when many secondary schools turned out few college bound graduates, when local school boards questioned expenditures for secondary education, when denominational schools and colleges provided significant competition, and when the high schools themselves remained dependent on a still developing primary school system, the secondary schools were hard pressed to raise the level of instruction as quickly as the University would have liked or to restrict their course offerings too narrowly.[57]

Several technical aspects of the certificate system had come in for criticism. Some charged that a few Michigan inspectors certified schools not on the basis of a thorough inspection, but by insuring that the textbooks employed were those authored by University faculty members. Another superintendent complained that some younger inspectors showed contempt at the practices of his high school and left him "in a position of great delicacy and embarrassment."[58]

On the surface, it may not be apparent why the secondary schools of Michigan put up with the certificate system's inconveniences. The answer was that most schools initially were not certain enough of their survival to turn down the opportunity of University sponsorship. As they grew stronger, the high schools discovered that the certificate system could facilitate college admission for those students intending to continue their education, while permitting emphasis on the large percentage of students who were not college oriented. This discovery formed the basis of another chapter in the history of college admissions policies.

CONCLUSION

No State seems to have succeeded better than Michigan in establishing a judiciously regulated and systematized relation between the public schools and the State University.

JAMES BRYCE[59]

Sixteen high schools had been granted certificate privileges during the 1870s. In 1887, 58 schools appeared on the approved list. The following year the number increased to 71, of which 46 were located in Michigan, 19 in Illinois, 3 in Minnesota, and 1 each in Pennsylvania, Ohio, and Indiana. During its initial phase, the certificate system had provided the University with a constant flow of students, while permitting it to increase gradually its entrance requirements. As secondary school enrollments increased, the University became an automatic beneficiary and by the turn of the century it had one of the largest student bodies in the nation.

Michigan's success in implementing the certificate system provided contemporaries with an important example of how admissions policies could be employed to bring about wider reform. Certificate admission demonstrated that by increasing the potential applicant pool to include all who completed programs in accredited high schools, increases in academic standards need not come at the permanent expense of enrollments. It further showed that colleges did not have to remain content with admissions judgments based on brief contact with prospective students during the artificial conditions imposed by entrance examinations. Most important, admission by certificate helped integrate the state's hitherto unrelated public educational institutions into a coordinated system.

That system provided for the successful selection of the University's entering class by the state's high schools. The criteria for selection were academic, but could be broadened. Finally, Michigan's reform established the growing university as an active social institution, one that could and would take initiatives with important social consequences. After 1870, American higher education slowly abandoned its status of marginal importance.

NOTES TO CHAPTER 2
SYSTEMS AND STUDENTS:
THE UNIVERSITY OF MICHIGAN AND CERTIFICATES

1. See Morton White and Lucia White, *The Intellectual Versus the City: From Thomas Jefferson to Frank Lloyd Wright* (New York and Toronto, Mentor Books, 1964).

2. John Parker Huber, *Toward Camelot: The Admission of Women to the University of Michigan* (Ann Arbor, Michigan Historical Collections, 1970); Dorothy Gies McGuigan, *A Dangerous Experiment: 100 Years of Women at the University of Michigan* (Ann Arbor, Center for Continuing Education of Women, 1970). The medical division refused to instruct men and women jointly for a number of years (Huber, *Toward Camelot*, p. 13). Interestingly, the admission of Michigan's first blacks went largely unnoticed (see Elizabeth Gaspar Brown, "The Initial Admission of Negro Students at the University of Michigan," *Michigan Quarterly Review* (Autumn, 1963), 2:233–236.

3. Joseph L. Henderson, *Admission to College by Certificate* (New York, Teachers College, 1912).

4. Tappan said that Erastus O. Haven, a Methodist clergyman who eventually succeeded Tappan as president, was the last faculty member to be appointed on the basis of his religious affiliation (see Elizabeth S. Adams, "The Administration of Henry Philips Tap-

pan," in Wilfred B. Shaw, ed., *The University of Michigan: An Encyclopedic Survey*, vol. 1 (Ann Arbor, The University of Michigan, 1941), p. 43.

5. See Elizabeth S. Adams, "The Administration of Erastus O. Haven," in Shaw, ed., *The University*, pp. 54–59.

6. Twice during Angell's presidency he again became Acting President. On each occasion Angell received leave to conduct diplomatic negotiations on behalf of the United States.

7. James B. Angell, "A Memorial Discourse on the Life and Services of Henry Simmons Frieze, Lh.D., Proffessor of the Latin Language and Literature in the University from 1854 to 1889," in Angell, *Selected Addresses* (New York, Longmans, Green, and Co., 1912), pp. 165–167; Angell, *The Reminiscences of James B. Angell* (New York, Longmans, Green, and Co., 1912), p. 237.

8. Henry Simmons Frieze, "Diaries of Henry Simmons Frieze in 1855–1856," vol. 1, pp. 53–56 in Michigan Historical Collections, Bentley Historical Library, The University of Michigan (hereafter cited as MHC), Henry Simmons Frieze Papers, Box I, file 10. Frieze noted that the collegium had less direct influence over teachers in cities.

9. Fritz K. Ringer, *The Decline of the German Mandarins: The German Academic Community 1890–1933* (Cambridge, Harvard University Press, 1969), pp. 26–34.

10. Only New York State, where the Board of Regents administered examinations to all students on completion of each secondary school course required for graduation, continued this practice in America.

11. See especially James B. Angell, "The Higher Education: A Plan for Making It Accessible to All," *Forty-third Annual Report of the Superintendent of Public Instruction of the State of Michigan with Accompanying Documents for the Year 1879* (Lansing, 1880), pp. 205–212.

12. Adams, "The Administration of Henry Philips Tappan," pp. 44–52. See also Howard H. Peckham, *The Making of the University of Michigan 1817–1967* (Ann Arbor, The University of Michigan Press, 1967), pp. 31–52.

13. Calvin O. Davis, Helen Travis, and Allen S. Whitney, "The Branches of the University and Secondary Education in Michigan," in Shaw, ed., *The University*, vol. 1, pp. 159–171.

14. Address of President William W. Folwell delivered August 24, 1870 before the Minnesota State Teachers Association. Reported in *Minnesota Tribune*, date unknown; copy in Scrapbook 265, Alexander Winchill Papers, MHC.

15. The University of Michigan, *The President's Report to the Board of Regents for the Year Ending June 30, 1870* (Ann Arbor, published by the University, 1870), p. 63.

16. In 1874, the high schools' future brightened when Judge Thomas Cooley, of the University's Law School faculty, declared in a case usually known as the Kalamazoo Decision that the state constitution permitted support of free public secondary education subsidized by general revenue. Cooley further stated that the state Constitution envisioned an integrated public educational system beginning with primary school and continuing through university training. See the *Thirty-Seventh Annual Report of the Superintendent of Public Instruction, 1873* (Lansing, 1874), pp. 399–407; *Thirty-Eighth Annual Report of the Superintendent of Public Instuction, 1874* (Lansing, 1875), pp. xc, 346–351; "The Free High School Tax," *Kalamazoo Gazette* (February 13, 1874); Daniel Putnam, *The Development of Primary and Secondary Public Education in Michigan* (Ann Arbor, George Wahr, 1904), pp. 75–97; and *Michigan Argus* (February 13, 1874).

17. Charles E. Stuart to Kalamazoo Evening Telegraph, August 23, 1880, in Records, 1874, of Kalamazoo Case, or Stuart et al. v School District No. 1, MHC.

18. "Public vs. Private Control of High School," *Detroit Evening News*, June 19, 1883; copy in Scrapbook 274, Alexander Winchill Papers, MHC.

19. Isaac N. Demmon, ed., *University of Michigan Regents' Proceedings 1837–64* (Ann Arbor, 1915), p. 211.

20. One denomination applauded the University's recognition of the need for Christian influence "by the election of Professors connected with the various denominations of Christians in the state" [see Willis F. Dunbar, "The Influence of the Protestant Denominations on Higher Education in Michigan" (unpublished dissertation, The University of Michigan, 1939), p. 211].

21. *Ann Arbor Courier and Visitant*, undated; copy in Scrapbook 271, Alexander Winchill Papers, MHC. The Frothingham case of 1883 in which a professor of medicine was attacked for allegedly making antireligious statements prompted another round of charges.

22. S. B. McCracken, *Religion in the University—A Review of the Agitation of the Subject Before the Legislature of Michigan During the Session of 1873* (Detroit, Detroit Free Press, 1873). See also *Michigan Chronicle* (April 18, 1873) 14:165; and Norman Drachler, "McCracken's Charge of Sectarianism Against the University of Michigan," in Claude Eggertsen, ed., *Studies in the History of Higher Education in Michigan* (Ann Arbor, School of Education, University of Michigan, 1950), pp. 1–11.

23. Charles True Goodsell and Willis F. Dunbar, *Centennial History of Kalamazoo College* (Kalamazoo, Kalamazoo College, 1933), p. 198; Willis F. Dunbar, *The Michigan Record in Higher Education* (Detroit, Wayne State University Press, 1963), p. 110.

24. Dunbar, *The Michigan Record*, pp. 108–130.

25. University of Michigan, *The President's Report 1881*, pp. 7–8.

26. M. Louise Jones to James B. Angell, May 3, 1886, James B. Angell Papers (hereafter cited as "Angell Papers"), MHC. Between the 1860s and the 1880s about half of all students in Michigan institutions of higher education enrolled in denominational colleges. In 1860 five church-related colleges were in existence: Kalamazoo, Adrian, Albion, Hillsdale, and Olivet. In 1864, the report of a committee that had inspected Olivet stated that of the 230 students attending college in Michigan, 120 enrolled at the University of Michigan while 90 enrolled in the five church-related schools (see Dunbar, *The Michigan Record*, p. 17). Dunbar claimed that a hostile state Legislature inhibited the growth of denominational colleges by refusing to grant additional charters for such schools. However, in 1883 the *Detroit Evening News* reported that "not withstanding the, in some reports, superior attractions afforded by the state institutions and the free tuition they furnish, more than 49% of the entire number of students are found in the denominational colleges." The newspaper reported that all such colleges were flourishing and that each had sufficient financial support to maintain that condition (see "The Cost of Education in Michigan," *Detroit Evening News*, July 20, 1883; copy in Scrapbook 274, Alexander Winchill Papers, MHC).

27. James B. Angell, "Inaugural Address of James B. Angell," *Thirty-fifth Annual Report of the Superintendent of Public Instruction of the State of Michigan with accompanying documents for the year 1871* (Lansing, 1872), p. 215; University of Michigan, *The President's Report 1870*, p. 62.

28. University of Michigan, School of Science, Literature and Arts, *Faculty Record*, vol. 3 (1864–1878), p. 292, MHC. The actual committee report was not transcribed into the *Faculty Record*, nor could it be located among the faculty's official reports.

29. *Ibid.*, vol. 3, p. 304.

30. "A Dangerous Experiment," *Michigan Chronicle*, (April 15, 1871), 2: 210–211. Whereas students who passed entrance examinations in most, but not all, required entrance subjects would be "conditioned" in those subjects they failed, students admitted on certificate had to have been deemed prepared in all subjects to have received their certificates. Thus, students admitted on certificate did not receive conditions.

have been deemed prepared in all subjects to have received their certificates. Thus, students admitted on certificate did not receive conditions.

31. *Michigan Chronicle* (April 29, 1871), 2:225–226. See also *ibid.* (May 13, 1871), 2:241–243, and (May 27, 1871), 2:259–260.

32. H. M. Campbell, "The Diploma System," *Michigan Chronicle* (December 11, 1875), 7:57.

33. Frieze to Angell, April 19, 1871, Angell Papers, MHC.

34. In other writings, Angell admitted that it was almost impossible for a high school to carry on a normal routine given the circumstances.

35. University of Michigan, *The President's Report 1870*, p. 63.

36. Charles Eliot to Angell, April 5, 1878 and April 24, 1878; Angell to Eliot, April 15, 1878, Angell Papers, MHC.

37. The report's authors argued that grades earned during subsequent years should not be taken into account, since "a year in college ought to be sufficient to obliterate distinctions, if any exist, arising from the differences in the preparatory schools." The implications of such logic are intriguing. If a year in college obliterated differences in preparation, did it really matter how students were admitted, or whether they had a strong or weak background? The tendency to use freshmen grades as a criterion for measuring effectiveness of preparation continued for many years.

38. University of Michigan, *The President's Report 1880*, p. 27. See also Shirly W. Smith, *James Burrill Angell: An American Influence* (Ann Arbor, The University of Michigan Press, 1954), p. 102.

39. The term "bad failure" was not defined in the tables or in the accompanying text.

40. University authorities considered the pattern evolved by Ann Arbor High School to be the model for emulation by other local school systems. The school's program centered around its college preparatory function. In turn, it had significant influence on the lower grades. "As the University gives tone and character to the work of the High School," wrote the local public school superintendent, "so the High School gives inspiration, aim and stability to the grades below" ["Superintendent's Report to the President and Board of Trustees of the Ann Arbor Public Schools," *Michigan Argus* (August 21, 1874), p. 1].

41. On most scales, the difference between the performance of certified and examined students was small. For example, the percentage of "bad" failures among certified students was 6.18: among examined students it was 6.09. The "success rate," defined as the percentage of entering freshmen who advanced to the sophomore class, was 88.91 for certified students and 87.22 for examined students.

42. Again, it should be emphasized that the faculty's main concern was for a drop in quantity, and therefore a negligible change in quality was acceptable.

43. George N. Carman to Angell, April 21, 1884, Angell Papers, MHC.

44. Frieze to Angell, April 25, 1881, June 10, 1881, and July 9, 1881, Angell Papers, MHC.

45. Charles Kendall Adams, Alexander Winchill, and Isaac N. Demmon, "Admission from High School on Diploma Without Annual Visitation," reported May 7, 1883, considered May 14, 1883. Recommended for revision as to form and substance, raised again January 28, 1884. Faculty and Committee Reports, Petitions, Resolutions, etc., 1878–1888, Registrar's Office Collection, MHC, 1882–1883 envelope, report no. XII.

46. A request for inspection by a secondary school within the three year period would be honored whenever practical.

47. Alexander Winchill, Martin Luther D'Ooge, William H. Payne, and Isaac Demmon, "Admission on Diploma from Schools Out of State; Admission from Other Colleges," April 14,

1884. Faculty and Committee Reports, Petitions, Resolutions, etc. 1878–1888, Registrar's Office Collection, MHC, "Resolutions and Reports, 1883–1884, first and second semesters envelope," report no 11.

48.   J. C. Jones to Angell, April 24, 1884, Angell Papers, MHC.

49.   W. H. Payne to Angell, April 13, 1876, Angell Papers, MHC.

50.   Henderson, *Admission*, pp. 68–69.

51.   Simon Wile to Angell, June 5, 1884, Angell Papers, MHC.

52.   M. Louise Jones to Angell, May 11, 1886, Angell Papers, MHC. See also Angell to Jones, June 9, 1886, *ibid.*

53.   The report on the Corunna High School was typical:

> The Corunna High School is under the charge of Mr. A. D. McIntyre, a graduate of Hillsdale College. The Preceptress, Miss Mary Eade, is a graduate of Detroit High School. The entire work of the high school is done by these two teachers. Classes in Chemistry, Physics, Botany and Latin under the instruction of Mr. McIntyre were visited and in Geography, History and English under the charge of Miss Eade. The work of both teachers was satisfactory, that of Mr. McIntyre being especially so. With very little apparatus and with few facilities for practical work he had introduced laboratory methods in all sciences taught and is exerting a strong personal influence for the development of solid and independent work.
>
> All our present requirements for the English course are met and it will be practicable to comply with increased requirements. Both Latin and German have been taught by the Superintendent and he wishes to prepare pupils for the Science and Latin courses of the University. This could readily be done if some additional help were provided in the high school but under present conditions does not seem advisable.
>
> It is recommended that the school be placed on the list of diploma schools for one year for the English course.

From Report on the Corunna High School, 1888, Faculty and Committee Reports, Petitions, Resolutions, etc., 1878–1888, Registrar's Office Collection, MHC, "Faculty Actions During the Year 1887–1888" file, "School Examinations—Report of Committees—Report on Chicago Suburbs" envelope.

54.   The secondary schools generally favored the changes. The substitution of German for French was especially popular in sections of the state settled by Americans of German descent. Since several accredited schools already offered advanced (that is, postgrammar school level) instruction in English, they had little objection to the University's proposal to require it for admission to the science course. The proposal to require botany for the classical course received a mixed response. Some believed it could be offered without crowding the preparatory course. Others wrote that the schedule would be so burdened that another year would have to be added to the high school curriculum (H. S. Tarbill to Angell, October 29, 1875; E. A. Strong to Angell, October 30, 1875, Angell Papers, MHC.)

55.   "Recommendations of the Committee on Revision of the Course of Study," March 15, 1881, in "Policy and Organization of the Literary School, I," MHC.

56.   W. H. Payne to Angell, April 13, 1876, Angell Papers, MHC.

57.   Superintendent Hathaway of the Flint Schools noted that the enrollment of a typical high school appeared to vary inversely with the importance of foreign languages in the curriculum. He concluded that those "city schools" with the greatest emphasis on foreign languag-

es (which formed the bulk of Michigan's entrance requirements) were "getting furthest away from our young people" (H. H. Hathaway to Angell, January 6, 1896, MHC).

58. Hathaway to Angell, January 6, 1896; Payne to Angell, April 13, 1876, Angell Papers, MHC.

59. James Bryce, *The American Commonwealth*, L. M. Hacker, ed. (New York, Capricorn Books, 1959), p. 473.

CHAPTER

3

The Spread of
the Certificate System

The academic world's reform wing must have breathed a collective sigh of relief sometime in the late 1870s. The Michigan experiment proved that significant dividends existed for any other college that emulated it. Not only had the University achieved a central educational role in the state; it achieved this status while raising entrance requirements maintaining (and later increasing) enrollments. Once Michigan demonstrated the system's viability other institutions, hesitantly at first and then with increased rapidity, followed suit.

During the 1880s and 1890s, the colleges and universities adopting the certificate system found that it helped them cope with additional problems emerging in the area of admissions. The "cost" of the plan, namely assigning the function of selecting the college student body to an outside agency—the secondary schools—appeared acceptable, if somewhat unsettling. The plan's attractiveness led all but a handful of colleges to adopt a version of it by 1915. Even the holdouts (mainly institutions with vast resources including faculty, curriculum, locale, and tradition) that continued to require entrance examinations for all applicants eventually made some concessions.

FACTORS DICTATING CAUTION

Few during the 1870s urged the rapid spread of the certificate system based on the Ann Arbor innovation. Michigan had modified its method of admission in response to a complex set of conditions. The University lacked the preparatory department then common to most American colleges and faced intense competition for students from local denominational colleges. The state's high schools faced strong political opposition despite the strong influence of German practices on many state officials. Observers at other universities at first concluded that Michigan's conditions were so idiosyncratic that its certificate system of admission would not be widely emulated. Other colleges considered adopting a similar system, but decided not to experiment until the success of the Michigan venture could be determined.

The colleges that did adopt new policies based on the issuance of certificates raised even more eyebrows than had Michigan. When Indiana implemented its program, its Board of Trustees announced that the state Board of Education (and not the University's faculty) would designate those high schools to be accorded certificate privileges and that the superintendent and principal of the Bloomington High School would henceforth examine students from other high schools. Some wondered whether substitution of public for University authority in the areas of accrediting and entrance requirements was the wisest course.[1]

At Michigan authorities argued that the certificate system would raise the level of instruction while maintaining the level of enrollment. The circumstances under which other colleges adopted the system proved to critics that enrollments, rather than academic considerations, were of prime concern. During the late 1870s Harvard increased the number of locations at which students might take its entrance examinations. Previously all applicants had traveled to the Cambridge campus for the tests. Williams College, for one, became apprehensive that this extension of Harvard's entrance tests would cut into the flow of students to Williamstown. Its authorities rejected retaliatory local administration of its own entrance examinations as too costly. Instead Williams adopted a certificate plan under which students would be admitted upon certification by their secondary school teachers that all of the College's entrance requirements had been met. Students who could not obtain such certificates would have to take the regular entrance examinations. The plan differed from Michigan's in that no provision existed for secondary school inspection. A teacher whose recommended students performed poorly in college found that his subsequent recommendations were disregarded.

Authorities at Williams termed the initial results acceptable. Enrollments had grown until Harvard (and Yale soon after) began its local examination program, after which they leveled off. President Edward Griffin of Williams concluded that adoption of the certificate plan had probably forestalled a major decline in enrollments. Its adoption did not, however, lead to recruitment of many students who might have gone elsewhere. He found the academic performance of certified students better than that of examined students, but stated that if the caliber of certified students began to fall off he would revert to the old method of administering entrance examinations, though at many more locations than before. Critics gave scant attention to Griffin's contentions about the academic performance of certified students and concentrated their attack on the willingness of colleges such as Williams to employ the certificate system to gain a competitive advantage in the drive for enrollments.[2]

Initial hesitancy in adoption of the certificate system mainly derived from the reluctance of most colleges to delegate the process of college admission to any external agency, including the secondary schools. During the 1870s and 1880s many feared that the high schools, freed from the necessity of preparing students for college entrance examinations, would attenuate their programs and let their instruction grow lax. Even some high school headmasters said that they did not want the power of selection and the accompanying responsibility. They considered it vital to retain an external standard (namely entrance examinations) by which the work of their schools and students could be judged. To critics of the certificate system, emulation of the German system appeared impossible, at least until American local government took the same interest in the secondary schools that German local government took in the gymnasia. Mere sponsorship by a university was deemed insufficient for establishment of an entire system along German lines.[3]

Supporters of the certificate system believed that its success depended on an effective inspection system in which the work of the schools rather than that of the students would be examined. University inspection would not only insure against laxity, but would compensate for lack of local support at a time when the high schools needed allies.

But the inspection system placed a considerable burden on the faculties of the certifying colleges, a burden that they sometimes accepted gracefully, but in other cases shirked. Travel to and from high schools desiring certificate privileges could be lengthy and, as the Michigan faculty discovered, often the longest trips produced the fewest students the following fall. As more high schools opened, the task became more onerous. By the mid-1880s midwestern colleges received greater numbers of requests for inspection of out-of-state high schools. This posed a dilemma of considerable proportions for certifying colleges since, like Michigan, few would forego the chance to increase out-of-state student enrollment, yet few would undertake or waive out-of-state high school inspection. A solution had to be found; students who could obtain admission by certificate to a local college were unlikely to take a long series of entrance exams for an out-of-state college that imposed a higher tuition.

FACTORS ENABLING SUCCESS

In the end the hope of increased student enrollments and the desire of many public universities to emulate Michigan's role in the educational structure of their respective states prompted many colleges to adopt a certificate system. At Rutgers, for example, authorities implemented the plan to offset the benefits derived by rival colleges that already admitted by certificate. When Rutgers' trustees expressesd opposition to the plan, the faculty responded: "We may mention that not a single classical student has been received this year from any of the schools in the Hudson Valley one of our greatest sources of patronage, those colleges which admit on certificates having drawn away all the pupils we should naturally get in this quarter." This was in 1881; it soon became commonplace for colleges like Rutgers to accept certificates for similar reasons.[4]

Advocates of the certificate system soon realized that the problems of inspection provided the main hindrance to the system's general acceptance. A number of interim solutions were proposed and adopted. Faculties followed Michigan's example and certified high schools for more than one year, thus reducing the inspections of schools of unquestioned excellence. Some universities hired permanent inspectors who held academic titles and perhaps had teaching responsibilities. Sometimes a state's education department employed an inspector, a fact that critics pounced on to prove that certificates led to abandonment of college control over admissions policies. Sometimes university authorities, again following Michigan's lead, delegated responsibility for out-of-state high school inspection to a competent local individual, for example a professor at a local college who was an alumnus of the certifying college. Several state universities exchanged lists of accredited schools. This practice never gained general acceptance because of the unwillingness of the stronger certifying colleges to accept the lists of the colleges with weaker entrance requirements.[5]

In the early twentieth century, regional associations of colleges provided a permanent solution to the out-of-state accrediting problem by assuming some responsibility for high school inspection within their jurisdictions. Initial plans for a Commission on Accredited Schools and Colleges to be located within the North Central Association of Colleges and Secondary Schools were announced in 1901, and their actual implementation ensued shortly thereafter. The Commission recommended inclusion of a school on its accredited list after its inspection, usually by the same officials who conducted local inspections. These inspectors applied far higher standards for regional than for statewide certification. In Michigan, for example, in the early twentieth century about three high schools received University accreditation for each school accredited by the North Central Association.[6]

In the East, the larger number of colleges and secondary schools, the close proximity of these institutions, and the greater propensity for students to cross state borders to go to college made inspection of high schools desiring certification even more difficult. The New England Certificate Board, the regional association of certifying colleges founded in 1902, therefore offered three-year renewable accreditation to secondary schools based on their graduates' performances in member colleges. The Board analyzed records of such students and removed from the accredited list those schools whose students performed poorly in college. Member colleges could continue to require specific subjects for admission but were bound to accept certificates from accredited high schools signifying completion of those subjects.

Although in one sense the Board symbolized a regression from the certificate system envisioned by Angell and Frieze, it improved existing conditions. New England's certifying colleges had been criticized for excessive liberality in accrediting neighboring high schools. Very often, accreditation by one college led to rapid accreditation by most neighboring colleges so that no competitor would derive an advantage in the contest for that area's college bound students. Cooperation through the Board led to a significant reduction in the number of accredited schools. Since information about the performance of each high school's graduates could be pooled, a better picture of each school's ability to prepare its students could be provided. Critics argued that without inspections the system was worthless, but the member colleges had neither the inclination to begin inspections nor the desire to give up certificates. Their attitude would remain the same as long as it appeared that certificates enabled them to hold their own against Harvard and Yale, which retained entrance examinations. Some local schools objected that their accreditation depended on the performance of students out of their control. Others welcomed the plan, knowing that their accreditation was assured, but that the fate of competitor schools was less certain.[7]

Generally, inspection and certification had a salutary effect on the nation's secondary schools, but their long-term improvement depended more on internal, structural reforms such as school consolidation, professionalization of the teaching staff, and the development of apolitical boards of education. From the point of view of the secondary schools, certification had its greatest effect in the early years, when in their struggle for survival they would accept a helping hand from anywhere. As these schools developed, they discovered that local pressures often exceeded the pressures from the colleges and that the direct advantages of certification had begun to diminish. But throughout the late nineteenth and early twentieth centuries, accredited high schools found that preparation of students for college was less of a problem than it was for high schools that still had to prepare students for entrance examinations.

From the colleges' point of view, the certificate system became increasingly attractive once it proved its viability. By facilitating communication between the secondary schools and the colleges, it permitted most colleges to divest themselves of the need to offer preparatory instruction. At the same time it insured that secondary school instuction fitted candidates for college level work. During the 1880s, a college graduate would be produced for every two high school students who had been graduated four years earlier.[8] During those years, high school officials knew that the success of their school would be measured largely by their ability to prepare students for college. Accreditation, especially after inspection, signified the offering of a high quality product. In return college officials received assurance that the high school followed a carefully prescribed curriculum. Colleges that continued to rely on entrance examinations often found that the high schools followed their own curriculum and that, to prepare students for the examinations, they offered "cram" courses during the senior year.

The intense competition for enrollments in which many colleges engaged further hastened adoption of the certificate system. In 1890, only about 5% of the seventeen-year-old population had been graduated from high school.[9] This tiny fraction, not all of whom desired to go to college, formed the pool of students from which the colleges could select a freshman class. Many institutions adopting the certificate system did so with the hope that additional students might be attracted by the waiver of the often difficult, always taxing, and ever-increasing barrage of entrance examinations. Colleges whose curricula were being followed in certified high schools realized that students who had spent several years meeting the entrance requirements of one college were less likely to spend their senior year and the following summer studying to pass the entrance examinations of another.

Thus the certificate system spread for both academic reasons and enrollment considerations. The plan would run into serious trouble only when further success in one area—enrollments—began to come at the expense of academic excellence.

CERTIFICATION, THE "NEW DISCIPLINES," AND UNIFORM ENTRANCE REQUIREMENTS

For most of the nineteenth century, the strong grip held by the classicists and the mathematicians on the undergraduate curriculum rendered fruitless efforts by representatives of all other disciplines to gain a foothold. Relegated to unimportant academic niches when permitted to function on the campus at all, those concerned with the social and natural sciences as well as those interested in the critical study of the humanities eagerly awaited the day when their numbers might increase sufficiently for them to become serious campus forces. The scholarly migrations between the United States and the great European universities, and the opening of graduate level institutions in America hastened the gradual shift in the balance of academic power on many campuses. The ultimate success of the newer disciplines in finding their way into college curricula led to further demands for inclusion in the list of college entrance requirements.

In 1870 a typical college offering a classical course required specific amounts of Greek, Latin, and mathematics for admission. Each subject would be further subdivided. For example, most colleges required preparation in arithmetic, algebra, and plane geometry. Although nearly all requested a grammar school knowledge of English, few required the passing of an entrance examination. By 1870, some colleges had added geography to the list of entrance requirements. Others asked for a knowledge of ancient history, which could be tested during the Greek and Latin examinations. In the "scientific" schools, which opened during the nineteenth century, preparation in the sciences could be substituted for knowledge of the classics.

A college's adoption of the certificate system did not necessarily imply any liberalization in the list of entrance requirements. However, representatives of the newer disciplines at certificating colleges found important allies among the principals and teachers at accredited high schools. The growth of such schools, owing in part to the certificate system, made them more attractive to increased numbers of students who did not wish to continue their studies into college. Concluding that the traditional classical curriculum would prove unattractive to such students, the high school principals had devised new curricula composed mainly of subjects such as English, history, and science— that is, the newer disciplines. To keep expenses within the prescribed budget (and often at the covert behest of college representatives of the new disciplines), these principals used the occasion of the annual inspection to request college faculties to liberalize their entrance requirements. Faced with strong pressure from two sides, many colleges began to make concessions. Generally, the addition of the "newer" subjects to entrance requirements lists took place more rapidly in areas where the certificate system facilitated the direct communication with secondary schoolmen.

The certificate system also helped mitigate the problems raised by the lack of uniformity in college entrance requirements, a difficult question even when the list of requirements was short, but which became compounded once the newer disciplines found their way onto the list. During the late nineteenth century, considerable divergence existed in the subject matter each college required the student to cover during his or her years of preparation. Even when colleges prescribed the same works, such as Xenophon's *Anabasis* and Homer's *Iliad* and *Odyssey* in Greek, or Caesar's *Gallic Wars*, Cicero's *Orations* and Vergil's *Aeneid* in Latin, they differed in the amounts of each work to be read and in the specific pages they prescribed. Although all agreed that the criterion for college entrance should be "thorough preparation" (no general aptitude tests existed), the colleges never arrived at a consensus on the level of mastery to be reached before admission to college. Not only did entrance examinations test for evidence of specific preparation, but certificating colleges expected certificates to attest to the student's precise completion of the stated requirements. At Dartmouth college authorities considered this point so important that they capitalized the relevant clause in the college catalogue.[10]

Secondary schoolmen catering to examining colleges complained that the lack of uniformity forced them to turn their senior class into many senior classes, each one preparing for a different set of entrance requirements. Their complaints became stronger as the colleges increased the required mastery levels, both in the traditional and the newer disciplines, making it impossible to provide specific instruction for each college during the portion of the senior year set aside for the purpose. When a high school desired certificate privileges from two colleges with differing requirements, the inspector from each college expected the entire preparatory curriculum to be in conformance with the entrance requirements of his college. The problem, as might be expected, proved expecially acute in the East, where the same high school might prepare students for a number of proximate colleges.

The high schools not only took umbrage at the often conflicting demands made by the colleges, but resented the more fundamental reality that the colleges largely determined the high schools' course content. Typical of this last point was the exasperation felt by the teacher who asked a student why he had not prepared his lesson for the day. "You forget . . ." he replied, "that I am going to Princeton, and we do not need the Ancient Mariner there."[11] The faculty at some accredited high schools may have early begun to reexamine the price they paid for being delegated the selective function. However, accredited high schools probably faced fewer difficulties than did schools that prepared students for examinations, if for no other reason than such schools could employ their leverage with the colleges to achieve rapid college adoption of uniform entrance requirements in each subject once the members of each discipline achieved consensus.

Not surprisingly, the first agreements on uniform entrance requirements came in subjects such as English and history, where tradition did not interfere with progress. The representatives of various college departments of English undertook the establishment of uniform entrance requirements in that subject in the late 1880s. They considered it important that the secondary school student come to college not only with a knowledge of English grammar and spelling, but also with some knowledge of English literature. Classicists objected that there was little written in English on a par with the best Greek and Roman authors and they often opposed efforts by English department members to gain access to the entrance subject list.

The first breakthrough came at Harvard in 1874. In the late 1880s, instructors of English, hoping to enlist the high schools as allies in their often frustrating battle, decided to issue an annual list of books upon which all colleges subscribing to the agreement would base their entrance examinations or certificates. In 1885, the New England Commission of Colleges issued the first such list in two parts. The first part consisted of books for "reading and composition" upon which general questions would be asked on entrance examinations, and the second of books for "study and composition" upon which specific questions as to character and plot would be emphasized. The Commission issued each list several years ahead of time to permit increased flexibility within the school curriculum. The Association of Colleges and Preparatory Schools of the Middle States and Maryland began to publish a similar list in 1887. In 1894 the two associations agreed on a mutually acceptable list, and subsequently both the Association of Southern Colleges and Preparatory Schools and the North Central Association subscribed to it. A National Conference on College Entrance Requirements, established in 1895, maintained jurisdiction thereafter. The Conference succeeded in convincing the high schools to accept their list of books, partly because the lists permitted the high schools to use the same curriculum for both preparatory and terminal students.[12]

In history, the first tentative steps toward establishment of uniform entrance requirements occurred in an 1892 conference held in Madison, Wisconsin. Although the conferees did not propose a specific set of requirements, the recommendations issued concerning the teaching of history indicated the general features of the system subsequently adopted. Three years later a conference called by the New England Association of Colleges and Preparatory Schools recommended that colleges adopt an entrance requirement in history. It suggested that colleges permit the student to offer two topics from a list of seven which it published, each of which could be covered in three periods a week over the course of an entire year. The Conference further advocated that high school courses, and the entrance examinations based on them, emphasize judgment and comparison on the part of the student, not mere memorization. In 1899, a Committee of Seven of the American Historical Association urged high schools to adopt a four-year course in history consisting of a year's study each of ancient history, medieval and modern European history, English history, and American history and civil government. It also recommended that each college require at least a year's study of history for entrance.[13]

It proved more difficult to agree on a set of uniform entrance requirements in the sciences. In fact it took until 1908 for agreement to be achieved in physics, the science most often taught in the high schools. The sciences had been taught in the public schools long before most colleges added them to the list of entrance requirements. The delay in establishing uniform requirements largely resulted from disputes between members of each discipline.[14]

Among the "older" disciplines, the nature of the material in mathematics necessitated fewer negotiations between colleges. By the 1880s, mathematicians realized that few high schools could devote more than two years to instruction in mathematics. They therefore set a two-year requirement as their goal and met general success in implementing it. During those two years, the student was expected to have completed algebra through the solution of quadratic equations and mastered the elements of plane geometry.[15]

So severe were the problems in the "classics" that several national conferences were held during the 1890s mainly to deliberate on them. From the secondary schools' point of view, Harvard's substitution in 1886 of a general sight translation requirement for the specific requirements it had listed until then intensified the confusion. Despite efforts by the National Education Association and the American Philological Association, entrance requirements in Latin did not achieve full uniformity even in the first decade of the twentieth century.[16]

These early efforts by the various disciplines to achieve uniformity in their entrance requirements did not solve all the problems at hand. Even after members of a discipline had reached agreement on entrance requirements, many other parties had to be convinced of the virtue of their efforts. Representatives of the older disciplines on many campuses delayed efforts by representatives of the newer disciplines to gain a place on the list of entrance requirements. Even when the classicists agreed to the principle of inclusion, faculty members often objected to adherence to requirements agreed on by an "outside" disciplinary or regional association. And even when a college faculty agreed on entrance requirement modification, high school acquiescence could not be taken for granted. Additional entrance requirements sometimes forced a high school in a poor neighborhood to hire an additional teacher or to build new facilities. At times, the high schools would not or could not make such expenditures.

Perhaps the chief flaw with a discipline-by-discipline approach to reform was that the colleges took few pains to assure that the high schools could complete instruction in all areas within four years. Although classicists did not have enough power to keep the newer disciplines off the list of entrance requirements indefinitely, they could assure that, for the time being, the newer disciplines would be required *in addition to,* not instead of, the older ones. And each discipline designed its entrance requirements to insure that a student arrived in college with more than a passing knowledge of that subject. If the typical complaint of the high school before 1895 consisted in the lack of uniformity in entrance requirements, the typical complaint after that date concerned their excessiveness. Here again, certificating colleges proved more responsive, although it would take more comprehensive efforts to modify college entrance requirements to solve this problem.

A BRIEF CASE STUDY:
THE UNIVERSITY OF ILLINOIS
AND THE CERTIFICATE SYSTEM

Some of the earliest efforts to solve the problem of excessive entrance requirements were undertaken at universities that had adopted the certificate system of admission. Because these colleges were in close contact with high schools which had the dual functions of college preparation and terminal education they became aware of problems regarding entrance requirements more quickly than did examining colleges. The modification of the University of Illinois's admissions policies in 1898 provides an example of how one institution set about to solve these problems.

The University of Illinois was founded under the provisions of the Morrill Act of 1862. The University's Organic Act, passed in 1867, provided that candidates for admission had to be at least fifteen years of age and be able to pass an entrance examination in common school subjects.[17] Faculty desire for elevation of academic standards was thwarted for more than a generation by the poor quality of public secondary education. In 1870 there were only 108 high schools in the entire state (about 1 per county), and although that number had officially doubled by the mid-1880s (University Regent Peabody thought that only 75 or 80 of these schools offered secondary level instruction), the average school had about 80 students and fewer than three instructors, most of them poorly trained.[18] Given the circumstances, it was reluctantly decided that the University would have to offer secondary education. Accordingly, it opened its preparatory school in the late 1870s, when other colleges were attempting to abolish their preparatory schools.[19]

The Illinois certificate system, begun in 1876, was similar to Michigan's, including initial reliance on the faculty to act as inspectors. Although the system was implemented with high hopes, it soon became apparent that the high schools applied for accreditation mainly to enhance their own prestige, not to improve articulation with the University. Only three-fifths of the schools on the accredited list sent any students in the first seven years of the system's existence and about three-quarters of all those who did enter on certificate came from Champaign or Urbana, the home of the University. In 1883 the faculty enacted some modifications, but concern persisted.

To forestall further criticism, Regent Peabody personally assumed much of the inspection burden. His personal investment in the visitation scheme, along with accelerated secondary school growth, accounts for the increase in the accredited list from 30 to 58 schools between 1883 and 1890. By 1893, the list included 113 schools.[20] The University eventually hired a permanent inspector and assigned him to the Department of Pedagogy. Since the bulk of his time was spent in the field, the inspector developed expertise in each school's conditions and a working knowledge of the relative conditions of the state's various schools.[21] Although the certificate system grew slowly in its early years, the faculty of the Protestant-oriented University procrastinated until the 1890s before permitting the state's private, mostly Catholic secondary schools to apply for certificate privileges.[22] As the certificate system began to produce desired results, agitation for the abolition of the University's preparatory school increased, and only the reluctance of Urbana and Champaign to establish a union high school with a special preparatory course prevented its closing in the early 1890s.[23]

During the presidency of Andrew Sloan Draper from 1894 to 1904, the University had to confront two problems with its admissions policies: the diverse admissions standards of its various undergraduate divisions, and the diverse courses of varying academic value offered by surrounding high schools.[24] Before 1898 a student could enter the University's School of Agriculture after completion of about two years of high school work. The College of Natural Science and the College of Engineering required slightly more preparation; the Liberal Arts College required three years. The considerable interdivisional rivalry and competition for students over the preceding decades might be blunted, officials hoped, by parity in entrance requirements.

Required subject distributions also varied by division. The course of study for Literature and Arts candidates was completely prescribed from a relatively restricted list of entrance subjects. Many high school principals asked the University to add or to permit students to offer more work in subjects such as civics, German, history, and physiography. All of these subjects were already taught in the state's high schools in amounts greater than could be applied toward admission to the University.

A faculty committee established to deal with these problems announced that it aimed to achieve internal uniformity while reducing the University's hindrance of the high schools' development. The committee recommended that a uniform admission standard of 33 credits (defined as the completion of a subject for a single trimester) be established for all divisions and that 26 of these credits be prescribed. This amounted to a 50% increase in the number of credits required for admission to the College of Agriculture, and smaller increases for the Engineering and Natural Science Colleges. The committee believed that most high schools could offer 33 credits without having to increase the length of their course.

A major disagreement arose over the number of foreign language credits to be required. Initially the Liberal Arts College held out for a three-year requirement, to be accommodated in entrance requirements totaling 36 credits. The College of Agriculture, which chronically suffered from low enrollment levels, led the opposition, arguing this number was excessive for its prospective students. The Liberal Arts faculty finally relented; the Agriculture School was allowed to waive the foreign language requirement completely on condition that students admitted to this division would complete two years of foreign language while in college. The Liberal Arts College did impose an exacting language requirement on the rest of the University, but at the cost of reducing the total number of required credits from 36 to 33.

The committee increased considerably the list of acceptable entrance subjects. Whereas in 1897 entrance requirements were dominated by the older disciplines, after the 1898 reform the list of acceptable subjects included astronomy, biology, botany, chemistry, civics, drawing, French, geology, German, Greek, history, Latin, manual training, physics, physiography, and zoology.

The state's high schools welcomed these reforms since they permitted greater curricular flexibility while insuring that students would complete their entire secondary course instead of entering the University after completion of only the first two years. Although entrance requirements were not precisely the same for all divisions, all agreed that the reforms eliminated most interdivisional competition for students.

Perhaps the most significant innovation in the long run was the provision that a student might offer seven credits in any subject on the acceptable list. Previously the University had restrained tightly students' options for meeting its entrance requirements. For example, a student might have been able to substitute French for German to meet the language requirement, but could not entirely neglect the language requirement in favor of manual training. Illinois's decision to permit entering students to elect seven credits from almost any subject offered in high school was typical of the certifying colleges of the period. Adoption of a liberalized elective system alleviated the problem of excessive entrance requirements, since students would select their secondary school courses on the basis of what could actually be completed within a standard high school course. If the high school deemed the entrance requirement in German to be excessive, it could steer its college bound students into the more reasonable course in French. The elective system permitted the high schools to regain some control over their own curricula and permitted students to study in their own areas of interest more than had been possible.

Taken as a whole, Illinois's reforms indicated a shift in the relationship between high school and college—at least between high school and certificating college. When Michigan first undertook certification in 1870, one goal had been to raise the level of high school instruction so as to free the University for more advanced instruction. The University correctly assumed that it was the dominant party in its relationships with the secondary schools. The struggling high schools accepted certification because they desired the University's sponsorship.

When in the 1890s an increasing percentage of students attended high school without desiring to continue their education in college, the high schools had to divert resources that had previously gone into college preparation. They continually urged the colleges to accept for college entrance those courses taught in the high schools to terminal students. They also urged the colleges to be realistic about what could be accomplished given their limited resources. The University of Illinois's actions reflect the responsiveness of certificating colleges to these pressures. Compared to these colleges, examining colleges gave less weight to the high schools' abilities to offer instuction in all required subjects—having less direct contact they usually assumed the high schools would do anything requested. They were also less inclined to offer options for meeting their entrance requirements.[25] Eventually high schools accredited by one or more colleges began to request permission to award certificates to any student who completed the high school program, no matter what subjects the student took. Most colleges did not abandon all their requirements.[26] But the actions of Illinois and of other similar colleges indicated the trend of the future.[27]

CERTIFICATION VS EXAMINATION

MR. [EZRA] CORNELL *[Founder of Cornell University]*:   These young fellows tell me you won't pass them, Professor.

PROFESSOR *[in charge of admissions]*:   No, Mr. Cornell, I have found it impossible to pass them.

MR. CORNELL: I should like to know why.

PROFESSOR: They don't know enough.

MR. CORNELL: If they don't know enough, why then don't you teach them?

PROFESSOR: I can't teach them the A B C.

MR. CORNELL: Do you mean to say they can't read?

PROFESSOR: That I don't know; but they can't spell.

MR. CORNELL: Well, if it comes to that, there aren't so very many persons who spell the English language correctly. I have known some people who simply never could learn to spell, but for all that were good and able men.

PROFESSOR: If you want us to teach spelling, Mr. Cornell, you should have founded a primary school and not a university.[28]

Originally, advocates of the certificate system argued that their plan permitted a significant increase in academic standards by allowing gradual relegation of introductory studies to the high schools. However, each effort to rationalize college admission in the latter part of the nineteenth century—to let nonclassical subjects satisfy entrance requirements, to arrive at uniform entrance requirements, and so on—stoked the apprehension of certain faculty members that academic standards would be impaired. These fears and the tendency to associate reform with the certificate system served to intensify the debate between examinationists and certificationists during the last decade of the nineteenth century.

E. C. Broome, author of an important work on college entrance requirements published in 1902, expressed as well as anyone the fears of many academics that certification opened the college to poorly trained students.

There is a growing tendency of late which may operate seriously in lowering everywhere the standard of work throughout our schools. Reference is here made to the deplorable desire of students to evade all thorough tests of accurate scholarship and of acquired mental power. The practice, generally prevalent, of advancing students from grade to grade in the elementary schools, from the grammar school into the high school, and from the high school into the college without examination is fostering that desire.

He argued that the absence of examinations at any level of schooling encouraged superficiality and deprived the student "of a valuable review and of an equally valuable intellectual exercise." [29] To the argument that certification was compatible with selectivity because high school principals were discriminating judges, Broome replied,

as a rule, entrance to college is the issue which decides for a young man whether he shall follow a professional or, better, an intellectual career, or one where intellectual training is a less important consideration. There are already too many fellows in our colleges who have got in easily and are there for no serious purpose . . .[All should be excluded] who have no serious purpose in going to college; and I believe that a thorough examination, administered judiciously, is at present the most effective means of maintaining the proper educational standards.[30]

Broome's critique included the inevitable list of abuses of the certificate system. He feared that the principal's judgment would be influenced by parents and by prominent local officials; that infrequent inspection might lead to undetected deterioration of secondary schools, and that the system would be impossible to administer effectively when visits to many schools at great distances were required. Finally, he and others expressed concern that the college preparatory function would take a subordinate role in the secondary school; the reforms implememted at Illinois and elsewhere gave credence to these fears. Such "concessions" as Illinois made operated against the certificate system's stated goal of raising academic standards, critics charged. The more options a college offered applicants for admission, the less the colleges could be assured that the students it admitted would have even minimal training in any given subject. Eventually the liberalized entrance requirements forced many colleges to offer elementary instruction in all subjects. Some rationalized that prescription of certain entrance subjects was not crucial so long as those subjects could be prescribed in the college curriculum. But this fallback position became untenable when the elective system became dominant in the colleges themselves.

Frightened rhetoric about the lowering of standards was not the exclusive property of the examinationists; some academics thought examinations were an equally porous and inept device. At most examining universities, responsibility for each examination rested with the senior professor of each required subject. A dearth of coordination between professors meant that some examinations were relatively easy, others unduly difficult. A frequent lack of consistency in examinations in different years led to schoolmasters' complaints that the preparation of students was impossible when the indications of what was desired were contradictory.

Secondary schoolmen applauded several innovations in the technicalities of test administration introduced in the late nineteenth century. At first, students attempted all entrance examinations on the college campus, just prior to the start of the fall semester. The lengthy series of examinations administered in a relatively impersonal setting far from home overwhelmed many students. They also found that the examinations covered material learned up to three years earlier, and that even a summer of intensive review proved insufficient to recall the content of three years of learning.

Criticism that examinations conducted under such circumstances imperfectly measured academic competence led examining colleges to undertake a number of reforms. Beginning in the 1870s, Harvard and Yale administered entrance examinations at a number of off campus locations—often the secondary schools which in the past had sent sizable numbers of students to those institutions. Other colleges soon emulated the practice. At the same time, some colleges flirted with the idea of accepting the results of entrance examinations offered by other colleges. Also, colleges increasingly permitted students to take some entrance examinations up to a year ahead of time, so that the material tested might be fresher in their minds. The Association of Colleges in New England sponsored an early agreement among examining colleges which exactly specified which subjects might be tested before the senior year and which had to be taken just before the semester of college entrance.[31] Last, a number of colleges began to offer entrance examinations in June, before the faculty departed from the campus for the summer, and while the material acquired during the senior year (including that portion specifically set aside for review) was still fresh.

Despite these reforms, many advocates of certification continued to criticize the use of entrance examinations on the grounds that no examination could indicate in an hour and a half what a teacher or principal could learn about a student in the course of several years of contact. They also argued that the lack of uniform entrance examinations created considerable confusion in the high schools' work, while the certificate system promoted more cordial relations between parts of the educational system. The examining colleges began to undertake further reforms in the late 1890s, but by then the certificate system had already proven too attractive to a large number of American colleges.

ATTITUDES OF THE SECONDARY SCHOOLMASTER

By the 1890s a new generation of secondary schoolmasters, fearful of academic inroads into their spheres of responsibility and jealous of their autonomy and status, made sure that their voices would be heard. Although they disagreed on many specific issues, all secondary schoolmasters agreed that the colleges would henceforth have to recognize the high schools as an equal partner in the educational process. The rise of schoolmasters' associations in many parts of the country indicated that they believed they could take on the colleges, if they acted collectively.

By and large, the secondary schoolmasters advocated rationalization of the college admission process—including increased entrance requirement uniformity and, usually, the certificate system of admission. They gladly cooperated with representatives of examining colleges to insure that the material mastered by the high school student would be the basis for the appropriate entrance examination. They also welcomed the liberalization of entrance requirements to permit the "newer" disciplines to be offered for admission. But they kept a vigilant watch to insure that neither the demands made by each discipline during the movement toward internal uniformity nor the number of disciplines required for admission increased too greatly. They feared preclusion of the option of doing anything but college preparatory work, and also feared that they would have to reduce the quality of preparation to compensate for the additional required quantity. They were not always successful.

Although some secondary schoolmasters objected to the responsibility imposed on them by the certificate system, most viewed it as a way of increasing the prestige of their schools while retaining some control over their own curricula. It did not take long for them to perceive that high schools with certificate relations experienced greater success in convincing the colleges to permit the student a wide latitude in choosing a high school course. This phenomenon prompted many high schools to apply for accreditation, especially as the number of terminal students began to dwarf the number preparing for college.[32] The financially weaker high schools were the primary beneficiaries, since they could least afford to devote a large proportion of their resources to college preparatory courses followed by a small percentage of their students.

For most secondary schoolmasters, pro forma consultation by college authorities was not sufficient. For if the colleges desired to impose an increasing proportion of the sifting process on the high schools, they could not treat the secondary schoolmaster's view lightly. Most colleges did modify their policies in response to such demands, and probably to a greater extent then they would have ideally desired. During the last fifteen years of the nineteenth century the nation's high schools and colleges engaged in a meaningful dialogue. Despite the existence of extremists on both sides, the two levels exerted a great amount of reciprocal influence. During the early twentieth century the secondary school moderates lost ground to extremists who denounced anything more than minimal cooperation with the colleges, while higher education moderates were eclipsed by extremists who criticized the high schools' continuing drift from an academic course of study.

CONCLUSION

By the 1890s the certificate movement had become national. Resistance was concentrated mainly in the Middle Atlantic states and among the institutions now known as the Ivy League schools. Such institutions opposed certification because it was new and they revered traditions; because it threatened their domination of the high schools and they were in the habit of domination; and because it implied that they were in competition for students, something their high enrollments did not support in fact and their high self-estimate did not allow in principle. Eventually even most Ivy League schools came to terms with the certificate system. Brown, Cornell, Dartmouth, and Pennsylvania all admitted students on certificate by the turn of the century.[33] Columbia, as we see later, led the movement for creation of the College Entrance Examination Board, but it did permit New York's public high school graduates to enter on Regents diplomas. Harvard, Princeton, and Yale never entirely caved in, but after 1910 each took steps toward consolidating their ever increasing number of entrance examinations. In the process, they permitted some students to skip examinations in some subjects studied for admission.

The certificate system grew most rapidly in the Midwest and in the New England states. Perhaps its rapid acceptance in the Midwest can be traced to the early sponsorship of the more powerful institutions in the area. In New England the plan counteracted the enormous regional influence of Harvard and Yale. It took additional time to get off the ground in the South, but once launched the plan gained rapid acceptance. Its expansion in the Middle Atlantic states was retarded by the lack of a regional accrediting commission similar to the Commission on Accredited Schools and Colleges of the North Central States or the New England College Entrance Certificate Board. The Association of Colleges and Preparatory Schools of the Middle States and Maryland, the logical association to sponsor such a service, was dominated by Columbia and Princeton which, for their own reasons, opposed any steps in that direction. Smaller colleges, denominational schools, technical institutes, and other such institutions eventually abandoned the traditional entrance examinations. Such institutions faced serious difficulties in attempting to accredit their feeder schools. The rise of regional associations partly solved the problem. In some states, especially in the South, the colleges joined together in a state accrediting association in which all colleges shared the burdens of inspection. In other states, the smaller colleges simply obtained the list of secondary schools accredited by the state university or by some prestigious neighbor and automatically granted similar privileges to all schools on the list.

Although only echoes of the certificate system have persisted in our time (the high school transcript is a direct descendent of the nineteenth century certificate), the plan left an impressive legacy. This included the accrediting system sponsored by the regional associations, an emphasis on performance during the entire high school course in determining college admission, legitimation of the newer disciplines in the list of entrance requirements (and indirectly into the college curriculum), and accelerated development of the nation's colleges and secondary schools. In its early years, when considerable personal contact typified relations between high school students and teachers, the system appears to have performed successfully. But after a while the system's momentum carried it to extremes which the moderate reformers who sponsored it in its early stages found increasingly objectionable. Demands for entrance requirement liberalization did not end with the incorporation of the newer academic disciplines. During the early twentieth century high schools used the same leverage to force the colleges to accept vocational subjects for entrance. At the same time some criticized the high schools for certifying too many students who did not appear to have the kind of thorough preparation they expected. After World War I, many college authorities concluded that the certificate system had outlived its usefulness, and a process of retrenchment began.

But during the plan's heyday some moderate reformers at examining colleges gazed enviously on it. These reformers knew that college admissions policies would prove a critical area for their plans to have higher education regulate access to the major social rewards America could offer. Believing that within the educational system the high school should have the major say in who would gain such access, they set about to find functional equivalents to the certificate system that would be acceptable to their college faculties and trustees. Foremost in this movement was Columbia University and its most important president, Nicholas Murray Butler.

NOTES TO CHAPTER 3
THE SPREAD OF THE CERTIFICATE SYSTEM

1. Joseph L. Henderson, *Admission to College by Certificate* (New York, Teachers College, 1912), pp. 53–54, 152–156; *Twenty-second Report of the Superintendent of Public Instruction of the State of Indiana Being the Seventh Biennial Report, and for the Years Ending August 31, 1873 and August 31, 1874* (Indianapolis, Sentinel Company, 1874), pp. 103, 108–111; James Albert Woodburn, *History of the Indiana University*, vol. 1: 1820–1902 (Bloomington, Indiana University Press, 1940), pp. 281–284. Only in 1888 did accreditation become contingent upon inspection. See Richard Boone, *A History of Education in Indiana* (New York, D. Appleton and Company, 1892), pp. 306–307.

2. E. H. Griffin to J. B. Angell, May 9, 1883, Janes B. Angell Papers, MHC.

3. Charles Eliot to Angell, April 24, 1878. Angell Papers, MHC. See also Harvard College, *President's Annual Report 1873–1874* (Cambridge, 1874), p. 12.

4. Richard P. McCormick, *Rutgers: A Bicentennial History* (New Brunswick, Rutgers University Press, 1966), p. 100.

5. Descriptions of these and other variations of the inspection system may be found in Henderson, *Admission*, passim.

6. Henderson, *Admission*, pp. 116–117. See also University of Michigan, *The President's Report, 1924–1925* (Ann Arbor, The University of Michigan, 1925), p. 246, and *The President's Report, 1925–1926,* p. 233. "The Association is conservative," stated a University of Michigan high school inspector, "believing that such a policy will eventually work to the highest interest of all. It aims to accredit only those schools which possess organization, salary policies, teaching force, standards of scholarship, equipment and esprit de corps of such character as will unhesitatingly commend them to any educator, college or university in the North Central territory. It is therefore a distinct honor for any high school to be recognized as a North Central School." *The President's Report, 1924–1925,* p. 146.

7. Henderson, *Admission*, pp. 100–102. See also Walter H. Young, "The High Schools of New England as Judged by the Standard of the College Certificate Board," *School Review* (February, 1907) 15:134–144, and Nathaniel F. Davis, "Is the Present Mode of Granting Certificate Rights to Preparatory Schools Satisfactory?" *School Review* (February, 1907), 15: 145–152.

8. Abbott L. Ferriss, *Indicators of Trends in American Education* (New York, Russell Sage Foundation, 1969), p. 110.

9. Ferriss, *Indicators*, p. 105.

10. John King Lord, *A History of Dartmouth College 1815–1909*, vol. 2 (Concord, The Rumford Press, 1913), pp. 400–402.

11. Frank A. Manny, "The Background of the Certificate System," *Education* (December, 1909), 30:205.

12. Joseph V. Denny, "English Requirements," *School Review* (March, 1898), 6:222–223; "Entrance Requirements in English," *School Review* (March, 1898) 6:222–223; Paul Monroe, ed., *A Cyclopedia of Education* (New York, The Macmillan Co., 1910), vol. 2, pp. 101–102; "Preparatory Course in English," *School Review* (September, 1897), 5:445–455; C. W. French, "Special Report of the Joint Committee on English Requirements," *School Review* (May, 1898), 6:344–349; "Uniform Entrance Examinations in English Language and Literature," *School Review* (November, 1894), 2:562–567; "Round Table in English," *Journal of Proceedings and Addresses of the National Education Association* 1897: 684–694.

13. B. A. Hinsdale, "Discussion of Entrance Requirements in History," *School Review* (June, 1896) 4:438–442; Monroe, ed., *Cyclopedia*, vol. 2, pp. 104–106; New England Association of Colleges and Preparatory Schools, "Report of the Conference on Entrance Requirements in History," *School Review* (October, 1895) 3:469–485.

14. American Society of Zoologists, "College Entrance Option in Zoology," *Science*, n.s. (December 16, 1904), 20:850–853; W. F. Ganong, "Suggestions for an Attempt to Secure a Standard College Entrance Option in Botany," *Science*, n.s., (April 19, 1901), 13:611–616; Monroe, ed., *Cyclopedia*, vol. 2, pp. 106–107; Charles S. Palmer, "Resumé and Critique of the Tabulated College Requirements in Natural Sciences," *School Review* (June, 1896), 4:452–460.

15. Paul H. Hanus, "College Admission Requirements in Mathematics," *School Review* (September, 1896), 4:535–538; Monroe, ed., *Cyclopedia*, vol. 2, pp. 102–103.

16. Remsin Bishop, "College Entrance Requirements in Greek," *School Review* (June, 1896), 4:437–447; Brother Giles, *Latin and Greek in College Entrance and College Graduation Requirements* (Washington, D.C., Catholic University of America, 1926); Francis W. Kelsey, "Entrance Requirements in Latin," *School Review* (June, 1896), 4:443–451; Monroe, ed., *Cyclopedia*, vol. 2, pp. 101–102; B. I. Wheeler, "College Requirements in Greek," *School Review* (February, 1893), 1:73–83.

17. Winton U. Solberg, *The University of Illinois 1867–1894: An Intellectual and Cultural History* (Urbana, Chicago, and London, University of Illinois Press, 1968), p. 81. See also Selim H. Peabody, "The University of Illinois," in President Selim H. Peabody, Speeches and Sermons, 1881–1891, 1894, Records Series 2/2/1, box 1, University of Illinois file, University of Illinois Archives.

18. Solberg, *The University of Illinois,* pp. 130, 235.

19. Solberg, *The University of Illinois,* p. 130.

20. Solberg, *The University of Illinois,* pp. 130–131, 235–236, 342–343.

21. Andrew Sloan Draper to Arnold Tompkins, June 1, 1895, Andrew S. Draper Letterbooks, box 1, April 8, 1895–September 20, 1895 book, pp. 223–225, and Draper to Burke A. Hinsdale, November 28, 1898, Andrew S. Draper Letterbooks, box 4, November 21, 1898–February 20, 1899 book, pp. 20–21, Record Series 2/4/3, University of Illinois Archives.

22. Solberg, *The University of Illinois,* pp. 131, 236, 342.

23. Solberg, *The University of Illinois,* pp. 342–343.

24. On Draper, see Ronald M. Johnson, "Captain of Education: An Intellectual Biography of Andrew Sloan Draper 1848–1910" (unpublished dissertation, The University of Illinois, 1970). Draper was formerly Superintendent of Public Instruction in New York City and was forced out for political reasons in the early 1890s. He subsequently made his reputation as a reformist educator in Cleveland. He would end his career back in New York State as the first Commissioner of Education under the 1904 Unification Act.

25. In a study of the practices of the leading examining and certifying colleges, Joseph Henderson found that the average number of subjects accepted by the four examining colleges he studied was seventeen, while seven major certifying colleges accepted twenty-six. He wrote, "More of the modern languages, more of the sciences and more of the vocational subjects are accredited by [certifying colleges] than are recognized by those institutions admitting students largely by entrance examinations" (Admission, p. 148).

26. C. P. Cary, the superintendent of the Wisconsin schools, argued that the state, not the University, should determine the secondary curriculum. He wrote that articulation was important when colleges had limited resources and taught only a few subjects. He concluded that this was no longer necessary since colleges offered beginning courses in almost every subject. He argued that any subjects successfully completed in high school should be accepted for college entrance (C. P. Cary, "Proposed Changes in the Accrediting of High Schools," School Review (April, 1909), 17:229.

27. T. J. Burrill to Draper, December, 1897, January 11, and January 12, 1898; E. B. Greene to Draper, January 15, 1898, Draper Faculty Correspondence, 1897–1898, box 4, A–D file, Record Series 2/4/2, University of Illinois Archives.

28. Morris Bishop, A History of Cornell (Ithaca, Cornell University Press, 1962), p. 124.

29. Edwin C. Broome, A Historical and Critical Discussion of College Admission Requirements (New York, Macmillan, 1903), p. 150.

30. Broome, A Historical and Critical Discussion, p. 151.

31. Charles Eliot, "What Has Been Gained in Uniformity of College Admissions Requirements in the Past Twenty Years?" School Review (December, 1904), 12:758.

32. "Where admission to college by examination alone has prevailed," wrote Henderson, "no doubt the preparatory schools were controlled in the selection of subjects to be taught, in a great measure, by the demands of the colleges; but where the certificating system has been used there has been a growing tendency to adjust college requirements to high school conditions" (Admission, p. 86.)

33. Walter C. Bronson, The History of Brown University (Providence, Published by the University, 1914), pp. 402, 476; First Annual Report of the New England College Entrance Certificate Board 1902–1903 (Providence, Snow and Farnham, 1904), passim.

II

COLUMBIA AND THE SELECTIVE FUNCTION

CHAPTER

4

Enter Butler

Name_____to enter in September, 19__.
What Professional School do you expect to enter later?
The first two lines of an application for admission to Columbia College from about 1920 to about 1940.

B y the turn of the century, college administrators and professors began to perceive that college admission policies had important consequences not only for their institutions (and for individual applicants) but also for society at large.

It began to dawn on academics, for example, that their willingness to recognize the language native to a particular immigrant group could bear on whether the first and second generation members of that group would go to college. As immigrants from such countries as Bohemia, Italy, Norway, Poland, and Sweden streamed into Chicago, local education officials asked whether the native language of students from those countries met the foreign language entrance requirement of the University of Chicago. University officials replied that just about any foreign language would be accepted for admission, but that all students were required to gain a reading knowledge of either French or German while in college. [1] The willingness of the universities and of the various state departments of education to recognize an academic credential acquired in the immigrant's native country also helped determine the immigrant's educational fate.

65

College admissions policies had direct and indirect effects on various economic groups. To the extent that the certificate system encouraged the growth of the public high schools, the opportunities available to those who could not afford the tuition charged by private academies increased considerable. More directly, legitimation of the newer disciplines as a comcomitant of certification permitted poorer students to acquire quickly the specific training they desired in both high school and college.[2]

Many, of course, were not aware of the broad social implications of admissions policies. Extremely parochial considerations often dictated decisions in this area. But challenges to such decisions in public arenas made the academic decision-makers conscious of their actions' consequences. Thus, for example, New York City's growing Catholic population made officials of the College of the City of New York aware that the institution's practice of limiting admission to graduates of New York's public schools was discriminatory.[3]

But at certain points in the academic universe, admissions policies were deliberately, self-consciously, and articulately manipulated to achieve broad social ends. At no place was this more the case than at Columbia University during the late nineteenth and early twentieth centuries. The social history of college admissions policies in this period would be grossly incomplete without reference to the pervasive influence of the Colossus on the Hudson, and of the extraordinary man who held it in charge, Nicholas Murray Butler.

This chapter outlines the problems faced by Columbia after the Civil War and shows why its authorities, notably President Frederick A. P. Barnard, considered inadequate any reforms short of thoroughgoing changes in the institution's mission. Butler's career, his proposals, and his actions concerning reform are then discussed. In the following chapters, we turn to a discussion of Butler's recognition of the selective function's importance in securing for the nascent university a central position in American society, and his attempts to reform college admissions policies nationally (Chapter 5) and locally (Chapter 6) so as to facilitate high schools' performance of the selective function.

Aware of the certificate system's success in enabling many high schools to exercise selectivity in sending its graduates on to college, Butler knew that different tactics would have to be employed in the East, where the certificate system had less legitimacy. Butler's counterrevolution against reforms largely of his making, and the reasons for this academic Thermidor, comprise the substance of Chapter 7. His conclusion that the high schools had failed to perform the selective function properly led him to reassign it, at least in Columbia's case, to his own internal bureaucracy where, at least, he could better control the criteria on which students could obtain admission to the undergraduate college. Selective admissions soon became the admissions policy of most of America's better private universities and colleges, and even of many public institutions. The final chapter in this part concerns Columbia's attempts and its ultimate failure to control access to all higher education within New York State. The chapter ends with a description of the price Columbia had to pay after World War II for abusing the public's trust in its performance of the selective function.

POST-CIVIL WAR COLUMBIA

The Columbia of the first decades after the Civil War was a small, unadventurous, local college. No match for Harvard and Yale in variety of offerings, or for Princeton and Cornell in breadth of constituency, it could hardly hold its own with its more immediate rivals—the College of the City of New York and the University of the City of New York (later New York University), which were more conveniently located than Columbia and were less expensive to attend.

During the 1850s Columbia had moved from its downtown location to temporary quarters on Madison Avenue and East 49th Street. The site overlooked the noisy New York Central Railroad yards and was not easily accessible from many parts of the city. Only at the turn of the century would Columbia find a permanent home in New York's Morningside Heights section.

Academically, Columbia relied almost entirely on its constricted liberal arts curriculum for students and their tuition. Attempts had been made during the 1850s to expand the undergraduate liberal arts college into something resembling a university. These attempts ended in failure, although the trustees established a School of Mines during the 1860s. The courses in medicine and in law were physically separated from the campus, and the latter was dependent on the charisma of one man, Theodore Dwight.[4]

As an urban institution, Columbia found itself dependent exclusively on the city's population for its student body. Small-town and rural parents were loath to send their children to any city because of fears which Columbia's post-Civil War President Frederick A. P. Barnard acknowledged were not imaginary:

It is not merely that in all large cities temptations are powerful and distractions are numerous, though this is with many an objection quite conclusive, but what is to the apprehensions of many more a source of graver apprehension still—it is true that in such cities, there exists a class of designing and plausible knaves who are ever on the watch to inveigle and mislead the unsophisticated, and whose malignant natures are never fully satisfied unless to the plunder of their victims they can add their moral ruin.

Dependence on the city did not bode well for Columbia's enrollment level since cities in general and New York City in particular had not yet cornered a dominant percentage of the population. Barnard understood that the only possibility of attracting out-of-town students lay in the building of expensive dormitories that would enable the College to "exercise over them something of the watchfulness which [their parents] might exercise over them themselves at home." But Barnard also knew that Columbia's treasury could not afford this—at least as long as Columbia remained on its "temporary" site.[5]

For many decades, Columbia tried to defend its territory by curbing its neighbors, especially its main competitor, the College of the City of New York. Founded as the Free Academy of New York in 1847, CCNY had secured legislative sanction to offer college level work in 1866, and had renamed itself to reflect this change. Columbia College considered this initiative pretentious because it was not *The* College of the City of New York (there being two others of importance), and because it considered the instruction offered at City College to be less exacting than that offered at Columbia.[6] President Barnard charged that City College offered "a sham education at a low price in labor and time." He further claimed that

it gives the academic degree for which other colleges demand a patient toil of seven or eight years, in consideration of the amount of hurried work which can be compressed into five years. And it holds out to young men the most seductive of all allurements which could be invented to entice them to give it their preference, viz., exemption from some years of distasteful though salutary preliminary drill in the secondary schools, and free and cordial welcome directly from the primaries.[7]

Barnard concluded that the key to City College's growth was the opportunity it gave potential students to enter its one-year preparatory course directly from grammar school. He discounted the effect of its free tuition policy after observing that the University of the City of New York had adopted a similar policy with no significant increase in enrollments.

City College officials responded that their students were usually unable to devote any more time to college studies than they were currently spending, and that its entrance examinations were a safeguard against any diminution of standards. They also contended that the usual high school and college courses were unnecessarily lengthy and were not relevant to the needs of many of the students who attended City College.

Barnard could see no short-run solution to the dilemma for Columbia posed by the policies of City College except

by a measure to which we shall never condescend—that of diminishing the amount of our exactions from those who come to us for education, and degrading our standard of scholarship, till a degree in arts shall be as easily achieved here as there; and, it may be added, when achieved, worth just as little . . . [Columbia College] will never be so false to her character or her trust as to seek to inveigle youth to her halls, by cheapening the quality of the article she offers them under the name of education; and whether those who come to her for knowledge be many or few, she will fulfil all her duties toward them with the same conscientious fidelity which has ever distinguished her hitherto.[8]

If no short-run acceptable solution were available, Columbia would have to transcend its historic limitations to grow and prosper. Under the leadership of President Barnard, this is precisely what was done. Barnard had been a prominent educational reformer and college president in the South prior to the Civil War. He assumed the presidency of Columbia during the War and served until the late 1880s. During the 1870s, Barnard secured faculty acceptance of an elective system for juniors and seniors—an innovation which, Barnard believed, when implemented at Harvard led to increased enrollments there.

The enthusiasm with which this reform was greeted by Columbia's students and faculty prompted Barnard to make further suggestions. Noting the initial success of Johns Hopkins after its opening in 1876, he urged Columbia's parsimonious trustees to provide for graduate instruction. This step would put Columbia on the road to becoming a great university and attract students from the entire nation. Strong graduate departments would in turn lead to a higher quality and a more diversified kind of undergraduate instruction. But instructors in some of the "newer" disciplines were scarce, and Barnard knew that it would take both financial and academic inducements to lure competent faculty to Columbia. He urged the trustees to provide newly recruited faculty with higher salaries and he hoped that the elective system would provide them with a sufficient number of disciples.[9] Recruitment of such a faculty would provide students with real options in planning their course work, and this in turn would, it was hoped, lead more students to seek Columbia out.

Barnard ultimately sought the establishment of a true "university." For him, and for his successors Seth Low and Nicholas Murray Butler, this implied more than the creation of a loosely related series of professional, graduate, and undergraduate divisions. A true university assumed the ultimate unity of all knowledge and required the integration of work offered in each division so that the relationship between what was taught in each classroom would become manifest.

The first step toward realization of Barnard's vision was the appointment of John Burgess to the Columbia faculty. Columbia lured Burgess, a professor of political science who was trained in Germany, from Amherst in 1876. In 1880 Burgess proposed the establishment of a new School of Political Science which would offer courses on the advanced undergraduate level to those primarily interested in careers in the public service. The trustees approved his proposal the same year, and the subsequent bulletins of that division described its courses as broad and generally oriented, and not narrow professional courses.

The creation of a Graduate School during the same year did not cause a stampede to the 49th Street campus. Its initial enrollment of six students had grown only to twenty in 1885. Subsequently, the faculties of philosophy (1890) and of pure science (1892) came into existence, and they, along with the faculty of political science, composed Columbia's three graduate faculties. At about the same time, the curriculum of the Law School underwent drastic revision and became integrated with the work of the rest of the University. The foundation laid by the School of Mines supported the new School of Applied Sciences. The rapid pace of these innovations made Columbia a nineteenth-century version of the multiversity.[10]

These reforms were not executed without opposition; economy-minded trustees, tradition-bound faculty members, and devotees of the old-time college were formidable foes. Barnard tried to meet the arguments concerning expense by stating that some financial expenditure was necessary to insure Columbia's long-run growth. He argued that revenue provided by the increased number of students who would be attracted to the University would eventually defer much of the additional expenditure. He told the classicists that they still held primacy in the undergraduate curriculum and that expansion of Columbia in the direction of graduate education would lead to increased prestige for their disciplines as well as for the "newer" ones.

Barnard told the friends of the old-time college that the relation between graduate and undergraduate education was not inevitably antagonistic.

It does not follow that, in aiming at something higher, it need suffer the undergraduate department to fall into neglect, or to be lost in the shadow of the superior development. The very contrary is more likely to be the case. In proportion as the College grows, in whatever direction, the impression of its importance and magnitude grows correspondingly upon the public mind; and this reacts to the benefit of all the departments.

He demonstrated that wherever graduate instruction was offered, undergraduate enrollments increased, while enrollments in colleges without the added towers tended to remain static.[11]

Finally, during the last years of Barnard's presidency and especially during the interregnum between Barnard and Seth Low from 1888 through 1890, it was necessary to keep in check an extreme prograduate faction that espoused elimination of undergraduate education. When the question of the future of the College was considered in 1887, Barnard's disciples were able to secure the continued growth of both graduate and undergraduate instruction by first voting with the faction that stood for the continuation of undergraduate instruction, and then with the other for the continuation of the various graduate and professional programs. After Columbia's reorganization, which was completed by 1890, opponents were never able to mount a serious challenge to Columbia's dominant educational vision—the type of reform advocated by Barnard, Burgess, Low, and by Nicholas Murray Butler.

NICHOLAS MURRAY BUTLER

To an extraordinary degree, the story of Columbia University is the story of President Nicholas Murray Butler, who was its official head for nearly half a century and its prime mover for almost two decades more. Butler was born in Paterson, New Jersey, to parents of English, Scotch, Irish, and Welsh descent. His father, a businessman, was always interested in the political life of the state. Raised in his mother's Presbyterianism, Nicholas shifted during his adolescent years to his father's more prestigious and ceremonial Episcopalianism, to which he made a lifelong commitment.

He was educated in the public schools of Paterson, attended Columbia College, and was graduated from its undergraduate School of Arts in 1882. After studying philosophy in Germany, he returned to New York to accept an instructorship at Columbia College. In his memoirs, Butler stated that about that time he decided that he could be of most service by permanently casting his lot with Columbia. In doing so, he turned down offers of high administrative positions at a number of important universities.[12]

Butler inherited his father's strong interest in politics, and participated in the activities of the Republican party from the late nineteenth century through the New Deal. Like many mugwumps of his time, he detested the New York City political machine and found natural allies in the business leadership of the city, some of whom Butler recruited as Columbia trustees. When President Seth Low of Columbia ran for mayor of New York in 1897, Butler served as his campaign manager. Both took an active role in the New York City consolidation movement, which culminated in the creation of Greater New York in 1898. Upon Low's election as mayor in 1901, Butler accepted the offer of Columbia's presidency. He subsequently remained politically active, but turned down opportunities to run for important elective offices in New York State to remain at Columbia's helm. He did make a run for the presidency in 1920, doing poorly at the Republican convention which eventually nominated Warren G. Harding. He also received votes for the vice presidency in 1912 when William Howard Taft's running mate died during the campaign. Butler's unwillingness to leave Columbia for anything less than national office indicated how important a political office he believed the Columbia presidency to be. He firmly believed that aside from the presidency of the United States no other office would give him as much influence over the country's political and social climate.

Butler's Vision

During the 1880s, after returning from an extensive tour of Europe, Butler served as professor of philosophy at Columbia. He later said that his European tour, along with discussions he held with Americans interested in pedagogical problems, led him to conclude that a real change in the intellectual capacities of youth took place about the time of the completion of the sophomore year of college.[13] After noting that most European countries recognized such a change by the termination of secondary and the commencement of university studies, Butler argued that in America the undergraduate college should be retained as a separate institution that would bridge this transition period. "The college as we have it here," Butler subsequently elaborated,

is peculiar to our own national system of education and is perhaps its strongest, as it is its most characteristic feature. It breaks the sharp transition which is so noticeable in Europe between the close surveillance and prescribed order of the secondary school and the absolute freedom of the university. Its course of liberal study comes just at the time in the student's life to do him most good, to open and inform his intelligence and to refine and strengthen his character. Its student life, social opportunities, and athletic sports are all additional elements of usefulness and of strength. It has endeared itself to three or four generations of the flower of our American youth and it is more useful today than at any earlier time.[14]

Butler later recounted that he had been strongly influenced by President Barnard's vision, and during the debate over Columbia's future in the late 1880s, he was a key member of the middle-of-the-road group. During that debate he first suggested his plan for the integration of graduate and undergraduate education—a plan designed to assure a smooth transition between prescribed order and absolute freedom while permitting students to complete their education in the least amount of time. The plan involved offering students who completed three years of undergraduate work the opportunity to take courses anywhere in the University for their fourth year and to have those courses credited both to their Bachelor's and to their professional or advanced degrees.[15] The Trustees adopted this scheme at the beginning of the Low administration in 1890. When Butler became president a dozen years later, he advocated that students be permitted to begin work on their professional degrees during their junior year.[16] This proposal met greater opposition, but eventually a number of professional divisions did permit undergraduates to register as candidates for two degrees after two years of college work.

Butler prompted reform, not in bits and pieces, but in keeping with a comprehensive, vision—not simply to get Columbia out of the doldrums but to project Columbia resoundingly into the world. His vision was a social one; his hope was that Columbia would play an important role in effecting social change. Influenced strongly by some of the prominent social theorists of his generation, Butler shared their concept of deferential democracy as the ideal of the good society and believed that the newly emergent university had to play an important role in the creation of an aristocracy of service. "I come back to the conception which Mazzini had of democracy," Butler told an audience at the University of California,

"The progress of all thru all, under the leadership of the best and the wisest." True democracy will carry on an insistent search for these wisest and best, and will elevate them to posts of leadership and command. Under the operation of the law of liberty, it will provide itself with real leaders, not limited by rank, or birth, or wealth, or circumstance, but opening the way for each individual to rise to the place of honor and influence by the expression of his own best and highest self. It will exactly reverse the communistic formula, "From each according to his abilities, To each according to his needs," and will uphold the principle, "From each according to his needs, To each according to his abilities." It will take care to provide such a ladder of education and opportunity that the humblest may rise to the very top if he is capable and worthy. . . .

The United States is in sore need today of an aristocracy of intellect and service. Because such an aristocracy does not exist in the public consciousness, we are bending the knee in worship to the golden calf of money. The form of monarchy and its pomp offer a valuable foil to the worship of money for its own sake. A democracy must provide itself with a foil of its own, and none is better or more effective than an aristocracy of intellect and service recruited from every part of our democratic life.[17]

According to Butler, the University would serve as the crucible of leaders. He believed, with some justice, that the academy had served that function in the early days of the Republic, had lost part of it in Jackson's America, had possibly slipped from even that low point in the America of Ulysses S. Grant, but was now at a crossroads. Recognizing that the nation's economic and political leadership had ceased to be overwhelmingly college-trained, though they were more so than the general population, Butler hoped to make the university an important, indeed, an inescapable training ground for the leaders of the emerging industrial-technical society. College had always served as a place where potential leaders could meet and could form social and political contacts. Butler knew that the university would continue to extend such possibilities, but also knew that the education received by these potential leaders had to prepare them to cope with the increasingly complex issues of the time, so that the general populace could safely put its trust in them. The twentieth century leader had to combine the best qualities of both the gentleman amateur and the competent professional. He would acquire the first set in college, and the second in graduate or professional school.[18]

The novelty lay in the layering of the college under the professional school. The state of education, both collegiate and professional, at the time of Columbia's reorganization was such that it would be years before Butler could hope to expose most potential leaders to both levels of instruction. Few students who attended a liberal arts college in the nineteenth century took up professional studies on completion of their courses. Throughout the nineteenth century, students in most collegiate departments looked down on professional students as intellectual inferiors, since it was possible to gain access to most professional schools on completion of the English (or nonpreparatory) secondary school course, or, in some cases, directly from grammar school. Moreover, it was not necessary to attend professional school to enter most professions. Most lawyers, for example, read the law in a law office and applied for bar membership after a specified time in apprenticeship.

Butler wanted to change this. To exalt the professions, he would make a collegiate education the prerequisite to professional study; to save the college (especially Columbia's) he would have the professional schools rely on a supply of college men. "It is our hope and wish," he wrote, "that those who hold professional and technical degrees from Columbia University will be not only soundly trained in their chosen professions, but liberally educated men as well."[19] He opposed direct access to professional schools by secondary school graduates on the grounds that however well taught, such individuals lacked "the more advanced discipline in the study of the liberal arts and sciences and [are] without that wider outlook on the world of nature and of man which it is the aim of the college to give.[20] He asserted that high school students were too immature to undertake professional study, and in turn that professional instruction of such students would inevitably be mediocre.

Butler's social or educational philosophy contained few original insights. But his organizational ability and political acumen, combined with his strategic position at Columbia, enable him to implement reforms that others simply talked about. Butler was more articulate than most reformers, a talent which put him in good stead at the various educational conferences at which so many reforms of that period were first suggested. As editor of perhaps the most important journal concerning contemporary educational questions, *Educational Review*, Butler had a nationwide audience to proselytize.

At Columbia during the late 1880s and the 1890s, he worked for an establishment of a combined undergraduate and graduate program that would train the leaders he desired at some saving of time for the student. Butler cited the success of the School of Political Science, which for almost a decade had been offering courses to advanced students in the undergraduate School of Arts as well as to incoming graduate students. He explained that he was simply advocating an expansion of this practice for all advanced studies.

Butler also played a pivotal role in the establishment of the Columbia

University Council, composed of representatives of each University division who would collectively determine academic policy. Given the growing number of graduate and professional schools at Columbia, the domination of such schools over the undergraduate liberal arts division in the determination of academic policy would be assured. Butler also pressed for the establishment of the graduate faculties of pure science and of philosophy and became the first dean of the latter in 1892. He pressured members of professional faculties to raise their entrance requirements and to make special accommodations for seniors in the undergraduate college who decided to exercise their professional option. He reassured the professional schools that the combined course would insure that any declines in enrollments would be only temporary.

Several professional schools needed such reassurance since they were in the process of undertaking fundamental reforms. For example, the Law School curriculum had been two years in length prior to reorganization. In 1890, President Low proposed that it adopt the increasingly popular case method of instruction and increase the course length to three years. The trustees adopted these reforms at the cost of Professor Dwight's retirement and the resignation of two other faculty members. The faculty also raised its admissions standards so that by 1903 a Bachelor's degree or its equivalent became mandatory for all students except those entering on professional option.[21]

Finally, to insure the growth of the various professional schools, Columbia required help from outside sources, such as the New York State Board of Regents and the State Legislature, which had ultimate authority in the area of licensure for the professions. During the nineties, for example, Butler and Low used their connections in Albany to try to get the Regents to require a three-year law course prior to admission to the bar instead of the two-year requirement then in effect. Although Columbia lost on that issue, the University enlisted the aid of the state on other occasions.[22]

Some critics, including representatives of competing professional schools and some elements of the press, charged that Butler's structural reforms would close the professions to the poorer elements of society. No doubt, the addition of three or four years of collegiate schooling to the three or more years of professional school did impose financial hardships on those who could ill afford to forego earnings for so long a period and pay the increased direct and incidental costs.

Butler was aware of these criticisms and replied that he did not desire to exclude anyone from his chosen profession as a result of his reforms:

the universities do not control admission to the practice of the professions, and it is not in their power, as it is certainly not their wish, to shut out from his chosen profession any competent person whatever his training or wherever it has been had. If the standards of professional study required by the universities are higher than the minimum fixed by law, no one will attend a university for professional study unless its standards appeal to him and unless he hopes to find ultimate gain by conforming to them at some expense of both time and money. On the other hand, if the universities make the minimum standards fixed by law their own—and only by doing so can they avoid discriminating against some one—then they seem to me to have abdicated their functions as leaders in American intellectual life.[23]

Butler believed that the professions had to demand lengthier preparations in response to rapid growth of knowledge, that his plan for the professional option would compress the preprofessional period to some extent without imperiling the existence of the college, and that the professions offered life-time monetary rewards that would amply compensate for earlier sacrifices.[24]

Butler and Undergraduate Reforms

Butler was by no means indifferent to collegiate education, or willing to have the college become simply a satellite of the professional and graduate schools. The college would serve all—no matter what profession each graduate eventually entered—as a place where the student could acquire the mental and moral habits required of a leader in the new industrial order. Butler believed that the rapid changes in American society provided the greatest test of true democracy and the greatest dangers to it. "True democracy creates leadership by its confidence and trust, and follows it . . . The true democratic representative is not the cringing, fawning tool of the caucus or of the mob, but he who, rising to the full stature of political manhood, does not take orders, but offers guidance." For Butler the college was the place where the potential leader would learn how to be the true democratic representative.[25]

This would be accomplished both inside and outside the classroom. The scientist Michael Pupin, an undergraduate at Columbia during the early years of the Butler era, wrote that "the recitation-room brought the student into touch with the personalities of the professors; college activities outside of the recitation-room, whether they were athletics or anything else [such as literary society, college journalism, glee-club practice, or the dramatic arts], brought the student into touch with the personalities of his fellow students." Pupin concluded that each set of influences had its own value "and contributed its distinct share to what is usually called the character-forming of the college student, but what [Lewis Morris] Rutherford, the Columbia College Trustee, called training in the principles of conduct becoming an American who is loyal to the best traditions of his country." "Neither one nor the other influence," Pupin concluded, "can be weakened without crippling seriously that great object which Trustee Rutherford called 'the historical mission of the American College'."[26] The college, Butler believed, was an absolute prerequisite for the professional training that more and more students also required.

Despite the continued importance that Butler attributed to the College, a shift in relative influence at Columbia from the undergraduate to the graduate and professional divisions had taken place. The University expended a greater proportion of its budget on the latter, and undertook many reforms during the 1890s to maintain their enrollments while raising their standards. After 1910, assured of the combined courses' success and of the professional schools' strength, Butler saw the necessity for a reemphasis on the liberal arts tradition as the foundation for professional education. This assuaged the faculty of the College, and appealed to the still significant percentage of College graduates who did not exercise the professional option—men who would become leaders perhaps in the business world or who came from well-connected families. Butler hoped to increase Columbia's enrollment of such students and continually emphasized that they were most welcome.

His desire to insure the exposure of all potential leaders to the moral influence of Columbia made him more than willing to accommodate the rich man's son who went to college to enjoy its social amenities rather than to acquire intellectual training.

It is now fashionable to go to college, at least to some colleges, and the attractions of college life and companionship are powerful motives in leading young men to strive to surmount the barrier of college admission. This new type of college student, whether he knows it or not, goes to college primarily for a social, not for an intellectual, purpose. His wish is to share in the attractive associations of an American college; he desires to participate in athletic sports; he hopes in after life to mingle freely and on terms of equality with college-bred men. It is a good thing that boys of this type should go to college, provided that the college will recognize their existence as a type and will deal with them accordingly. To try to turn such young men into scholars is a hopeless task. They are not fitted for high scholarship and they do not desire it. On the other hand, to bring down the level of scholarship of all college students to meet the capacities and ambitions of this type of student is to do a grievous wrong to scholarship itself and to those who would like to become scholars.[27]

Thus Butler would turn part of the University into a country club if that was the only way to attract budding merchants, financiers, and corporate officials to the campus.

To accommodate such students, Butler had an honors system introduced at Columbia, which in effect gave recognition to the existence of two classes of students on the campus. It rewarded students with serious intellectual interests by the granting of various academic honors, while placing no stigma on those "social students" who could earn the regular Columbia degree by expenditure of a minimum amount of intellectual energy. Butler also hoped to attract such students through the opening of dormitories and through the promotion of a wide-ranging extracurriculum including a vigorous fraternity system. Thus, the College would serve a dual purpose. Several years after implementation of his plans he wrote,

> While we have at Columbia now closely interwoven two or more years of college study with a later study of law, of medicine, of engineering, of architecture and of teaching, we have none the less held fast to the older conception of college work. We need at Columbia more men, not fewer, who pursue a college course with no vocational aim in view, but who wish to furnish the mind for enjoyments, for happiness and for worth in later years.[28]

For both purposes, he took aim against classical learning—traditionally defended as the key to a college program. As early as 1890, Butler critically noted that a student could be graduated from Columbia College without having any courses that would reflect the intellectual and scientific advances of the nineteenth century, and that would equip him for professional study. "Manifestly a training of this kind," he wrote,

> whether or not it is entirely satisfactory as a preparation for a higher study of theology or classical philology, is by no means what is required to enter upon a course of university instruction in modern philology, in the experimental sciences, in the historical and political sciences, in philosophy as it is now studied, or in law; while to the study of medicine it has no reference whatever. It is moreover my personal conviction that such a curriculum as we now offer is both too rigid and too narrow to be the most desirable even for the average student who has no intention of entering upon a university or professional career.[29]

He was exceedingly impatient with the view that the classics alone offered the benefits of "mental discipline." He did not dispute the contention of the classicists that mental capacities can be trained to operate more efficiently and that such training constituted one of the chief purposes of liberal education. But he did not agree that the classics alone were so empowered; other fields of study could do the same.[30] And in back of this arraignment of the pretentions of the classics lay his fear that students would forego the option of attending a liberal arts college as long as it was dominated by a classical curriculum. He noted at Columbia that members of professional school faculties were more willing to raise their entrance requirements to include a year or two of mandatory college work when the undergraduate curriculum contained generous helpings from the "newer" disciplines.

CONCLUSION

Butler's vision demanded certain human material—a steady and heavy flow of able students from the high schools, a smaller but appropriately prepared flow of students into graduate and professional schools from the college. This, in turn, required a student recruitment net spread wider than the locality or even the region. It also demanded curricula that would be tied into a large design and that would not impose irrelevant barriers between one training entity and another. Finally, it demanded a system of selection at the crucial breakpoints to insure that people and programs would be well matched. As Butler well knew, and knew from the start, everything he cared about would depend on the adoption—by Columbia, her peers, and her suppliers—of an adequate admissions policy.

NOTES TO CHAPTER 4
ENTER BUTLER

1. Ella Flagg Young to Henry Pratt Judson, March 4, 1913; Judson to Young, March 7, 1913, and James R. Angell to Judson, March 8, 1913, University Presidents' Papers, 1889–1925, University of Chicago, Special Collections, Ella F. Young file.

2. See James B. Angell, "The Higher Education: A Plea for Making It Accessible to All," *Forty-third Annual Report of the Superintendent of Public Instruction of the State of Michigan with Accompanying Documents for the Year 1879* (Lansing, Michigan, 1880), pp. 205–212.

3. Recognition of this condition led City College authorities to petition the Legislature of New York State to permit it to accept any qualified graduates who resided in New York City, whether they were publicly or privately educated. See S. Willis Rudy, *The College of the City of New York: A History 1847–1947* (New York, The City College Press, 1949), pp. 125–126.

4. Dwight taught on Lafayette Street, several miles from the main campus, so that his students could take his courses and still work at the various law firms as apprentices. Until the 1880s, the physical and financial connections between Columbia and the law course appear to have been tenuous at best.

5. Frederick Barnard, *Causes Affecting the Attendance of Undergraduates in the Incorporated Colleges of the City of New York* (New York, D. Van Nostrand, 1872), pp. 4–5.

6. Rudy, *The College*, pp. 103–104.

7. Barnard, *Causes*, p. 10.

8. *Ibid.*, p. 15. Barnard may also have interpreted City College's request to admit graduates of private schools as a further infringement (see Ruby, *The College*, pp. 125–127).

9. *Annual Report of the President to the Trustees, 1879–1880* , as quoted in William F. Russell, ed., *The Rise of a University* (New York, Columbia University Press, 1937), vol. 1, pp. 152–153. Barnard wrote:

   Should the measures now pending before the Trustees meet with favor [namely, steps toward the establishment of graduate studies], it is the full conviction of the undersigned that the desired result will speedily follow, and that the growth of the College in its under-graduate department in the next ten years will be such as to surprise the most sanguine of its friends.

   It will, of course, be understood that the scheme of higher teaching which it is proposed immediately to inaugurate is only a beginning. With succeeding years this scheme will naturally be amplified, not only in the departments already represented in it, but by the opening of new ones. This, of course, will require the creation of new chairs and the appointment of new officers, and this will entail upon us constantly new expenditures. But with increasing expenditures will also come increasing revenues; and if the growth of revenue from sources now distinctly visible should not keep pace with growing needs, we may safely count that new sources, discernable already to the eye of prophecy, will open up to us.

10. James Martin Keating, "Seth Low and the Development of Columbia University, 1889–1901" (unpublished dissertation, Teachers College, Columbia University, 1973), pp. 66–71, 107–118, 129–146, 178.

11. As quoted in Russell, ed., *The Rise of a University*, pp. 149–150.

12. Nicholas Murray Butler, *Across the Busy Years: Recollections and Reflections* (New York, Charles Scribner's Sons, 1939), vol. 1. See also W. F. Russell, "Nicholas Murray Butler, 1862–1947," *Teachers College Record* (January, 1948), 49:229–231. Obituaries of Butler may be found in *Current Biography* (December, 1947) 8:8–9 and the *New York Times*, December 7, 1947, p. 1.

13. Butler, *Across the Busy Years*, vol. 1, pp. 144–146.

14. Columbia University in the City of New York, *Annual Reports of the President and Treasurer to the Trustees with Accompanying Documents for the Year Ending June 30, 1902* (New York, Printed for the University, 1902), p. 48.

15. Butler, *Across the Busy Years*, vol. 1, p. 139.

16. Columbia University in the City of New York, *Annual Reports, 1902*, pp. 37–43.

17. Nicholas Murray Butler, "True and False Democracy," *Educational Review* (April, 1907), 33:330–331.

18. Columbia University in the City of New York, *Annual Reports, 1902*, pp. 35–38.

19. *Ibid.*, p. 34.

20. *Ibid.*

21. Julius Goebel, *A History of the School of Law, Columbia University* (New York, Columbia University Press, 1955), pp. 120–158, 187; Keating, "Seth Low," pp. 129–146. The two professors who resigned, George Chase and Robert Petty, subsequently founded the New York Law School to perpetuate Dwight's methods.

22. Seth Low to "Dear Sir," February 15, 1897, Seth Low Papers, Columbia University Archives, Butler Library (hereafter referred to as CUA), Box 13 (1890–1897), January, 1897–February, 1897 file. Relations between Columbia and State authorities are discussed in Chapter 8.

23. Columbia University in the City of New York, *Annual Reports, 1902*, pp. 32–33.

24. Butler wrote, "the whole tendency of our present educational system is to postpone unduly the period of self-support, and I feel certain that public opinion will not long sustain a scheme of formal training which in its completeness includes a kindergarten course of two or three years, an elementary school course of eight years, a secondary school course of four years, a college course of four years, and a professional or technical school course of three or four years, followed by a period of apprenticeship on small wages or no wages at all" (*Ibid.*, p. 35).

25. Butler, "True and False Democracy," pp. 332–333.

26. Michael Pupin, *From Immigrant to Inventor* (New York, Charles Scribner's Sons, 1960 [1922]), pp. 128–129.

27. Columbia University in the City of New York, *Annual Reports, 1909*, pp. 26–27.

28. Columbia University, *Annual Report of the President and Treasurer to the Trustees with Accompanying Documents for the Year Ending June 30, 1919* (New York, Columbia University, 1920), p. 25.

29. Butler to Low, October 11, 1890, Columbia University Files (hereafter referred to as CUF), Nicholas Murray Butler 1890–1894 file.

30. Walter B. Kolesnik recently defined the concept of mental discipline as "nothing more than the psychological view that man's mental capacities can somehow be trained to operate more efficiently 'in general,' and the philosophical conviction that such training constitutes one of the chief purposed of schooling" [Mental Discipline in Modern Education (Madison, Wisconsin, The University of Wisconsin Press, 1962), p. 3.]

CHAPTER

5

From the Committee of Ten
to the College Board

Columbia College, wrote President Butler in 1916, "is the door—or better, the vestibule—through which great numbers of students constantly pass on their way to highly organized professional study of one sort or another." If the College were to perform a function quite removed from its older one of providing a standard classical education, its admissions policies had to be liberal and its curriculum had to be broad enough to accommodate the diverse student body attracted to the College.

It is therefore imperative that the College program shall be broad enough and flexible enough to be readily adjusted to the needs of these various and varying types and groups of students. Columbia College is not at liberty, therefore, to insist stubbornly upon some preferred type of general education, however highly it may value that type. It must, in order to serve the University and the public, meet the demands which a university puts upon a college which is embedded in its educational system.[1]

Admission to college would henceforth mean admission to the professions and upper middle class America. Facilitation of college entrance would insure that students who had studied high school subjects other than Greek, Latin, and mathematics would not be denied access. But at the same time the colleges, and especially Columbia, wanted to assure a high standard of secondary school instruction which would provide students of true leadership caliber. Butler knew that Columbia could accomplish this only in conjunction with its peers, and for that reason placed great hope in the work of the Committee of Ten.

THE COMMITTEE OF TEN OF
THE NATIONAL EDUCATION ASSOCIATION

To the participants in the annual convention of the National Education Association of 1892, the goal of closely relating the coursework of the secondary schools and the colleges appeared distant. In many disciplines and in certain geographical areas, few initiatives had been undertaken in this direction. When such efforts had been undertaken, they had not resulted in success because, contemporaries believed, they had not engaged the most prestigious universities or academic statesmen of the day and because they were too piecemeal, each subject putting in its claims without concern for overall effects. The Committee of Ten, created by that convention, was designed to overcome these faults.[2]

A geographically diverse group of academic leaders were members of the Committee, including Eliot of Harvard and Angell of Michigan. Secondary schoolmasters on the committee included John Tetlow, headmaster of the Girls' High School and the Girls' Latin School of Boston, and Oscar D. Robinson, principal of Albany, New York High School. Another member was the leading educational philosopher-bureaucrat of his day, United States Commissioner of Education William Torrey Harris.[3] Some of the most illustrious academics of the generation served on the subcommittees organized by disciplines: Florian Cajori, Albert B. Hart, George Lyman Kitteridge, Simon Newcomb, James Harvey Robinson, Woodrow Wilson. Their presence insured that the programs of study they recommended would be sufficiently rigorous to prepare students for a high level of college work.

The chairman of the Committee of Ten, and its leading spirit, was Charles W. Eliot of Harvard. After assuming Harvard's presidency in 1869, Eliot became absorbed in the problems of Harvard's curriculum and its relations to Harvard's entrance requirements. This concern led him to think seriously about the work of the secondary schools. During the early years of his presidency, Eliot worked to raise the level of instruction at Harvard, and continually pressed for rigorous entrance examinations which would test the applicant's mastery of increased amounts of preparatory work. By the late 1870s, Harvard's feeders complained that they could not add any more material to the load that Eliot already asked them to bear. Faced with these complaints as well as with charges of economic and cultural elitism and with the possibility of losing able students, Eliot turned his attention to "broadening the road" to Harvard. This especially involved the elimination of Greek as an entrance requirement, a move he had favored even before he was chosen to be Harvard's president. After almost twenty years of frustration, Eliot succeeded in obtaining a compromise with the Harvard faculty resulting in what might be called the "multiple road" approach. Students could subsequently enter Harvard by following the traditional road, by offering elementary Greek and Latin plus advanced work in other fields, or by offering mathematics and physics as substitutes for all preparatory work in Greek. The compromise did not work (as late as 1894, only seven percent of the candidates for admission omitted Greek).

Eliot's role on the Committee of Ten was influenced by and in turn influenced the course of academic reform at Harvard. The Committee's deemphasis of Greek and its corresponding emphasis on the "newer" disciplines guided a Harvard faculty committee, established in 1894 to prepare new entrance requirements, toward recommending considerable liberalization. This would be accomplished through establishment of a "point" system and the expansion of "options" which the student could pursue in secondary school to include significant amounts of sciences, modern languages, and history. After resistance by the Harvard Board of Overseers led to some modifications in the scheme, it was accepted by all parties. Subsequently, Harvard required only one ancient language for admission, and the broader curriculum already implemented in many of Harvard's feeders was legitimized.[4]

Conversely, Eliot's experience at Harvard guided him in the writing of the *Report of the Committee of Ten.*[5] His observation of the evolution of secondary education in New England convinced him that the colleges should no longer dominate the secondary schools by requiring them to be academic preparatory institutions. In a passage that would be frequently quoted, Eliot wrote, "The secondary schools of the United States, taken as a whole, do not exist for the purpose of preparing boys and girls for colleges. Only an insignificant percentage of the graduates of these schools go to colleges or scientific schools . . . . A secondary school programme intended for national use must therefore be made for those children whose education is not to be pursued beyond secondary school." Eliot did not mean that colleges should refrain from making demands on the secondary schools—only that the colleges' demands should not be so constrictive. After issuance of the *Report*, he wrote to Columbia's President Low,

As you may have read between the lines of the Report of the Committee of Ten, I am very much interested in promoting a great widening of the requirements for admission to our colleges. I want to see substantial requirements arranged in History, Chemistry and Physics, and Natural History; so that the colleges can safely accept these subjects for admission on a level with the traditional subjects. I believe that this change would greatly improve the public secondary schools, and greatly broaden the foundations of our colleges in the schools below them.

The Committee of Ten's agreement on a list of disciplines for which subcommittees on entrance requirements would be established proved a major breakthrough. The list contained many of the "newer" disciplines, and mere existence of entrance requirements in these disciplines—entrance requirements that had been agreed on by prestigious academics and by secondary schoolmen—gave the secondary schools additional bargaining power when they discussed entrance requirements with conservative colleges bent upon retaining the triumverate of Greek, Latin, and mathematics.[6] Eliot called the attention of the colleges to the work the secondary schools were already offering in the newer disciplines. He asked the colleges to permit applicants to count these disciplines toward admission and thereby recognize that aptitude for college could be demonstrated in a variety of courses. In return, he requested that the secondary schools adopt the various recommendations of the Committee of Ten's subcommittees as the basis of the curriculum for *all* of their students.[7]

Eliot had commented that "preparation for the duties of life" rather than merely for scholastic success should be a key goal of the high school. He believed that true preparation for life involved the rigorous study of the disciplines discussed in his *Report*. He further hoped that his suggested reconciliation of curricula for terminal and continuing students would have another added benefit, that of solving the problem of the "late decider." "Their parents often do not decide for them four years before the college age that they shall go to college, and they themselves, may not, perhaps, feel the desire to continue their education until near the end of their school course." In the past, college entrance requirements had not only forced the student to decide to go to college, but to choose a specific college well before he could make intelligent decisions. Eliot believed that by having all students follow the liberalized but demanding curricula suggested by the Committee of Ten, the decision on college attendance could be safely delayed.[8]

The Committee's main curricular proposals reflected the goal of legitimizing the newer disciplines. The Committee recommended reducing the Greek requirement in the secondary school curriculum from three years to two years.[9] Although its report has been analyzed and criticized on many accounts since 1894, contemporaries spent most of their time and energy in debate over this recommendation. Some wanted the committee to go even further and delete Greek from the list of suggested required courses, but Eliot feared that most college faculties were not ready for this and he did not wish to jeopardize the entire report for this point. Sooner or later, he assumed, the now legitimated newer disciplines would force Greek out. Latin would be joined either with Greek to compose one track, or with science to compose another, and the committee also suggested alternative high school courses (modern language and English) that would not require any classical study.[10]

The committee suggested four curricula for the nation's high schools, all of which were demanding: a minimum of four years of English, three years of history, three years of mathematics, and three years of science. The required levels of mastery were high. This was moderate revisionism, quite in line with what a Harvard reformer would desire.

BUTLER AND THE COMMITTEE OF TEN

Nicholas Murray Butler played an important behind-the-scenes role for the Committee of Ten. Butler pressed for the establishment of the committee at the 1892 NEA Convention, he suggested the names of those who would ultimately serve on the committee, and he hosted its first meeting when it was formally established.[11] Subsequently the committee met for most of its sessions at Columbia. It would not have been uncharacteristic of Butler to have used these occasions to inform the committee of his views. Later, he would be one of the *Report's* prime defenders at the various educational conferences at which it was discussed. He also gave it favorable publicity in the pages of his *Educational Review* and elsewhere.[12]

Butler derived his views about the function of secondary education from his general notions about the need for an educational system that would adequately train the nation's leaders. To reserve the facilities of the University for those students who would take the most advantage of them, Butler argued that admission to the University had to become selective—that is, that the educational system had to exercise a certain degree of care in deciding which students should be encouraged to continue with their studies. It was Butler's hope that the selection of potential leaders would be undertaken by the growing numbers of high schools. The selective function, he argued,

is of unusual importance in this country on both social and political grounds. Democracy needs intelligent and trained leadership—leadership in public policy, leadership in industry, in commerce, in finance, leadership in arts and in letters. The basis of training for leadership is laid in the secondary schools, where the directive capacity of the nation is serving its apprenticeship. There the majority of the men and women who are to guide the destinies of the next generation are putting forth their powers and testing their strength: out of a variety of intellectual interests, nature and environment lead them to make a selection. Training—persistent, thorough, broad—in the field chosen, is the surest guarantee, if one can be given, of future success and future usefulness.[13]

Butler knew the day was not far off when primary education would become universal in the United States and when the high school would become the educational institution in which students would make their career choices. He believed that secondary schoolteachers and officials had to play a vital role in influencing those who could perform leadership functions to complete high school and go on to college. Students who were not leadership material would be given instruction that would make them productive citizens of the True Democracy. Butler did not expect such students to continue their high school studies to the point of graduation, but he hoped that a year or two of high school would serve both a vocational and a social purpose.[14]

Butler's rhetoric was not his only manifestation of concern over the crucial role to be played by the secondary schoolteacher.[15] His active participation in the founding of Teachers College, his interest in the public school system of the City of New York, and his support, after its establishment in 1900, of the teacher-oriented Columbia University Summer Session are further indications of Butler's desire that secondary schoolteachers be inculcated with the proper standards by which to judge and guide their students.[16]

Butler shared with Eliot the knowledge that the relationship between the secondary schools and the colleges was undergoing considerable change. In 1898, a few years after the issuance of President Eliot's report, Butler identified this phenomenon in almost the same words. The role of a secondary school was expanding so rapidly that

it cannot give its pupils the best possible secondary education, and at the same time have its efficiency judged by its ability to fit some or all of its graduates to pass the tests prescribed in a thousand forms for college entrance. My mind is perfectly clear that the relation usually existing hitherto between secondary school and college must be reversed; instead of the secondary-school programme having to conform to college entrance requirements, college entrance requirements must be brought into harmony with secondary-school programmes. Only an insignificant percentage of secondary-school pupils go forward to a higher institution of learning. It is important for our civilization and for our culture that this percentage should be largely increased.[17]

Butler understood that if the high schools were to perform the selective function, it was necessary to remove all academic roadblocks. The courses offered by the high schools in the newer disciplines had to be accepted for admission by the colleges, not only to aid in the development of the high schools but to facilitate the professional education of continuing students. He also understood that if this were to happen, the disciplinary value of these subjects had to be increased. High school programs included "too many subjects pursued for too short a time," Butler commented.[18] But if the content of these courses was prescribed by a prestigious committee of high school and college instructors who were experts in each discipline, it would be more difficult for conservatives in college faculties to object to the inclusion of such subjects as entrance requirements on the grounds that they afforded little mental discipline.[19] Thus, Butler pushed hard for the establishment of the Committee of Ten and was more than satisfied with its report.

But the millenium did not arrive immediately upon publication of the *Report.* Butler and Eliot understood that further efforts toward rationalization of the relations between high school and college would have to be conducted locally. The *Report of the Committee of Ten* did, however, stand as the reference point for all of these efforts.

THE COLUMBIA CONFERENCES

About a year (1895) after the issuance of Eliot's report, Wilson Farrand, headmaster of the Newark Academy, a Columbia feeder, and a central figure in the movement toward uniformity in entrance requirements, sent President Low a copy of a speech he was to make to the local Schoolmasters Association at its next meeting. In the text, Farrand took the colleges to task for the lack of uniformity in their entrance examinations, the uncertainty and inaccuracy of their administration, and the specific and detailed character of the examinations which the preparatory schools deemed restrictive and confining.

Farrand's language was particularly harsh when he treated the problem of uniformity of college entrance requirements. "[The] establishment by any college," he thundered, "of a requirement not in harmony with those prevailing in other colleges, is a direct blow at the cause of sound education . . . [No] college founded for the advancement of sound learning and devoted to the furtherance of education has any moral right to hamper the work of secondary education by thus laying down an arbitrary, individual requirement."

He generally agreed with the recommendations of the Committee of Ten and expressed disappointment that, despite considerable discussion, little progress had been made by most colleges in acting upon those suggestions. He called for the establishment of committees of college and secondary school representatives to propose uniform entrance requirements to be seriously considered by the faculties of the invited colleges.

After reading Farrand's speech, President Low invited representatives from Harvard, Princeton, Yale, Cornell, and from his own faculty to such a series of conferences at Columbia.[21] His motives for issuing such an invitation were complex. He understood that a successful set of conferences would go far to secure Columbia's position among the foremost leaders of American education. He and Butler believed that the recommendations of the Committee of Ten and other groups had not been implemented because academic conservatism, "intercollegiate jealousies and differences of points of view have prevented thoroughly harmonious action up to this time."[22] It took considerable courage to advocate, much less implement, major reforms in entrance requirements in the face of resounding jeremiads pronounced by defenders of the old order. It took even more strength to admit that one's own set of entrance requirements was not necessarily the only set—or the best set possible. Low and Butler hoped that the changes jointly negotiated by the major institutions of the East would find easier going if each faculty knew that all others were considering or had already adopted similar reforms.

Charles Eliot promptly responded to Low's invitation, viewing such a conference as a logical next step after the issuance of the Committee of Ten *Report*. The Harvard president agreed to cooperate with Columbia alone or with any of the other invited colleges. His internal problems had been resolved for the moment, and the time seemed ripe for the establishment of uniform entrance requirements. Princeton also expressed its willingness to participate.[23] Yale had always been hesitant to participate in any such ventures with other colleges. President Dwight wrote, "I cannot but feel that it is very questionable whether our Colleges should all put themselves on a common level—which, because all must agree, is too liable to be a lower, rather than a higher, level. I think there are manifest advantages, to say the least, in the reserving on the part of an individual College for itself the right and privilege of establishing conditions of its own."[24] However, it ultimately sent representatives to the Columbia Conferences.

Cornell's president, Jacob Gould Schurman, believed it would be more politic to let the Middle States Association, composed of secondary schools and of the greater and lesser colleges in the region, take the lead. Farrand strongly objected to this suggestion, arguing that a successful effort required the active participation of the leading colleges, including Harvard and Yale, which were not Middle States Association members. Farrand also recalled that in the past the Middle States Association had failed in several efforts to achieve limited agreements on uniform entrance requirements.[25] When apprised of Farrand's views, Schurman also agreed to send representatives. Columbia's faculty expressed its sympathy with the object of the conference and encouraged Low to pursue it. Finally, Farrand suggested the addition of the University of Pennsylvania to the list of invited colleges, although it was considered academically suspect by some of the other invited colleges. Low assented.[26] The Schoolmasters Association of New York City and Vicinity appointed secondary school representatives.

The Columbia Conferences began on February 1, 1896. Six conferences met—one for each of the classical triumvirate as well as for French, German, and history. Each conference had for its goal "some agreement . . . as to the form and content of college entrance requirements."[27] Each conference eventually reported success in settling on an agreeable list; however, unlike the Committee of Ten, no supervisory committee or board coordinated the work of the conferences.

Delegates to several conferences based their recommendations on their own entrance requirements and on work undertaken at previous forums. Thus, the history conference urged partial adoption of the report of the New England Association of Colleges and Preparatory Schools. The commended sections dealt with the kinds of written work to be required of students in their secondary courses, the general format of any entrance examination to be offered (emphasis on comparison and judgment, rather than memorization, and specific provision for tests of geographical knowledge), and the principle that students should be allowed to select topics for study from a broad list. On the other hand, the conference modified the subjects on the New England Association's list and went beyond it by suggesting a second list of topics from which the student could offer additional work or could obtain advanced standing.[28] Just as the Columbia Conferences relied upon others' work, Low and Butler hoped subsequent committees would employ the results of this endeavor.[29] They specifically had in mind the Committee on College Entrance Requirements of the National Educational Association, which would report in 1899.[30]

Although more limited than the list of subjects considered by the Committee of Ten, the group considered at the Columbia Conferences included subjects not yet accepted for admission at some of the participating colleges. For example, President Low asked Dean Burgess of the graduate faculty of political science to send a representative to the conference in history, even though Columbia had no requirement in that subject, "so that if we want to move in that direction, we can do so in harmony with our colleagues."[31] Thus, despite the absence of conferences for certain disciplines, notably in the sciences, Low considered the scope of the conferences adequate.[32] Initially the Columbia president reacted favorably to the general unanimity denoting the work of all conferences except Latin. Even in that discipline a consensus would ultimately be reached.[33] He called the results "gratifying" and "remarkable."[34]

Low's optimism was not to last. Examining the conference report in Greek, he noted its recommendation that in case of need any subscribing college could conduct two sets of entrance examinations, one based on the generally negotiated requirements, and another based on requirements established to meet local "necessities." This did not discourage Low immediately—he noted the high quality of the Greek conference's recommendations and reasoned that the goal of the conferences would be served as long as students had the opportunity to prepare for entrance under the uniform requirements. He thought that most secondary schools would shift to using these requirements even if all the colleges merely adopted them as one of several alternative sets.[35]

More disheartening was the criticism leveled by James MacKenzie, a member of the Committee of Ten and the headmaster of the Lawrenceville School, a Columbia feeder. MacKenzie chastized Low for not coordinating the conferences to insure that the requirements agreed upon fell within the high schools' capacities. After examining the proposals, he concluded that his own school and a handful of others in the Middle Atlantic states would have no trouble meeting them, but "the remaining two or three thousand small schools, public and private, in the Middle States, have not thus far attempted more than one-half or two-thirds of what is now proposed." A supervisory committee that had the function of assigning amounts of time to be devoted to each subject would have immediately seen the infeasibility of the proposals. He concluded that a subject-by-subject approach almost inevitably had to lead to disastrous results, since "like the Judges in the Bible each conference is determined to do that which seems in its own eyes right."[36]

Although the Columbia Conferences had significant long term results, the recommendations for uniformity in entrance requirements met only a mixed fate at the hands of conference participants. Columbia's faculty accepted the reports after a year's delay.[37] The two weakest colleges in attendance, Cornell and Pennsylvania, also adopted the recommendations. Harvard had completed a revision of its entrance requirements in 1895 and, although Eliot appeared to concur with the recommendations of the conferences, he was only able to promise that his faculty would take them into account when it next examined the question of entrance requirements. His faculty's hesitation may be partly explained by the decision of Princeton and Yale not to accept the results of the conferences. Their motives are not entirely clear. Most probably, the faculties decided that acceptance of the recommendations would have meant considerable modification of the demands made on their feeders—changes they were unwilling to impose at that time.[38]

Although Butler had permitted Low to stand in the limelight surrounding the Columbia Conferences, he was as usual active behind the scenes. He took advantage of the initial optimism surrounding the work of the conferences to undertake yet another initiative, this one involving not only the establishment of uniform entrance *requirements*, but the establishment of uniform entrance *examinations*.

BUTLER AND UNIFORM ENTRANCE
EXAMINATIONS—EARLY INITIATIVES

Butler's efforts to reform college admissions policies aimed ultimately at the assumption of the selective function by the secondary schools. If a principal or headmaster thought a student to be leadership material, the college had no business imposing artificial impediments to college entrance. Butler repeatedly called for an increase in the percentage of American youth attending college. Without this increase, he feared, a considerable portion of future American leadership would not have had the benefit of exposure to the moral and intellectual training offered there.

Establishment of uniform entrance requirements and acceptance of the newer disciplines for college entrance were only two methods of overcoming previously existing impediments. As early as 1893, Butler called for the establishment of uniform entrance examinations as a further move in this direction. In that year, Butler introduced a resolution before the Columbia faculty calling for negotiations leading to the establishment of a board that would administer uniform entrance examinations. The Columbia faculty showed little interest in the proposal at the time, but when the early results of the Columbia Conferences became known, Butler seized the opportunity to secure passage of his resolution. He then bided his time until the reaction of the other participants at the Columbia Conferences to its recommendations became clear.[39]

When it became apparent that only Harvard offered a glimmer of hope for favorable action among the colleges requiring entrance examinations (Cornell and Pennsylvania accepted students on certificate), Low initiated correspondence with Eliot concerning the possibility of jointly administered entrance examinations.[40] Eliot had made the first public proposal for establishment of a board offering uniform entrance examinations in 1877.[41] His interest in this reform never waned. Low's overture on the subject struck a responsive chord in Eliot, and he told the Columbia president that he believed the moment in American education to be the right one for such an undertaking. But he also told Low that the kind of scheme he had in mind would involve the participation of more than two colleges, and that it should include schools not on the East coast.[42] Finally, he suggested to Low that his faculty had decided to reexamine its own entrance requirements, and that he was reluctant to begin any cooperative efforts until internal revision had been completed.[43] What he did not tell Low directly was that if Harvard offered cooperative examinations, its faculty would prefer to do so with Yale rather than with Columbia, whose undergraduate department was not considered first-rate.[44]

Butler and Low fully understood that establishment of such a relationship with Harvard would immensely add to Columbia's prestige. For this reason, Low pursued the matter, telling Eliot he would be amenable to a wide consortium consisting of representatives of various areas. He explained that his suggestion for cooperation with Columbia was a fallback to be resorted to in case no other school expressed interest at that time. Eliot told Low that he preferred to drop the subject. As an excuse he mentioned the attempts being made at that time by several disciplines to define uniform entrance requirements, and said that administration of uniform entrance examinations should await publication of their recommendations.[45]

Columbia's efforts to bring the other colleges into cooperative agreements had run its course for the moment, and Butler began to look in new directions in his attempt to facilitate the selective function.

BUTLER AND THE TURN
TOWARD CERTIFICATION

Reaching an impasse with Harvard in the fall of 1896, Butler and Low began seriously to consider the possibility of adopting the certificate system of admissions—a move that would have meant the waiving of all examinations for students recommended by the principals of accredited high schools. The reorganization of the New York City public school system, a reform in which Butler played an important part, occasioned this turnabout. Prior to 1896 a Tammany-dominated citywide school board appointed a local school board to administer the schools in each of New York City's twenty-four wards. Once appointed, these local boards became virtually autonomous. Educational critics such as Butler castigated the boards, especially for making teacher appointments part of the Tammany patronage system and for retarding the introduction of any administrative or pedagogical reform.

In 1896, Butler and other reformers secured passage of the Pavey Bill in the New York State Legislature. This act abolished the ward school boards and concentrated all real power in a central school board appointed by the mayor. Executive authority would be placed in the hands of a city superintendent of schools who would supervise appointment of teachers using meritocratic criteria such as educational attainment. When the legislature enlarged New York City to include the counties of Kings, Queens, and Richmond in 1897, it incorporated these reforms into the Greater New York Charter. Within a short period of time, three public high schools, the city's first, opened, and a movement for the establishment of an entire system of such schools gathered momentum.

Butler had been in the forefront of the school reform movement. He took a hand in organizing the Public Education Association, which disseminated propaganda against the ward system; in the forming of the Committee of Seventy, dedicated to the ouster of the Tammany machine and pledged to public school reform; and in the establishment of the Citizen's Committee on Public School Reform, which secured passage of the Pavey Bill.[46]

He believed that the New York reforms would serve as a model for reform in other major cities, and that one of its benefits would be the growth of public secondary education. He was further convinced that reform control would make public education more attractive to the many young men of leadership caliber who found it impossible or undesirable to pursue their education. "The colleges are doing admirable work," he said, "but not enough of it. They need more students. The public high schools will furnish them if permitted to do so."[47]

Locally, he believed that Columbia could capitalize on the impending major expansion of the city's public school system. He could imagine the schools sending 150 (1897 estimate) or even 200 (1899 estimate) students to each freshman class, thus more than doubling its size. As a consequence he could see Columbia finally outdistancing archrival City College.[48] Already, Columbia had begun to move ahead in enrollments as a result of its graduate and professional offerings; with an era of good feelings between Columbia and the high schools, it bid fair to dominate the local student market, or so he thought.

As these hopes rose, so did Butler's interest in the certificate system. He thought that certification had greatly contributed to the growth of the public high schools throughout the Midwest, and therefore to the rapid growth of a number of Midwestern state universities. He thought that adoption of a similar system by Columbia would produce similar results.[49]

Although the system of entrance examinations had been under attack for many years, Butler held aloof from this battle; now he entered it with full force. Tipping his cap at President Eliot, he conceded that the entrance examinations of some colleges (such as Harvard) had "done much to uplift and inspire the general educational work of the country." But in general the tests had the opposite effect. "For the sake of broadening college influence," he concluded, "I would do away with the entrance tests." Speaking before a receptive audience at the 1897 convention of the National Educational Association, held in Milwaukee, Butler praised the positive results of the certificate system and concluded,

When Columbia became a university, in 1890, we decided that the graduate of any reputable college should be admitted on the face value of his diploma. His work after entrance would be determined by us. It would be preposterous for universities to take the same attitude toward colleges as colleges take toward the high schools. There is no reason why colleges should not receive pupils from reputable high schools without entrance tests.[50]

The many beneficial changes that appeared to have accompanied the inspection of the states' high schools intrigued Butler. He concluded that no better way existed for the high schools to be apprised of exactly what kind of human material they should send on to college and what they should sift out.[51]

In 1898 he attempted to establish an institution-based inspection system, similar to Michigan's, at Columbia. He envisioned that Low would play a ceremonial part in inspections similar to that played by Angell at Michigan:

I think that it could be done if you and the Dean [Van Amringe of Columbia College] would be willing to visit the schools once or twice during the year, delivering each time a brief, say five minute, address to the students, and bringing Columbia prominently before them in the person of its highest officers. I feel sure that we have an opportunity here of great promise.[52]

Low agreed, and suggested that inspection might be conducted by a permanent inspector who could be given an appointment on the Teachers College Faculty. Butler replied,

[Your suggestion] contemplates what I believe to be the ideal method of dealing with the matter under discussion. There is no disguising the fact that the large majority of our own professors are neither competent nor otherwise qualified for dealing with the work of the secondary schools. The few who are competent and qualified are overworked already. Everything, however, depends upon the man selected. . . .[53]

Butler convinced the faculty to accept the diploma of one private school, the Horace Mann School. But he encountered opposition when he recommended to the faculty committee considering the question of certification that other private—and the better public—schools be included. Many on the Columbia faculty equated the certificate system with the lowering of academic standards. Others found virtues in the administration of entrance examinations which they were loath to give up. The faculty committee investigating the problem insisted that whatever system Columbia adopted had to apply to all schools. As a result, the faculty revoked the Horace Mann School's privileges.[54] It soon became apparent that the Columbia faculty would not sanction adoption of a certificate system. The matter came to naught.

BUTLER AND UNIFORM
EXAMINATIONS—AGAIN

The same faculty committee examining adoption of the certificate system at Columbia made alternative recommendations that it hoped might achieve some of the goals shared by Butler and Low. It suggested that Low again communicate with the other colleges that attended the Columbia Conferences to determine their interest in establishing a common board of examiners to administer uniform entrance examinations valid for admission to all member colleges. Knowing Low's and Butler's stance, the committee hesitated to reject out of hand all changes in admissions policies and hoped its president and dean would interpret this suggestion as indicating willingness to accept significant steps in this area.

Although a joint examining board had been in operation in England for some time, in the United States only halting steps had been taken in this direction.[55] At best, these involved unilateral decisions by one college to accept the entrance examinations of another. Usually such decisions were reciprocated. The faculty committee here proposed a set of uniform examinations, the scores of which would give evidence of preparation to any admission committee that desired the information.

Given the mood of the Columbia faculty and the example provided by the British system, Butler and Low decided that another attempt at establishing uniform examinations might be profitably undertaken. At this point, Butler abandoned his flirtation with certificates.[56] However, he always retained his admiration for at least the inspection features of the system and on more than one subsequent occasion expressed his hope that one function of a uniform examinations board might be "to supervise the inspection and accrediting of the secondary schools."[57]

When Low suggested to the presidents of the universities represented at the Columbia Conferences that they send delegates to a preliminary conference to consider the idea of common examinations, he received favorable replies from all except Yale.[58] At the conference held in December, 1898, Low proposed the establishment of a single board to compose entrance examinations on behalf of the participating colleges. Knowing that the colleges would be reluctant to abandon their individual examinations without any guarantee of the scheme's success, Low suggested that the undertaking be limited at first to New York City. His hope was that it would spread "by reason of its intrinsic merits, if it spreads at all."[59] Low told the delegates that the lack of uniform entrance requirements burdened the preparatory schools in the New York City area more than any other problem. He also noted that administration of common entrance examinations would enable out-of-town colleges to tap the new supply of students likely to be produced by the opening of the city's public high schools. The delegates at the conference asked Low to suggest to the presidents of their universities that such a board be established. Low left it open whether the board or the institutions would grade the examinations and whether, in the latter case, the grade given by one institution would be accepted by another. The main question put to the presidents was whether they would be willing to replace their own examinations with those drafted by a central board (on which they would all be represented).

Eliot's reply to the proposal revealed the institutional snobbery that Harvard's representatives had usually taken pains to conceal:

A preliminary difficulty seems to me to be the weakness of the proposed group of institutions. The University of Pennsylvania has but a very small department of arts, being in the main a school of medicine and of law. At Columbia also the undergraduate department has by no means the importance of the professional schools. Cornell is a vigorous youngster, but has the defects of youth and inexperience. At Princeton the standard of admission seems to us at Harvard distinctly low, although it has improved of late years. *Our Faculty would feel very much the absence of Yale from the group.*[60]

Low concluded that "it is probably not practicable to make progress with this movement at the present time."[61] Ever jealous of their institutional autonomy, usually suspicious of the motives of their peers, and never wishing to do anything for the first time, the Ivies backed away from the proposal.

BUTLER AND THE CREATION OF
THE COLLEGE ENTRANCE EXAMINATION BOARD

. . . the matter was carried forward by a system of trench warfare without, though, I think, the use of any poison gas . . .

NICHOLAS MURRAY BUTLER, recounting the creation of the CEEB.[62]

As a last resort, Low and Butler turned to the Middle States Association, the organization they spurned a few years before. By now they gathered that Harvard's faculty was unwilling to take any steps toward establishment of uniform examinations without Yale, and that Yale was adamantly opposed to the idea. But the constant criticism offered by the New York Schoolmasters Association concerning the unreasonable demands made by neighboring universities and Butler's impatience after almost five years of frustration led him and Low to make use of the one alternative that still seemed open.

At the annual meeting of the Middle States Association for 1899, held in Trenton, New Jersey, Butler read a paper calling for the establishment of a board of examiners that would administer uniform entrance examinations based on mutually agreeable entrance requirements. The paper elicited some negative responses, notably from President Warfield of Lafayette College.[63] Butler quoted Warfield as saying that he could not agree to the proposal since Lafayette did not want an outside board telling it whom to admit or reject. If the school wanted to "admit the son of a benefactor or the son of a trustee or the son of a member of the faculty, and if they thought such action to be in the interest of the college, they would not be prevented from doing so by any board." Charles Eliot, attending the meeting as an observer since Harvard was not a member of the Association, saved the day for the Board. He told Warfield that he had misunderstood Butler's proposal. The purpose of the Board, Eliot explained, was not to admit students but to define entrance requirements acceptable to all member colleges, to administer exami-

nations based on these requirements at many different locations, and to issue
certificates of performance to students attempting them. He told Warfield
that under this plan "it will be perfectly practicable . . . for Lafayette College to say, if it so chooses, that it will admit only such students as cannot pass
these examinations. No one proposes to deprive Lafayette College of that
privilege."

According to Butler, the debate ended with a roar of laughter. The Association thereupon adopted the principles of Butler's schemes. Butler concluded
that "This might never have happened if President Eliot had not come down
from Cambridge to support the proposal and make that kind of a speech."[64]

There was a serious point in Warfield's remarks. A uniform grading standard applied to uniform examinations (for this was the system endorsed) would
expose the colleges to invidious comparisons when average college entrance
scores were announced. Nevertheless, the vote at Trenton committed no college to relinquish its own examinations in favor of those furnished by the
Board. The tool was invented, but it could be ignored.

The proposal, as finally implemented, provided that the College Entrance
Examination Board would be composed of each member college plus five
secondary school representatives. Membership would be open to all recognized colleges, not to members of the Middle States Association alone. The
Board would offer entrance examinations every June in many locations
throughout the country, and eventually throughout the world. Entrance requirements on which the examinations would be based would be taken from
the *Report of the Committee on College Entrance Requirements,* just issued by the
National Educational Association. The Board would subsequently rely upon
the various associations representing the scholarly disciplines for modifications in those requirements.

Although member colleges could retain their own entrance examinations,
they were obliged to accept certificates of the Board as proof that a candidate
had met the college's entrance requirements in the tested subjects. They were
not obliged to admit the student if they deemed his performance on the
examinations to be of insufficient quality. Examinations would be graded by
the Board, using representatives of the disciplines recruited from the faculties
of member colleges. The Board would attempt to insure that its examinations
in the various disciplines were of relatively equal difficulty and that examinations would be graded according to clearly specified standards. Finally, the
Board would not prescribe which examinations a student was required to
take for admission to any member college. Such prescriptions would continue
to be made by each school.

Getting colleges to accept the Board's examinations did not prove an easy
task. Low and Butler went to work immediately to line up participant institu-

tions. They enlisted the aid of Middle States Association members in drafting a formal Plan of Organization. Besides containing a description of the Board's responsibilities, it would publish a list of subjects in which examinations were to be offered as well as detailed syllabuses for each. At the behest of Butler, exams would be held in many of the "newer" disciplines.

When the Board held its first formal meeting in November, 1900, it had eleven members, enough to get the program of examinations started. At that meeting, Low was elected the Board's first chairman, and Butler its first secretary. Low resigned from the Board when he was elected mayor of New York City in 1901 and was replaced by Butler, who served in that capacity until 1914. After considerable preparation, the first examinations were administered in June, 1901.[65]

But getting the Board started and insuring its success were two different matters. The better Eastern colleges held aloof, partly because of the low repute of the Middle States Association, and partly because of an unwillingness to "experiment" in an area as important as examinations. Indeed, the Columbia faculty itself was slow in giving full approval to the scheme so ardently urged by its president and dean.

COLUMBIA COMMITS ITSELF TO THE CEEB

It is easier to move a graveyard than to move a college faculty.

STEVEN MARCUS, Columbia General Education Seminar 1975.

Until Columbia's reorganization was completed in 1889, control over admissions rested in divisional committees. Reorganization resulted in the transfer of considerable authority to the "department," an interdivisional unit composed of all instructors in a given discipline. Responsibility for composing and grading entrance examinations was henceforth vested in the hands of the senior professor of each department. The actual administration of the exams was often delegated to a junior member.

Several of Columbia's senior professors exercised their power in this area in ways considered unfair and arbitrary by secondary schoolteachers in the New York vicinity. For example, in 1892 several local schoolmasters accused Professor Harry Thurston Peck, chairman of the Latin Department, of authoring difficult exams based on obscure portions of required works and of ignoring all pleas for help in establishing uniform entrance requirements. Peck defiantly replied that the schoolmasters were not really interested in increasing scholarship standards. He downplayed the importance of uniformity:

Now as the head of a department has, as a rule, his own way of developing his subject and his own views of what are the necessary preliminaries to his development, it follows that the nature of an entrance examination will differ in different universities. As I am at the present time arranging my work upon certain definite principles, and as I am teaching in my own way, I must necessarily be the best judge of the sort of preparation required for this particular kind of work, and my opinion is embodied in the questions asked of the students who present themselves in my subject.[66]

When the schoolmasters' complaints continued, Low intervened on their behalf.[67] During the 1890s, a series of reforms was instituted resulting in the transfer of authority from the department heads to divisional committees. In 1894, the School of Arts, the undergraduate liberal arts division soon to become known as Columbia College, gave its Committee on Entrance Examinations final authority over admissions decisions, although it still permitted department chairmen to compose and grade the actual examinations.[68]

In response to complaints that the level of difficulty of Columbia's examinations varied widely both from year to year and between different subjects, the Committee on Entrance Examinations in 1896 received the authority to review exams before their administration. However, grading responsibilities remained in the hands of the departmental chairmen and the complaints persisted.[69]

The stalemate was finally broken three years later when a Columbia College faculty committee complained that the departments were shouldering too much of the burden of administering entrance examinations including "proctoring examinations," "supervising the printing and distribution of examination papers," and "interviewing the schoolmasters, parents and candidates in regard to the character of the examinations and the correctness of the reports." The committee recommended that the departments be relieved from these tasks and that administration of the tests be centralized.

Acknowledging the continuance of schoolmasters' protestations concerning the inconsistency of the examinations, the committee suggested that centralized responsibility for their administration and evaluation would insure greater uniformity "in regard to the length and difficulty of the examination, the standards observed in making up the reports, and the time at which these reports are rendered."[70] The chairman of the Committee on Admissions, Thomas Scott Fiske, seconded the recommendations since he found himself performing considerable drudgery owing to the absence of many department heads at the postcommencement June examinations.[71]

Low, seizing on the mood of the faculty as reflected in its committee, endorsed Fiske's suggestion that uniform entrance examinations be administered for all undergraduate divisions of the University including Columbia, Barnard, and Teachers Colleges, and the Schools of Applied Sciences.[72] The

Columbia College faculty, with some reluctance, agreed to this after receiving informal assurances that the chairman of the new universitywide committee would be a member of the Columbia College faculty and that the standards used in composing and grading the examinations would be comparable to those then employed in the College. Separate divisional committees on admission were maintained to pass on their applicants after completion of the examinations.

When the concurrence of the other divisions was obtained, Low wrote to Eliot, "You will perceive that we have succeeded in doing for ourselves what we have often discussed as desirable on a much larger scale."[73] Butler's influence over these events is difficult to determine, but it is significant that this reform was similar to that accomplished at the University of Illinois just two years earlier. Illinois's President Draper and Butler were close friends and were in frequent contact.

Once Columbia reached the halfway house of universitywide examinations, it could with less fear and trembling move on to common external examinations. The departments were out of the picture; the various undergraduate faculties were becoming less parochial, and there were always the placative entreaties of President Low and Dean Butler. Two months after the ratification of resolutions concerning universitywide entrance examinations, Butler and Low requested and received approval of the CEEB's Plan of Organization.[74]

But the College faculty feared that the secondary schools would find the entrance requirements published in the Plan of Organization too exacting, and to spare them they voted to retain Columbia's own examinations, based on a different set of requirements. At the same time, they expressed their willingness to accept certificates of the CEEB in lieu of Columbia's entrance examinations.[75]

Knowing that acceptance of the plan by other colleges depended on substitution of the Board's entrance requirements for Columbia's, Low elicited letters from local headmasters and principals showing that they much preferred the Board's universal examinations to Columbia's idiosyncratic ones.[76] Low indicated that he was willing to make temporary provisions for students who had been preparing for Columbia's entrance exams, but warned the faculty that it had to take the plunge lest its delay be interpreted as "indicating a certain hesitation on our part in regard to the movement."[77] A conference among interested parties seems to have cleared up the matter, for the College faculty agreed to the substitution of the Board's exams for the University's in time for the Board's maiden effort in June, 1901.[78] The importance of this step to the Board's future was borne out at that first series of examinations: of the 973 candidates taking the exams, 758 sought admission to Columbia or Barnard.[79]

With the support of their own faculty thus assured, Butler and Low turned to the problem of gaining acceptance of the nation's major colleges for their Board.[80]

CONVERTING THE HEATHEN

Once it demonstrated ability to administer entrance examinations, CEEB membership gradually increased. Examining colleges were attracted by the prospect of reaching all potential sources of students without having to conduct their own entrance examinations at remote sites at a great cost in time and money. From the start, the Board offered examinations throughout the East, and soon examination centers appeared everywhere. A stipulation that a member college could continue to offer its own entrance exams in addition to accepting those of the Board made membership even more attractive. By 1905, twenty-seven colleges and universities had become Board members.[81] A number of others refrained from joining, but accepted the Board's certificates. A few in this latter group, notably Princeton, modified their own entrance requirements in the direction of the Board's.[82]

Colleges that accepted students on certificate found that they had to maintain entrance examinations for those few students who came from nonaccredited high schools or who did not receive the certificate of their principal attesting to their fitness for college work. Many such colleges, especially those of New England, found it easier to have their examinations administered by the Board and became members despite their minimal use of CEEB facilities.

Butler realized that the long-run success of the Board depended on securing the membership of all the major Eastern colleges, especially Harvard, Princeton, and Yale. The haughty manner in which these three institutions resisted Board membership caused resentment among the other members. Cornell, in fact, abolished a long-standing practice and refused to accept the results of entrance exams taken at the three colleges as equivalent to its own examinations. (Since the CEEB administered examinations only in June, member colleges continued to administer their own tests in September. Students living some distance from the university of their choice sometimes took some of the CEEB's exams in June and completed their tests the following September at a nearby college whose examinations were acceptable for that purpose by the applicant's chosen college.) Columbia considered following Cornell's lead, but did not, partly because it feared the Big Three might retaliate and partly because of impolitic timing.[83]

After almost a decade of persistent prodding, Eliot had finally convinced the Harvard faculty that much benefit could be derived from cooperation. In May, 1904, almost four years after the Board had begun to function, Eliot elatedly wrote Butler:

The Harvard Faculty moves slowly, but it moves. It will be ten years next November since I outlined a general admissions examination board to the New England Association of Colleges and could not interest the Association at all, or the Harvard Faculty. Yesterday, our Faculty voted by a large majority to go into your Board. You and Mr. Low have done the thing. . . .The country will thank you twenty years hence. I want to congratulate you now.[84]

The constitutional provision that membership be confirmed by vote of the College Board membership at its annual November meeting was suspended, and Harvard was immediately admitted by mail vote.[85] By 1910, both Princeton and Yale had applied for and obtained membership in the Board. For the Big Three a major motivation for joining appears to have been their desire to facilitate the recruitment of students from considerable distances.

CONSOLIDATION AND REASSESSMENT

Although established under the auspices of a regional association, the College Board aspired to a national standing. Thus, when a Southern Examination Board was established in 1905, Butler moved quickly. He told Fiske that he knew about it,

but I think it will not amount to very much and its certificates will have no weight outside of a few southern states. At the same time we ought to head off its growth by getting the best southern institutions in our Board. These are the University of Virginia, Vanderbilt University, Tulane University, and the University of Texas. I should think that tactful negotiations with these institutions, begun without delay, indicating the character of our Board's membership and the pleasure we should all have in the addition of southern institutions, would not be without some good results.[86]

The standards of the Southern universities were distinctly below those of schools in other sections of the country, and the Southern institutions were reluctant to push far beyond the capabilities of the surrounding secondary schools. Butler and his associates tried to convince the major colleges of that section that CEEB membership would aid them in their efforts to raise the level of education there, and would enable them to gain new ideas from discussion of practices at other major universities. His recruitment effort met with some success, but the real breakthroughs in Southern education came from other sources.[87]

When the Association of State Universities called a national conference "in reference to the standardizing of entrance requirements," Butler appointed a representative. "Of course this is just what our Board has done and is doing," he remarked, "but it may be that this conference will afford an opportunity to extend the scope of our influence."[88]

Looking back on the first decade of the College Board, Butler could take considerable satisfaction in the great extension in the scope of his influence.

By 1910, the "newer" disciplines had been fully accepted in the list of college entrance subjects in all significant American colleges. Entrance requirements had been standardized within each discipline, and complaints of arbitrary grading or poor administration of entrance exams had practically ceased. The colleges had learned to cooperate with one another, and to an extent unthinkable a generation earlier. The quality of instruction in the secondary schools and the range of offerings vastly improved.

Butler had also accomplished much for his alma mater, which in 1890 still viewed City College as its main competitor. By 1910 Columbia was housed in the pantheon of great American universities. And yet, things had not worked out quite the way Butler had expected.

There were still problems with the working of the College Board. The Board never resolved the schoolmasters' complaints concerning the excessiveness of entrance requirements. It could offer no recourse when even the best schools found that, say, the four-year Latin curriculum provided by the American Philological Association could not be completed in less than five years unless a high school skimped instruction in some other subject.[89] "The things that cause trouble are requirements that have been adopted in unison with other institutions," wrote Wilson Farrand in 1906. "These have generally been framed by bodies of specialists, and their recommendations have been accepted without revision by any central authority, with the result that there has been an increase in the amount called for in almost every subject. The great need at present is of an adjustment, and, if possible, of the establishment of some permanent method of adjustment."[90]

The following year, the CEEB modified its original policy of reliance on requirements formulated by the appropriate disciplinary associations by establishing a Committee of Review that continously studied the workings of the entrance requirements and arranged for modifications as they proved desirable. It usually accomplished this by appointing a representative commission in a given subject including both secondary school and college representatives and including individuals who worked for the CEEB as examiners or readers and thus having practical experience.[91] A decline in interest in entrance requirements on the part of the disciplinary associations (only the National Conference on Uniform Entrance Requirements in English remained in continuous existence for any length of time), and an increase in the CEEB's prestige permitted this reform to be implemented with little controversey. The continued large numbers of students admitted conditionally to the major examining colleges attested, however, to the Board's essential failure to resolve this problem.[92]

More fundamentally, Butler had intended to make the College Entrance Examination Board the ultimate arbiter of academic standards in America and the primary point of reference for the secondary schools in performing the selective function. By 1910 he knew that he had not succeeded. Almost all American colleges admitted students on certificate, not by entrance examination. The 3731 students who took CEEB tests in 1910 were a small proportion of those who entered college the following fall. Although the CEEB probably had an indirect effect on entrance requirements at certificating colleges, Butler thought the general standards of those colleges were far too low, and he believed the Board could do little to affect them.[93] It was true that students could offer many more subjects for college admission, but by 1910 Butler had become alarmed that many reputable colleges accepted considerable amounts of vocational work toward college admission. In short, Butler realized that efforts to facilitate the selective function were being abused, and that in some areas the secondary schools did not perform this function at all.

Butler's plan for controlling secondary and higher education by influencing all the powerful universities of the nation through the College Board never fully succeeded, but he was not without alternative plans. As president of an important university he could propose revisions in Columbia's own policies that might be widely adopted. Further, as the most prominent institution of higher education in New York State, Columbia could be a model of benevolent domination, perhaps even outdoing the success of the University of Michigan in this role. It is to these stratagems that we now turn.

NOTES TO CHAPTER 5
FROM THE COMMITTEE OF TEN
TO THE COLLEGE BOARD

1. Columbia University in the City of New York, *Annual Reports of the President and Treasurer to the Trustees with Accompanying Documents for the Year Ending June 30, 1916* (New York, Columbia University, 1916), p. 11.

2. There is a growing bibliography concerning the Committee of Ten. Theodore Sizer's *Secondary Schools at the Turn of the Century* (New Haven, Yale University Press, 1964) is entirely devoted to an analysis of the report and a discussion of the circumstances surrounding its issuance. See also Edward A. Krug, *The Shaping of the American High School 1880–1920* (Madison, Milwaukee, and London, The University of Wisconsin Press, 1969), especially chapters 2 and 3; Hugh Hawkins, *Between Harvard and America—The Educational Leadership of Charles W. Eliot* (New York, Oxford University Press, 1972). pp. 232–245; Henry J. Perkinson, *The Imperfect Panacea: American Faith in Education 1865–1965* (New York, Random House, 1968), pp. 134–138; Lawrence A. Cremin, "The Revolution in American Secondary Education, 1893–1918," *Teachers College Record* (March, 1955), 56:295–308: and Richard Hofstadter, *Anti-Intellectualism in American Life* (New York, Vintage Books, 1962), pp. 329–332.

3. The other members of the committee were James M. Taylor, president of Vassar College; James H. Baker, president of the University of Colorado; Richard H. Jesse, president of the University of Missouri; James C. MacKenzie, headmaster of the Lawrenceville School, Lawrenceville, New Jersey; and Henry C. King, professor of philosophy at Oberlin.

4. Hugh Hawkins, *Between Harvard and America*, pp. 171–176.

5. National Educational Association, *Report of the Committee on Secondary School Studies Appointed at the Meeting of the National Educational Association, July 9, 1892* (Washington, Government Printing Office, 1893). A copy of the report appears as an appendix in Sizer, *Secondary Schools.*

6. National Educational Association, *Report of the Committee on Secondary School Studies,* pp. 51–52. Eliot to Low, October 26, 1895, CUF, Uniform Entrance Requirements file. Subcommittees were established in Latin; Greek; English; Other Modern Languages; Mathematics; Physics, Astronomy, and Chemistry; Natural History (Biology including Botany, Zoology, and Physiology); History; Civil Government and Political Economy; and Geography (Physical Geography, Geology, and Meteorology). Eliot wrote in the *Report,* "The Conferences which found their tasks the most difficult were the Conferences on Physics, Astronomy and Chemistry; Natural History; History, Civil Government, and Political Economy; and Geography; and these four Conferences make the longest and most elaborate reports, for the reason that these subjects are to-day more imperfectly dealt with in primary and secondary schools than are the subjects of the first five Conferences. The experts who met to confer together concerning the teaching of the last four subjects in the list of Conferences all felt the need of setting forth in an ample way what ought to be taught, in what order, and by what method. They ardently desired to have their respective subjects made equal to Latin, Greek and Mathematics in weight and influence in the schools; but they knew that educational tradition was adverse to this desire, and that many teachers and directors of education felt no confidence in these subjects as disciplinary material. Hence the length and elaboration of these reports. In less degree, the Conferences on English and Other Modern Languages felt the same difficulties, these subjects being relatively new as substantial elements in school programmes" [*Report of the Committee on Secondary School Studies,* p. 13].

7. Eliot's definition of the "newer" disciplines did not include vocational subjects, and his suggested curricula provided for only token amounts of them.

8. Sizer, *Secondary Schools,* pp. 260–261.

9. The subcommittee on Greek had recommended continuation of the requirement of at least three years of Greek. The committee itself recommended only two years.

10. See Sizer, *Secondary Schools,* pp. 122–128.

11. [Nicholas Murray Butler], "Editorial," *Educational Review,* 2:238; 4:203–204, 514–515; 5:96–99, 207–208; 6:98–99, 409, 514–515; Nicholas Murray Butler, *Across the Busy Years: Recollections and Reflections* (New York, Charles Scribner's Sons, 1939), vol. 1, pp. 17, 197.

12. Richard Whittemore, *Nicholas Murray Butler and Public Education* (New York, Teachers College Press, 1970), pp. 78–88. William T. Harris, "The Committee of Ten on Secondary Schools," *Educational Review* (January, 1894), 7:1–10; Charles W. Eliot, "The Report of the Committee of Ten," *Educational Review* (February, 1894), 7:105–110; Charles De Garmo, "Report of the Committee of Ten: From the Point of View of Educational Theory," *Educational Review* (March, 1894), 7:275–280; Cecil F. P. Bancroft, "Report of the Committee of Ten: From the Point of View of the Academy," *Educational Review* (March, 1894), 7:280–285; John E. Bradley, "The Report of the Committee of Ten: From the Point of View of the Smaller Colleges," *Educational Review* (April, 1894), 7:370–374; John S. Clark, "The Report of the Committee of Ten: Art in Secondary Education—An Omission by the Committee of Ten," *Educational Review* (April, 1894), 7:374–381; Francis W. Parker, "The Report of the Committee of Ten: Its Use for the Improvement of Teachers Now at Work in the Schools," *Educational Review* (May, 1894), 7:479–491; Julius Sachs, "The Report of the Committee of Ten: From the Point of View of the College Preparatory School," *Educational Review* (June, 1894), 8:75–83; Charles W. Eliot, "The Unity of Educational Reform," *Educational Review* (October, 1894), 8:209–226; Nicholas Murray Butler, "Regulation of

Secondary Education," *The Nation* (January 18, 1894), 58:44–45; Nicholas Murray Butler, "The Reform of Secondary Education," *Century* (June, 1894), 48:314–316.

13. Nicholas Murray Butler, "The Scope and Function of Secondary Education," *Educational Review* (June, 1898), 16:26–27.

14. Butler often used the term "citizenship" in this connection. In a True Democracy, it was just as important for those who followed to understand the need for according deference as it was for those who ruled to do so in the best interests of all. The high school could serve the purpose of thus educating those who would not go to college, either directly in civics courses, or indirectly by giving them the sense that they had failed where others had succeeded in completing the high school course. The "cooling out" function operated at the high school level at the turn of the century.

15. Butler, "The Scope and Function," p. 25. Butler hoped that the status of the teaching profession could be elevated to the point where secondary schoolteachers were truly competent to make such important decisions. Drastic steps were necessary because of the poor state of the profession at the turn of the century. A contemporary wrote that the class of teachers was far from first-rate, that uncertainty and insecurity of position were common, that salaries were so low as to attract only the mediocre, and that few had any professional preparation. "Professionalization is still an ideal, the dream of the educational optimist. The lower positions are supplied to-day with the young, the immature, the poorly equipped. These young people pay a small price to get into teaching; they work little and they gain little" [Lotus Delta Coffman, *The Social Composition of the Teaching Population* (New York, Teachers College, 1911), pp. 84–85].

16. See Richard Whittemore, *Nicholas Murray Butler;* Lawrence A. Cremin, David A. Shannon, and Mary Evelyn Townsend, *A History of Teachers College, Columbia University* (New York, Columbia University Press, 1954); James Earl Russell, *Founding Teachers College, Reminiscences of the Dean Emeritus* (New York, Teachers College, 1937); and David C. Hammack, "The Centralization of New York City's Public School System, 1896: A Social Analysis of a Decision" (unpublished masters essay, Columbia University, 1969).

17. Butler, "The Scope and Function," p. 22.

18. Ibid., p. 23.

19. Butler posited something of a subject hierarchy based on informational and cultural, rather than disciplinary, value. "The exercise of a free choice does undoubtedly tend to develop responsibility and so character, but it is also to be remembered that the educational experience of the race is of some value. I take it that this experience points decisively to some academic disciplines as of more value for information, for culture, and for practical life, than others. Without some knowledge of the civilization and literature of antiquity, of the history of the race and particularly of one's own country, of mathematics and the natural sciences, of the modern languages, and of the laws and processes of thought, an education can hardly be called liberal" (Butler to Low, October 11, 1890, CUF, Nicholas Murray Butler 1890–1894 file.

20. Wilson Farrand, "The Reform of College Entrance Requirements," attached to Farrand to Low, October 18, 1895, CUF, Far file.

21. Low to Eliot, October 23, 1895, CUF, Uniform Entrance Requirements file.

22. Butler to Low, October 26, 1895, CUF, Uniform Entrance Requirements file.

23. Francis L. Patton to Low, November 13, 1895, November 22, 1895 and December 7, 1895, CUF, Uniform Entrance Requirements file.

24. Timothy Dwight to Low, November 1, 1895, December 18, 1895; Low to Dwight, December 10, 1895, CUF, Uniform Entrance Requirements file.

25. J. G. Schurman to Low, October 28, 1895 and November 9, 1895, CUF, Uniform Entrance Requirements file; Low to Farrand, October 31, 1895, and Farrand to Low, November 1, 1895 and November 5, 1895, CUF, Far file. Farrand charged that an attempt by instructors in history to establish a conference on entrance requirements under the association's auspices was blocked and that a similar conference in English had nearly been wrecked twice. Farrand feared that the association would reject a conference committee report.

26. Farrand to Low, November 12, 1895, CUF, Far file; Low to Charles C. Harrison, December 17, 1895, CUF, Uniform Entrance Requirements file.

27. [Nicholas Murray Butler, C. H. Coole, William H. Maxwell and Addison B. Polant], "Editorial," *Educational Review* (March, 1896), 11:305.

28. Paul Monroe, ed., *A Cyclopedia of Education* (New York, The Macmillan Co., 1910), vol. 2, pp. 105–106.

29. [N. M. Butler et al.], "Editorial," 305.

30. National Educational Association, *Report of the Committee on College Entrance Requirements* (Washington, D.C., The Association, 1899). Augustus F. Nightengale, Superintendent of the Chicago public schools, chaired the Committee.

31. Low to Burgess, January 6, 1896, CUF, Professor John W. Burgess 1890–1900 file; Low to Patton, January 11, 1896, Low to Dwight, January 11, 1896, CUF, Uniform Entrance Requirements file.

32. Butler's *Educational Review* specifically criticized the undertaking for excluding the sciences. See [Butler et al.] "Editorial," 305–306. Eliot offered a similar criticism. See Eliot to Low, December 26, 1895 and December 31, 1895, CUF, Uniform Entrance Requirements file. Low had not overlooked the sciences; he suggested they be dealt with at some future time "as that raises other and complex questions" (Low to Patton, December 10, 1895, CUF, Uniform Entrance Requirements file).

33. "Conclusions as to Uniform College Entrance Requirements Reached by the Conferences Held at Columbia College on February 1, 1896 and the Following Days," *Educational Review* (May, 1896), 11:494–501; Low to Eliot, February 5, 1896, G. M. Whieber to Low, June 1, 1896, CUF, Uniform Entrance Requirements file.

34. Low to Eliot, February 27, 1896, CUF, Charles W. Eliot file.

35. Thomas Day Seymour to Low, February 22, 1896; E. D. Perry to Low, February 22, 1896; Low to Seymour, February 24, 1896; Seymour to Low, February 25, 1896, CUF, Uniform Entrance Requirements file; Low to Eliot, February 27, 1896, CUF, Charles W. Eliot file; Eliot to Low, February 29, 1896, CUF, Uniform Entrance Requirements file.

36. MacKenzie to Low, March 4, 1896, CUF, Ma file; MacKenzie to Low, March 9, 1896, CUF, Uniform Entrance Requirements file.

37. John H. Van Amringe to Low, January 27, 1897, CUF, Professor John H. Van Amringe file; Columbia University *Minutes of the Faculty of Columbia College September 29, 1892 to May 25, 1900,* February 26, 1897, p. 144 (hereafter cited as *College Faculty Minutes 1892–1900*). Low to Eliot, March 11, 1897, CUF, Charles W. Eliot file.

38. Butler to William Beebe, March 17, 1898, CUF, Nicholas Murray Butler, 1898–1900 file; Eliot to Low, March 10, 1897, CUF, Charles W. Eliot file.

39. Krug, *The Shaping*, pp. 147–148.

40. Low to Eliot, October 7, 1896, CUF, Charles W. Eliot file.

41. Claude M. Fuess, *The College Board: Its First Fifty Years* (New York, Columbia University Press, 1950), p. 9.

42. He specifically mentioned the University of Michigan. It should be recalled that certificating colleges still offered entrance examinations to students from nonaccredited high schools.

43. At that time it took a student preparing for Harvard a year longer to complete its entrance requirements than it took a student to prepare for just about any other college. Low informed Eliot that Columbia would not raise its own requirements and Eliot knew that the chances for agreement were slim unless he could convince his own faculty to enact some reductions.

44. Eliot to Low, October 9, 1896, CUF, Charles W. Eliot file.

45. Low to Eliot, October 12, 1896; Eliot to Low, October 13, 1896, CUF, Charles W. Eliot file.

46. Whittemore, *Nicholas Murray Butler*, pp. 64–68.

47. Nicholas Murray Butler, "Discussion [of the 'Report of the Chairman of the Joint Committee on College-Entrance Requirements']," *Journal of Proceedings and Addresses of the National Educational Association,* 1897:652–653.

48. Butler to Low, August 7, 1897 and October 26, 1899, CUF, Nicholas Murray Butler 1890–1897 and Nicholas Murray Butler 1898–1900 files.

49. Butler was not the first major Columbia academician to consider the possible benefits to that university of implementation of a certificate system. During the early 1870s, when the threat posed by City College led to considerable discussion about all of Columbia's academic policies, President Barnard advocated adoption of a modified certificate system. Under his plan, all students who could produce a certificate from their preparatory instructors indicating that they had met all of Columbia's entrance requirements and were well prepared to enter their chosen course of study would be admitted for a probationary period of one or two months. To be retained on the rolls of the College after that period had expired, the student would have to attain a specific numerical average. To Columbia's trustees he argued that the entrance examinations were physically and mentally onerous and could lead to permanent damage to students rejected after undergoing the stress and anxiety they entailed. He also argued that the bestowing of certificate privileges on worthy preparatory schools would add to Columbia's prestige in the eyes of the public. He concluded that American education would be the beneficiary if Columbia would only let its "power be felt." "Nothing is needed but a judicious application of the means at her command to enable her to take her place in the foremost rank of the agencies which are hereafter to give direction to the entire current of educational effort in this country" [William F. Russell, ed., *The Rise of a University,* vol. 1, *The Later Days of Old Columbia College* (New York, Columbia University Press, 1937), pp. 3–16].

50. Butler, "Discussion [of the 'Report of the Chairman], p. 653.

51. Even Harvard's Eliot showed some respect for this aspect of the certificate system. Between 1892 and 1896, Harvard sent inspection teams to private New England schools on invitation and provided those schools with confidential evaluations. They were solely for the information of the preparatory schools and in no way affected admission of their students to Harvard (see Hawkins, *Between Harvard and America*, p. 353).

52. Butler to Low, October 26, 1899, CUF, Nicholas Murray Butler 1898–1900 file.

53. Butler to Low, December 5, 1898, CUF, *Ibid.*

54. Low to Dr. Julius Sachs, December 22, 1898, CUF, Professor Julius Sachs file; Fiske to Prettyman, June 21, 1900, CUF, Virgil Prettyman file.

55. The Oxford and Cambridge Schools Examinations Board, composed of an equal number of representatives from both universities, had been intended to examine preparatory schools upon the application of the headmaster. Instead, inspectors began to examine individual students during their visits. Passing of the examination entitled the student to admission to almost any of the colleges of the two universities. The examinations were conducted in many parts of England, were credited with considerable improvement of English secondary education, and brought added prestige to the sponsoring universities (see Russell, ed., *The Rise of a University*, pp. 12–16, 27–28).

56. When Butler offered a defense of uniform entrance examinations over certification at a meeting of the Commission of Accredited Schools of the North Central Association in 1902, his friend Andrew Sloan Draper, still president of the University of Illinois, reproached him for going over to the enemy (see Krug, *The Shaping*, pp. 153–154).

57. Possibly he had not abandoned all hopes of adopting a full-fledged certificate system since on a major occasion, he suggested that the ultimate purpose of inspection might be the acceptance of "the credentials issued by this board, without a special formal admission examination" [Nicholas Murray Butler, "Uniform College Admissions Requirements with a Joint Board of Examiners," *Educational Review* (January, 1900), 19:68–74]. For the position of the Columbia faculty, see Low to Dr. Julius Sachs, December 2, 1898, and December 22, 1898; and Sachs to Low, December 3, 1898, CUF, Professor Julius Sachs file.

58. Schurman to Low, December 9, 1898; Patton to Low, December 10, 1898; Eliot to Low, December 10, 1898, December 21, 1898 and December 27, 1898; Harrison to Low, December 20, 1898; J. H. Penniman to Low, December 28, 1898, CUF, Uniform Entrance Requirements file.

59. Low to Eliot, January 26, 1899, CUF, Charles W. Eliot file.

60. Eliot to Low, January 25, 1899, CUF, Charles W. Eliot file. Italics mine.

61. G. R. Carpenter to Low, January 3, 1899, CUF, Uniform Entrance Requirements file. Low to G. R. Carpenter, February 25, 1899, CUF, Professor George R. Carpenter 1893–1903 file.

62. Nicholas Murray Butler, "How the College Entrance Examination Board Came to Be," in College Entrance Examination Board, *The Work of the College Entrance Examination Board* (Boston, Ginn and Company, 1926), p. 4.

63. Association of Colleges and Preparatory Schools of the Middle States and Maryland, *Proceedings of the Thirteenth Annual Convention, 1899*, pp. 43–86.

64. Butler, *Across the Busy Years*, vol. 1, p. 199. For another description of the meeting, see Edward Krug, *The Shaping*, p. 148.

65. Butler to Low, December 4, 1899, CUF, Nicholas Murray Butler 1898–1900 file; College Entrance Examination Board of the Middle States and Maryland, *Annual Report of the Secretary, 1901*. The first eight reports of the CEEB were reprinted in Butler's *Educational Review* in the October issue.

66. Peck to Low, November 15, 1892, CUF, Professor Harry Thurston Peck file.

67. In 1892 the dean of Columbia's School of Mines sided with schoolmasters' complaints about the difficulty of the examination given by Professor of French Adolph Cohn. Cohn's reply to Low, who seemed to side with his critics, was similar to Peck's. See Low to Cohn, November 11, 1892; Cohn to Low, July 29, 1893, CUF, Adolph Cohn file. See also T. S. Fiske to Low, July 1, 1899, CUF, Thomas S. Fiske file.

68. *College Faculty Minutes 1892–1900.* April 27, 1894, pp. 92–94.

69. *Ibid.*, December 18, 1896, pp. 136–137. Two years later, the chairman of the Committee on Admissions wrote that the percentage of students passing the 1898 entrance examinations

varied widely from 47% in French to 82% in Mathematics (Low to Fiske, September 29, 1898, CUF, Thomas S. Fiske file).

70. *College Faculty Minutes 1892–1900,* February 24, 1899, pp. 265–268.

71. T. S. Fiske to Low, March 15, 1900, CUF, Thomas S. Fiske file. Fiske had previously requested of Low that he be given additional help in the carrying out his administrative duties (see Fiske to Low, January 6, 1899, CUF, Thomas S. Fiske file, and Low to G. R. Carpenter, January 14, 1899, CUF, Professor George R. Carpenter, 1893–1903 file).

72. Fiske to Low, March 15, 1900, CUF, Thomas S. Fiske file.

73. Low to Eliot, May 14, 1900, CUF, Charles W. Eliot file.

74. *College Faculty Minutes 1892–1900,* May 25, 1900, pp. 333–335.

75. Columbia University, *Minutes of the Faculty of Columbia College, October 26, 1900 to June 13, 1908,* November 23, 1900, pp. 365–366 (hereafter cited as *College Faculty Minutes 1900–1908*).

76. "Be assured . . .," wrote one, "that I shall be sincerely glad to make any contribution toward the successful work of the Board that can be given by urging our boys to take their examinations under the guidance of the Board and its committees" (Lawrence C. Hull to Low, January 5, 1901, CUF, Hu file).

77. Low to Van Amringe, January 8, 1901, CUF, Professor John H. Van Amringe, 1896–1905 file. Low made good on his promise. When schoolmasters objected that the proposed CEEB exam in Attic prose would put their students at a disadvantage, Low authorized the acceptance of certificates in that subject (Fiske to Low, April 4, 1901, CUF, Thomas S. Fiske file). See also *College Faculty Minutes 1900–1908,* October 25, 1901, p. 412.

78. Columbia continued to offer its own examinations in September but control over these was nominal since "it is necessary in order to avoid confusion and injustice to the candidate for admission, that the September examinations follow as closely as possible the pattern set by the Intercollegiate Board in June" (*College Faculty Minutes 1900–1908,* March 27, 1903, p. 16).

79. College Entrance Examination Board, *The Work,* p. 81.

80. Faculty resentment over lost authority in the area of admissions manifested itself sporadically. In 1903 the College Faculty rejected a proposal to grant students advanced credit for completion of extra work as measured by their performance on their entrance examinations on the grounds that acceptance of CEEB results for such a purpose meant the surrender of "the control of our own standards for the Bachelor's degree" (*College Faculty Minutes 1900–1908,* March 27, 1903, p. 16). Fittingly, Professor Peck initiated a last attempt at unilateral action in 1908. Although the University Committee on Entrance Examinations commended the general principle behind the proposed changes in the University's Latin requirements and commented that they would place preparatory studies of Latin "on a more rational and scientific basis," it rejected the changes on the grounds that unilateral action would injure relations between Columbia, the CEEB, and the secondary schools. Its suggestion that Peck seek the support of other major colleges shows how far the movement had come (*College Faculty Minutes 1900–1908,* April 10, 1908, pp. 107–108). In 1910, the final decision on admission to Columbia College was placed in the hands of a universitywide Committee on Undergraduate Admissions.

81. CEEB, "Annual Report of the Secretary, 1905," *Educational Review* (October, 1905), 30:250.

82. Wilson Farrand, "Five Years of the College Entrance Examination Board," *Educational Review* (October, 1905), 30:217–230.

83. Clarence Young to Butler, February 25, 1904, CUF, Dr. Clarence H. Young file.

84. Eliot to Butler, May 18, 1904, CUF, Charles W. Eliot file. See also Butler to Eliot, May 4, 1904, CUF, Charles W. Eliot file for details of the negotiations.

85.   See *The Harvard Graduates Magazine,* 13:434–435. The faculty took pains to point out that "it must not, however, be inferred that in becoming a member of the College Entrance Examination Board, Harvard is necessarily making her entrance requirements in any subject the equivalent of any one or more of the other colleges and universities belonging to it." It noted that Harvard would continue to offer its own extrance exams as alternates, that applicants in any case would have to take Harvard's exams in advanced Greek and German, in elementary and advanced Latin, and in mathematics since Harvard's requirements "are not fully met by the Board exams," that the CEEB exams could be read by Harvard graders if desired, and that Harvard was free to establish its own passing grade on CEEB papers.

86.   Butler to Fiske, March 2, 1905, CUF, Thomas S. Fiske file.

87.   Nelson G. McCrea to Butler, December 28, 1907, CUF, Dr. Nelson Glenn McCrea file. Carnegie Foundation for the Advancement of Teaching, *Third Annual Report of the President and Treasurer,* pp. 65–71.

88.   Butler to Farrand, November 17, 1905, CUF, Far file.

89.   Farrand to Butler, November 20, 1905, November 22, 1905, and January 11, 1906; and Butler to Farrand, January 8, 1906, CUF, Far file.

90.   Farrand to Butler, January 16, 1906, CUF, Far file.

91.   Wilson Farrand, "A Brief History of the College Entrance Examination Board," in College Entrance Examination Board, *The Work,* pp. 24–25.

92.   Butler to Farrand, April 11, 1906, CUF, Far file.

93.   College Entrance Examination Board, *The Work,* p. 106; Butler to Farrand, November 17, 1905, CUF, Far file.

CHAPTER

6

Internal Improvements

The issuance of a report by the Committee of Ten and the establishment of a College Entrance Examination Board did not by themselves bring on a new era in high school–college relations. For significant change to come about, the suggestions contained in the report and the services offered by the Board had to be adopted by the major colleges. Fully understanding the reluctance of college faculties to deviate from the tried and true ways, Butler attempted to convince the faculty of Columbia College to fulfill a historic role by responding to the challenges posed by the breakthroughs of the 1890s.

COLUMBIA'S ENTRANCE REQUIREMENTS
AND COLUMBIA'S CURRICULUM

When Nicholas Murray Butler assumed Columbia's presidency in 1902, he asked his registrar, George Germann, to compare the admissions requirements of the College in that year with those of 1860. Germann found that entrance requirements had grown more demanding[1] (see Table 6.1). Using the metric employed in 1902, he estimated that, whereas the students entering the College in 1900 had to complete fifteen points of studies to gain admission, they had had to satisfy only half of that number in 1860. He found that the amount of Greek and Latin required for admission had not varied during those forty years, but that the amount of math—the third of the

113

triumverate that made up the 1860 entrance list—had significantly increased in this period.

Germann concluded that greater subject competence required in 1902 was due primarily to the inroads of the new disciplines, not to the raising of the level of required mastery of the old.

Generally, once a subject gained academic curricular recognition, pressure was exerted by its representatives on the faculty to make some kind of propaedeutic work in that subject a prerequisite for entrance into the institution; moreover, once the high schools, partly in response to these pressures, placed the subject in their own curricula, pressures were exerted by headmasters to gain acceptance of that subject as one that would fulfill an entrance requirement.

Table 6.1. Columbia Entrance Requirements: 1860–61, 1880–81, and 1901–02 (optional units in italicized numerals).

	1860–61	1880–81	1901–02[d]
Latin	4[a]	4	*4*
Greek	3	3	*3*
Math	1	2 or 3[b]	3
English		0[c]	3
Geography		0[c]	
French			*2*
German			*2*
Spanish			*2*
History			*1*
Physics			*1*
Chemistry			*1*
Botany			*1*
Physiography			*1*
Zoology			*1*
Total required for entrance	8	9 or 10	15

SOURCE.   Germann to Butler, June 19, 1902, CUF, Dr. George B. Germann file.
[a]Relative values of subjects determined by 1900 requirements.
[b]Value of mathematics in 1880–81 could not be precisely determined.
[c]Only a grammar school knowledge of these subjects required.
[d]Maximum of 4 units permitted in modern languages, and of 2 in sciences. One additional point permitted for advanced work in each of French, German, Greek, history, Latin, mathematics, and physics.

In 1890 Butler had written that Columbia College's curriculum was typical of many contemporary colleges, sharing "the fate of all the older courses of study, mainly literary in character, in which the pressure of circumstances has forced, first, some instruction in natural science and, secondly, some instruction in the modern languages, and which have not been entirely reconstituted with reference to the changed educational conditions."[2]

The few changes that had occurred in the Columbia College curriculum to that point affected only the junior and senior years: some course work in the "newer disciplines," including the sciences, history, and modern languages was added to the prescribed curriculum, and some further work was made optional.[3] After reorganization in 1889, seniors could take course work anywhere in the University. But the freshman and sophomore curricula remained completely prescribed and monopolized by the traditional subjects. As long as that situation remained unchanged, so did Columbia's list of entrance requirements.

Representatives of the new subjects had no desire to wait until a student's junior or senior year before exposing the student to their disciplines. Not only were they impatient to introduce the student to subject matter that they considered a vital part of a liberal education, but they felt at a severe competitive disadvantage in attempting to recruit students to professional work in their disciplines. Exposure to six years of classical instruction (four in high school and two in college) and no years of chemistry or history was considered unfair by men who considered the classical subjects to be "mere disciplines" and who were about to effect an Academic Revolution.

Butler and others knew that once the classicists relinquished the freshman and sophomore bastions, they could no longer insist on a monopoly of subjects needed for entry. Thus, reform of the lower college curriculum and of entrance requirements were bound together. Butler objected to Columbia policies that permitted freshmen to enter the College knowing nothing of French or German, physics or chemistry. He objected more vigorously to policies that permitted a student to be graduated without exposure to any of the biological sciences save botany. Recalling that reorganization included establishment of a professional option, Butler concluded that the College's entrance requirements and curriculum were not adequate prerequisites for graduate or professional work in almost any subject.[4]

At the same time that the classics were attacked from "above," objections to Columbia's curriculum and entrance requirements from the secondary schoolmasters became more vocal. In 1894 a group of headmasters, although hesitant to request the complete elimination of Greek as an entrance requirement, asked that Columbia and neighboring colleges offer instruction in elementary Greek for those not having adequate opportunity to pursue it in high school. The schoolmasters justified this on the ground that so many new courses had been added to the secondary curriculum that "few high schools could spare the time and the effort necessary to fit pupils for college in Greek."[5]

Within two years, Greek would cease to be prescriptive; the handwriting had been on the wall even before the schoolmasters issued their request. In 1892, the first break in the lower college curriculum occurred when students in the College were given the opportunity to study chemistry instead of one language during the sophomore year. The move elicited some of the expected jeremiads. "You are doing a most radical and far-reaching thing: a thing untried (I believe) anywhere and unsupported by any authoritative advice, so far as I know, in any quarter save that of the scientific world of which some citizens would sacrifice Greek on any terms as a mere enemy," said Professor George Woodbury.[6]

Some classicists argued that students interested in the study of sciences might be offered a separate course. Permitting the substitution, they argued, "fills the required hours to such a degree with other and less disciplinary studies, that it denies to the classics the opportunities which they have so long had, and which from their disciplining and humanising character they so justly deserve." Implementing the reform, they concluded, "would result in lowering the standard of the college and in degrading the degree of A.B."[7]

One classicist disagreed with his colleagues. Professor of Latin Harry Peck argued that implementation of the reform would not spell the end of classical study, since many students voluntarily pursued advanced classical studies and exposure to significant work in one classical language would still be required. He chided his colleagues for overestimating the unique disciplinary value of the classical languages and stated that all subjects have "much that is dry, and much that entails real though necessary drudgery." He said that it would be better for a student to learn patience and perseverence "in that work wherein his hope of ultimate success gives him the powerful stimulus of expectation, rather than that he should perform the same toil with no motive before him but the motive that animates a dog in a treadmill." A believer in the importance of the growth of the College, Peck concluded that an expanded curriculum would attract many new students "who are at present repelled by the inflexibility of the course."[8]

Several factors led to a change in the academic balance of power in the 1890s with important implications for the liberalization of entrance requirements and the college curriculum. The resignation and death of some of the most vocal antiuniversity diehards, including Professor Henry Drisler's retirement in 1894, took place in this decade. At the same time, an onslaught of *wissenschaft* scholars offering instruction in the newer disciplines appeared.

Finally the report of the Committee of Ten and the constant demands of the secondary schoolmasters had a strong cumulative effect.

The end for Greek as a prescriptive entrance requirement came about shortly thereafter. In the fall of 1894 a College faculty committee recommended acceptance of advanced mathematics and either advanced study of a modern language or study of a natural science (physics, chemistry, or an equivalent) as a substitute for that classical language. Further review revealed that the proposed substitution of modern languages was excessive. As finally passed the requirement was that a student not offering Greek had to offer advanced mathematics and both an elementary language and a science. When President Low made a public statement announcing these permitted substitutions, he took pains to state that the new substitutions "received the affirmative vote of all the classical professors in the College."[9]

During the three years that these substitutions were permitted prior to further liberalization, the trend away from Greek became unmistakable. Whereas in the first year only 13 of 108 students entered the freshman class without Greek (12%), the ratio increased to 24 of 126 students (19%) during the second year, and to 34 of 104 (33%) in the third year.[10]

Other subjects would similarly enter the list of entrance subjects as substitutes for Greek, after gaining a niche in the lower College curriculum. In 1895 the faculty accorded history elective status in the freshman course. In 1898, it accepted one year of secondary school history from students not offering Greek for admission. In the same year, students not offering Greek were permitted to offer both elementary German and elementary French for admission. At the same time, the faculty upgraded the entrance requirement in English to reflect the agreements voted at meetings of the New England and Middle States Associations in 1894. In its new form, English became prescriptive for all applicants.[11]

Perhaps the most important liberalization of the College's entrance requirements occurred in 1900, when Latin became an optional requirement for admission. President Low argued that the many students who might decide to attend college late in their high school careers and who therefore had not taken a college preparatory course found themselves unable to attend Columbia College because of its requirement that Latin be studied throughout high school. Elimination of required Latin was the next logical step in the process of facilitating college admission. Low wrote, "a student can begin in the College the study of Greek, the modern languages, and any of the natural sciences. I am under the impression that it will only be necessary to make provision for the elementary study of Latin within the College to accomplish fully what I have proposed."[12]

Supporters concluded that so long as Latin was prescribed for graduation, it did not really matter whether it was studied in secondary school or taken up only after admission to college. When the College faculty adopted this change, it emphasized that its goal was not to change the requirements for graduation, but "to provide that when a student presents himself for admission, after a thorough high-school course, but without some one or more of the subjects insisted upon by this Faculty for the degree of A.B., he shall be given the opportunity to make good his deficiency during the college course."[13]

The drop-off in the percentage of students offering Latin for admission was gradual. Eight years after implementation of the reform, three-quarters of Columbia's entering class still offered Latin, and some of these also presented Greek (see Table 6.2). The reason for this may have been that most secondary schools continued to require Latin for graduation regardless of the changed conditions at Columbia. Further, Latin remained a graduation requirement for all Columbia College students until 1905 and for students desiring a B.A. for a decade after that.

The collapse of Latin, although not accompanied by the apocalyptic rhetoric invoked during the collapse of Greek, proved even more important. It permitted the candidate for admission to gain exposure while in secondary school to almost all the "newer" disciplines, if he so chose. It also permitted the high school to allocate its resources more equitably among terminal and continuing students. Although some schools and some students were slow in coming around, the classics would never again attain the preeminence they had until the turn of the century.

Coincidentally, it was this modification in entrance requirements that oc-

Table 6.2. Students Offering Greek and Latin, Latin Only, or Neither for Entrance to Columbia College: 1901–08.

	Class Entering							
	1901	1902	1903	1904	1905	1906	1907	1908
Latin and Greek	54%	50%	41%	40%	30%	22%	20%	16%
Latin only[a]	40	43	49	48	55	63	65	59
Neither	6	7	10	12	15	16	15	25
Number of students[b]	103	125	123	113	123	168	173	153

SOURCE.   Columbia University, *Annual Report of the President of Columbia University, 1902–1909.* The annual reports supply statistics for these years only.

[a]Students offering Greek but not Latin not included. The expectation and the reality were that there were few such students.

[b]Not counting transfers or students entering on Regents Academic Diplomas.

casioned the adoption of a unit system for the calculation of entrance credits at Columbia. The transmutation of qualitative requirements into quantitative ones marked the triumph of the doctrine of equivalence, the notion that no academic subject was inately superior to any other in terms of academic knowledge or ability to "discipline" the mind. Adoption of the unit system permitted somewhat more freedom for a student in choosing his secondary school program. Since, for all students, whether or not they offered Greek or Latin, some secondary units were not prescribed, the faculty merely had to lengthen the list of courses the student could take to fill those optional units in order to further liberalize the College's entrance requirements. In this manner did drawing, music, physiography, shop work, and zoology join the list of acceptable entrance subjects.[14]

B.A. OR B.S.?

At bottom, the issue involved in all of these changes could be summed up in a single question: What should be required of a student attempting to acquire a liberal education at a university? Butler answered that a liberal education should be a broadening experience, yet should have relevance to the student's future plans. Butler, Low, and others insisted that liberal education was not identical with classical education and the reforms they instigated reflected this belief.

The classicists on the Columbia faculty executed a graceful retreat, perhaps believing that ground could be yielded in the area of entrance requirements as long as the classics remained on the list of graduation requirements. It would be beneficial for the student to have been exposed to classical training while in high school, but since for many students this might be unrealistic, a specified minimum of college training would have to suffice. No classicist assumed that a student could receive a Bachelor of Arts, the symbol of acquisition of a liberal education, without at least the Latin classics. All believed that a majority of the College faculty, whether they represented the older or new disciplines, would agree with them. And for a quarter century after reorganization, they were right.

At many other universities, students could obtain a degree without completing work in the classics, but usually the degree awarded would be the Bachelor of Science or the Bachelor of Philosophy degree rather than the Bachelor of Arts.[15] At Columbia, such a solution was not possible. The classicists had the votes, and despite sporadic suggestions that a second degree be awarded they insisted that "they would grant no degree other than that of Bachelor of Arts, and would not grant that degree without some knowledge on the part of the candidate of at least one ancient language."[16] Students not wishing to pursue classical studies in college could enter another undergraduate institution, or they could enter the College and transfer to a professional school after meeting the prerequisites of that school. However, students following this latter course would only receive the professional degree unless they completed all prescribed College work and had a minimum number of years of College residence before transferring—and this included classical study.

The opposition to the classicists agreed that the College should offer only the Bachelor of Arts, but wanted the definition of liberal education extended to include the knowledge acquired by students whether their courses were preprofessional or were simply aimed at acquiring a "well-trained and cultivated mind." Butler remained in the forefront of this group from 1890 to the ultimate resolution of the question in 1916. The entire reform movement at Columbia, he argued, attempted to make liberal education a necessary foundation for professional study. It would be manifestly absurd, he continued, while insisting on this, not to offer preprofessional courses that would serve as an introduction to specialized studies. The only alternative would be to insist that the traditional curriculum was the best possible preparation for professional study—a proposition that Butler considered absurd.[17]

At first only a small minority advocated establishment of a nonclassical course within the College leading to a degree other than the B.A. But the sciences were popular among students, and professors of science believed that undergraduates could obtain adequate scientific training only if the classical requirements were drastically reduced. Pressure for establishment of a scientific course constantly rose; by 1905 it became irresistible. In that year, the College faculty adopted parallel curricula for classical and scientific study leading to the degrees of Bachelor of Arts and Bachelor of Science, respectively. The classicists yielded and permitted students to be graduated from the College without completing any work in the classics. On the other hand Butler lost his battle to retain one degree for all students completing a Columbia College course of study. He accepted his defeat philosophically, reasoning that "the line of distinction between the two degrees is so thin that it will not take long to wear it away." Expresident Low, now retired after defeat in his 1903 bid for reelection as mayor of New York, was not quite as reserved in his comments. He wrote Butler that Columbia College

has hitherto stood firmly, despite all temptations to depart from it, for the idea that its aim is to give a liberal education; that the traditional reward for such an education is the degree of A.B.; and that it would not multiply College degrees, upon the theory that part of its work was liberal and part was not. To depart from this policy now, when the whole conception of a liberal education has already broadened so much and is still broadening, seems to me like a step backward. I should as soon think of the City of New York abandoning the underground trolley to go back to horse cars as of Columbia taking such a step.[18]

It would take Butler another eleven years before he finally got his way on this issue. While he waited for his faculty to see the light, he could take solace from the important substantive changes he had brought about in the nature of a liberal education. And under his leadership, Columbia would continue to introduce the major innovations in liberal education for many years to come.

THE RECONCILIATION OF
THE DESIRABLE WITH THE POSSIBLE:
CONDITIONED ADMITTANCE

As Registrar Germann found, the addition of new subjects to the College's list of entrance requirements did not simply come at the expense of Greek and Latin. Over the years, the number of "units" required for admission to Columbia had doubled, signifying that the faculty required study in newer disciplines *in addition to* and not simply *in place of* the classical subjects. As the number of required admissions units increased, so did the number of entrance examinations. By 1910, a student wishing to enter Columbia—or any other college still mandating entrance exams—confronted as many as eleven tests. Given the different capabilities of students and the different capacities of the various high schools for instructing them in each subject, an obviously well-qualified student would frequently fail one or more examinations. Most faculty members agreed that a failure in one entrance examination should not suffice to exclude a student from college. At the same time, they concurred that a failure in all entrance examinations implied obvious unfitness. The problem of what to do with students who failed an exam or two in subjects they had studied in high school continually vexed faculty and administrators at all colleges that clung to the examination system.[19]

The most common solution of this problem was the "conditioning" of such students. A student failing the entrance examination in, say, history would still be admitted if he had passed the remainder of his exams. Usually he would be given a semester or a year to make up his condition, either by completion of introductory course work in history in college or by outside study and passing another administration of the failed examination. During the 1890s the Columbia faculty gave a student a year to make up his conditions, and placed him on probation until he did. After one semester, the student could be dropped if he had not made "satisfactory progress" in all of his courses.[20]

In the early twentieth century, the convergence of several factors led to receipt of conditions by an increasing proportion of the freshman class. The number of subjects required for entrance led many secondary schoolteachers to claim that they were excessive and that thoroughness of preparation had to be sacrificed to achieve breadth of preparation.[21] Students who decided to attend college late in their secondary careers often had taken courses not on Columbia's list of acceptable entrance subjects and consequently had to be conditioned in those courses. Further, any discretion that Columbia professors might have had in grading of entrance exams ended with the shift of that responsibility to the College Board, which did its work "in a thoroughly impartial and businesslike manner."[22] Scanty statistics exist giving the percentage of Columbia freshmen entering with conditions. The percentages for students taking the June exams in 1903 and from 1905 to 1908 were 58% (N = 50), 53% (70), 52% (66), 70% (57), and 52% (89).[23] In 1907, 67% of the 126 students taking the June and/or September exams entered on condition.[24]

The director of admissions at Columbia summed up the situation:

if there were complete adjustment between school and college, if all subjects were well taught in school, if every student knew several years in advance to what college he would go and could make sure of including all required subjects in his curriculum and if every student worthy of higher training were reasonably good in all the subjects required for admission, there would be little excuse for admitting students with conditions.

Butler called it "inconceivable" that such a large proportion of the freshman class entered with conditions and became "thereby severely handicapped at the time when they should be most free to adjust themselves and their mental life to the new work of the College." He asked the faculty to investigate the problem.[25]

In response the College faculty appointed a Special Committee on the Relations Between the College and the Secondary Schools. The committee found that in 1907 two-thirds of those admitted to the freshman class received conditions, with the average conditioned student having three conditions (that is, completing twelve of the required fifteen points). It termed justifiable most of the conditions issued. Some disparities existed in the level of difficulty of the exams, and the committee singled out in this regard the tests in advanced mathematics and Latin prose. However, it discovered that a significant proportion of conditions were given to students with grades of between 50% and 59% on their exams—a range the committee considered "doubtful," rather than "failing." The committee believed that a recent ruling by the University Committee on Entrance Examinations, permitting the College Committee on Admissions to take a candidate's average on all exams into account in determining the number of conditions to be imposed, would go far to remove many freshmen with only one or two doubtful grades from the list of conditioned students. The committee also found that students readily made up their conditions. Only about one-fifth of those entering in the fall of 1907 with conditions had made no progress toward removing them during the fall semester, and some of these had dropped out. The committee did not prescribe any major changes in policy and justified conditioned admittance in light of the large proportion of students who proved themselves acceptable after their first semester in the College.[26]

THE CARNEGIE FOUNDATION
AND CONDITIONED ADMITTANCE

By 1905, the use of conditions had become so widespread among examining colleges that it began to draw considerable attention. Notable among the critics was Henry S. Pritchett, the administrator of the Carnegie Foundation for the Advancement of Teaching.

When Andrew Carnegie established a fund designed to provide pensions to retired professors from "eligible" colleges, he hired Henry S. Pritchett, president of the Massachusetts Institute of Technology and a friend of Butler, to supervise disbursements. Pritchett quickly realized that the definition of "eligible" could be manipulated to raise academic standards. Thus, he defined a college as "an institution, the faculty of which contained at least six professors giving full time to their teaching and research, which offered a course of four full years of instruction in liberal arts and sciences, and which required for admission not less than four years of high-school training in addition to preacademic or grammar-school studies." Similarly, he defined a high school as an institution that offered between fourteen and sixteen units of preparatory courses in the academic disciplines. A unit was a subject studied for five hours weekly for a full year. Although the term had been employed for almost a decade, in the future it would popularly be referred to as the "Carnegie unit." [27]

In his effort to upgrade academic standards, Pritchett considered the amount of preparation required for college admission to be critical. Labeling entrance requirements the factor underlying all that "influences the final efficiency or dynamic force of a college," he concluded they were "the sole feasible means of securing a fair degree of unity in our system." During the foundation's early years, Pritchett strived to raise the standard of admission to American colleges to at least fourteen Carnegie units, and to insure that the content of these units roughly paralleled the requirements accepted by the College Entrance Examination Board.[28] Within a few years, he found that the carrot of Carnegie funds had led many colleges to institute reforms in this direction.[29]

Pritchett believed that the conditioning of students undermined much of his efforts. Charging that "leniency, theoretically justifiable if involving one or two slight conditions, has developed into indiscriminate charity," he argued that the practice hurt the secondary schools by promoting competition between them and the colleges.[30] When he inquired of Butler about the large number of students admitted to the College with conditions, the Columbia president, relying on his faculty's report, defended the College's practices. He termed the old admissions process at Columbia "almost mechanical in character." It "denied admission to every incoming student who did not comply completely with the technical requirements, or whose conditions were not so slight as to be quite unimportant." Following such a policy had led to "serious educational injustice and grave wrong to many students." At his insistence the various committees on admission had begun to take the "human element" into account. He considered the results largely satisfactory. "[T]he Registrar informs me," he told Pritchett, "that some students most heavily conditioned at admission have been some of the most successful in their college work."[31]

REFORM IN THE PROVINCES

Pritchett aimed his criticisms not at Columbia alone; he offered stinging rebuke to the other examing colleges appearing to abuse the practice of conditioning. It probably was no coincidence that shortly after 1910 Harvard, Princeton and Yale, under attack by the Carnegie Foundation on one flank and by the certificate system on the other, all modified their admissions policies.

Harvard, which had routinely expected applicants to complete up to eleven entrance exams, permitted students with satisfactory secondary school records in a program that included language, history, mathematics, and science to take only four comprehensive examinations. The new examinations' comprehensiveness derived from their coverage of all parts of a subject in one text. Until this time, Harvard offered separate exams testing the various aspects of the discipline, say Latin, such as grammar, reading ability, and composition. The students permitted to elect this option took exams in English; Latin (or French or German for Bachelor of Science candidates); mathematics, physics, or chemistry; and one other area to be selected from chemistry, French, German, Greek, history, mathematics, or physics.

Conservatives objected that Harvard had switched to the certificate system, at least for the subjects not included in the comprehensive examinations, and that students would take tests only in the subjects in which they were the strongest. Supporters of the change replied that careful examination of the secondary school record would prevent abuse of the system. Critics further argued that by judicious choice of examination subjects, a student could be examined in as few as half of the credits they studied in high school. This would occur, for example, if a student took comprehensive examinations in

English, elementary French, physics, and chemistry. They conjectured this might lead to neglect of subjects not offered for examination. Supporters offered an empirical response: at least in the beginning only the best students applied under this new plan and abuse had been minimal.[32]

Princeton adopted a similar scheme. A student with good grades in high school only had to take tests covering the advanced portions of the Latin, English, mathematics, and Greek entrance examinations. Princeton's entrance requirements offered less latitude for students than those of most other colleges, and if it is assumed that passage of the advanced portion of an examination implied competence in the elementary portion, Princeton still required examination in most of its required units.[33]

Yale also began to experiment. Its admissions committee actively solicited comments from secondary schools concerning its entrance examinations. Although it still required exams in each required subject, it began to administer "comprehensive" tests. Yale employed the school record in marginal cases, and in extraordinary situations permitted the substitution of subjects other than those prescribed.[34]

During the teens, Harvard convinced the CEEB to offer comprehensive exams similar to those it had been administering. Although defenders of the certificate system criticized these reforms as inadequate, the changes did significantly reduce the number of students admitted on condition, an accomplishment in which mild reformers, such as Pritchett, could take satisfaction.

THE "HUMAN ELEMENT" AT COLUMBIA

In a period of two years, Butler had completely reversed his views on the admission of conditioned students. In 1907, he attacked the faculty for permitting the wholesale award of conditions. Two years later Butler accepted conditioning as the inevitable consequence of Columbia's lengthy list of entrance requirements and even justified the practice to Pritchett.

Butler still deemed the University capable of further growth, and considered such growth compatible with the maintenance of academic standards. But by 1910 he concluded that the mechanistic requirements, considered a reform a decade earlier, had become a hindrance. He told Pritchett that the question of college admission was generally in an unsatisfactory state and that "it would be better educational policy to admit every student who offered himself without any examination or test of any kind, excluding at the end of a term those who had not been able to carry the work satisfactorily, than to fix upon 14½ or 15 points as an absolutely irreducible minimum and reject all who did not come up to that standard."

At this point, Butler's education credo still included the precept that "no student of serious purpose ought ever to be turned away from Columbia University"—that there ought to be room for all academic aspirations to be satisfied. Although all students would not be degree candidates, the important goal was "the opening of new doors of acquisition and reflection to serious students, however defective their former preparation may have been." [35]

If Butler could not convince the undergraduate faculties to make their entrance requirements less "excessive," he could effect other reforms that might diminish their harm. In 1909, he convinced them to abolish their divisional admissions committees and to place responsibility for all admissions decisions in the hands of a single administrator and faculty committee. Butler chose for this position a former professor of philosphy at Columbia and at Princeton, Adam Leroy Jones. Jones assumed responsibility for Universitywide admissions in 1915 and would serve as Columbia's chief admissions officer for the next quarter century.

Along with the establishment of a bureaucratic admissions apparatus, Butler convinced the undergraduate faculties to permit Jones to make use of high school grades in making the final judgment on admissions. Thus, if a student did poorly in an entrance examination, reference to his secondary school record would reveal if the deficiency was due to a poor showing on a given day or to poor preparation. Butler hoped that this innovation would considerably reduce the number of students admitted on condition. Although admittedly making a concession to the certificate system, the faculties did not immediately envision any further steps in this direction.

Initially, the Committee on Undergraduate Admissions cautiously used the high school record as a supplement to the entrance examinations. Butler criticized its reluctance to use the school record to compensate for a grade of less than 50% on an examination.

That is practically to nullify the value of the whole school record. In my judgment, the school record should be given weight even if the candidate had a grade of 10%, or of nothing at all, for it is precisely in such a situation as this that it is desired to arrive at an equitable judgment by weighing a good performance for four years against a poor performance in an hour and a half. In bringing the plan forward my thought was that the school record would be given at least equal weight with the examination mark, no matter what the candidate's record at examination. Otherwise, we have no plan at all, but simply a very limited readjustment of examination ratings. Unless we grasp the nettle firmly in our hands we shall not get school records that are worth much, and we shall not improve the situation as to our admission examinations, which is now held by many to be very unsatisfactory.[36]

The committee did permit Jones to exercise his judgment within the 50% to 59% range (the passing grade was 60%), but asserted that any good student should do better than 50% on the tests. In fact, according to Jones, "comparatively few cases would be affected by accepting lower grades for the reason that a student with a good school record from a good school almost invariably receives a grade of at least 50 in examinations." But Jones did promise increased attention to the exceptions. He challenged Butler's contention that entrance examinations should be weighed equally, arguing that this would aid the academically inferior school which gave a student respectable grades.[37]

If Columbia's admissions policies took no further steps toward implementation of a certificate system, they would continue to make increasingly greater use of the human element.

CONCLUSION

The cautious introduction of subjective judgment, or what Butler called the "human element," into the admissions process marked the end of a long period of adjustment of the relations between high school and college. The inclusion of many new subjects both in the college curriculum and in the list of subjects acceptable for entrance marked the first half of this period at Columbia and other institutions. During the second half, concern increased that the inclusion of these new subjects had imposed excessive demands on the high school and that this had retarded admission and progress of many students. The admissions committee could look to the high school record to see whether the entrance exams had screened out any serious students.

Butler's dissatisfaction with Columbia admissions policies before the 1909 reforms should not be allowed to obscure all that had been achieved. Greek and Latin no longer had special status among entrance subjects, nor among graduation subjects after 1916. College offerings and requirements had been expanded to conform to the work then done in the best high schools. This congruence, and the gradual raising of mastery levels required for college admission also provided a goal for the weaker high schools. Uniform entrance examinations administered by a single board and based on uniform entrance requirements automatically widened the applicant pool for institutions joining the CEEB. American high schools and colleges engaged in a meaningful dialogue resulting in a level of articulation greater than that achieved previously or subsequently. Changes in entrance requirements and in the college curriculum enabled professional schools to expect reasonably their applicants to have completed at least some college work.

Butler's dissatisfaction with the general status of admissions policies in 1910 stemmed from more than a belief that they had outgrown their "mechanistic" stage. He had encouraged the facilitation of college access on the assumption that the high schools would effectively perform a selective function. This not only involved encouraging qualified candidates to prepare for college, but also the discouraging of candidates who lacked the qualifications. As is discussed later, Butler viewed with concern the growth of a certificate system vulnerable to what in his view were increasingly unreasonable demands being made by secondary school teachers—especially for the inclusion of vocational courses among the list of subjects acceptable for college entrance. But what provided immediate cause for alarm was the failure of many students being graduated from Columbia's feeders and entering the College to meet one major unwritten criterion for access to the upper and upper middle classes—they were not gentiles.

NOTES TO CHAPTER 6
INTERNAL IMPROVEMENTS

1. Germann to Butler, June 19, 1902, CUF, Dr. George B. Germann file.

2. Butler to Low, October 11, 1890, CUF, Nicholas Murray Butler 1890–1894 file.

3. Until the early 1880s the School of Arts had a uniform curriculum consisting of Greek, Latin, mathematics, and some history, chemistry, physics, and English. Seniors could pursue philosophy and a second year of one science. During the early 1880s, a year of required geology and a semester of required political economy were added to the curriculum (a second year of political economy became optional). German was offered as a short course that could be taken at any point in the student's career. By the mid-1880s, most junior year courses became optional and botany, additional political economy, astronomy, and additional German and philosophy could be elected. Required history was added to the junior curriculum just before reorganization.

4. Butler to Low, October 11, 1890, CUF, Nicholas Murray Butler 1890–1894 file.

5. G. R. Carpenter and William Hallock to Low, January 5, 1894, CUF, Professor G. R. Carpenter, 1893–1903 file.

6. Woodbury to Low, June 23, 1892, attached to Harry J. Carman to Roger Howson, February 22, 1945, Harry J. Carman Papers, CUA, Series II–5, G–H (1940–50): H(4) file.

7. A. B. Merriam to Low, September 28, 1891, CUF, Professor A. B. Merriam file.

8. Peck to Low, October 4, 1891, CUF, Professor Harry Peck file.

9. *College Faculty Minutes 1892–1900,* November 23, 1894, pp. 10, 12–13; December 20, 1895, following p. 95; January 14, 1896 ("Report of a Subcommittee on curriculum to take into account Professor Cohn's objections"); February 28, 1896, p. 105, and March 27, 1896, p. 110. Columbia College, *Seventh Annual Report of President Low to the Trustees, October 5, 1896* (New York, Printed for the University, 1896), pp. 11-12.

10. Columbia College, *Ninth Annual Report of President Low to the Trustees, October 3, 1898* (New York, Printed for the University, 1898), pp. 31–32; Columbia College, *Tenth Annual Report of President Low to the Trustees, November 6, 1899* (New York, Printed for the University, 1899), p. 33; *Eleventh Annual Report of President Low to the Trustees, October 1, 1900* (New York, Printed for the University, 1900), p. 100.

11. Low to Burgess, January 14, 1895, CUF, Professor John W. Burgess 1890–1900 file; *College Faculty Minutes 1892–1900,* March 25, 1898, p. 196; May 24, 1895, pp. 55–57.

12. Low to Van Amringe, December 5, 1899, CUF, Professor John H. Van Amringe file.

13. *College Faculty Minutes 1892–1900,* January 26, 1900, pp. 309–310.

14. Fiske to Butler, January 2, 1900, CUA, Thomas S. Fiske papers, 1899–1901 box, B file.

15. The dropping of the B.S. and the B. Phil. degrees at Cornell in the 1890s, which had the effect of granting all graduates the B.A. whether or not trained in the classics, caused a large uproar. See Morris Bishop, *Early Cornell 1865–1900* (Ithaca, N. Y.; Cornell University Press, 1962), p. 324.

16. *College Faculty Minutes,* January 26, 1900, pp. 307–308.

17. Butler to Low, October 11, 1890, CUF, Nicholas Murray Butler 1890–1894 file.

18. *College Faculty Minutes 1900–1908,* January 22, 1904, p. 77; February 26, 1904, pp. 85–86; April 28, 1905, pp. 167–170; Butler to Low, January 18, 1905 and Low to Butler, January 16, 1905, CUF, President Seth Low file.

19. Some students came from high schools that did not offer all the subjects required for college admission. Their failure to pass the entrance exams in subjects they had not studied concerned the faculty, but it was envisioned that this problem would be alleviated as the list of subjects considered acceptable for admission was increased.

20. Administrative responsibility for conditioned students shifted several times during the 1890s, but it was eventually delegated to the Dean of the College. See *College Faculty Minutes 1892–1900,* March 24, 1893, p. 36; March 16, 1894, p. 82; May 25, 1894, p. 100; March 22, 1895, pp. 37–38; and April 22, 1898, pp. 208–209.

21. The secondary schools also objected that conditioning undermined the four-year preparatory course. "It is an open secret," reported a Columbia College faculty committee, "that any boy of reasonable attainments can enter Columbia after 3 and one half years of preparation in the New York City high schools and after three years if he passes the subjects completed and will take some conditions" ("Report of the Special Committee of the College Faculty on the Relations Between the College and the Secondary Schools," p. 15, in *College Faculty Mintues 1900–1908,* May 15, 1908, after p. 116).

22. Fiske to Butler, February 17, 1903, CUF, Thomas S. Fiske file.

23. *College Faculty Minutes 1900–1908,* October 23, 1903, p. 50; October 27, 1905, p. 208; October 19, 1906, p. 253; October 11, 1907, p. 11; Columbia University, *Minutes of the Faculty of Columbia College October 16, 1908 to May 15, 1916,* p. 149 (hereafter cited as *College Faculty Minutes 1908–1916*).

24. *College Faculty Minutes 1900–1908,* December 6, 1907, p. 35.

25. Adam Leroy Jones to Butler, May 9, 1913, CUF, Professor Adam Leroy Jones file; *College Faculty Minutes 1900–1908,* October 11, 1907, pp. 1–2.

26. "Report of the Special Committee of the College Faculty on the Relations Between the College and the Secondary Schools," in *College Faculty Minutes 1900–1908,* May 15, 1908, after p. 116.

27. Abraham Flexner, *Henry S. Pritchett: A Biography* (New York, Columbia University Press, 1943), pp. 95, 123. See also R. L. Duffus, *Democracy Enters the College: A Study of the Academic Lockstep* (New York, Charles Scribner's Sons, 1936), passim; and the Carnegie Foundation for the Advancement of Teaching, *First Annual Report* (New York, 1906), pp. 38–39. Butler sat on the Foundation's Board of Directors. The Foundation at first excluded from its benefits professors from denominational and public colleges on the grounds that the denominations and the states should provide pensions. This expectation was erroneous. See Flexner, *Henry S. Pritchett,* pp. 91–92.

28. College Entrance Examination Board, *The Work of the College Entrance Examination Board 1901–1925* (Boston, etc., Ginn and Company, 1926), p. 106.

29. During 1907–08 for example, 56 colleges raised their published unit requirements for admission. See Carnegie Foundation for the Advancement of Teaching,*Third Annual Report* (New York, 1908), pp. 92–93. For examples of Foundation leverage on two universities, see Herman F. Eschenbacher, *The University of Rhode Island: A History of Land Grant Education in Rhode Island* (New York, Appleton-Century-Crofts, 1967), p. 90: and Richard P. McCormack, *Rutgers: A Bicentennial History* (New Brunswick, N. J., Rutgers University Press, 1966), p. 156.

30. Carnegie Foundation, *Third Annual Report*, p. 107.

31. Butler to Pritchett, March 29, 1909, CUF, Henry S. Pritchett file.

32. "Admission to Harvard College," *Science,* n. s. (July 7, 1911), 34:23; "Harvard's New Entrance Tests," *Nation* (January 26, 1911), 92:80–81; F. W. Johnson, "The New Harvard Entrance Requirements," *School Review* (June, 1911), 19:412–413; J. H. Ropes, "New Harvard Entrance Requirements," *Science* n. s. (May 26, 1911), 33:793–801; Howey N. Davis, The New Harvard Plan for College Admission," *Journal of Proceedings and Addresses of the National Education Association,* 1911:567–571; and Clifford H. Moore, "New Plan of Admission to Harvard College," *Educational Review* (June, 1911), 42:71–78.

33. Adam Leroy Jones, "Some New Methods of Admission to College," *Educational Review* (November, 1913), 46: 351–360.

34. Ibid.

35. Butler to Pritchett, March 29, 1909, CUF, Henry S. Pritchett file.

36. Butler to Jones, October 24, 1911, CUF, Professor Adam Leroy Jones file.

37. Jones to Butler, October 26, 1911, CUF Professor Adam Leroy Jones file.

7

Repelling the Invasion: Columbia and the Jewish Student

Columbia University is a Christian Institution . . .

PRESIDENT NICHOLAS MURRAY BUTLER[1]

Those who ruled Columbia dreamed that their institution might become the center for the training of the nation's future leaders. They expected that the high schools would select and prepare and send along to college students who exhibited social and intellectual qualities desirable in members of the upper and upper middle classes. Most reforms undertaken at Columbia between 1890 and 1910 facilitated admission for those who demonstrated academic and social competence but who might have been dissuaded from attending college by sterile preparatory and collegiate curricula.

The University adopted few measures specially designed to attract students with the social qualities thought necessary in members of those classes—traits such as "poise," "character," and "ability to lead"—since it correctly, at first, assumed that the secondary schools encouraged most students exhibiting these qualities or the potential to acquire them. Nor did Columbia and its sister institutions take many steps to insure the exclusion of those deemed academically or socially unfit. Academically unqualified students, everyone assumed, would not survive the preparatory curriculum offered by Columbia's feeders. It was just as univerally assumed that the secondary schools would not encourage those without the desirable social qualities. Of course, the students admitted posed disciplinary problems which gave faculty, administrators, and trustees pause, but such problems were believed to be endemic to youth. They would be overcome with maturity and with further exposure to collegiate norms.

Specifically, most academic officials exhibited little concern about the ethnic and religious composition of the Columbia College student body, at least until after 1905. Most College students were native Protestants. Those few Catholics and Jews who did enroll exhibited the desired social traits: that is, in Michael Pupin's phrase, they "played the game." All at Columbia were conscious of the great waves of immigrants who had settled in New York City since the 1880s—there was no way to ignore them or the enormous political, economic, and cultural changes they had brought about. At the same time, few believed that more than a handful of such immigrants would ever perceive that anything of value took place on Morningside Heights. And, even among those who did, many might disqualify themselves as "socially unprepared." "Columbia College," wrote Pupin, "a daughter of great Trinity Church, an alma mater of men like Hamilton, Jay, Livingston, and of many other gentlemen and scholars who guided the destiny of these United States—can that great institution, I asked myself, afford to enroll a raw Serbian immigrant among its students; train me, an uncouth employee of a cracker factory, to become one of its alumni?" The fine words contained in the Declaration of Independence did not persuade Pupin that he was the equal of the American boy who could meet the unstated requirements for which no prescribed examinations existed. "The college of Hamilton and of Jay expected certain other things which I knew I did not have and could not get from books. A jump from the Cortlandt Street factory to Columbia College . . . appeared to me like a jump over Columbia's great and venerable traditions."[2] Yet Pupin himself overcame his hesitation and so did hundreds of others, essentially convinced of the truth of the American Dream.

It was precisely the reforms instituted by Butler and Co. that attracted to the Colossus on the Hudson first and second generation Americans desirous of attaining social mobility through the growing professions. Columbia had continually pressured the New York State Legislature to require more and more education for admission to each licensed profession. It increased professional school admission requirements until such divisions became graduate—or at least advanced undergraduate—level institutions. And, of course, Columbia authorities had taken many pains to facilitate access to the undergraduate divisions.

Although many other colleges instituted similar reforms, the financial constraints facing an immigrant family residing in New York limited most students to whatever options were available in New York City. Many enrolled in City College, which charged no tuition, while others availed themselves of New York University's conveniently located facilities. But Columbia's combined course, along with its growing academic reputation, made that university particularly attractive to the upwardly mobile immigrant.

By 1915 a large proportion of Columbia undergraduates consisted of first and second generation Americans, mostly East European Jews. Their presence posed a major dilemma for Columbia authorities—a dilemma that ultimately resulted in major changes in the method by which many American students of all backgrounds were admitted to college. In this chapter, we argue that Columbia's attempt to limit attendance of Jewish students led it to assume the selective function that its leaders had helped relegate to the secondary schools a generation before. Since the high schools failed to eliminate students Columbia considered socially unqualified, university authorities would have to employ their newly created bureaucratic apparatus to do the job themselves.

DRAWING BATTLE LINES:
STUDENTS, ADMINISTRATION, AND TRUSTEES

Think of it! Herbert Spencer preferred to a fairy story by boys and girls.

NEW YORK CITY POLICE COMMISSIONER MCADOO[3]

The happiness and sorrow, aspiration and anguish that constituted Jewish life on New York's Lower East Side at the turn of the century has been depicted with special poignancy in the recent writings of Irving Howe. His description of a deep impulse common to the immigrant population helps to explain the remarkable drive for education seemingly characteristic of almost all immigrant sons. "America was different from all other countries," they believed. "America—land of sweat and swineishness!—meant that the sons could find a path such as Jews had never before been able to discover. The fathers would work, grub, and scramble as petty agents of primitive accumulation. The sons would acquire education, that new-world magic the Jews were so adept at invoking through formulas they had brought from the Old World."[4] And education provided access to the professional and business worlds in which the young would obtain the material gratification the elder generation was fated never to experience. The son's responsibility of having to live for two generations led most to the public school system, and drove many to remarkable educational attainments.

In describing the amazingly rapid Jewish influx into the public school system, Moses Rischin noted, "in 1891, of some 60,000 East Side children, only 1000 received no education and most of these soon would be in class-rooms; on the Lower East Side, a school absenteeism rate of 8 percent was caused almost entirely by sickness."[5] Throughout the period of mass Jewish migration many children had to await construction of new classrooms before gaining admission to the city's schools. Between 1905 and 1910, the Camp Huddleston Hospital Ship, berthed at the foot of Corlears Hook, absorbed an overflow of about 10,000 public school children.[6]

These same Jewish students lost little time in exploiting the good relations President Nicholas Murray Butler had cultivated with the New York City high schools. "[Of] all the races represented in considerable numbers," one contemporary observer noted, "the Hebrews far exceed all others, including the native born Americans, in their appreciation and use of the New York City high schools."[7] "Appreciation and use" meant college and professional preparation. The same observer noted that the only boys who completed their high school course were those "to whom a high school education is an abso-lute necessity, as a means of preparation."[8] Since within a decade of the opening of the city's first public high schools at least 41% of their graduates were Jewish, Columbia soon found its assumptions about its student body severely challenged.[9]

Columbia did not face a similar influx of Catholics. During the nineteenth century New York's Catholics had established an entire educational system parallel to the public system, for which they read "Protestant" system. Sever-al colleges, notably Fordham, capped this system, and the lower units encour-aged students seeking a higher education to do so within the framework of the Catholic system. Partly for this reason, and partly because Catholic immi-grants were not as quick as the Jewish immigrants to "appreciate and use" the education system as a vehicle of social and economic mobility, few Catho-lics applied for admission to Columbia College before World War I.

By 1910, about half of the students attending the New York City public high schools were immigrants or the children of immigrants.[10] The mounting stream of Jewish high school graduates foretold a heightening wave of Jewish students seeking entry into college and from thence to graduate and profes-sional schools. Columbia's administrators had rapidly become aware of this—more so than at other colleges—for their institution was where the tidal wave was highest. Few administrators of a major university were more inclined to regard this wave as a *problem*, and one that for want of proper handling could turn into a disaster. Frederick P. Keppel, dean of Columbia College from 1910 to 1918, spoke of this matter publicly and with a good deal of delibera-tion. His public comments offer us some insight as to why Columbia leaders viewed the growing number of academically-oriented and well motivated Jewish candidates not as an opportunity or as good fortune, but as occasion for anxiety.

The heart of "the problem" was that a large influx of Jews at Columbia might drive away Columbia's "natural" constituency, or, to use Keppel's language, Columbia's "position at the gateway of European immigration" could make it "socially uninviting to students who come from homes of refinement." The dean concluded that this was not likely to happen, first because "more Jewish parents are realizing the advantages to be obtained from sending their boys away from home." Second, he argued that the Jewish segment of the student body was smaller than usually thought. Last, he maintained that the Jewish students who did attend Columbia were not all socially retarded.

By far the majority of the Jewish students who do come to Columbia are desirable students in every way. What most people regard as a racial problem is really a social problem. The Jews who have had the advantages of decent social surroundings for a generation or two are entirely satisfactory companions. Their intellectual ability, and particularly their intellectual curiosity, are above the average, and the teachers are unanimous in saying that their presence in the classroom is distinctly desirable.

Most of the Jews Keppel deemed "desirable" had Spanish or German origins and had migrated between the mid-seventeenth and late nineteenth centuries. The East European Jew, considered socially backward and difficult to assimilate, much less to socialize to upper middle class values, belonged in a different category. In this published statement, Keppel urged a liberal attitude toward this group of students.

There are, indeed, Jewish students of another type who have not had the social advantages of their more fortunate fellows. Often they come from an environment which in any stock less fired with ambition would have put the idea of higher education wholly out of the question. Some of these are not particularly pleasant companions, but the total number is not large, and every reputable institution aspiring to public service must stand ready to give those of probity and good moral character the benefits which they are making great sacrifices to obtain.

Keppel prophetically concluded that the "problem" of Jewish assimilation into undergraduate life would have to be faced "by every college of the first class" since "they will go to no other." This apparently liberal statement should be understood in its context. He believed that Columbia's location placed it at a relative disadvantage in dealing with the "Jewish problem" but reassured Columbia's traditional constituency that the situation would soon affect all good schools proportionately. His statement might also be interpreted as a subtle attempt to dissuade Jewish readers residing in New York from enrolling their offspring at Columbia by convincing them that their best interests lay in sending their children away from home.[12]

Keppel's private attitude will be discussed later. His statement reflects the concern that many officials at elite universities privately expressed. Social anti-Semitism was not peculiar to Columbia. It was relatively widespread among the private liberal arts colleges which by this time had begun to take the airs of private clubs. And yet, there was something special about Columbia's social anti-Semitism. Located in New York City, Columbia was the first university with elitist pretensions to be confronted with a large influx of Jews. Its admissions policies had been designed to facilitate the entrance of New York City high school graduates to the College, a situation that hastened the influx. Finally, the men who became Columbia trustees during these years displayed an intense social anti-Semitism. In fact, the trustees' attitude probably made Columbia's "Jewish problem" among the most significant issues that university faced during the teens.

Columbia's trustees considered themselves members of New York's upper class; they considered the Board to be "the highest honor that a man can receive in that line."[13] But, in reality, they were a cut below the top. Instead of conveying prestige to the Board by their service, they derived prestige from that service. This fact made them highly status-conscious, which in turn led to a social snobism that had a definite ethnic cast. The Jews were beyond the pale because they would not defer to the leadership of such men or to the social system they represented. The attitude of the trustees toward the Jews may best be indicated by a series of brief examples.[14]

THE SELECTION OF A JEWISH TRUSTEE

The considerations involved when Columbia's trustees pondered admittance of a Jew to trusteeship reflect their attitudes when other questions involving Jews came before them. "We can both of us recall many times when free discussion in the Board would have been very seriously handicapped by the presence of one of this [sic] people," wrote Trustee William Barclay Parsons to Chairman George Rives in 1913. Several of these discussions concerned restrictions on admission of Jews to the College.[15]

When Kings College, chartered by the king of England in 1754, was renamed Columbia College and granted a new charter by the State of New York, the Legislature provided that the clergy of each religious denomination in the state could elect one regent of the University of the State of New York. These regents would collectively exercise supervisory authority over the reopened College. For this purpose New York's Jews held denominational status and the state's Jewish clergymen chose Gershom Sexias, a Jew of Spanish background. Sexias sat as a regent, and later as a trustee of Columbia College, for a generation. No other Jew served as Columbia trustee until the election of his descendant Benjamin Cardozo in 1928.[16]

The unsuperceded Charter of 1810 provided for a self-perpetuating board and made no reference to denominational representation. Agitation for the appointment of a Jewish trustee began at the turn of the twentieth century. Columbia's trustees strongly resisted these pressures. They rationalized their reluctance by stating they did not want to choose a colleague on the basis of his race or faith, and on the grounds that they feared criticism for choosing a Jew because of his wealth. For some trustees, these may have been sincere reasons. But for many others, they were disingenuous arguments. A number of prominent Jews were as qualified to be trustees as those sitting—qualified, that is, if the criteria for selection consisted of concern for the University, philanthropic intention, and ability to devote time to trustee business. Moreover, the very fear that the appointment of a Jew would be seen as inspired by mercenary considerations testified to prejudice, for it presumed that Jews were undesirable on all other grounds.

This prejudice cost Jacob Schiff board membership. Schiff's money had helped to build Teachers College as well as Barnard, the undergraduate college for women. He had been in constant contact with President Low during the 1890s, most notably in attempting to effect a merger between Columbia and the University of the City of New York, now known as New York University. As early as 1891, Schiff attempted to elicit from Low a commitment to nominate a Jewish trustee.[17] In 1900 he criticized the trustees for "the injustice done both to the best interests of the College as well as to the race I come from, by keeping, apparently through a tacit understanding, any member of the latter from the government of the University." He expressed regret at having contributed to a fund for the payment of Columbia's debts: "I have by no means the intention to recall what I have once promised, but I do feel that the beginning of the twentieth century should not see unjustified race-prejudice perpetuated in these United States of America, and at the fountain-head of learning, study and culture."[18]

Low answered Schiff warmly, citing his appointment of four Jews to the University faculty, an achievement which Low thought unmatched in any other American university, as an indication of his personal sympathies. He commented, "If no such trustee has yet been chosen, it does not indicate, I am sure, an illiberal spirit, but the fact that when vacancies have occurred other considerations have prevailed." He told Schiff that he believed Columbia to have "shown itself so liberal that it ought to be free from misinterpretation, because in one direction it has not moved along these lines."[19] The Columbia president subsequently recommended that the trustees elect a "representative Hebrew" to one of two existing vacancies. He suggested that Isaac N. Seligman, a Columbia alumnus, would bring Columbia "into closer touch with the business community," and would "secure the hearty support of this element by giving it representation on the Board of Trustees."[20] He found himself unable to make any headway at that time.

By 1907, Schiff's patience was exhausted, and he informed Butler, Low's successor, that he did not intend to make further contributions to Columbia until the trustees appointed a Jewish member. He wrote:

I feel that, so long as representatives of the citizens of Jewish faith are, by a tacit understanding, kept out of the Government of Columbia University, the Metropolitan Museum of Art, the Museum of Natural History and other leading communal corporations, prejudice is being kept alive against the Jewish population, which those who lead public opinion should do everything in their power to eliminate. It cannot be expected that the stream run pure, so long as its source is contaminated. [21]

When Horace Carpentier, a trustee, heard about Schiff's criticism, he offered to resign and "make way for the election of an able, liberal and representative Jew who will do more for Columbia than I can." [22] Carpentier was dissuaded from resigning and again no Jew was elected. [23]

The question continued to smolder, and forcefully reemerged in 1913 on the death of the New York merchant Benjamin Altman. Altman, a Jew, had bequeathed his stock, with a value estimated at between $25 and $30 million, to the recently established B. Altman Foundation, which would make grants "for the benefit of such charitable and educational institutions in the City of New York" as the foundation's directors may approve. [24] Certainly Columbia, which always appeared to be in financial difficulties, would be a prime candidate for such funds, but its refusal to elect a Jew to trusteeship was an obvious impediment. Discussion between Trustees and President Butler took place on the question, but when Trustee William Barclay Parsons learned from Chairman George Rives of the movement afoot, he said such a step would be a mistake. He noted that the trustees' policy of refusing admittance to Jews was "recognized generally" and that a change in this policy at that point would jeopardize the high esteem in which the board (and, he might have added, its individual members) was held. He did not find his understanding of the Jewish personality to be congenial to trustee membership.

In character they are terribly persistent. They realize that there has been for 2000 years or more a prejudice against them, and they are always seeking after special privileges for themselves and their people. They have retained their special calendar, their holidays differ from those of everybody else, and they want those holidays recognized generally, and in some cases I believe by law. They certainly do seek special privileges by law. They form the worst type of our emigrants, they supply the leaders to anarchistic, socialistic and other movements of unrest. In the recent election the socialistic vote was confined largely to the East Side and to Brownsville, in Brooklyn, where they live.

Finally, he suggested that positive action at this time would subject the University to criticism, perhaps justified, that its decision was affected by the Altman will provisions. [25]

When Rives asked Butler to comment on Parsons's statements, Columbia's president replied that his comments about "the race" were "as true as Gospel." But he was not willing to dismiss the election of a Jewish trustee out of hand. He said he could not decide whether Columbia would gain or lose by taking this step, but he feared that criticism offered by Schiff and others would someday force the board to take the plunge. In that case, it might be better to elect a Jew as an act of free will, rather than appear to succumb to outside pressure.[26] But the opposition of Parsons, of John B. Pine, secretary to the trustees, and of other trustees, put the matter to rest.[27]

Although agitation persisted through the 1910s and 1920s, Columbia did not elect a Jewish trustee until 1928. During the previous decade, the "Jewish problem," insofar as it affected students, was largely resolved to the trustees' satisfaction. A Jewish trustee elected in the late 1920s could no longer challenge the steps Columbia had taken in this area—even if disposed to. The time was propitious for several other reasons. Parsons, who was by then chairman of the trustees, and who continued to oppose election of a Jewish trustee, gave indications that he might relent. Further, Benjamin Cardozo, the logical candidate, indicated that if elected he could take an active role in some of the trustees' activities, a guarantee he could not make earlier. At the time, Cardozo, a Columbia graduate, was chief justice of the New York State Court of Appeals.[28]

Convinced that the election of a Jewish trustee could no longer be postponed, Butler approached Parsons tactfully and tried to overcome all rational objections. "Judge Cardozo," he said,

is not only the most distinguished of our alumni of his race, but he is perhaps the most distinguished Columbia man of this generation. He is profoundly interested in the life and work of the University, and keeps in constant touch with the life of the School of Law. No one could accuse us of having chosen him because of his wealth, and yet, being an outstanding member of his race, his election ought certainly to meet the views of those who think that for reasons of catholicity and general policy a member of that race should be elected a trustee. The election of so outstanding an alumnus, whose achievements and accomplishments entitle him to consideration anywhere, would I think raise his choice above the plane of any possible dispute.[29]

Parsons finally gave in to Butler's arguments and Cardozo's name was placed in nomination at the trustees' meeting of February, 1928. Since Trusteeship was traditionally accorded by unanimous vote,[30] the objection of one member at this meeting placed his election in jeopardy. Butler determined that the opposition was not based on Cardozo's religion and set upon winning over the dissenting member.[31] Arguing that rejection of Cardozo's nomination would be embarrassing to him and to the trustees if word of it ever got out, Butler finally succeeded.[32] The trustees unanimously elected Cardozo to membership at the March meeting. The election in 1944 of the next Jewish trustee, Arthur H. Sulzberger, publisher of the *New York Times,* after another lengthy and commented upon hiatus, marked the beginning of fairly routine elections of Jews to "the highest honor a man can receive in that line."[33]

SETH LOW'S RESIGNATION
AS A COLUMBIA TRUSTEE

The trustees' attitude toward the Jews ultimately claimed Seth Low as a victim. Perhaps more than any other trustee, Low recognized the Jews as an integral part of the city to which Columbia was inextricably bound and therefore an important University constituency. During his presidency, he recruited four Jewish faculty members and sympathized with Schiff's pleas for election of a Jewish trustee. His relationship with Dean Burgess of the faculty of political science cooled in the early 1890s when the latter defeated Low's plan for coeducation by suggesting that such a step would turn Columbia into "a female seminary, and a Hebrew female seminary, in the character of the student body, at that."[34]

Although Low resigned from the Columbia presidency during his successful campaign for mayor of New York City in 1901, he retained his position as trustee. In 1911 he resigned that office when he and Butler took opposite sides in discussing the ramifications of a proposal permitting the Protestant Episcopal Church to use Columbia's facilities for its annual conference. The proposal met with the trustees' approval, but a controversy arose when they attempted to establish a policy for future similar requests.

Columbia had always maintained ties with the Episcopal Church (its president was traditionally Episcopalian, and the rector of Trinity Church and the Episcopal bishop of New York were customarily elected trustees), but the University professed a welcome for all Christian sects. For example, Butler wrote upon the opening of the new campus chapel:

Columbia University is a Christian institution, and by its charter and traditions its Christianity is truly catholic, and the spirit of St. Paul's Chapel will be as broad and as tolerant as the spirit of the University . . . The Chapel pulpit will be free to any Christian minister or other speaker who may from time to time be invited to occupy it.[35]

In accordance with this tradition, the trustees decided to grant Columbia's facilities to any other Christian denomination making a similar request.

At this point, Low asked if the trustees would grant similar privileges to a Jewish group which petitioned for them. When Butler and the other trustees refused to commit themselves in advance of receiving an actual request, Low protested. He had reservations about the wisdom of permitting the Episcopalians to use the University's facilities, but insisted that if the trustees decided to go ahead with the project they should issue a statement of policy, which must "if we are to be true to ourselves, be broad enough to include the Jews as beneficiaries of the policy." Butler told Low that "all non-Christian bodies, religious or ethical in character, come under a different category" and that an application from any such group would be treated on its merits, just as an application from historians, economists, natural scientists, or philosophers would be treated. In judging such an application, Butler would "make sure that the University, its name and its prestige, are not exploited in the interest of all sorts of fads and isms of one kind or another." [36]

But "fads or isms of one kind or another" did not concern Low; the rights of practitioners of an ancient religion were at stake. He indicated that much of Columbia's endowment had been received from New York State (specifically Columbia's Upper Estate on which Rockefeller Center is now located) and that New York City's Jews had contributed to the growth and prosperity of the city, and hence to Columbia's growth in endowment, as much as any other group. He noted that Columbia's charter did not recognize special treatment for any religious sect. Finally he argued that Columbia accepted gifts from sympathetic Jews and that "it ought to be a point of honor with the University not to accept gifts from people whom it proposes to discriminate against in any matter of general policy." He cited several examples during his own tenure as president in which he declined to participate in certain church-related functions so as not to create the danger of misinterpretation of the relationship of the University to the Episcopal Church. [37]

When it became apparent that the conflict would not be resolved, Low found himself in an awkward position. He, the expresident of Columbia, disagreed with the current president on an important matter of policy. Low believed that under such circumstances he should resign as a trustee so that the judgment of the president would not be brought into question. Despite the pleas of Butler and several colleagues, Low would not change his mind, although he agreed not to formalize his resignation. Knowing that a recorded resignation would have meant disclosure of the reasons behind it, Low merely ceased to attend trustee meetings after this incident. He submitted a formal resignation in 1914. [38] Ironically, Low's absence removed one of the major obstacles to the imposition of additional restrictions on Jews by the remaining trustees.

THE THEODORE ROOSEVELT PROFESSORSHIP

In 1905, James Speyer, a wealthy Jew and a friend of President Butler, endowed an exchange professorship under the terms of which a distinguished

American professor would lecture for a year in Prussia. The German Ministry of Education established a similar Kaiser Wilhelm Professorship which provided funds for the maintenance of a German professor for a year in the United States. Speyer wished Butler and the trustees, as administrators of the Theodore Roosevelt Professorship, to make an effort to appoint regularly a Jewish scholar to the post.

Butler refused to place such a stipulation in the formal documents establishing the professorship, telling Speyer "that such a provision would expose you to criticism and misunderstanding and might, in a way, seriously damage the interests which both you and I have it in mind to advance." Asserting that "action is better than words in this manner," Butler suggested that "for us to appoint a competent and distinguished Jewish scholar among the first three incumbents and to follow this appointment up with another similar one within a few years would fix the matter beyond peradventure in the public mind both here and in Germany, without running any risk of misunderstanding or criticism."[39]

Several years later, Speyer told Butler that he had understood the President as agreeing

that no discrimination should be shown, either in theory or practice, as to the religious belief of anybody to be nominated for that Professorship, and that from time to time, say every third year, if possible some suitable person of Jewish belief should be nominated. You told me at the time that it was better not to put this in the deed, but that you could consult with me, and that we could no doubt arrange it in some way.[40]

Butler did arrange for the appointment of Felix Adler, the founder of the Ethical Culture movement in the United States, and a professor of social and political studies at Columbia since 1902. Adler came from a German-Jewish background, and as such a number of important German academicians found him objectionable. "The men here [officials in the Prussian Ministry of Education] are afraid that the German professors will not show Adler social attention. They say that is something that cannot be controlled by the higher powers," wrote John Burgess from Germany.[41] The ministry also expressed concern that Adler would use his professorship as a pulpit in advocacy of his faith. Butler reassured the ministry that Adler prepared seriously for a series of lectures on ethical problems in America, and would not abuse his appointment in any way. He subsequently told Speyer that when the ministry delayed acceptance of Adler's nomination, Adler suggested that his name be withdrawn. Butler would not assent to this "because we were engaged in establishing a principle and I in carrying out my personal obligation to you." He summed up, "It required all the pressure that I could bring to bear, and all the influence that I could exert in the highest quarters, finally to secure Dr. Adler's appointment."[42]

Thus Butler carried out his view of the agreement he had reached with Speyer. On the other hand, he agreed with John Burgess, the first Roosevelt Professor, that "it is simply absurd for us to send German Jews as Roosevelt Professors." Burgess said that the German academicians desired "genuine Americans of the old stock as representatives of American culture and not German Jews."[43] When Speyer exerted pressure for additional Jewish appointments, Butler informed him that the objection was not Columbia's, but originated in Prussia. This was probably the truth, but Butler was willing to acquiesce because he believed the Prussian position to be correct.[44]

In 1911, in response to renewed pressure by Speyer, Butler brought the matter to the attention of the trustees' Committee on Education.[45] The committee supported Butler's position.

The Committee on Education do not believe it would be judicious or in the interest of the greatest usefulness of the Roosevelt Professorship to make a practice of appointment representatives of the Hebrew race thereto at stated intervals or at any particular time. The appointment of Dr. Adler to the Professorship for the year 1908–09 made it plain in Germany, as well as in the United States, that there was no discrimination on account of race or creed in the filling of the Professorship. It is the expressed wish of the Prussian authorities and of many university professors in Germany that the men appointed to the Roosevelt chair should be of native-born American stock who can represent American institutions and ideals not only by word of mouth, but by instinct, by association, and by inheritance. The Committee find themselves in agreement with this view.[46]

The following year the committee informed Speyer that it could not accede to his request that a Jew be regularly appointed to the professorship. Its chairman told him that the committee members

regret extremely that you have had any expectations as to the character of the nominations made to this professorship that have not been fulfilled. It is the wish of the Committee, as it is of the Trustees as a whole, to make every possible recognition of your friendly and generous support. It is, however, quite beyond the power of the Committee or of the Trustees to make the religious tenets of any appointee a condition of his appointment. The charter of the College and the unbroken traditions of the Trustees for more than a century and a half require that there shall be absolutely no discrimination made on account of religious belief.[47]

The committee offered to return Speyer's gift if he were under any "misapprehension" as to the conditions under which the trustees could accept it. Having taken a position on the high ground of nondiscrimination, and conveniently failing to recall its past resolve to appoint professors of native-born American stock (a definition which effectively excluded German-Jewish Americans), the committee placed upon Speyer the onus for ending the professorship. Speyer did not withdraw his support under these circumstances.

However, the entire issue soon became academic (in the other sense) with the termination of both the Roosevelt Professorship and the Kaiser Wilhelm Professorship during World War I.[48]

The debate between Butler and Speyer was whether nondiscrimination implied nonexclusion, as Butler claimed, or definite inclusion, as Speyer defined it. But Butler did not intend even to honor his own definition of nondiscrimination as implying no more than nonexclusion. In the cases of a Jewish trustee and of a Roosevelt professor, Columbia asked the interested parties to await selection of members of their group in the natural course of events. When such selections did not occur, Columbia authorities dismissed objections to this apparently exclusionary policy with the comment that selection of a member of any group would imply discrimination in favor of that group—a violation of fundamental academic policy. This double-edged sword rationalized the thwarting of Jewish access to trusteeship and to other positions for many years.

THE INVASION OF JEWISH STUDENTS: FIRST SKIRMISHES

When it came to students, the "Jewish problem" took on a different cast. The issue the trustees faced was not whether to grant or to withhold a prize from outstanding Jewish individuals, but whether to accept or delimit the ingress of Jews to Columbia en masse. One involved the conferment of status in a way that only marginally touched the interests of the University; the other involved the present and future demography of Columbia's student body. Still, the attitudes displayed on the first set of issues—the stereotyping of Jews, the high premium on old-stock backgrounds and values, the variance between private and public statements—carried over to the second.

The increase in Jewish applicants to Columbia College would not have gone unnoticed in any case, but the phenomenon elicited considerable attention once, to use William Barclay Parsons's phrase, they began by "seeking special privileges," even before gaining admission. The remarkable propensity for Jewish holy days to fall during entrance examination week created the problem. In 1904, a student petitioned for a special examination on the grounds that a required entrance examination was offered only on Saturday, the Jewish Sabbath. Clarence Young, chairman of the University Committee on Entrance Examinations, obtained a ruling that examination dates, part of the announced academic calendar, were not to be altered. Columbia authorities reasoned that successful Jewish applicants would have to violate their

Sabbath sooner or later, since courses required for graduation met on Saturdays.[49]

Young soon requested another ruling to cover the case of the Jewish High Holy Days. Recognizing the bureaucratic difficulties involved in scheduling special examinations, yet feeling that Jewish students would be placed at a severe disadvantage unless some provision were made, Butler proposed that students who observed the Holy Days and had done well on their entrance examinations be admitted with conditions in those subjects which they did not attempt because of "conscientious scruples." Students in this category could remove their conditions by taking the missed examinations when offered the following January.[50]

Many Jewish students objected to adoption of this solution, since College rules prohibited them from taking college work in subjects in which they received conditions. Instead, they urged, special examinations should be administered just after the regular entrance examination week in September. When they gained a partial victory on that front in 1907, they agitated for the abolition of the $5 fee imposed upon them for taking the examinations at a time other than that prescribed.

Faced with the same problem every autumn since he assumed responsibility for the administration of entrance examinations, Professor Young finally exclaimed in exasperation,

My *impression* is that the candidates have been told that they would be admitted with conditions in subjects scheduled for their holy days and could try to pass the subjects in January. My *impression* also is that 9 out of 10 there upon forgot their scruples and took the examinations in September.

Personally I have no patience with those who raise this point. If they wish to attend a Christian college, let them submit to its requirements or *stay away*. If I wished to attend a Jewish college, I should go prepared to work on Sundays. If religious scruples prevented my doing this, I should not go to a Jewish college. Why in the name of the Olympian deities can they not do the same?[51]

Young was put out of his misery two years later when the functions of the committee he chaired were assumed by the Office of Undergraduate Admissions, under the directorship of Adam Leroy Jones.

THE INVASION OF JEWISH STUDENTS: COLUMBIA OUTFLANKED

At the same time, the Columbia faculty became concerned about the disturbing changes in the composition of the entering class apparently brought about by a long-standing series of policies. Beginning in the 1870s, the New York State Board of Regents, which had general supervisory authority over all matters of public education within the state, required all students to pass an examination upon completion of each academic subject offered by the state's public high schools. Throughout the 1890s, Columbia had accepted in place of its own entrance examinations certificates signifying completion of Columbia's entrance requirements and the passing of the accompanying Regents examinations.

During the 1890s, this exemption proved limited because of Columbia's dependence on private schools which, though accredited by the Regents, did not require their students to take Regents examinations in any subject. Columbia retained the provision mainly to keep in the Regents' good graces and "to keep in touch with the work of the public high school throughout the State, as far as possible." [52] For years, the Columbia faculty took exception to this practice on the grounds that the Regents examinations were unsatisfactory substitutes for Columbia's own entrance examinations. [53]

Although the provision ceased to be a dead letter after the opening of the first public high schools in New York City at the end of the 1890s, as late as 1908 only a small percentage of Columbia's entering class offered the Regents alternative. [54] After that date, a change in Columbia's regulations permitted students to offer Regents work which covered only a part of Columbia's entrance requirements. [55] The change led to a considerable increase in this percentage (see Table 7.1).

Gradually, as the number of students with Regents credentials increased, and as the proportion of these students coming from New York City rather than from upstate, appeared to grow, the faculty raised new reservations about the policy of granting automatic credit for these credentials. The academic caliber of such students troubled some; the growing numbers of Jewish students concerned others; the increasing parochialism of the student body which these proportions seemed to suggest worried still others. [56]

Columbia's authorities were not ready at this time to close the back door. Jones argued that Columbia's support of the Regents examinations, which had helped to raise secondary school standards throughout the state, was a necessary measure of academic citizenship. At the same time, this program continued to be the mechanism of admission for "most of our students from the country and the smaller parts of the state." To cut them off would make the student body even more parochial. [57] To the faculty's persistent criticism that the Regents examinations were inferior to Columbia's or the CEEB's, Jones responded that although students admitted on Regents credentials were not as successful in college as students admitted without conditions, "they were on the whole satisfactory and distinctly above those admitted with con-

Table 7.1. **Percentage of Students Admitted to Columbia College by Entrance Examination, Regents Credential, and Transfer, 1903–1915 (fall percentages only).**

	Examination[a]	Regents[b]	Transfer	Number
1903[c]	73.1	17.2	9.7	134
1904	n.a.[d]	n.a.	n.a.	163
1905	82.1	11.0	6.9	173
1906	75.1	12.4	12.4	177
1907	79.7	13.3	7.0	158
1908	68.2	19.3	12.5	192
1909	51.5	34.5	14.0	171
1910	51.3	38.9	9.8	193
1911	41.4	50.7	7.9	215
1912	45.5	46.1	8.4	191
1913	27.2	65.4	7.4	243
1914	n.a	n.a	n.a	300
1915	19.9	73.2	7.0	302

SOURCE. Columbia University *College Faculty Minutes, 1900–1908*, October 23, 1903, p. 51; October 27, 1905, p. 208; October 19, 1906, p. 253; October 11, 1907, p. 11; Columbia University, *College Faculty Minutes, 1908–1916*, October 16, 1908, p. 149; October 15, 1909, p. 247; October 21, 1910, pp. 324–325; October 13, 1911, p. 386; October 20, 1913, p. 8; November 15, 1915, p. 153. Figures not recorded in 1904 and 1914.
[a]Includes examinations offered by Columbia and by the CEEB.
[b]Includes students admitted partly by entrance examination and partly on Regents credit (from 1910 to 1915). The number of such students for each year was: 1910, 21; 1911, 51; 1912, 29; 1913, 34; 1915, 85.
[c]Figures for 1903–1909 and for 1911 are for students admitted. Figures for 1910 and for 1912–1915 are for students matriculated. During these years, between 80% and 90% of all students admitted actually attended.
[d]Not available.

ditions by our entrance examinations." The faculty's reservations did not gain the upper hand until after World War I when the postwar climate caused a massive change in Columbia's admissions policies.

DEVISING STRATEGIES: THE PRETTYMAN REPORT

At the same time that Columbia received more graduates of the New York City public high schools, it received fewer graduates of the Horace Mann School. Although Columbia's Teachers College housed, administered, staffed,

and supplied it, an average of only 53% of its college bound graduates attended Columbia in the century's early years. Since the percentage had been
considerably higher in the recent past, and since Horace Mann's graduates
were thought desirable, Butler asked Virgil Prettyman, the school's headmaster, to chair a committee of Columbia faculty and administrators which
would investigate the reasons for the decline and offer suggestions for a rever-
sal of the trend. Butler could not have been unaware that Horace Mann had
historically limited enrollment of Jewish students.[58]

Prettyman's report, filed late in 1908, turned into a full-fledged indictment
of much of Butler's work of the previous decade. "[The] University," he
charged, "has repeatedly shown its desire to accommodate the [public] High
Schools and to adapt itself to the system of public education in the State, and
has thereby established a Columbia sentiment in these schools, which it has
made little or no effort to duplicate in the better private schools of the country." Thus Horace Mann was only the most notable example of a general
problem.

Butler stood guilty as charged. He believed that most private schools were
wedded to the traditional classical curriculum and would not expand their
offerings to accommodate the many students with the ability to do college
work but without a desire to master Greek and Latin. On the other hand, the
public high schools, at least the better ones, had a far more diversified curriculum and accommodated many students who, both intellectually and socially, were the kind of students Butler hoped to recruit for Columbia. He assumed that the high schools would channel only such students toward
Columbia. Butler did not envision that the high schools would become vehi-
cles for upwardly mobile but socially undesirable Jews.

Prettyman told Butler that the prevalent view among parents who sent
their children to private schools was that "the University undergraduate
body contains a prepondering element of students who have had few social
advantages and that in consequence, there is little opportunity of making
friendships of permanent value among them." As a result, most of these
parents sent their children out of the city for college.[59]

The Prettyman report concluded that for Columbia to change the undesirable situation in which the College was "neither receiving its share of students from the better families of the City, nor even holding the sons of its own
trustees, Professors and alumni," it would have to take into account the real
reasons why many students went to college.

The conditions and environment in which youth is to pass into manhood, the associations and friendships which may be formed within the student body, are popularly
esteemed not less important factors in the value of a college education than the

academic training and knowledge that may be acquired. Every undesirable student admitted is not an advantage but a detriment to the University.

Prettyman's committee therefore recommended that "only such students should be admitted [to Columbia] as are susceptible of education and *as may be of benefit to the student body.*"[60] Students with few social advantages (recall that Keppel used the same term), by which it meant East European Jews, did not fit this last criterion. But, the committee concluded,"it is plainly impossible to draw racial or class distinctions between applicants for admission." With the exception of those admitted on Regents credentials, Columbia still relied exclusively on its entrance examinations for admission at the time of the Prettyman report. It would have been too obvious, and politically untenable, for the College suddenly to request information concerning the applicant's religion and then reject Jewish applicants who may have scored as well on the entrance exams as non-Jews who had been accepted.

The committee could only recommend an indirect course: "the solution of the difficulty must be sought in the careful construction of new channels which will bring desirable candidates and the careful turning in other directions such streams as have proved deleterious." This diversionary process would be accomplished in part at least by exploitation of Columbia's uptown neighbor. "In the latter connection, a generous recognition of the many and great educational advantages of the C.C.N.Y. and moral support in still further increasing these occur to the committee as possibly useful." Thus, by 1908, Columbia no longer viewed City College as a competitor but as a potential ally that might absorb students whom the former institution did not find desirable.[61]

Prettyman recommended the hiring of a permanent administrator who could devote all his time to constructing "new channels" for the recruitment of the "better" students who attended private secondary schools now that immigrants largely populated the public high schools. Such an official could keep in contact with local headmasters and regularly visit the preparatory schools to explain to the students the advantages of a Columbia education. The committee urged that high school grades be taken into account by the admissions committees not only to reduce the number of conditioned admittances, but also to facilitate the admission of students with high grades from good schools. The report concluded that

to attract a better class of students to Columbia College is vitally and urgently necessary to the continued well being of the whole University and that were any serious efforts to be made in this direction it would command the support of many of the better New York families. The equipment and staff of the University is as a whole of the highest rank. It can offer to its alumni resident in New York privileges of continued university association, lectures, colloquia, the use of library, laboratories, Faculty Club and athletic field—such as no other University can extend, and which cannot be duplicated in the city. That these privileges should be extended to those best fitted to profit by them and who are best able to contribute to their permanent value is something which is of the utmost importance not only to the University but to the City as a whole.[62]

Shortly thereafter, an office of Undergraduate Admissions, staffed by an administrative officer, was established at Columbia. Although the primary impulse for the office's establishment came from the problems raised by conditional admittance, Butler certainly had Prettyman's recommendations in mind when he suggested the innovation. The office not only made possible greater leeway in evaluation of academic admissions criteria; it also permitted the future addition of nonacademic criteria that could be subjectively evaluated.

In the short run the Prettyman committee did not stem the Jewish invasion. It did identify an area of increasing faculty concern and recognized that existing admissions mechanisms could not deal with the problem. Further strategies had to be contemplated.

DEVISING STRATEGIES: HALFWAY MEASURES

Immediately after his appointment as dean of Columbia College in 1910, Frederick Keppel took stock of the "Jewish problem." Columbia University had aspired to be a national institution. It wished to attract students with desirable character traits and family background so that it would produce well-placed and wealthy alumni. It found itself again engulfed by the metropolis it had fled to Morningside to escape. It found that children from the older families of New York, including the children of Columbia's own trustees and faculty, shunned its urban locale for greener pastures. For Keppel, as for all of Columbia's leaders, the animus against Jews was an expression of a broader fear; to some extent, perhaps, "Jew" was the shorthand for all that represented the gap between reality and desire.

The dean criticized Columbia's handling (or, better, lack of handling) of the Jewish problem to that point. He understood that no measure or combination of measures would lead to the complete elimination of Jewish students from the College, but he hoped to confine the Jewish element to the "desirable" ones who came to college with "social advantages" and somehow eliminate the "undesirable" ones, who came despite social disadvantages. He told Adam Leroy Jones, the admissions director, to be less concerned with the number of students admitted to the freshman class each year and more concerned with their quality: "Where an undesirable citizen could, with justice, be left outside the walls, I am sure that in the long run his room would be more advantageous than his company." He was especially concerned about "a number of ill-prepared and uncultured Jews" who were "trying to obtain a cheap College degree by transferring, usually in February, from the City College, which they entered after only a three-year High School course."[63]

Jones defended the policies of his office, and in doing so revealed one mechanism by which Columbia tried to modify the composition of its entering class. He reported that not only were the students just admitted better prepared than applicants of previous years, they were also "very much more desirable." He noted that many of them had to be conditioned in, at most, two or three units. Jones had discovered that the practice of conditioning permitted the use of subjective criteria in evaluating candidates. Did a student from a good preparatory school just miss passing an exam or two? Wouldn't he be likely to benefit from the "Columbia Experience"? Might he not emerge as a leader of other students, and ultimately as an important member of the community? Questions such as these significantly departed from a strict meritocratic standard and Jones's decision to admit on condition students for whom the answer to these questions was "yes" and reject those for whom the response was negative permitted him to alter the "mix" of the student body.[64]

During the teens, Butler, Keppel, Jones, and other administrators, as well as the Columbia trustees, considered further methods of regulating the composition of the College's student body, short of outright limitation of Jews. Butler and Keppel thought that the will of Joseph Pulitzer, publisher of the *New York World,* could be exploited for this purpose. Pulitzer had provided for the endowment of scholarships "to enable poor boys of ability to enter the professions and overcome the handicap of poverty which might otherwise prevent their achieving success."[65] Students awarded the scholarships would receive a stipend that could be applied to their expenses at any college. However, if the student chose to attend Columbia, he would also be exempted from paying tuition. Since the scholarships were restricted to graduates of the New York City public high schools, it was not surprising that a majority of those receiving Pulitzer awards were Jewish and that of these most decided to attend Columbia.[66]

Columbia's authorities made several proposals for changing the terms of the awards. Butler suggested that upstate New York students be made eligible, hoping this would attract needy gentiles from upstate. Keppel, theorizing that gentile Pulitzer scholars would be more likely to use their scholarships at an out-of-town college, suggested that all Pulitzer winners be required to attend Columbia. He also recommended that preference in the award of Pulitzers be given to students intending to embark on careers in journalism. Not only would this encourage the growth of Columbia's new School of Journalism, the endowment of which was also provided by the terms of Pulitzer's will, but it "might also give us a larger proportion of Gentiles among the Scholars; for Journalism is not sufficiently lucrative a profession to be particularly attractive to the Jew." All these schemes came to naught when it was determined that the provisions of Pulitzer's will could not be altered.[67]

At about the same time, Keppel and the College Committee on Scholarships agreed upon the need for intensified recruitment of students from outside the New York City area. "From the nature of the population of New York City," Keppel wrote, "a considerable portion of the local matriculants will be of foreign birth or parentage. Most of these are excellent and desirable students, but the danger of their preponderating over the students of the older American stocks is not an imaginary one. This has already happened at the New York University and at the College of the City of New York." To save Columbia from the fate of its neighbors, he recommended increased attention to widening the College's geographic constituency. "The number of students now coming to Columbia College from outside the metropolitan district is already considerable and is growing," he reported. Such students seemed to be largely self-reliant and self-supporting, and their recruitment would be facilitated by the establishment of a system of scholarships. He suggested that a competitive scholarship covering tuition and fees be established for each state and for each province of Canada. Not only would this bring in many desirable students and make the College truly national in scope, but it would also "bring Columbia College to the attention of many students and parents throughout the country who now know very little about it."[68] Lack of funds ultimately led Columbia to reject the scheme. Its significance lies in its implied recognition that Columbia could do little to attract gentiles living in New York City and would have to make special efforts to attract a broad-based clientele.

The Scholarships Committee then proposed a more limited scholarship program. In 1912, the New York State Legislature had approved a scholarship program for state residents who intended to attend college within the state. The scholarships would cover about half of Columbia's tuition fee of about $150. The faculty therefore suggested that Columbia provide supplemental funds to cover tuition for State Scholars *residing outside of New York City* "who may elect to study in Columbia College and who, for financial reasons, would otherwise be unable to do so."[69] The faculty's Committee on Instruction said that such a program "would do more than any one other thing to attract resident students of a desirable type."[70]

The trustees' Committee on Education debated the merits of the various proposals for scholarships, but put off a final decision until they had more information as to the kind of students who were winning state scholarships. Keppel provided precisely the information they desired. Of the 58 state scholars who entered Columbia in the fall of 1913,

6 of these would have, in any case, won Pulitzer or other competitive scholarships. Of the others, so far as I can judge, 43 are desirable citizens, not only academically but socially. This number included perhaps a dozen of the better type of Jewish students. 9 are of a less desirable type.

The winners of scholarships from districts outside the boroughs comprising the city of New York are, with but a single exception, Gentile boys of a desirable social type.[71]

The College implemented a small-scale scholarship program in 1914. Scholarships were placed at the disposal of several private secondary schools which "in the past sent us a series of conspicuously good men" or which were "competent to do this but who have not hitherto sent us many students of any kind." Scholarships would be awarded without regard to financial need.[72]

At the same time, the trustees considered a more comprehensive solution. If the "Jewish problem" could be remedied by encouraging the attendance of out-of-town students while discouraging local students, why not require all freshmen to reside in the dormitories on the Columbia campus? The growth of a campus-oriented student community had proved attractive at Harvard and Yale; perhaps required dorm residence would have the same effect at Columbia. It would at least discourage the attendance of those who attended Columbia because it was within daily commuting distance, thus saving at least $150 a year in supplementary expenses. The idea appeared so promising to the trustees that they kept it under active consideration for more than a year.[72]

When Butler sounded out Keppel and the College faculty, he did not expect their completely negative reaction. Their sympathy for the goals underlying the proposal was tempered by awareness of its inability to produce the desired result. Calling the idea "suicidal," the College Committee on Instruction said that "our cue is to emphasize the advantages of our place in the city rather than to seem to apologize for it, by copying too obviously the conditions of a rural institution."[74] Keppel said that the plan would not "make Columbia in any sense a fashionable college."

For boys whose families are in New York society the tendency to go out of New York for school and college is too strong. There is indeed a certain justification for it, because the boy whose friends are in the city is under constant, and for most boys, irresistible temptation to neglect his College opportunities, both scholarly and social, in favor of downtown entertainments of various sorts, and residence in the dormitories would not solve this problem. To put it frankly, I do not think such a plan, or any other, would bring to us the sons of men like Mr. Rives, Mr. Cutting and Mr. Parsons.

Keppel also argued that such a requirement would not discourage the attendance of Jewish students since that constituency comprised "a fair proportion" of those already living in the dormitories. He conjectured that should the plan be implemented, "many sons of rich New York Jews would engage rooms and continue to spend most of their time in their own family circles."

Finally, he warned the trustees to remember that the College fed the University's professional schools and that the added expense of compulsory dormitory residence might lead professionally-oriented students, especially those taking a combined course, to go elsewhere.[75]

Both the Committee on Instruction and Keppel agreed that only gradual change should be undertaken in this direction. Initial steps might include charging freshmen a minimal rental to induce them to reside in the dorms and required residence of all freshmen who did not live at home or who entered on conditions (while placing more emphasis on "the educational and social needs of the University in the administration of the halls"). The adverse reaction of the dean and his faculty convinced the trustees to abandon their plan, but sentiment in this direction lingered and the issue was resurrected after World War I.

Along with the use of conditons, altering the Pulitzer scholarships, attracting upstate and out-of-state students, and compelling dormitory residence for freshmen, another strategy was suggested—and eventually adopted. In 1913, Dean Keppel suggested "limiting in some equitable and intelligent way the number of students admitted each year to the College." Such a proposal challenged the prevailing belief in the desirability of expanded student enrollments for reasons of prestige (the "best" colleges were those with the largest enrollments) and of finance (larger numbers meant increased revenue from tuition). Noting that "the physical limit for effective College work with our present equipment is . . . in sight," Keppel argued that instead of expanding, as Columbia had done in similar situations in the past, the College should be content to maintain enrollments at the level of full employment of existing facilities. When the number of qualified applicants began to exceed this level, the Admissions Office could choose among them using criteria such as "personal qualities" or it could give "preference in the registration to boys who would live in the Residence Halls."[76]

The dean discussed at length what he knew would be the trustees' major objection to such a proposal. He admitted that its financial aspects were "problematical," but suggested that a considerable increase in enrollment might entail "added expenditures for equipment and other purposes that would more than counterbalance the increase which would come from tuition fees." The 900 students currently enrolled already had to contend with an inadequate library collection and study area which forced students to sit "on the radiators in the College Study," overcrowded the science laboratories, and fully utilized classroom space.

The dean argued that the College's prestige was not measured by its numbers, but by its "attention to the interests and needs of the students." For the maintenance of this personal relationship between College and student, in face of expanding enrollments the trustees would have to make additional expenditures for the offices of admissions, the registrar, the health service, and the dean. Thus, unchecked increases in enrollment at this time could lead to a decline in the College's prestige, not an increase.[77]

The inertia generally typical of universities led to a continuation of Columbia's old policies through World War I.[78] The trustees contemplated the effects of lost tuition revenues as they considered methods of limiting enrollments while maintaining academic and increasing social standards. The war itself ultimately spurred the trustees to action by demonstrating the practicality of one such method.

HEAVY ARTILLERY:
SHIFTING THE SELECTIVE FUNCTION

Soon after President Woodrow Wilson asked Congress for a declaration of war in April, 1917, the "cream of American youth" offered their services at their local army recruiting stations. Although most of the nation responded warmly to this expression of patriotism, Columbia's rulers saw it as a mixed blessing. Although the size of the College's freshman class did not decline the following fall, Butler commented that its "quality" was "depressing in the extreme." "It is largely made up of foreign born and children of those but recently arrived in this country," he lamented. "The boys of old American stock, even many of them under draft age, have sought opportunity for military or other public service and have no time to go to college."[79]

Shortly thereafter Butler publicly advocated a limitation in the College's enrollment. (He also noted the existence of considerable congestion in certain departments of the graduate school.) He characterized Columbia's past policy as accepting "any one as student who is not shown to be unfit or unprepared." Stating that the University overtaxed its resources and the energies of its teachers by this policy, he urged a retreat from it "in order to fortify and to hold the position that the University should itself, by an affirmative process of selection and not merely by a negative process of exclusion, choose those upon whom it wishes to expend its funds and its energies." Admitting that such a policy would be questionable if "there were but a single college and a single university in the United States," Butler went on to say that the widespread opportunity for both higher and professional education that existed in the United States would permit Columbia to effect its retreat "without public damage." Although he said that students should be selected on the basis of "their record, their personality and their promise," and that existing academic entrance requirements should be retained "solely for the purpose of creating an eligible list," he was vague as to the actual criteria that might be employed in making selections. He merely said that Columbia would choose students "by such process as it deems fit" but employing a maximum of careful discretion, work, and responsibility.[80]

Those assigned the task of specifying selection criteria faced a formidable task. One way to limit enrollment would have been simply to raise the academic criteria for admission: for example, to raise the passing grade on the entrance examinations or to raise the high school grade that could overcome a failing score on the tests. This was considered but rejected since it would have done little to alter the social mix of the student body. But for social characteristics to be considered relevant in admissions decisions, it became necessary first to define desirable characteristics and then to elicit information necessary to determine which candidates had them.

Jones and the College faculty set to work on listing these characteristics, which turned out to be those the high schools should have been looking for if they had properly performed the selective function. The criteria finally settled upon included personal background (new application blanks would ask for the candidate's place of birth, religious affiliation, and father's name, place of birth, and occupation), leadership in school (measured not only by academic excellence, but also by participation in activities such as school publications, musical and other organizations, athletics, patriotic activities, debating, student government, and by the receipt of honors and prizes), leadership in the community (including patriotic activities, religious and other organizations, as well as employment), breadth of interests (as measured by outside readings), and finally motivation and potential (measured by an essay on why the applicant wished to go to college, why he selected Columbia, and what he expected to make of himself).[81]

The College's position as "vestibule" for entrance to the entire University made the candidate's career plans as important as his personal traits in making judgments on admissions. By the onset of the war, all of Columbia's major professional schools required some college-level study for admission and depended on the College for their supplies of students. Keppel noted that a limitation of enrollment would lead to an increase in the proportion of "desirable" students entering these schools, but cautioned that "the limit set would have to be sufficiently high to provide an adequate quota of firstrate Columbia material for six professional schools as well as for the Faculty of Political Science, Philosophy and Pure Science."[82] To meet this concern, after implementation of the new admissions system in 1919, the first question asked of the candidate on the new application blank (after his name) was his probable occupation.

Having determined the necessary information for making admissions decisions, Jones and the faculty discussed the possible methods of eliciting it. They decided to rely on an extensive application to be completed by the student, a photograph to be submitted with the application, and a personal interview with as many of the applicants as possible. Finally, they requested three letters of recommendation, including one from the applicant's high school principal. Columbia had required a principal's evaluation for several years, but in most cases considered itself fortunate to receive a halfway complete transcript, let alone a serious discussion of the candidate's attributes. Jones hoped that in the future principals would take this responsibility more seriously.[83]

Assuming that the applicants would truthfully answer all the questions, Jones could have proceeded to modify the composition of the entering class along any number of lines, including a strict limitation on the number of Jews, the restriction of Jewish admittances to those "of a desirable kind," or the rejection of all but a specified number of New York City residents. And yet, Columbia did *not* at this time adopt what would later be called a quota system—that is, setting aside a predetermined number of places for Jewish applicants in a freshman class of limited size. This might seem surprising since, unlike the situation at the time of the Prettyman report, Columbia now had a bureaucratic apparatus to regulate admissions. Concern with the Jewish problem was perhaps at its height.

Several complementary explanations may be offered for Columbia's reluctance to fire its heavy artillery. First, Butler's announcement of enrollment limitations and the assignment of the selective function to a bureaucratic office under the University's own control received considerable attention, and some already suspected invidious motives behind these changes.[84] Second, exclusion of undesirables could have involved a large financial cost unless the vacated seats could be filled with other tuition-paying customers. Third, and related to the second, Butler desired implementation of an affirmative process of selection. Mere exclusion of Jews was as "negative" as rejection of the academically unqualified. Butler still evisioned Columbia's mission as educating the next generation's leaders; removal of those elements preventing attainment of this goal was a necessary but not a sufficient accomplishment.

Fourth, some had been reluctant to employ social criteria at the expense of academic criteria. The director of admissions, Adam Leroy Jones, belonged in this category. A few years earlier, he mused over the question in a memorandum to Butler. "If a college were devoting itself to training men for leadership demanding public spirit and unselfish devotion to the common good, as well as integrity and trained intelligence," he said, "it is conceivable that the promise of those other qualities should also be considered" along with intellectual and narrowly defined moral qualities. But, "such qualities can rarely be detected with certainty in young boys," and "to exclude those who showed no promise of them would undoubtedly result in sending away many who might later go farthest." He suggested that the college could best achieve this result "by providing as teachers those who have the desired qualities."

He contended that Columbia's own experience as well as recent scientific studies demonstrated that those with the requisite intellectual qualities seemed also to possess the other desirable qualities. "In any case," Jones concluded, "many would hold that since intellectual training is after all the business of a university, other than intellectual qualities were not matters of primary interest to it."[85] Coming from the man who would implement Columbia's new policy, this viewpoint had to be kept in mind by those who had fewer qualms.

Fortunately for Columbia, at just this moment, there appeared a new instrument that seemed to meet everyone's needs. It appeared to limit the number of Jewish students while increasing Columbia's constituency to include areas where the pervasiveness of the certificate system had heretofore dissuaded most students from attempting the entrance examinations of any Eastern college. It measured intellectual qualities without sacrificing social qualities. In short, *intelligence* tests employed in conjunction with selective admissions appeared to be deadly, yet acceptable, weapons.

SATC AND IQ

Fielding an army required no little effort in a nation that had been at peace for many years. Although the United States War Department retained for itself the job of recruiting and training an infantry, it delegated the task of selecting and instructing its officers to the universities, through the Student Army Training Corps. More than 150 campuses suspended their normal routine for the duration and devoted their full resources to this service. At Columbia, the normal divisional lines were erased and the entire faculty pooled its efforts to instruct several thousand potential officers. Preparation for the program continued throughout the 1917–18 academic year in anticipation of the first SATC class to be admitted in the fall of 1918.[86]

Because the minimum qualifications set by the War Department for admission to the program were liberal, Columbia found itself deluged with applications.[87] The War Department permitted each university to choose from among those applicants meeting these qualifications. According to Director Jones, there were "hundreds of applicants . . . wholly unsuited by personality to become army officers." Among those who passed the personality test, many "did not possess the necessary mental alertness and power."[88] Using the discretion granted him, Jones required that each SATC candidate undergo a personal interview with a faculty member selected for this purpose and submit three letters of recommendation.

"To measure the mental alertness of the candidates," Jones said, "we required them to take the Thorndike Tests for Mental Alertness." Designed by

E. L. Thorndike of Teachers College, these tests were thought to measure the "intelligence" or "quality of mind" of each applicant. Unlike the traditional entrance examinations, intelligence tests (often called psychological tests by contemporaries) did not test acquisition of a specific body of knowledge. Instead they measured a characteristic believed to be inherited by an individual at birth—the ability to learn how to respond to a given situation. Instead of measuring what had already been accomplished by an individual, the tests attempted to predict what an individual would accomplish in the future.

The possibility of employing intelligence tests as part of Columbia's admissions apparatus had been discussed before the war, but was rejected on the grounds that they had not been sufficiently tried.[89] Selection of an SATC class provided Columbia with an ideal opportunity to perform an experiment. The experiment was a success. Of the fifty students entering the College through SATC who were advised to withdraw after their freshman year, only three attained a B on the intelligence tests.[90]

Thus assured that reliance on intelligence tests would not prove academically detrimental, Columbia proceeded to integrate the test into the admissions process. In 1919, Butler announced that henceforth all applicants to Columbia College would be required to take either the Thorndike Tests or the comprehensive entrance examinations devised by Harvard several years earlier and subsequently prepared by the CEEB. Students taking the intelligence tests could present a certificate attesting to their completion of Columbia's entrance requirements.[91] At the same time Butler declared that Columbia would no longer accept Regents credentials in lieu of the entrance examinations. This practice, he said discriminated against the out-of-state student who often had decided to go elsewhere rather than spend considerable time and effort in preparation for the entrance examinations. As a result of these changes, Columbia hoped that "a very desirable type of students from outside the metropolitan district will be able to enter college and by virtue of his native intelligence as indicated by the psychological tests, more than hold his own."[92] Butler announced that henceforth a maximum number of places in the freshman class would be designated and that selection to the class would be based on performance on the intelligence tests or comprehensive examinations, and on the information provided by the applicant on his application and letters of recommendation.

These steps were not only aimed at attracting the good gentile out-of-state student; they also enabled Columbia to "limit the number or proportion of foreign students without adopting a policy of exclusion."[93] The concept of intelligence was closely associated with the eugenics movement and with the racist ideologies that held forth during the early twentieth century. Many thought it would be found in greater quantities in certain "racial stocks," especially the "Nordic," which populated much of northern and western

Europe. They thought it relatively lacking in two other racial stocks, the Alpine, mainly East European Slavs, and the Mediterranean, those who lived in southern Europe. Although some contemporary literature attributed a high degree of intelligence to the Jews,[94] the quantitative research performed by the intelligence testers seemed to demonstrate the reverse. Carl Campbell Brigham, who supervised the administration of Army Alpha intelligence tests given to American troops in World War I, cited census figures to demonstrate that at least half of his sample of Russian immigrants who took the Alpha Tests were Jewish and that between a fifth and a quarter of "Alpines" were Jewish. He concluded:

Our figures, then, would rather tend to disprove the popular belief that the Jew is highly intelligent. Immigrants examined in the army who report their birthplace as Russia, had an average intelligence below those from all other countries except Poland and Italy. It is perhaps significant to note, however, that the sample from Russia has a higher standard deviation (2.83) than that of any other immigrant group sampled, and that the Alpine group has a higher standard deviation than the Nordic or the Mediterranean groups (2.60). If we assume that the Jewish immigrants have a low average intelligence, but a higher variability than other nativity groups, this would reconcile our figures with the popular belief, and at the same time, with the fact that investigators searching for talent in New York City and California schools find a frequent occurrence of talent among Jewish children. The able Jew is popularly recognized not only because of his ability, but because he is able and a Jew.[95]

Brigham neglected to add another factor that explained the success of native Americans on the intelligence tests: the tests were written in English, which might not have been the soldier's first language. When "the success of the Army Alpha mental tests in the cantonments became known," Butler, Jones, et al. lost their last hesitations about the usefulness of intelligence tests for Columbia's purposes.[96]

Herbert Hawkes, Keppel's successor as dean of Columbia College in 1918, succinctly described Columbia's expectations with regard to the intelligence tests. He distinguished between the student "grind" who did not have much native intelligence, but who had enough persistence in his studies to do well in the traditional entrance examinations, and the student with genuine intelligence, who might also have done well in the tests, but whose success stemmed from native ability. Hawkes thought that the former type of student (read Jew) should be discouraged from going to college since there appeared to be a high correlation between intelligence and success in college. From this observation, he concluded that the grind would not be able to keep up with the pace at Columbia since he could not indefinitely work above his native capacity. "What we have been trying to do," he wrote just after the tests were introduced, is to eliminate the low grade boy. We had 1200 applications for admission last fall and could accommodate only 550. This meant that somebody had to lose out. We have not eliminated boys because they were Jews and do not propose to do so. We have honestly attempted to eliminate the lowest grade of applicant and it turns out that a good many of the low grade men are New York City Jews. It is a fact that boys of foreign parentage who have no background in many cases attempt to educate themselves beyond their intelligence. Their accomplishment is over 100% of their ability on account of their tremendous energy and ambition. I do not believe however that a College would do well to admit too many men of low mentality who have ambition but not brains. At any rate this is the principle on which we are going.[97]

IN THE PROVINCES

When a few years later Harvard confronted its "Jewish problem," the affair made national headlines.[98] In announcing that Harvard had decided to study the feasibility of limiting its undergraduate enrollment, President Abbott Lawrence Lowell, who had succeeded President Eliot in 1909, also stated that as part of the study, Harvard would consider the possibility of limiting the admission of Jewish students.

It was Eliot's opinion that Lowell privately hated Jews and feared them as well.[99] However, the position Lowell expressed to friends and supporters had a broader rationale. Having watched the proportion of Jews at Harvard triple during the first decades of the twentieth century, Lowell argued that the "Jewish problem" did not consist primarily in the undesirability of traits present in individual Jews, but in the trait of "clannishness" that was supposedly inherent in the Jewish group as a whole. This self-imposed segregation offended other groups and eventually drove them off. And since the presence of gentiles had originally attracted the Jews in large numbers, their departure would quite rapidly lead to a loss of interest among the Jewish clientele.

When pressed that perhaps the Jew remained clannish in response to gentile prejudice, Lowell replied that it was useless to trace the source of the problem since the problem existed in any case and could only be solved by limiting the number of Jewish students to a proportion that the gentiles found acceptable.[100] This limitation would work to the benefit of Harvard by enabling it to retain its character as a "democratic, national university; drawing from all classes of the community and promoting a sympathetic understanding among them." It would work to the benefit of the Jews by resolving in an assimilationist direction the great question currently confronting American Jews: Whether they "were to persist as a separate group in the community or to be merged in the body of unhyphenated American citizens."[101]

Lowell rejected the use of character tests and other aspects of selective admissions designed to weed out undesirability in individuals, and urged that the faculty and corporation not employ subterfuges, but announce a policy aimed at Jews alone and state the reasons for the policy's adoption.[102] He envisioned a quota of about 15% to 16%, as opposed to an estimated current enrollment of about 20%. He cited the large Jewish enrollment at Columbia College as the reason why it had never realized its potential and called for the Harvard community to recognize the urgency of the problem.

Critics attacked Lowell on a number of grounds: his ironic use of the word "democratic" in defense of a discriminatory mechanism, his paternalistic attitude toward a people he did not understand, his unilateral decision about their destiny in America and his willingness to use Harvard to implement it, and his assertion that the establishment of a quota system would reduce rather than aggravate intergroup tensions.

To Harry Starr, a Jewish student at Harvard who became involved in the controversy, no "Jewish problem" existed—the Jew was a problem only to those who made him so. Upon reflection, he understood the importance of the principle at stake: "that no self-respecting Jew can allow any talk which would cast a shadow over the Jew as an American with the right to domicile not only on the soil but in the institutions arising from that soil." As for the desirability of assimilation, he asked to what the Jews were supposed to assimilate. In other words, what was the true American? It might well be argued, he said, "that precisely those qualities of a race which seemed to the Anglo-Saxon mind as 'unassimilable' were the very qualities which that race might most usefully contribute to the great American race to emerge." In this way, the presence of individuals possessing those qualities might be an asset, not a liability.

These arguments all reflected one basic proposition: "that the position of the Jew at Harvard depended not on his complacent acceptance of an immobile standard of thinking or living, but on his eagerness to share in the creation of newer and better standards in a society whose outlines were still shadowy in their very greatness."[103]

Harvard did not adopt a quota system at that time, although it did adopt policies aimed at widening the geographic distribution of its freshman class.[104] During the twenties, a number of private undergraduate colleges as well as many medical and other professional schools affiliated with private universities did restrict access of Jewish students, either directly or indirectly. Most of these barriers would not come down until after World War II.

SELECTIVE ADMISSIONS IN OPERATION

A few years before the adoption of selective admissions, Butler had suggested that each candidate for graduation from Columbia College be favorably recommended by the College's Committee on Instruction "*on the basis of his character, personality and general bearing while in College residence.*" He envisioned a procedure analogous to that submitted to by "a candidate for admission to a Club, that is, having his personal qualifications examined." [105]

The analogy was appropriate. Graduation from college—especially from a college as prestigious as Columbia—implied admission to a rather select circle, namely the upper strata of American society. It was only natural that those already among the elect would attempt to prescribe the qualifications necessary for joining them. During the late nineteenth and early twentieth centuries, the demand for expertise occasioned by a rapidly industrializing economy necessitated a widening of elite circles, and the university had undertaken the task of training new recruits in the social and professional skills demanded of their new members in a complex society. But, by the onset of World War I, some university authorities concluded that any further increase in enrollments would reduce the effectiveness of their programs.

Thus, even without a "Jewish problem," limitation of enrollment would have eventually occurred at many elite universities. But, at schools like Columbia where any further increase in Jewish attendance meant a corresponding decrease in gentile attendance, those in authority tried to insure the continued access of "desirable streams." Selective admissions permitted them to make college entrance, rather than college graduation, the cutoff point.

From Butler's point of view, the system got off to a good start. After the Armistice, Columbia received applications from many of the same students who had forsaken the campus for the cantonments when war was declared. Given this enlarged pool of applicants, Jones was able to employ the various admissions devices, the psychological tests (which within a few years became mandatory for all applicants), the interviews, the information on the application blanks and letters of recommendation, as well as academic criteria, to obtain an entering class far more to Columbia's liking than those admitted immediately before the war. Along with the traditional academic criteria, "a purely objective use of the Thorndike Psychological Tests," reported Hawkes, "afford a student body that is reasonably well-balanced." He found, as expected, that no group did significantly better than any other on the tests—or at least well enough "to disturb the balance here mentioned." [106]

Columbia's conception of a "reasonably well-balanced" student body included room for at least some Jews. "I have no desire whatever to eliminate the Jew from Columbia College," wrote Dean Hawkes.

Situated as we are in New York we ought to furnish the very best education we can to a good many of them and as a matter of fact the cream of the Jews constitutes a very fine body of people in my opinion. I believe that we ought to carry at least 15% of Jews and I do not think that 20% is excessive for Columbia College.[107]

But the 40% or more of the entering class that was Jewish before adoption of selective admissions was excessive. "Every college should be ready to admit as many divergent types of students as it can assimilate," Hawkes said. But at the same time, "for a college to consist entirely or almost entirely of newly arrived immigrants makes it impossible for them to gain the contacts that they need and should have." Although Hawkes believed in the melting pot image of American society, he commented that "the pot will not melt if too much cold metal is put in at once."[108] By 1921, with selective admissions well launched, Jews comprised only 22% of the College's entering class.[109]

But by 1925 there were signs that despite Columbia's elaborate plans selective admissions yielded at best only a temporary change. Although no other tabulations of the religious affiliations of college freshmen could be located, two surrogate indicators are available, namely geographic origin and nationality. In the first two years in which the Thorndike Tests were used, 33% and 28% of Columbia's student body came from "remote points," which meant from beyond New York City and its suburbs. The percentage then fell to 20% and remained there through the mid-1920s. Figures on the nationality of the student body revealed that at all times through the mid-1920s at least 40% of the freshman class was from immigrant families.[110]

The increase in students from the New York metropolitan area and the constancy in the percentage of foreign-born students may appear surprising in light of Columbia's efforts to change these trends. Continued dormitory construction (John Jay Hall, the largest dorm to that point, was opened in 1926) and reorganization of the scholarship program had augmented selective admission.[111] Concerning scholarships, for most of the twenties and early thirties two-thirds of the scholarship holders were "American-born sons of American-born parents." Protestants received about two-thirds of all awards (a percentage that increased to 88% by 1937); Catholics received most of the rest. What little scholarship aid went to Jewish students was provided through the Pulitzer awards.[112] In petitioning for a liberalization of Columbia's loan policy, Dean Hawkes suggested that it too could be employed to keep away "from an exclusively New York registration."[113]

But on further reflection, the high ratios of New York City and European-born students are not surprising. Despite Columbia's concern about the composition of its student body, it retained a meritocratic urge which for a long time worked in favor of the local boy. During the teens, Butler had noted that the "alarming" increase in enrollment had taken place "in the face of steadily advancing standards of admission and of graduation." The "endless thousands of ambitious men and women" who were "ready to meet any test of time or scholarship" in order to matriculate at Columbia still streamed from the New York City high schools in the twenties.[114] Columbia still hoped to enroll the best of these "but to add to these men those of equal ability and preparation from other parts of the country." But, wrote a Columbia admissions officer, "the great difficulty in arriving at the solution is the difficulty of enrolling a sufficient number of men from other states who can measure up to the standards of ability and preparation set by the students of New York City,"[115] Even if the Admissions Office could identify and admit such students, Columbia College officials conceded their inability "to overcome with any great success the handicap" that the University's inadequate financial aid program "would impose on the College in the direction of discouraging out-of-town students of American parentage."[116]

The problem persisted through the thirties, when Dean of Students Nicholas McKnight commented that emphasis on geographic distribution and on the qualities of character and leadership led to the recruitment and subsidy of students "less well-prepared for the Columbia College program of study than the students from New York and its environs."[117] Columbia never fully abandoned its desire for solid academic preparation, but whereas in earlier times, when the College had a relatively homogeneous student body, academic preparation constituted the primary admissions criterion, by the twenties it had become one of several important criteria.

Columbia's concern for scholarship was not the only factor that accounted for the continued high percentage of local and foreign-born students in the College. The surge in applications to the College after the Armistice subsided within a few years, and Columbia found itself with a smaller pool of applicants from which to select. Finally, as the General Education Board noted prior to World War I, all schools of higher education, even the national ones, tended to recruit the bulk of their students within a fairly narrow circumference.[118] Adam Leroy Jones suggested that as local colleges all over the country grew in importance their increased attractiveness would divert even more students from the "national" colleges. To some extent, at least, this happened at Columbia during the twenties.[119]

Upon introduction of selective admissions to Columbia, Dean Hawkes had sounded an ominous note. "When a man is responsible for the development of an institution involving as it does traditions and a heritage which may have required decades to develop," he said,

It is certain that he bears a very heavy responsibility to his institution and to the community. He has no right to take steps that will destroy the value of the institution. For instance, if a thousand men from France should present themselves to Columbia College for admission and were better qualified to pass our entrance examinations than young men from our local clientele, I should feel that some steps ought to be taken so that it would be impossible to admit them all. It would so modify the work that we are trying to accomplish that in a short time the work of 150 years would largely be undone. The same kind of remark may be made in regard to Jews, colored people, and other groups which are more or less distinctive. We ought to be glad to have as many of each kind as in our judgment the institution can stand but to say that there should be no limit to the number of men of a given type who may present themselves to College, seems to me a surrender on the part of the administration of one of the most important responsibilities that they bear.[120]

If "objective" criteria of admissions such as psychological tests could not enable Hawkes to meet his responsibility, selective admissions could be used invidiously to this end.

THE ULTIMATE WEAPON

The Columbia campus was anything but idyllic during the worst years of the Great Depression. In 1932 the administration expelled from the College Reed Harris, editor of the *Columbia Spectator,* on the grounds of misrepresentation and repeated discourtesy in his accusations concerning management of the University dining halls. The University's action prompted a large demonstration and a "strike" on the Columbia campus.[121] The following year, further demonstrations took place over the nonreappointment of a communist junior faculty member.[122] The conduct of some students during these demonstrations prompted Nicholas Murray Butler to examine anew the familiar question, "Who should be admitted to Columbia?"

"I don't know whether it is at all practicable," Butler told Hawkes, "but it would be highly judicious if . . . some way could be found to see to it that individuals of the undesirable type did not get into Columbia College, no matter what their record in the very unimportant matter of A's and B's."[123] By "undesirable," Butler meant students who "have shown themselves to be so lacking in any spirit of University loyalty or any concern for the welfare of the University as such and its public reputation that their presence is really a nuisance and a source of damage." He believed that many students of a "higher type" put Columbia on the same plane as City College "and look upon both as more or less of a nuisance, the outgrowth of metropolitan conditions which must be borne with as patiently as may be, but which should not be patronized."

Butler knew that the situation had to be handled delicately. "Our principles and our traditions," he told Jones, "would prevent our imitating even at a long distance the Nazi policy in Germany which is endeavoring to cast all students in a common mold. On the other hand it is important that we should not permit a publicity-loving minority to do real and continuous damage to our reputation and influence." Although Columbia's New York City location made the "undergraduate problem" very difficult, Butler believed that "having New York University and the College of the City of New York as an alternative, we should not be depriving young men of an opportunity for a college education if we should tell them that they are not desired at Columbia."[124]

Jones replied that he had been giving close attention all along to reports concerning the applicant's conduct as citizen as well as to his intellectual, social, and moral qualities. His records for the troublesome students indicated nothing "which would have given us reason to suppose that they would become academic nuisances." These students represented more or less a cross section of the student body, and Jones attributed their deviant behavior to the growing-up process. Contemporary students, he concluded, had more political awareness than students of earlier generations, but they did not have a correspondingly greater sense of responsibility.[125]

Butler largely agreed with this analysis, and did not request specific action at that time.[126] When Jones died several months after this exchange, Frank H. Bowles, a graduate of Columbia College and Jones's assistant for the previous four years, replaced him. Aware of his superiors' concerns about the nature of the student body, and perhaps hoping to make a good impression with them, Bowles had less hesitancy about an invidious use of selective admissions, including a set quota of Jewish students to be admitted, if it would widen the University's influence and attract "desirable students of upper middle class American stock."

In reporting to Butler and the trustees concerning the composition of the first College freshman class over which he had ultimate responsibility, Bowles demonstrated his concern with the question of Jewish admittance, which lurked just below the surface of the entire discussion of citizenship, as Butler's reference to Nazi practice indicates. At the same time, Bowles understood the College's role as a major gateway to Columbia's professional schools and he continued to regulate admission to the College with their needs and desires in mind.

Bowles expressed general satisfaction with the College's admissions policy, expressing unhappiness only with the small number of Catholic applications, which forced him to admit too many professionally-oriented, first generation, Italian Catholics. The large number of applications received from Jewish applicants permitted him to select a Jewish contingent that was less professionally oriented. "About one out of every seven Jewish applicants is admitted, particular emphasis being placed on personal qualifications, academic ability, and choice of future career." He reported that only 60% of those admitted planned on a professional career, although 80% of those who applied had such intentions.

Bowles's comments on Jewish and Catholic students indicate that as an early step in the admissions process, he classified applicants according to religion. Then he grouped them by professional orientation within each religious group. He made final selections on the basis of all available evidence, including "personal contact," which permitted the gathering and use of "a great mass of information that does not and can not appear in an application blank." Bowles desired to insure that the student body would be geographically diverse and that those students of all religions offered admission had personality and character traits that would make them respectable members of the upper strata.

Stating that "selective admission has affected greatly the makeup of our freshman classes," Bowles reported that, in the fall of 1934, 572 freshmen matriculated of which 58% were Protestants, 25% were Catholics, and 17% were Jewish. Bowles provided statistics that indicated that three-quarters of all Columbia freshmen came from public high schools (although a greater percentage of Jews than gentiles came from them), and that 59% of all freshmen came from New York City and State (87% of all Jews, 62% of all Catholics, and 50% of all Protestants).[127]

Butler expressed satisfaction with Bowles's report and encouraged him to "continue to build up the Freshman Class in the College along the lines that have recently been followed." He specifically applauded the goal of making the "student constituency be geographically as wide as possible consistent with excellence" and "the tendency to put more and more stress on personal and family background, character and personality, and not to depend exclusively upon the results of formal examination tests." This was a far cry from the Butler of 1900.[128]

In 1931, Heywood Broun and George Britt, in their study of discriminatory practices against Jews, wrote of the College's admissions procedure:

Columbia's machine for regulating the flow of Jewish students through its classrooms is one of the most elaborate ever devised. Armed with its eight-page blank, its talk of scholarship standards, its personal interviews, psychological tests, physical examinations, and passport photograph requirements, Columbia can select exactly the applicants it desires, keep the Jewish quota down to the fractional percentage it may determine, and defy anyone to slip by unnoticed. With this minute sifting for good material and testing for young scholars of promise, if Columbia fails to produce the bulk of the nation's future leaders, it will be a discouraging blow to human foresight.[129]

Hawkes had met his responsibility. After many modifications, Columbia College had an admissions policy that stopped the invasion.

SELECTIVE ADMISSIONS AND THE PROFESSIONAL SCHOOLS

The Medical School

Since most of Columbia's professional schools relied heavily on Columbia College for their supplies of students, admission to these schools was not a very complicated affair. Students exercising their professional option gained admittance as a matter of course, while graduates of the College obtained acceptance after the most cursory examination of their credentials. Applicants from other schools were ordinarily admitted after officials ascertained that such students had met the minimum requirements for admission, which usually consisted of completion of a specified number of years of college work and sometimes a minimum age and health standard.

Columbia's Medical School was the first professional school to depart from these practices when it adopted a selective admissions policy in 1918. A deluge of applications was partly responsible, but the policy seems to have been adopted as a part of a general effort to upgrade the school—an effort highlighted by affiliation with Presbyterian Hospital, located in Washington Heights, New York.

Before implementation of selective admissions, Jewish students typically composed about half of an entering class. Jewish enrollment peaked in 1919, and from then on, the percentage of Jewish students declined in each subsequent entering class. By 1924, the proportion had declined to 18% to 20%. In the late 1920s and early 1930s, the general trend temporarily reversed itself and the proportion of Jewish students reached 33% one year. But another downturn reduced the percentage to 10% to 12% of some entering classes. During World War II, when Columbia was assigned students by the Army and Navy, the percentage increased to about a quarter of each class[130] (see Table 7.2).

When in 1930 the publisher of a local Jewish newspaper published statistics which he interpreted as indicating discrimination against Jewish students, authorities at the Medical School defended themselves by asserting that the statistics appeared to be based on the results of applications submitted by students from CCNY. Dean William Darrach admitted that few students from CCNY were admitted, but "not because they are Jews but because they seem to have less desirable qualifications than many of our applicants from other colleges." He estimated that about a quarter of the current entering class was Jewish but commented that "even if we take the figure of 20%, I believe that to be a fair proportion considering the percentage of Jews in New York State," Darrach did not say whether this percentage of Jews accurately reflected the percentage of Jewish applicants.[131]

Associate Dean of Admissions Frederick Van Buren explained how the medical school's use of selective admissions might be interpreted as discriminatory:

We have no prejudice against Jews, as Jews, or against any other religious affiliation. We have a strong disinclination to admit to the privileges of the Medical School of Columbia University the inferior type of man, of whatever race or creed and, where

Table 7.2. School of Medicine, Columbia University, Jewish Student Enrollment 1908–1946

Year of Admission	Enrollment	Number of Jewish Students	Percentage of Jewish Student Enrollment
1908[a] (Class of 1912)	96	22–26	23–27
1909 (Class of 1913)	93	18–19	19–20
1910 (Class of 1914)	76	18–20	24–26
1911 (Class of 1915)	81	26–28	32–35
1912 (Class of 1916)	89	23–26	26–29
1913 (Class of 1917)	108	28–36	26–33
1914 (Class of 1918)	132	40–44	30–33
1915 (Class of 1919)	136	53–61	39–45
1916 (Class of 1920)	144	44–54	31–37
1917 (Class of 1921)	213	91–105	43–49
1918 (Class of 1922)	100	42–49	42–49
1919 (Class of 1923)	98	48–52	49–53
1920 (Class of 1924)	94	44–47	47–50
1921 (Class of 1925)	103	40–43	39–42
1922 (Class of 1926	103	27–30	26–29
1923[b] (Class of 1927)	104	28–30	27–29
1924 (Class of 1928)	108	19–22	18–20
1925 (Class of 1929)	113	34–36	30–32
1926 (Class of 1930)	111	17–20	15–18
1927 (Class of 1931)	112	21–25	19–22
1928 (Class of 1932)	110	19–23	17–21
1929 (Class of 1933)	115	25–30	22–26
1930 (Class of 1934)	114	27–31	24–27
1931 (Class of 1935)	115	28–35	24–30
1932 (Class of 1936)	115	33–38	29–33
1933 (Class of 1937)	112	25–32	22–28
1934 (Class of 1938)	109	14–22	13–20
1935 (Class of 1939)	113	17–23	15–20
1936 (Class of 1940)	115	12–16	10–14
1937 (Class of 1941)	113	16–20	14–18
1938 (Class of 1942)	108	11–15	10–14
1939 (Class of March 1943)	107	12–17	11–16
1940 (Class of December 1943)	110	13–18	12–16
1941 (Class of September 1944)	126	15–23	12–18
1942 (Class of June 1946)	116	18–22	16–19
1943 (Class of 1946)	119	29–32	24–27
Jan. 1944 (Class of 1947)	115	19–25	17–22
Oct. 1944 (Class of 1948)	119	29–35	24–29
1945 (Class of 1949)	114	29–34	25–30
1946 (Class of 1950)	111	30–36	27–32

we have so many applicants that (as last year) eight must be denied admission for every one that can be accepted, the selection of candidates is a difficult and tedious process. I can hardly conceive how the fact of rejection could be understood otherwise than as a discrimination and I can readily understand that, by one who looks upon himself as at least the equal of all other men, it may be regarded as unfair discrimination. But we can certainly not avoid the fact of discrimination (nor would we wish to) so long as the ratio of applicants to places remains as large as it is.[132]

Butler asked that the question on religion be deleted from the application blank. "Questions as to nationality and race are entirely beyond criticism," he commented, "but it is the question as to religion which stirs up these criticisms."[133] Dean Darrach complied. Thus, in this division, Columbia restricted the number of Jewish admittances without resorting to a numerus clausus, at least until the Bowles years.

The Law School

Although enrollments in the College and the Medical School taxed the capacity of those divisions just after World War I, the Law School accommodated all qualified applicants for another decade. Registration had wavered during the first decade of the century due to poor administration and the imposition of a more difficult curriculum. It began to expand during the teens and continued to do so at a rapid pace during the twenties.

In 1928, Dean Young B. Smith of the Law School announced that since Kent Hall, the Law School's home, was incapable of absorbing any more students, enrollment would henceforth be limited.[134] He also announced adoption of a selective admissions policy in the hopes of recruiting an entering class from a wider constituency.

it is highly desirable that a group of men selected to engage in the study of law, a subject which involves the interests of all classes of people and all sections of the country, should be fairly representative of the class and sectional interests which are involved. It is therefore important that there should be included among the list of applicants from which the student body is chosen, a substantial number of capable men from all classes and all sections.[135]

SOURCE. "John G. Saxe File," CUF, May 1, 1947.

[a]For the years 1908–1922, Columbia calculated the number of Jewish students "after an examination of one or more persons acquainted with each class, together with all other evidence." Prior to 1923, no question as to the religion of a student was asked.
[b]Between 1923 and 1931 application blanks asked the applicant's religion. Between 1928 and 1946 the registration card signed by each student after admission contained a question "Religious Preference (answer voluntary). . . ." Since 1931 twenty percent of the first year students did not answer this question. For the years 1923–1946 minimum figures on the table were based on written declarations furnished by the students while the larger figures comprised "a conservative estimate based on a careful survey of all available information."

During the twenties, the percentage of local students in the Law School student body probably increased. We know that over half of the increase in the size of the Law School student body between 1921 and 1928 came from an increase in the number of CCNY graduates entering the school (see Table 7.3).

Despite the adoption of a selective admissions policy, the composition of the Law School did not seem to change radically. One contemporary, writing a few years after the system was implemented, observed.

Anyone entering Kent Hall at noon might suppose it almost entirely Jewish. The Law Review board of editors whose members are automatically chosen from the scholastically highest of the class, is usually Jewish in the majority; and of the last nine editors-in-chief, six have been Jews. But this condition is very simply accounted for by the fact that New York is so largely a Jewish city and law a profession attractive to Jews. There is no other first rate law school in the city, and Columbia must absorb the large contingent from City College and the Jewish students from New York who return from other colleges.[136]

Except for the small, relatively peripheral schools of Architecture and Journalism, during the 1920s and 1930s Columbia's other professional schools recruited from an applicant pool composed mainly of local residents and Columbia College graduates. A few of these schools directly benefited from the selective policies of the others. Bowles attributed an increase in the quality of applicants to the School of Optometry to the difficulty students with scientific aptitudes had in gaining admission to medical schools: "Their decision to avoid the medical field is undoubtedly influenced by the fact that the majority of them are Jewish. They recognize that most of the large schools of

Table 7.3. Enrollment of Former City College Students at the Law School: 1921–22 through 1927–28

	CCNY Graduates	Total Law School Enrollment	% CCNY Graduates
1921–22	78	689	11.3
1922–23	84	705	11.9
1923–24	93	705	13.2
1924–25	101	723	14.0
1925–26	114	712	16.0
1926–27	124	756	16.4
1927–28	148	821	18.0

SOURCE. Columbia University in the City of New York, *Annual Report of the President and Treasurer to the Trustees* (New York: Columbia University, 1928), pp. 107–111.

medicine have established limitations on the number of Jewish students admitted."[138] At all times, a significant percentage of the entering class of the major professional schools came from Columbia College.

CONCLUSION: THE DESIRABLE STUDENT

We suppose . . . that a young Bernard Shaw might well flunk a character test and be sent down because of conditions in Reverence. Of course, he might try to brush up on it during the summer months, but we doubt whether he could ever pass.

HEYWOOD BROUN[139]

"Columbia has amorous dalliance only with those whom, with reasonable expectation of success, she can label the embryonic good citizens," wrote an anonymous staff member of the 1932 Yearbook. Although not versed in the mechanics of selective admissions, he perceived that the world view of those in charge of admissions so circumscribed their thought processes "that they will admit an applicant who comes with undistinguished marks from a recognized preparatory school and who looks as if, in time, he might turn out to be a respected bond salesman or an honest stockbroker in preference to a far more sophisticated creature from a public high school who has the sharp cast to his features which indicates quite clearly that he will make a very bad citizen, and, we might add, a very intelligent one." Contrary to the impression outsiders had of the University, Columbia College, he said, was as snobbish as Princeton or Yale. The only difference was that Columbia's snobbery was puny and sordid.

Writing during the midst of the Depression, our critic concluded that Columbia continued to provide fresh grist for a broken down mill while closing its doors to those who might be the nation's salvation, "the embryonic bad citizen." He argued that Columbia should be preparing the leaders of the next generation, but that those leaders should be completely "unbound by heritage and tradition," a notion totally rejected by the Admissions Office. Thus, instead of getting men who can "set our sails for the new port we must achieve," Columbia admitted

small time panhandling politicians, a great number of 18 year old mediocrities who think they have been elected God when they get drunk on phony brotherhood at one of the neighborhood lodge houses for mysterious Greeks, and a sprinkling of pseudo-literateurs who drool regularly in campus publics. We also have a splendid body of athletes, clean limbed young men, overdeveloped in the torso and underdone in the head, who learn the grand game of life by getting cracked on the skull in a football game.

Admittedly, Columbia had a handful of intellectuals, but they were the "queer ones," the "grinds," the "smacks" who were always socially ostracized. "How they ever got into college," our critic concluded, "even they don't know."[140]

Butler would agree with his nameless critic that Columbia aimed to produce the leaders of subsequent generations. But for the Columbia president this implied training the "embryonic good citizen." This training involved both the liberal education necessary to give a man breadth, to understand his heritage and traditions and to learn how to make decisions for the general good, as well as specific professional training necessary to perform tasks required by a modern industrial society.

Butler's aspirations in this respect failed. Twentieth century New York City was no place to teach aspiring professionals to be nineteenth century gentlemen. This point was perhaps best made by M. G. Torch, a pseudonym for a contemporary observer.

As one casually observes the men of the College, one is struck by the complete lack of a Gentile undergraduate atmosphere about any group of them. Singularly absent is the grace, the swagger, the tall attractive sleekness which, if it does not always dominate the usual college group, at least always touches it importantly. These men, one senses at once, are not of the highest caste, nor have they among them an influential sprinkling of members of the highest caste for their models. About them is none of the romantic swank of the college student, none of the not-unpleasant affectation. Seen quickly, there is even a certain grubbiness about them. One somehow expects them all to be Jews, for it is usually the Jewish members of such a group who lower the communal easy handsomeness.[141]

And yet, most of the students in the College were gentiles. This created a split in the collective College personality. Because Columbia tended away from "conventional Nordicity," it tried to make up for this by manufacturing the atmosphere and traditions of other colleges. "Columbia deeply wants these manifestations of its conventionality to be as perfect as they can be." But deeply too it was cynically indifferent to them. "When the officers of the R.O.T.C. lined up in fullest regalia on South Field to be decorated in the sight of President Butler, it was not righteous anti-militarism that brought the College to the dormitory windows to cat-call and irreverently whoop, but a proper cynical sense of the ridiculousness of the occasion." Torch concluded that in the spirit and movements of the College, there is always something Jewish. "It may be asked, 'Is this not metropolitan rather than Jewish?' Perhaps. And perhaps Jews act like Jews only because they, too, are metropolitan. Nevertheless, they act like Jews."[142]

Many major changes in college admissions policies were implemented almost all at once at Columbia. Other colleges and universities would adopt those devices to achieve their own ends, often noninvidious. However, at Columbia the evidence strongly suggests that the motives behind the adoption of these devices were, to say the least, not always the most honorable. But New York City could not be entirely denied. From Torch's comments, we may infer that the denouncer of Columbia's embryonic good citizens was being a trifle too cynical—in good Columbia fashion. Within the context of a changing New York City, the gentlemen who opened shop on Morningside had become an alien force, and, like many other alien forces in the past, they found their institution succumbing to the mores of the surrounding culture. Perhaps there had always been an unconscious recognition of this. After all, Columbia's full corporate title is "Columbia University *in the City of New York.*"

NOTES TO CHAPTER 7
REPELLING THE INVASION: COLUMBIA
AND THE JEWISH STUDENT

1. Columbia University in the City of New York, *Annual Report of the President and Treasurer to the Trustees with Accompanying Documents for the Year Ending June 30, 1906* (New York, Printed for the University, 1906), p. 2.

2. Michael Pupin, *From Immigrant to Inventor* (New York, Charles Scribner's Sons, 1960 [1922]), p. 104.

3. W. McAdoo, *Guarding a Great City* (New York, 1906), p. 143, as quoted in Moses Rischin, *The Promised City: New York's Jews 1870–1914* (New York, Corinth Books, 1964), p. 199.

4. Irving Howe, "Immigrant Jewish Families in New York: The End of the World of Our Fathers," *New York* (October 13, 1975), 8:67. See also Irving Howe, *World of Our Fathers: The Journey of the East European Jews and the Life They Found and Made* (New York, Harcourt Brace Jovanovich, 1976).

5. Rischin, *The Promised City*, p. 200.

6. *Ibid.*, p. 100.

7. Joseph King Van Denburg, *Causes of the Elimination of Students in Public Secondary Schools of New York City* (New York, Teachers College, 1911), p. 38. He also suggested that "the Hebrews despite all limitations of poverty or deprivation send from the very first their children to the high schools in large numbers."

8. Van Denburg, *Causes*, pp. 102–103. He found that one-half of all entering students dropped out before completing their second year (pp. 88–90).

9. *Ibid.*, p. 127.

10. *Ibid.*, p. 38.

11. Frederick Paul Keppel, *Columbia* (New York, Oxford University Press, 1914), pp. 179–180.

12. Keppel returned to this subject in another book entitled *The Undergraduate and His College* (Boston and New York, Houghton Mifflin Company, 1917):

    "The presence in college of a 'Jewish problem,' which means a situation where the Jews are not readily assimilated, is really a compliment, though sometimes an embarrassing one. The Jew more than any other group looks upon the college course from the point of view of an investment. Both the young fellow and his parents know exactly what he could have been earning in the years he spends in college, and they see that he spends them under the most favorable possible conditions. One will find very few of them in the poorly equipped colleges. For this reason, although the total proportion throughout the colleges is said to be less then four percent, the figure in certain institutions will run much higher. The Jews being essentially urban and domestic, their presence in large numbers was felt first in the city institutions; but with their settling in the small towns throughout the country, and the rapid increase in wealth of those remaining in the large cities, they are now being much more generally distributed among the stronger institutions" (pp. 83–84).

13. William Barclay Parsons to George Rives, November 8, 1913, CUF, William Barclay Parsons file.

14. See E. Digby Baltzell, *The Protestant Establishment: Aristocracy and Caste in America* (New York, Random House, 1964): and John Higham, *Strangers in the Land: Patterns of American Nativism*, 2nd ed. (New York; Atheneum, 1969). That the trustees derived rather than conveyed prestige was unconsciously revealed when Trustee Parsons related an incident in which he was called upon by a member of one of the city's commercial agencies. "At the end of the interview," Parsons said, "I casually mentioned that I was a trustee of Columbia. The man laughed and said, 'I wish you had said that at the outset and I would have saved you a great deal of trouble. . . . We regard that Board as giving any man a special rating.'" (Parsons to Rives, November 8, 1913, CUF, William Barclay Parsons file).

15. *Ibid.*

16. John B. Pine, comp., *Charters, Acts of the Legislature, Official Documents and Records* (New York, Columbia University, 1920), vol. 1, p. 39.

17. Schiff to Low, March 2, 1891, CUF, Jacob H. Schiff file.

18. Schiff to Low, December 24, 1900, CUF, Jacob H. Schiff file.

19. Low to Schiff, December 26, 1900, CUF, Jacob H. Schiff file.

20. Low to William Bayard Cutting, August 22, 1901, CUF, W. Bayard Cutting file.

21. Schiff to Butler, January 30, 1907, CUF, Jacob H. Schiff file.

22. Carpentier to Edward W. Mitchell, February 4, 1907, CUF, Hon. Edward Mitchell file. Carpentier also commented, "I have repeatedly expressed the opinion that it would be well to have a Jew in the board of trustees and that to refuse would be a mistake. I think that this should have been conceded before it was demanded. I do not quite like the characteristic tone of Mr. Schiff's letter, but in the administration of Columbia there is no place for resentments."

23. Apparently Edward Mitchell, another Columbia trustee, dissuaded Carpentier (Mitchell to Butler, February 5, 1905, CUF, Hon. Edward Mitchell file). But Schiff's pressure had struck a raw nerve and Butler felt the need of soliciting reassurance from his Jewish friend James Speyer that Columbia was acting liberally in the area of religion and that Schiff did not "represent the feeling of a great many Jews in New York although he likes to be the self-appointed spokesman of all the Jews" (Butler to Mitchell, February 14, 1907; Mitchell to Butler, February 19, 1907, CUF, Hon. Edward Mitchell file).

24. *New York Times*, October 15, 1913, pp. 1–2.

25. Parsons to Rives, November 8, 1913, CUF, William Barclay Parsons file.

26. Butler to Rives, November 13, 1913, CUF, George L. Rives file.

27. Pine told Butler, "I am greatly relieved to hear that the idea of electing a Jew has been so

generally discountenanced and I hope we may be spared further discussion on the subject" (Pine to Butler, December 15, 1913, CUF, John B. Pine 1913–1914 file).

28. Cardozo had previously been considered in 1917, but John G. Milburn, an attorney, was elected instead (*Minutes of the Trustees of Columbia University*, November 5, 1917, p. 112).

29. Butler to Parsons, January 12, 1928, CUF, William Barclay Parsons file.

30. Frederic R. Coudert, a trustee and a friend of Cardozo, was fearful of the effect that a rejection might have on the Judge. "I called upon my friend this morning and had a most satisfactory talk with him. His sister, the only remaining member of his family, has had a second stroke of apoplexy, and when she goes he will be left entirely alone. You can realize how unhappy I would be should the matter turn out to be the cause of wounding the susceptibilities of such a dear and respected friend at this time" (Coudert to Butler, February 8, 1928, CUF, Ci–Cu file).

31. Butler told Coudert that the trustee who expressed disapproval was "anxious to fill the existing vacancy by the election of a man of the Jewish race, and has had in mind one of the commercial or industrial class, on the theory that that would give us new and helpful contacts with men of means." Butler commented, "If it were ever to get abroad that a man were elected trustee for any reason save his personal standing in the community and his ability to serve the University by counsel, it would do us infinite harm. This is not theory but the result of watching action of this kind taken elsewhere. There is also one very striking case in our own corporate history, of which I will remind you when we meet" (Butler to Coudert, February 9, 1928, CUF, Ci–Cu file).

32. Milburn to Butler, February 15, 1928; Butler to Milburn, February 16, 1928, CUF, John G. Milburn file. Milburn wrote, "To withdraw the nomination is just as damaging as an adverse vote. It will get about that the nomination was made and had to be withdrawn and there can be no explanation or defense. The position of those who insist that there is a policy of exclusion could not be more effectively strengthened" (John G. Milburn to Frederic R. Coudert, February 27, 1928, attached to Coudert to Butler, February 28, 1928, CUF, Ci–Cu file). Coudert had an additional meeting with Cardozo before the March trustee meeting. Cardozo had been hesitant before the February meeting and when the delay in his confirmation occurred, he had to be convinced that such delays were not out of the ordinary. Coudert insisted that when the trusteeship was offered, as he was confident it would be, Cardozo should accept. "He replied that he loved the University, felt he was a part of it, and, although he doubted whether he could bring it any strength, he was entirely willing to serve if they desired to have him do so. We discussed fully various matters relating to the Board and I explained to him with the frankness prevailing only between old collegemates, the situation regarding the prejudice question" (Coudert to Butler, February 28, 1928, CUF, Ci–Cu file).

33. Joseph M. Proskauer to Butler, February 24, 1943, and Butler to Proskauer, February 25, 1943, CUA, Butler Papers, Joseph M. Proskauer file. Sulzberger was identified with the more politically conservative Jewish organizations. An anti-Zionist, he had come from a German-Jewish family that urged the rapid assimilation of East European Jews into the population and opposed efforts of the latter to perpetuate their old culture. Gay Talese, author of *The Kingdom and the Power*, a history of the *New York Times*, stated that Sulzberger was one of a group of influential Jews who in 1939 "urged President Roosevelt not to appoint Felix Frankfurter to the Supreme Court because they believed that it would intensify anti-Semitism in America, a notion that Roosevelt resented and ignored" [Gay Talese, *The Kingdom and the Power* (New York and Cleveland, The World Publishing Company, 1969), p. 91]. Shortly after the story got out, Sulzberger encountered Harold Laski, the English scholar. Laski expressed interest that Sulzberger had sold the *Times*.

Sulzberger replied, "I can't imagine what gave you that idea." Laski replied, "Well, you told Roosevelt that giving the Jews more power by giving one of them a seat on the Supreme Court would retard their reconciliation with the general populace. But, after all, isn't the *New York Times* more powerful than any single justice of the Supreme Court?" (author's interview with Shad Polier, February 2, 1972).

In light of this, it was ironic that Sulzberger accepted his appointment as trustee since having a Jew on a board seemed, even as late as the 1940s, to antagonize some incumbents. His nomination had been screened by Harry Pelham Robbins, who had consulted with his brother-in-law, Undersecretary of State Sumner Welles. Welles's resignation from that position was due in part to the publicity given in the *Times*, in columns written by Arthur Krock, to disputes between Welles and his boss, Cordell Hull. Thus when Welles gave Sulzberger a favorable recommendation, Columbia's trustees gave it considerable weight. Robbins reported to Butler, "I asked my brother-in-law for a quite confidential expression of opinion, knowing that not only had he contact with Mr. Sulzberger but also that his eldest son now with the army in North Africa had been well acquainted with Mr. Sulzberger's nephew, Cyrus, who had written some very interesting articles from the Near East." Robbins concluded, "In view of Sumner's comments I would feel that if we are to elect a Jew to the Board of Trustees of Columbia, we would certainly be making a wise choice in Mr. Sulzberger" (Robbins to Butler, January 15, 1944, CUF, Ro file).

34. John W. Burgess, *Reminiscences of an American Scholar: The Beginnings of Columbia University* (New York, Columbia University Press, 1934), pp. 241–242.

35. Columbia University in the City of New York, *Annual Reports of the President and Treasurer to the Trustees with Accompanying Documents for the Year Ending June 30, 1906* (New York, Columbia University,1906), pp. 2–3.

36. Low to Butler, January 11, 1911; Butler to Low, January 12, 1911, CUF, Seth Low file.

37. Low to Butler, January 17, 1911; Low to the Committee on Education of the Trustees of Columbia University, January 31, 1911, CUF, Seth Low file.

38. See *Columbia University Quarterly* (March, 1914), 16:190–191.

39. Butler to Speyer, September 25, 1905, CUF, James Speyer file.

40. Speyer to Butler, December 27, 1910, CUF, James Speyer file.

41. Burgess to Butler, January 8, 1907, CUF, Professor John W. Burgess 1901–1910 file.

42. Butler to Speyer, February 8, 1912, CUF, James Speyer file.

43. Burgess to Butler, April 6, 1910, CUF, Professor John W. Burgess 1901–1910 file.

44. Butler's position became untenable when the Prussian Ministry invited Professor Hugo Munsterberg of Harvard, who was Jewish, to the position of Harvard exchange professor at Berlin for 1910–11. Butler wrote Burgess, who was then in Germany, "What now becomes of the official objections to Adler, which were based, first upon his being German-born and second upon his race? Both objections apply to Munsterberg, who is, in addition, far below Adler in ability and representative character. What have I now to say to Mr. Speyer when another Hebrew is proposed for the Roosevelt Professorship?. . . Hereafter, he will be justified in thinking that the objections to a Hebrew as Roosevelt Professor come really from us and not from Berlin" (Butler to Burgess, March 1, 1910, CUF, Professor John W. Burgess 1901–1910 file).

Burgess responded that Speyer had taken an active role in Munsterberg's appointment. Speyer had endowed the newly-established American Institute in Berlin, and, according to Burgess, allowed Munsterberg to say that it was he who had persuaded Speyer to donate the money. Burgess conjectured that Munsterberg hoped that Speyer's offer would be sufficient to modify the Ministry's attitude toward the appointment of Jews and that he, Munsterberg, would be the beneficiary of such a change. He lamented that the American Institute "has now fallen into the hands of the Jews for the commercial reason that they have furnished the money." He reported that the Faculty of the University of Berlin disapproved of the exchange system falling into the hands of "an international brotherhood." Burgess concluded:

"it is stupid for the Prussian Ministry of Education to place a German Jew, and especially such an one as Munsterberg, at the head of anything called American. You know that personally I have no prejudices, at least no pronounced prejudices, against the Jews and that I am inclined to defend the acts and measures of the Prussian government. . . . The Prussian Ministry had indeed placed us in a very unenviable situation. It protested against German Jews as Roosevelt Professors until we had to accept their view. In this I think the Ministry was right. But now without a word of explanation, they not only accept Harvard's nomination of a very offensive German Jew, but put him for a year at the head of the American Institute, which is bound to be an offense to every genuine American. As you say, their act has apparently compromised us; but please do not let Speyer think that you are imposed on by the idea that the Prussian Ministry has done this thing of its own motion and without the influence of Jew money. When Speyer knows that you understand that, I don't think he will chaff you any more on the subject" (Burgess to Butler, April 6, 1910, CUF, Professor John W. Burgess 1901–1910 file).

Butler requested that Burgess discuss with the Prussian Ministry

"the whole international academic situation so that they may know and appreciate that our attitude at Columbia is solely one of helpfulness; that we have no personal ambitions to serve and no personal vanities to gratify; neither are we concerned with advancing or retarding the interests of the Jewish people. All that we ask is to be permitted, in peace and quiet and dignity and without friction, to work out our part of the great international program agreed at Wilhelmshohe in those important days in 1905" (Butler to Burgess, April 18, 1910, CUF, Professor John W. Burgess 1901–1910 file).

45. Butler insisted that the principles of the agreement were fully carried out "when we see to it that no discrimination is permitted against any suitable person because of his religious belief." He claimed not to have personal knowledge of the religious beliefs of any appointee, save Adler (Butler to Speyer, February 8, 1912, CUF, James Speyer file). He did, however, have knowledge of their social background. One was "a typical American of the combined New England and Western types." Another was "a cultivated Southern gentleman with none but American blood in his veins for several generations back" (Butler to Burgess, April 18, 1910, CUF, Professor John W. Burgess 1901–1910 file.)

46. Committee on Education, Memorandum undated, CUF, James Speyer file.

47. T. M. Chessman to Speyer, March 5, 1912, CUF, James Speyer file. See also Butler to Speyer, January 19, 1912, January 25, 1912, February 8, 1912, February 19, 1912; Speyer to Butler, January 24, 1912, January 29, 1912, February 16, 1912; and Pine to Butler, January 27, 1912, CUF, James Speyer file.

48. After the war, Speyer donated funds to Johns Hopkins University and underwrote the cost of bringing German scholars to America for two-month periods. Speyer's correspondence with Johns Hopkins officials indicates no dissatisfaction with the method in which the University administered this endowment. This exchange program ended when the Nazis came to power in 1933 (see material in Box 927, Johns Hopkins University Archives, Milton S. Eisenhower Library).

49. Keppel to Young, May 17, 1904, CUF, Dr. Clarence H. Young file.

50. Butler to Mr. Myers, September 10, 1904, Nicholas Murray Butler 1901–1904 file.
51. Young to Keppel, August 15, 1909, CUF, Dr. Clarence H. Young file. Italics his.
52. Low to A. B. Merriam, December 7, 1892, CUF, Professor A. B. Merriam file.
53. *College Faculty Minutes 1892–1900*, December 23, 1892, p. 16. See also F. H. Lane to Melville Dewey, September 24, 1894; and Low to Van Amringe, October 11, 1894, CUF, Professor John H. Van Amringe, 1890–95 file.
54. See statistics on secondary education of Columbia graduates in Columbia College Senior Books for 1903, 1904, and 1905.
55. Butler to Andrew Sloan Draper, December 18, 1908; and Draper to Butler, December 21, 1908, CUF, Andrew S. Draper file. See also extract from Minutes of University Committee on Entrance Examinations, January 8, 1909, CUF, Dr. Clarence Young file. For earlier legislation see George R. Carpenter to Fiske, February 11, 1902, CUA, Thomas Scott Fiske Papers, catalogued correspondence; Fiske to Van Amringe, April 23, 1902, CUA, Thomas Scott Fiske Papers, 1901–04 box, V file; and Carpenter to Keppel, October 15, 1902, CUF, Professor George R. Carpenter, 1893–1903 file.
56. *College Faculty Minutes 1900–1908*, March 27, 1903, p. 16. See also undated, handwritten Resolutions in CUF, Dr. Clarence H. Young file, filed with September, 1907 papers.
57. Jones to Butler, October 25, 1910 and May 9, 1913, CUF, Professor Adam Leroy Jones file.
58. "Diary of Richard J. H. Gottheil," September 28, 1898, Richard J. H. Gottheil Collection, American Jewish Historical Society (*P.–49).
59. Although it was not the main thrust of his report, Prettyman noted in passing that students may have been diverted elsewhere for academic reasons: "The educational good name of the University has been seriously impaired by the ease and frequency with which indifferent students, deficient in school work, by passing a portion of the entrance examinations have been permitted to enter with conditions."
60. Italics mine.
61. About five years later, Dean Keppel of Columbia College proposed that City College offer a professional option similar to Columbia's. He listed two ways in which this might help Columbia: "it would provide well prepared professional students who might otherwise go to institutions like the New York Law School and on the other hand it would relieve Columbia College of a certain number of students less desirable from the College standpoint, whose only reason for coming here is to save the year in the total period of their study" (Keppel to Butler, November 24, 1913, CUF, Dean Frederick P. Keppel 1910–1913 file).
62. "Report of the Special Committee Appointed to Consider the Establishment of Closer Relations Between Horace Mann School and the Colleges and Schools of Columbia University," December 11, 1908, CUF, Virgil Prettyman file.
63. Keppel to Butler, September 15, 1910, CUF, Dean Frederic P. Keppel 1910–1913 file. In a formal memorandum to the Columbia College Committee on Instruction, Keppel urged "careful and sympathetic consideration of the Hebrew problem." He stated, "It is obvious that much of the education which these students most need cannot be organized into courses. . . . [Enlist] some distinguished Jewish alumnus like Mr. I N. Seligman or Mr. Oscar Strauss to meet the Jewish students of the University and to give them some much needed advice" ("Confidential Memorandum of matters to be thought over during the summer by the Committee on Instruction, July 19, 1910," CUF, Dean Frederic P. Keppel 1910–1913 file).
64. Jones to Butler, October 25, 1910, CUF, Adam Leroy Jones file.

65. Harry Schwartz, "Preliminary Report: The Survey of Successful Pulitzer Scholars, " attached to Frank H. Bowles to Philip Hayden, August 3, 1939, CUF, Frank H. Bowles file.

66. Frank H. Bowles and Harry Schwartz, "The Pulitzer Scholars: A Record of Fifty Years," *Columbia University Quarterly* (September, 1939), 31:263–71.

67. Keppel to Butler, January 27, 1912, CUF, Dean Frederick P. Keppel 1910–1913 file; Pine to Butler, October 31, 1912, CUF, John B. Pine 1910–1912 file.

68. Keppel to Butler, October 4, 1912, CUF, Dean Frederick P. Keppel 1910–1913 file. Though initially enthusiastic about the proposal, Butler had no success in funding a scheme of this scope (Butler to Keppel, October 7, 1912, CUF, Dean Frederick P. Keppel 1910–1913 file).

69. Keppel to Butler, April 22, 1913, CUF, Dean Frederick P. Keppel 1910–1913 file. The faculty noted that Columbia sponsored at least four scholarship programs restricted to New York City residents.

70. "Copy of extract from Report of Committee on Instruction April 1913, Regarding Resident Students," CUF, Dean Frederick P. Keppel 1910–1913 file. The Committee believed the scholarships would attract desirable city residents to Columbia since "within the State we have no real rival for the city boy."

71. Butler to Keppel, October 3, 1913; Keppel to Butler, November 11, 1913, CUF, Dean Frederick P. Keppel 1910–1913 file.

72. Butler to Keppel, January 27, 1914; Keppel to Butler, June 2, 1914, CUF, Dean Frederick P. Keppel 1914–1918 file.

73. Butler to Keppel, May 6, 1913, CUF, Dean Frederick P. Keppel 1910–1913 file.

74. Keppel to Butler, October 13, 1913, CUF, Dean Frederick P. Keppel 1914–1918 file.

75. Keppel to Butler, May 13, 1913, CUF, Dean Frederick P. Keppel 1910–1913 file.

76. Columbia University in the City of New York, *Annual Reports of the President and Treasurer to the Trustees with accompanying documents for the year ending June 30, 1913* (New York, Columbia University, 1913), pp. 56–57; Keppel to Butler May 13, 1913, CUF, Dean Frederick P. Keppel 1910–1913 file.

77. Keppel to Butler, October 14, 1914; Butler to Keppel, October 30, 1914, CUF, Dean Frederick P. Keppel 1914–1918 file.

78. But the preoccupation with "The Problem" never ceased. Sometimes it colored thinking on topics at best tangential to it. Thus Keppel and the Committee on Insturction objected to a proposed tuition increase for College students on the grounds that the College was "just finding itself under the new conditions which have arisen in the last ten years," and in particular it did not want to discourage attendance of students from outside the metropolitan district. Butler retorted that other factors predominated. The money was needed for salaries and equipment, and the proposed increase was "almost infinitesimal." But he also asserted that tuition was the last element taken into account when a student chose a college. In fact, many seemed to prefer "the institution charging the highest fee on the shrewd assumption that that is probably where they will get more for their money than elsewhere." Soon after, tuition was increased by a dollar a point. Butler to Keppel, January 17, 1914 and January 24, 1914; Keppel to Butler, January 23, 1914, CUF, Dean Frederick P. Keppel 1914–1918 file.

79. Butler to Parsons, October 2, 1917, CUA, Nicholas Murray Butler Papers, Parsons, William Barclay (Folder 2) file.

80. Columbia University, *Annual Report of the President and Treasurer to the Trustees with accompanying documents for the year ending June 30, 1917* (New York, Columbia University, 1917), pp.

13–15. The day after Butler published his suggestion, Columbia College students began to circulate petitions opposing the proposed change. According to the *New York Times,* the secretly circulated petitions received many signatures within a short period of time. Those circulating the petition said that "any restriction upon entrance to an educational institution based upon other than scholarship standings is out of place in any but a Prussianized system" (*New York Times,* December 19, 1917, I 20:4).

81. Columbia University, *Annual Report of the President and Treasurer to the Trustees with accompanying documents for the year ending June 30, 1919* (New York, Columbia University, 1920), p. 236.

82. Keppel to Butler, October 14, 1914, CUF, Dean Frederick P. Keppel 1914–1918 file.

83. Columbia University, *Annual Report of the President . . . 1919,* pp. 234–235. The principal was asked for an evaluation of the candidate's native ability, industry, and faithfulness, originality, integrity, straightforwardness, cleanmindedness, fair play, public spirit, interest in fellows, and leadership.

84. See *New York Times,* December 7, 1917, I 20:4.

85. Jones to Butler, May 9, 1913, CUF, Adam Leroy Jones file, pp. 19–20.

86. See William Summerscales, *Affirmation and Dissent—Columbia's Response to the Crisis of World War I* (New York, Teachers College Press, 1970), passim.

87. The War Department prescribed that all candidates must have completed a four-year high school course or its equivalent and must have passed a medical examination.

88. Columbia University, *Annual Report of the President . . . 1919,* pp. 232–233. See also Ben D. Wood, *Measurement in Higher Education* (Yonkers–on–Hudson, N. Y., World Book Co., 1923) p. 16.

89. Columbia University, *Annual Report of the President . . . 1918,* pp. 205–206; *Annual Report of the President . . . 1919,* pp. 233–234.

90. Columbia University, *Annual Report of the President . . . 1919,* pp. 84–85.

91. *Ibid.*

92. *Ibid.,* pp. 36–39, 88–89.

93. Herbert E. Hawkes, "The Limitation of Numbers Entering College," *Columbia Alumni News* (November, 1923), 15, 7:79.

94. See, for example, Thorstein Veblen, "The Intellectual Preeminence of Jews in Modern Europe," in Max Lerner, ed., *The Portable Veblen* (New York, The Viking Press, 1948), pp. 467–479.

95. Carl Campbell Brigham, *A Study of American Intelligence* (Princeton, Princeton University Press, 1923), p. 190. In a footnote, Brigham said, "There is no serious objection from the anthropological standpoint, to classifying the northern Jew as an Alpine, for he has the head form, stature and color of his Slavic neighbors. He is an Alpine Slav."

96. Wood, *Measurement,* p. 16.

97. Hawkes to E. B. Wilson, June 16, 1922, CUF, Herbert E. Hawkes file.

98. See *New York Times,* June 2, 1922.

99. David Gordon Lyon, Diary, January, 1922, David Gordon Lyon Papers, Harvard University Archives.

100. Abbott Lawrence Lowell to William Earnest Hocking, May 19, 1922; Lowell to Rufus S. Tucker, Esq. , May 20, 1922, Abbott Lawrence Lowell Papers, Harvard University Archives, 1919–1922 section, folder 1056, Jews.

101. Henry Aaron Yeomans, *Abbott Lawrence Lowell 1856–1943* (Cambridge, Mass., Harvard University Press, 1948), pp. 209–212.

102. Among the subterfuges was limitation of enrollment. Harvard could have absorbed more students, but Lowell's main goal was the establishment of the correct proportion between Jewish and Gentile students. Harvard's initial public statement, which couched restriction of Jews in the general problem of limitation of enrollment, indicates that Lowell was not dogmatic on the question of subterfuge suppression. See Abbott L. Lowell to Langdon P. Mervin, June 10, 1922, Abbott Lawrence Lowell Papers, HUA, 1919–1922 section, file 1056, Jews.

103. Harry Starr, "The Affair at Harvard—What the Students Did," *The Menorah Journal* (October, 1922), 8, 5:263–276.

104. The Harvard Affair has been discussed frequently. See Heywood Broun and George Britt, *Christians Only: A Study in Prejudice* (New York, The Vanguard Press, 1931), pp. 53–54; Stephen Steinberg, "How Jewish Quotas Began," *Commentary*, (September, 1971), 52, 3:67–76; and an exchange between myself and Steinberg in *Commentary* (January, 1972), 53, 1:20–24. Marcia Synott's "A Social History of Admissions Policies at Harvard, Princeton and Yale" (unpublished dissertation, University of Massachusetts, 1974) is an important in-depth study. See also B. S. Hurlbut to E. D. Burton, President, University of Chicago, April 2, 1923, University President's Papers, 1889–1925, Department of Special Collections, The University of Chicago Library, box 54, file 15: Racial Question file.

105. Butler to Keppel, January 27, 1914, CUF, Dean Frederick P. Keppel 1914–1918 file. Italics his.

106. Herbert E. Hawkes, "The Limitation," pp. 79–80.

107. Hawkes to Wilson, June 16, 1922, CUF, Herbert E. Hawkes file.

108. Hawkes, "The Limitation," p. 79.

109. These figures have often been quoted and first appeared in "May Jews Go to College?" *The Nation*, (June 4, 1922). They appear to be based on surveys of the College student body conducted by the Columbia University Christian Association. See "Frosh Statistics Show Religious Preferences," *Columbia Spectator*, October 27, 1921, p. 4.

110. Hawkes to Butler, September 18, 1925, CUF, Herbert E. Hawkes file.

111. After World War I, serious consideration was given to the establishment of a residential college. Under the plan the College would have been divided into a preprofessional school for those who looked "upon their College course as a rather prescribed channel through which they must pass before entering upon the most important part of their education," and a residential college for the student who, though having a definite ambition, "regards his college residence with all that it implies in its opportunities for companionship, college activities, reading, study and reflection, as a part of his life, rather than merely as a preparation for a profession or a career." Envisioned as representative geographically, by social types, by economic groups, and by racial stocks, the Residential College would have had "as its purpose the training of leaders for the Nation" in a proper environment. The plan was called "an attempt to fulfill the obligation of the University toward the community in which we are placed without endangering the solidarity and homogeneity of the group that must, in a leisurely and thorough manner, absorb the learning of the past, and observe dispassionately the events of the present in order to be prepared to meet the tremendous problems of the future." After considerable discussion, the project was abandoned (Herbert E. Hawkes for the Committee on Instruction of Columbia College, "Memorandum regarding the establishment of A RESIDENTIAL COLLEGE," undated (1919), CUF, Herbert E. Hawkes file. See also Adam Leroy Jones, "MEMORANDUM REGARDING THE SELECTION OF STUDENTS FOR A RESIDENCE COLLEGE," attached to Jones to Butler, February 26, 1918, CUF, Professor Adam Leroy Jones file).

112. Nicholas McKnight to Frank Fackenthal, November 29, 1937, CUF, Mc file. At least two scholarships awarded by the University were formally restricted to students of Christian parentage. These were the Frances S. Bangs and the George DeWitt Scholarships offered by the Law School. In 1927, an offer of a scholarship restricted to Jewish students prompted Butler to reconsider the propriety of offering restricted scholarships. He requested and received permission of the donors to remove the formal restrictions although he told one donor there would "be no difficulty in carrying out your wishes in connection with the fellowship" (Butler to Milburn, April 28, 1927, May 4, 1927; Milburn to Butler, May 3, 1927, CUF, John G. Milburn file; Butler to Helen Bangs, May 6, 1927, May 12, 1927, May 16, 1927; Bangs to Butler, May 15, 1927, CUF, Ba–Bl file; Butler to Mrs. George DeWitt, May 6, 1927, May 18, 1927, September 27, 1927, October 4, 1927; DeWitt to Butler, undated (received May 18, 1927), October 2, 1927, CUF, D file).

113. "Comments on Application for Loan," August 28, 1925, CUF, Herbert E. Hawkes file.

114. Columbia University, *Annual Report of the President . . . 1917*, p. 12.

115. Harold K. Chadwick, "Why the Columbia College Student Body Is Becoming More National in Character," *Columbia Alumni News* (April, 1922), 13:366.

116. "Comments on Application for Loan," August 28, 1925, CUF, Herbert E. Hawkes file.

117. McKnight to Fackenthal, November 29, 1937, CUF, Mc file.

118. The General Education Board, *The General Education Board: An Account of its Activities 1902–1914* (New York, General Education Board, 1915), pp. 119–143.

119. "Report of the Director of Admissions." *Columbia Alumni News* (December 7, 1917), 9, 11:262.

120. Hawkes to Wilson, June 16, 1922, CUF, Herbert E. Hawkes file.

121. Justus Buchler, "Reconstruction in the Liberal Arts," in Dwight C. Miner, ed., *A History of Columbia College on Morningside* (New York, Columbia University Press, 1954), p. 86.

122. Jacob J. Weinstein, "Jewish Students at Columbia," *Menorah Journal* (Spring, 1934), 22:53.

123. Butler to Hawkes, May 16, 1933, CUF, Herbert E. Hawkes file.

124. Butler to Jones, August 10, 1933, CUF, J file.

125. Jones to Butler, August 15, 1933, CUF, J file.

126. Butler to Jones, August 17, 1933, CUF, J file.

127. Bowles to Butler, January 31, 1935, CUF, Frank H. Bowles file.

128. Butler to Bowles, February 2, 1935, CUF, Frank H. Bowles file.

129. Broun and Britt, *Christians Only*, p. 102.

130. College of Physicians and Surgeons, School of Medicine, Columbia University, "40 Entering Classes," May 1, 1947, CUF, John G. Saxe, February 1–June 30, 1947 file.

131. Louis D. Gross to Butler, January 16, 1930, February 8, 1930, February 11, 1930; Butler to Gross January 16, 1930, CUF, Gl–Gu file; Darrach to Butler, February 4, 1930, CUF, William Darrach file.

132. Van Buren to Butler, February 3, 1930, CUF, Frederick Van Buren file.

133. Butler to Darrach, February 7, 1930, CUF, William Darrach file.

134. He gave as a further reason the high failure rate among students already attending the Law School.

135. Columbia University, *Annual Report of the President and Treasurer to the Trustees with accompanying documents for the year ending June 30, 1928* (New York, Columbia University Press, 1928), p. 80. See also Young B. Smith, "Admission to the Columbia University Law School,"

School and Society (May 26, 1928), 27:636–638. In this article Smith said considerable emphasis would henceforth be placed on candidate performance on "capacity" tests.

136. M. G. Torch, pseud., "The Spirit of Morningside: Some Notes on Columbia University," *Menorah Journal* (March, 1930), 18:253. Since most graduates intended to practice law in New York, Jewish students who intended to practice law there had trouble finding employment. "There are enough Gentile firms to absorb the Gentile graduates," wrote Torch. "But the Jewish firms are about saturated. Not a few Jewish firms, when vacancies occur, write to the School asking for Gentile graduates. Some imply that they will accept either Jews or Gentiles. Almost none ask definitely for Jews."

137. Frank H. Bowles, "A Study of Applications for Admission 1934–38 to the School of Architecture," attached to Claire Dickenson to Fackenthal, December 7, 1939, CUF, Frank H. Bowles file and "A Study of Admissions 1934–38 to the School of Journalism of Columbia University," attached to Bowles to Fackenthal, June 13, 1940, CUF, Frank H. Bowles file.

138. Frank H. Bowles, "A Study of Admissions 1934–1938 to the Courses in Optometry of Columbia University," attached to Dickenson to Fackenthal, December 7, 1939, CUF, Frank H. Bowles file. Bowles noted that 82% of the applicants to the courses in optometry during the late 1930s were Jewish.

139. As quoted in *The Literary Digest* (June 24, 1922), 73:28.

140. *1932 Columbian,* pp. 4–5.

141. Torch, "The Spirit," 255.

142. *Ibid.,* pp. 256, 261.

CHAPTER

8

Who Runs New York?

In its usual sense, a college's admissions policy consists of determining the criteria for evaluating an application for admission to that college. Will we accept a student with a B or a C average? Should we give preference to children of alumni or to students with athletic prowess? Is our entering class geographically balanced? Do our students come from a wide variety of backgrounds? Selective admissions provided administrative officers with the tools necessary to make such decisions.

But in a wider sense, an admissions policy consists of all the actions a college undertakes to affect the size and composition of its student body. Should it open a new division in a part of the state undersupplied with higher educational facilities? Should it construct a new dormitory? Should it offer new programs? Although such decisions are not usually delegated to the admissions officer, they have a profound effect on the composition of the entering class since they define the boundaries within which the admissions officer must operate.

Thus, admissions policies are not tangential to the main concerns of an institution of higher learning. In establishing such policies, a college is forced to define its purpose if it has not already done so. Admissions policies and "institutional goals" have a reciprocal effect on each other. Every college attempts to devise an admissions policy that will attract and select students who will help it fulfill its mission. But at the same time the students who are finally admitted make demands on the college that are not entirely anticipated—demands that force modifications in the institution's goals.

Similarly, the university's mission has been, at least during this century, largely determined by more general social and economic conditions. It was no coincidence that the university movement in the United States occurred at precisely the time when the process of industrialization proceeded most rapidly. The incorporation of the professional schools into the American university similarly appears to have been a response to a general rise in the status of most professions and to an increased demand for expertise.[1]

But if the aims of a college (and hence its admissions policies) are affected by the world around it, the goals it adopts and their method of implementation have an effect on the larger society. But regulating access to the professions, the colleges have affected the nature of social mobility in American society and, more intangibly, the nature of the decisions made by those in authority.

Nicholas Murray Butler understood the complexities of these relationships between admissions policies, institutional goals, and general social conditions. All of Butler's schemes and proposals had for their end the increased involvement of the university in society—and this involvement was seen as a prerequisite for effecting societal change. On the national level he intended to make the university a more significant social institution and to place Columbia in the forefront of the university movement. At Columbia he aimed to provide a model for other universities to follow.

Butler further understood that for higher education to achieve significant influence over society, the major institutions had to work together. Unlike most European nations, the United States had no national university, nor did it have a formal, centralized educational system. On the contrary, American education on all levels was typified by an intense parochialism. The institutions of higher learning, thought Butler, must overcome this parochialism and establish an informal education *network* based on voluntary cooperation. Armed with agreements on key questions such as college entrance requirements, each university could set the academic standard in its own region.

Situated in a great cosmopolitan center, Columbia hoped to exert its influence over the other educational institutions—both public and private in that region, in part to provide a model for other universities. During the years before World War I, in addition to the general steps undertaken to strengthen Columbia's ties with the secondary schools in the area, Butler undertook a series of specific initiatives aimed not only at further improvement of relations, but at elimination of any potential competition for the position of capstone of New York's educational system. By the onset of the war,

Columbia had outrun its competitors and could insure that no new ones would emerge for more than another generation. However, by the close of World War II, its position became untenable.

GAINING DOMINANCE—MERGERS

During its years of transformation from college to university, Columbia kept a vigilant watch for signs that another college within New York State had embarked on a similar undertaking. Low and Butler thought that only a true university could dominate education within the state in the way that Michigan and other powerful state universities did in the midwest. Within New York City, only CCNY and NYU were its potential rivals; outside the city only one or two colleges were taken seriously. Even Cornell was considered too remote to attract significant numbers of graduate and professional students or to be able to influence the work of the state's major public and secondary school systems.

Columbia's authorities were more concerned with the two major colleges in New York City. Low and Butler thought that one way to end the threat they posed was to acquire their plants and terminate their corporate identities. Although they never seriously considered merger with the publicly supported City College, they did contemplate such a step with privately controlled New York University. In 1891, Jacob Schiff, a member of the NYU Board of Trustees as well as a Columbia benefactor, suggested the possibility to President Low. Schiff believed that this combination would eliminate needless duplication of effort and would permit the rapid emergence of a first–rate institution in a city with a growing demand for higher education.

Low would consider a merger if NYU made most of the concessions. "[There] is absolutely no basis of union which has occurred to me which would be advantageous to the city of New York on the line of two independent organizations, each attempting to cover the whole ground of a university for this city." [2] But there was more than one way to eliminate competition, and if Schiff's initiative failed, Columbia's strategy was "to place Columbia on record as being open to any reasonable proposition for the consolidation of the University [of the City of New York], and to place the University on record as refusing to make any such proposition." By making it appear that the "Presbyterian prejudice" of NYU's trustees and its chancellor, James McCracken, prevented them from initiating negotiations with Episcopalian dominated Columbia (a change not devoid of merit), Low and the Columbia trustees calculated that "Mr. Schiff and others holding his views" would discover "the narrowness and bigotry which characterizes the University." Of course, this would mean more donations to Columbia and fewer to NYU. [3]

It did not take the NYU authorities long to realize that merger was only possible at the cost of their institutions's identity, a price they were unwilling to pay. This effort came to naught, as did a subsequent initiative undertaken by President Butler in 1905.[4] Columbia's strategy of placing the blame on NYU apparently succeeded since Schiff told Butler that McCracken's opposition would prevent successful negotiations as long as he remained NYU's Chancellor.

In 1911, Low asked Butler to reopen the question, but by that time the relationship between the two institutions had significantly changed. Columbia had clearly emerged as the area's most important educational institution, and it had come to view NYU and CCNY not as competitors but as institutions that might help Columbia retain its dominant position. Butler hoped they would absorb those students desirous of a college education, but not qualified to attend Columbia because of academic or social reasons. In fact, when Butler first suggested that Columbia College limit its enrollment, he specifically mentioned both NYU and CCNY as alternatives open to her unsuccessful applicants.[5]

Columbia also contemplated affiliation with several marginal institutions located in New York City, including Adelphi College and the Packer Institute, in the expectation that some students would be tempted to apply to a more proximate institution affiliated with the University rather than to Columbia College. Students attending such an affiliate would probably stay long enough to acquire preprofessional training needed to gain admission to some local professional school. Because such arrangements were financially impractical, and because the prospects of directing applicants from Columbia College to such affiliates (at least until the adoption of selective admissions) were even more questionable, Columbia took no further steps in this direction until the late 1920s.[6]

GAINING DOMINANCE:
MANIPULATING THE CEEB AND
THE STATE EDUCATION DEPARTMENT

In 1904, as a result of persistent behind the scenes efforts by Butler and a number of his Republican allies, the New York State Legislature passed a Unification Act which placed direct responsibility for all public education under the authority of the Regents of the University of the State of New York. Previously, responsibility for primary and normal education had been in the hands of the New York Department of Instruction, which, Butler charged, was subject to corrupt political pressure. The Regents, who served for longer terms and managed to avoid political controversy, had supervised only the secondary schools, colleges, and universities. Executive authority in this new unified system was assigned to a Commissioner of Education. For this position, Butler secured the nomination of his old friend, Andrew Sloan Draper, president of the University of Illinois.[7]

Shortly after Draper assumed his duties, Butler wrote that both New York State and New York City (whose public schools were administered by William Maxwell), were now supervised by "ideal educational leaders."[8] He omitted that both men were personal friends and political allies, and that both were indebted to him for their positions. Butler quickly exploited his relationships with these men in an attempt to establish closer ties between his College Entrance Examination Board, and the city and state educational bureaucracies.

In 1902, not long after the first administration of CEEB examinations, Maxwell petitioned the CEEB for permission to use its exams as final subject tests offered in the New York City high schools. Three years later, Draper similarly petitioned the CEEB for permission to use its exams in place of the "Regents" examinations the State required upon completion of major subjects in the state's secondary school curriculum. Maxwell left the method of evaluation of the exams open to negotiation; Draper requested that the CEEB evaluate the examinations of college bound students and reserved the evaluation of terminal student's exams to his own department.

These ambitious proposals bore the definite stamp of Nicholas Murray Butler. Coming shortly after the first colleges agreed to the establishment of uniform entrance requirements and examinations, they embodied Butler's plan for extending the CEEB's influence over the public educational system of a major state. Not only would adoption of the proposals permit Columbia and the other CEEB members to determine the level of difficulty of examinations required for high school graduation, they would also have given the CEEB an important say in determining the content of courses for which examinations were required. The rationale for these steps came directly from the *Report of the Committee of Ten*; the Committee recommended that the same course content be offered to students whether or not they intended to continue their education past high school. At this time, Butler was still attempting to facilitate performance of the selective function by the secondary schools. He urged CEEB acceptance of these proposals as a way of assuring that the academic criteria by which the secondary schools would judge who had college ability would be acceptable to the colleges.

Although Butler had little trouble gaining acceptance for these schemes from the relevant public authorities, he had severe problems with the CEEB, which rejected both proposals. Butler had convinced Maxwell and Draper that college bound students would have to take CEEB examinations for admission to most colleges in any case, and that consequently their acceptance of these exams in lieu of the "Regents" and city-sponsored tests merely ended a wasteful duplication of effort. He tried to convince the CEEB that acceptance of these proposals would not only make several thousand additional students eligible for admission to member colleges, but would also swell the organization's coffers.

Opponents of the proposals argued that they were too ambitious for an organization still in its infancy. They also claimed that unsolvable problems would arise in implementing the proposals. Who would grade the exams of students undecided about college? What if a student failed CEEB-graded exams? Would they have to be regraded by the New York State authorities to determine if the student should be graduated from high school? Butler knew that these objections had some merit, but told Draper that the real reasons for the proposals' disapproval were conservatism and jealousy. "It was . . . the very largeness and boldness of the plan that staggered our colleagues," he wrote. The out-of-state colleges "seem to be afraid of some gain accruing to New York State colleges from so close an alliance with the city and state high school systems." Since Columbia already accepted Regents programs culminating in Regents examinations in lieu of its own entrance examinations, the plan would only have assured Columbia that the students who passed the examinations were of good academic quality. Butler did not advocate the scheme with the notion of gaining a temporary edge in the competition for students, but with the idea that it would form the cornerstone for the national educational network he envisioned.

The failure of the Draper proposal caused a considerable strain in his relationship with Butler, who had virtually assured the commissioner that CEEB consideration would be a mere formality. Butler subsequently stood aloof from such ambitious schemes and concentrated his efforts on exerting subtle influence in support of gradual implementation of his goals.[9]

GAINING DOMINANCE:
OPPOSITION TO A PUBLIC UNIVERSITY

During the early twentieth century, it became apparent to Butler that neither NYU nor CCNY posed an immediate threat to Columbia'a educational dominance. The former had some pretensions, but could not marshall the resources necessary for an all-out effort; the latter seemed content to introduce some undergraduate professional training, and to cater to the demands of its local constituency.

Butler therefore turned his attention to assuring that no new competitive institution would be established. There was no public university within New York, that is, no institution composed of undergraduate, graduate, and professional schools supported by public funds. But, because of rapid population growth within the state during the early part of the century, demands for the establishment of such an institution began to echo through the state legislature.

Butler had to maintain a delicate balance in stating Columbia's position concerning such demands. On one hand, he would countenance no proposals to establish another university that might successfully compete with Columbia. On the other hand, he recognized that some provision for higher education had to be made for students desiring a college education but lacking the academic and social qualities that would make them Columbia material. He hoped that NYU and CCNY would absorb such students.

Representatives from Brooklyn were especially adamant in demanding public higher educational facilities. During the first decade of the century, several bills were introduced into the Legislature calling for establishment of a university in Brooklyn that would be to that borough what Columbia was to Manhattan.[10] Such bills gained passage in both the 1906 and 1907 legislative sessions, but suffered gubernatorial vetoes.

Butler, exploiting his powerful position in the state Republican party, exerted considerable behind the scenes influence with the Legislature, the State Education Department, and the Governor in opposition to those bills. Recognizing the need for additional educational facilities in that populous borough, but opposing construction of a full-scale university, Butler suggested that CCNY open a new branch there. Such a course would "not depart from precedent," namely CCNY's emphasis on undergraduate education, nor would it "launch us out on new and uncertain, and possibly ridiculous seas," that is, establish an institution that would duplicate Columbia's efforts. He also argued that general revenues should not be expended on a project that would benefit the residents of only one of the city's boroughs.[11]

The vetoes of the Brooklyn University Bills did not end the demand for new college facilities there, and Butler continued to urge the opening of a Brooklyn unit of CCNY.[12] Such an institution would serve one additional function from Columbia's viewpoint—it would absorb many Brooklyn high school graduates now making the daily trip to Morningside, "fully half of which were 'undesirables' residing in the Brownsville section" who corresponded "much more closely with the type of student attending the College of the City of New York than with our type of boy."[13] Columbia's merger talks with Adelphi and other minor Brooklyn institutions were intended to accomplish the same goals in case CCNY decided not to expand.

Columbia did not resolve the situation before World War I. CCNY did not expand. Financial considerations prohibited Columbia from sponsoring a local college in Brooklyn, and Brooklyn students continued to apply for admission to colleges in Manhattan, including Columbia. Limitation of Columbia

College's enrollment after the war served to reduce the number of these students at Columbia, but in the long run, it also upset Columbia's delicate balance. Access to Columbia became more difficult just at the time when a greater proportion of the age cohort wanted to go to college and when young men returning from armed service swelled the applicant pool even further. To make matters worse, colleges in other states confronted with similar pressures began to limit their enrollment. State universities, for example, established sharp restrictions on admission of out-of-state students. New York students, unable to gain access to the better colleges within New York State (since they emphasized geographic distribution in their student bodies) or elsewhere, began to demand establishment of a state university that would not only provide undergraduate education, but also graduate and professional training—likewise more difficult to obtain.

In the late twenties, Columbia attempted to head off such demands by opening Seth Low Junior College in downtown Brooklyn. The school offered a two-year curriculum, mainly to students of "foreign parentage" who would then continue their education at local professional schools (such as Brooklyn Law School) which admitted students after two years of college. Columbia authorities did not permit students who completed the Seth Low course to transfer into the College with its system of professional options. Those who desired a Columbia bachelors degree could enroll in its evening division, University Extension, and work toward a Bachelor of Science.[14]

Columbia briefly considered the possibility of acquiring Seth Low's chief Brooklyn competitor, Long Island University, as a way of saving expenditures on additional plant.[15] But when it learned that as a result of the reorganization of the municipal college system a new public college, similar to CCNY, was soon to open in Brooklyn, it dropped its own plans for further expansion in that borough.[16] Brooklyn College, a four-year municipal college with a more varied curriculum than either Seth Low or LIU, opened in 1932.[17] Soon thereafter, Columbia announced that Seth Low would close as soon as its current students had completed their courses of study. Thus, Columbia forestalled demands for a major unit of public higher education by establishing a smaller, nonthreatening one, and by encouraging the founding of a public municipal college in an area with a chronic demand for college facilities.

Calls for the creation of a state university persisted through the twenties and thirties, but Butler and his allies in the State Education Department and on the Board of Regents had no intention of heeding them. In the late thirties, when the Regents instituted a full-scale investigation into all aspects of education within the state, the author of the summary report, Luther Gulick, concluded that "New York is adequately supplied with private colleges, universities and public and private professional schools though it does not have a state university." He recommended that "no additional state funds should be spent this generation to set up new colleges or independent professional schools."

Gulick did acknowledge the existence of "youth qualified for college and professional schools who are now debarred from advanced education for economic and other reasons." Even though the need for additional facilities was "acute in specific areas and specific places," Gulick recommended that the public "rely on the New York State school system, not on the western public university system, for the realization of greater equality at the college and university level."[18]

Columbia did not defend the status quo by itself during the twenties and thirties. Many other private colleges throughout the state feared the adverse effects of a state university. This fear of diminished enrollments and even closing heightened during the Depression when only income from tuition fees kept some colleges out of the red. But Columbia could never silence those who contended that the lack of public higher educational facilities deprived many deserving students of access to college. After World War II, the private colleges recognized that they could no longer convincingly respond to that contention.

DENOUEMENT:
THE STATE UNIVERSITY OF NEW YORK
AND THE FAIR EDUCATIONAL PRACTICES ACT

As long as Nicholas Murray Butler remained president of Columbia University, no serious challenge arose to Columbia's primacy within New York State. But in 1945, after 43 years in office, the trustees retired the aging and infirm man who had become the symbol of the Colossus on the Hudson. His successor, Frank Fackenthal, had stood in Butler's shadow for many years as his assistant and had performed most of Butler's functions in the years preceding his retirement. Even after Butler had left the scene, Fackenthal's stature never matched Butler's. And even had post-World War II conditions remained the same as those before the war, Columbia's influence over state affairs would have significantly decreased.

But post-World War II New York was different, and the differences made Columbia's position even more untenable. The country was about to experience a period of relative prosperity and peace after fifteen years of depression and war. Many returning GIs wanted to used their veteran's benefits to complete their education. At the same time, the world realized the extent of the Holocaust, which had almost put an end to European Jewry. In America, a heightened sensitivity to the plight of the Jews and of other recently arrived groups resulted. These groups also began to express a greater militancy. Thus the American Jewish Congress created a Committee on Law and Social Action, responsible for challenging formal legislation as well as informal practices that it considered discriminatory.

Not long after V-J Day, minority groups and liberal politicians registered the first demands for construction of additional higher education facilities within the state. And even before that date, the AJC charged that Columbia employed discriminatory admissions policies. Fackenthal consulted with many interested parties, including trustees, the University attorneys, administrators, and faculty in his attempt to develop a response to these demands and charges. His consultants agreed that establishment of a state university could no longer be opposed. "New York State," wrote Dean Caswell of Teachers College, "through a long-term policy of reliance on private support of higher education, has achieved a position in this field far below that of which she is capable, and below that of her best self interest." John Godfrey Saxe, the University's chief attorney told Fackenthal that he understood Caswell to be correct in this statement, but suggested "for purposes of official reports or addresses, to adhere to Dr. Butler's side of the picture," which demonstrated "the tremendous service which our non-profit, voluntary educational institutions have rendered to the State and Nation."[19] But if in public Columbia would extoll the virtues of private education, in private it would do nothing to prevent the establishment of additional public facilities.

Fackenthal did, however, resolve to use all weapons at his command to oppose outside interference with Columbia's internal admissions policies. During World War II, Columbia had again given over its facilities to the military and had suspended its regular admissions procedures. After the war, religious discrimination does not appear to have resumed.[20] In 1945, already under attack by some Jewish groups and perhaps feeling guilt about its pre-war policies, Columbia demonstrated its good faith by removing questions concerning an applicant's religion and nationality from the College's application blank.[21] But if Columbia no longer intended to discriminate, it did intend to continue admitting a national student body. In fact there was some agreement with Dean Caswell's remark that creation of a state university might actually facilitate this objective by reducing efforts at state control over the private colleges and by leaving Columbia "greater freedom to be selective in the objectives we emphasize and the students we accept." Caswell concluded, "Our national and international character could receive comparatively greater emphasis."[22] In any case, Fackenthal believed that any concessions in this area would jeopardize Columbia's standing as a major institution, and he resolved to oppose adamantly all legislative attempts to regulate its admissions policies.

The American Jewish Congress had indicated in no uncertain terms that such attempts would be forthcoming. During 1945 and 1946, it employed several different forums in New York City to gain publicity and support. Its first attack came in the summer of 1945 when it charged the New York City Tax Commission with erroneously granting Columbia a tax exemption as a nonprofit and exclusively educational institution. The New York State Tax Law stated that no tax-exempt educational corporation could deny the use of its facilities to anyone otherwise qualified on the grounds of race, color, or religion. The AJC charged that Columbia's admissions policies in effect denied students the use of its facilities on precisely these grounds.

Judge James B. McNally of the State Supreme Court threw out the suit, arguing that the law's intent was not to deny tax exemption to institutions that invidiously discriminated, but to compel tax-exempt institutions not to discriminate. Thus, the law permitted petitions only from an individual who believed he was the victim of discrimination and who desired to gain access to the institution practicing discrimination.[23]

A few months later, New York City Councilman Eugene Conolly introduced a resolution calling for Tax Commission investigation of Columbia's tax status. It prompted the City Council to verify the charges of discrimination made by the AJC and others. Concentrating its attack on medical school admissions, where it believed discrimination to be the most blatant, the AJC provided statistics purporting to demonstrate "a constant and precise decline in Jewish boys and girls being admitted to Columbia University['s Medical School]." Columbia provided its own statistics supporting its contention that it had not practiced discrimination in the past. These hearings and subsequent ones concerning the admissions policies of all New York City medical schools generated considerable publicity, but resulted in no legislation.[24]

The Mayor's Committee on Unity, established after the 1943 Harlem riots to investigate their causes and the reasons for intergroup tensions within the city, became the third official forum involved in the discrimination controversy. Composed of citizens of various racial, ethnic, religious, and economic groups and chaired by Charles Evans Hughes, Jr., the Committee had found itself deflected from investigation of underlying social conditions and involved in several immediate controversies. Complaints by students that they had been victims of discrimination in the treatment of their applications for admission to New York City private colleges prompted the Committee to undertake its own investigation of those schools' admissions policies. "Many of us felt," said Dan Dodson, the Committee staff's director, "that it [discrimination in admission to college] was one of the key problems, since we saw Nazism in Germany starting at this point. It was thought that, since the colleges set the moral tone and climate for the nation, discrimination on the campus might lead to further discrimination elsewhere."[25]

Although a staff report contained serious charges of discriminatory practices on the part of private colleges, the Committee took no action on it until its report was leaked to the *New York Times* in April, 1946. The AJC charged that the unnamed authorities who according to the *Times* report admitted to the existence of quota systems at their colleges were Dean Harry Carman, Hawkes's successor as dean of Columbia College, and Professor Harrington of Barnard College's Committee on Admissions. According to Dodson, Carman had told the staff that Columbia could fill every seat in its freshman class with students from Brooklyn without lowering its admissions standards, but that a policy of geographic distribution was defensible on other grounds. Many college authorities were angered and embarrassed by the report; the Committee emphasized that it was a staff report and that the Committee had yet to act upon it.[26]

Public pressure resulting from leakage of the report prompted Hughes and the Committee to issue its own official report, more conservative in tone, yet forceful in its conclusions. "As herafter shown," it said, "there can, in the opinion of the Committee, be no reasonable doubt of the prevalence of quota systems or other discriminatory practices in institutions of higher learning in this State and indeed in the Nation."[27] The Committee recommended that the New York State Board of Regents examine the problem and either promulgate regulations outlawing all discrimination in the colleges and universities in the state or, if the Regents determined that their powers were too narrow to make such a proscription, recommend legislation that would serve this purpose.[28]

All sides took some satisfaction from the Hughes Report. Columbia was relieved that neither it nor any other college was condemned by name. The American Jewish Congress applauded its findings of widespread invidious discrimination and its call for governmental intervention.

The AJC and its allies understood that neither the litigation over Columbia's tax exemption, the City Council's hearings, nor the Report of the Mayor's Committee on Unity could compel any changes in the admissions policies of Columbia and the other private colleges. These groups did believe that such actions convinced the public of the inadequacy of self-regulation and the need for state intervention. They hoped that this public sentiment could be translated into action by the New York State Legislature.

New York State had already prohibited discrimination because of race, creed, or color in such areas as jury service, the right to practice law, admission to public schools and places of public accommodation, public employment, and membership in cemetery associations. It also forbade tax-exempt institutions to deny the use of their facilities on account of race, color, or religion. The 1938 New York State Constitution forbade any discrimination against a citizen because of race, color, creed, or religion "in his civil rights by any other person or by any firm, corporation, or institution, or by the state or any agency or subdivision of the state."[29] In 1945 a Fair Employment Practices Act became law. It established a State Commission Against Discrimination composed of five full-time, salaried commissioners who would hear complaints and hold hearings when a charge of unfair employment practices was filed. Subject to judicial review, the Commission had the power to issue cease and desist orders and to compel affirmative action such as the rehiring or reinstatement of employees.[30]

Assemblyman Bernard Austin and Senator Francis Mahoney, both New York City Democrats, introduced the first Fair Educational Practices Bill during the 1946 legislative session. Drafted by the AJC, and modeled after the Fair Employment Practices Act, the bill would have given the State Commission Against Discrimination power to issue cease and desist orders and to order loss of tax exemption whenever an institution was found to have committed an unfair educational practice (including inquiry of applicants as to race, creed, color, national origin or ancestry, either oral or written). In making such a determination, the Committee would be permitted to take into account evidence, statistical and other, that might "tend to prove the existence of a pre-determined pattern of admission of students or employment of members of instruction or research staff." Religious institutions were specifically exempted from the provisions of the Act, at least insofar as giving preference or restricting admission and employment to members of the sponsoring sect.[31]

The Austin-Mahoney legislation had been introduced late in the session, timed to coincide with the AJC's publicity campaign in New York City, and passage was not expected until the next session. The following fall, those favoring the bill conducted a concerted campaign to obtain commitments from candidates for election to the Legislature and for Governor.

Columbia's authorities found the proposed legislation totally unacceptable. Saxe found especially objectionable a provision stating that an institution which admitted applicants "not solely and exclusively on the grounds of their intellectual ability and moral character but aims . . . at the satisfaction of racial and religious prejudices" was not an educational institution within the meaning of the law. In an effort to prevent invidious discrimination, Saxe commented, "it would put in our statute law definitions of the 'purposes and functions of education and educational institutions,' *as these functions are conceived by the American Jewish Congress.*" He contended that selective admissions employed other, legitimate, noninvidious criteria besides academic excellence and "moral character." Capacity for future usefulness, record in relation to associates and surroundings, extracurricular activities, leadership and personality were all equally valid criteria, he contended.[32]

Columbia considered several strategies in an attempt to head off passage of the Austin-Mahoney legislation. First, behind the scenes influence would be employed whenever it seemed likely to achieve positive results. Public statements would be avoided, however, since anything that Columbia said would likely be turned against it.[33]

Second, Fackenthal and his advisors contemplated enlisting the suppport of the more conservative Jewish organizations against the AJC. "I can think of nothing that would do more to help in this whole difficult area of discrimination," wrote Fackenthal, "than to have a clean-cut line drawn between the right-thinking Americans of Jewish background and the agitating, deliberately trouble-making, more recent arrivals."[34] This strategy was abandoned when trustee Arthur Hays Sulzberger reported that two "guinea pigs" with whom he discussed the possibility thought it would be unwise.[35]

Third, Columbia decided to enlist the aid of all the private colleges in the state, saying that the proposed legislation would impose admissions criteria and definitions of "educational function" that each of them might find unacceptable. Fackenthal hoped to demonstrate that opposition was not confined to those institutions directly attacked by the AJC and that the legislation, though perhaps well intended, jeopardized the legitimate interests of the private colleges and universities within the state. Henceforth, Columbia would act through the Association of Colleges and Universities of the State of New York, an organization in existence for some time but previously the object of little interest. Throughout most of the ensuing controversy, its chairman was Father Robert I. Gannon, president of Fordham University.

As the 1947 legislative session approached, Fackenthal and his advisors were apprehensive about their chances of thwarting passage of antidiscrimination legislation. The AJC had claimed that a majority of legislators in both the State Senate and the State Assembly favored the bill.[36] It had also sponsored several major "Marches on Albany" and had mounted a large-scale publicity campaign, including petitions, endorsements by local officials, rallies, and school programs. Even the student newspaper at Columbia endorsed the legislation.[37] Finally, the bill had been amended to place the power of enforcement in the hands of the State Education Department, a move designed to mute opposition on jurisdictional grounds.[38] The presidents of several other important private colleges expressed pessimism about the outcome of the forthcoming debate.[39]

When matched against the AJC's efforts, the opposition offered by the private colleges seemed woefully inadequate. But suddenly on February 27, 1947, just as momentum in favor of the Austin-Mahoney legislation reached a peak, New York Roman Catholic Archbishop Robert McIntyre announced his opposition, saying that it was anti-American in its purposes, that it seriously affected the freedom of educational institutions in the state, that it infringed on the fundamental rights of parents, and that it seemed certain of passage without time for proper debate. McIntyre showed special concern for the exception of sectarian institutions since there were many Catholic colleges within the state.

Austin-Mahoney proponents speculated that Father Gannon had alerted McIntyre to the bill, and especially to the provisions concerning sectarian institutions.[40] Columbia's attorneys had argued that the bill's language on exemptions was ambiguous; that the exemption granted was "limited and qualified." According to their interpretation, "a sectarian institution may select its students and faculty 'exclusively' from members of its own faith, and may give 'preference' to such persons; but if it admits *any* others, as students or as faculty, their admission is regulated and controlled by all the provisions of this bill."[41]

Shad Polier and Will Maslow of the AJC hurried to the bill's defense. Polier charged that McIntyre favored turning back the clock to a time when private institutions could act with no responsibility to the public. Maslow contended that McIntyre's general charges could be refuted by careful reference to the legislation's provisions and that the exemption of the sectarian institutions was "unequivocal." He added, "If the language is not sufficiently clear, I am sure that the sponsors of the bill would accept any other provision proposed by the Catholic Welfare Committee [the Catholic legislative watchdog] to make unmistakable the legislative purpose not to interfere with sectarian, denominational or parochial schools."[42]

Sensing that the tide had turned against the legislation, Father Gannon rejected Maslow's offer and announced that the Association of Colleges would not accept any bill produced by the current legislative session. Although the bill's supporters made further attempts to secure its enactment, a friend of Saxe in Albany reported the Legislature "to be sick and tired of the bill, and that very possibly it is beaten."[43] By March 6, both Austin and Mahoney had withdrawn their bills.[44]

A few days later, Fackenthal commented that, indeed, "it is the Catholic Church that rescued us" from proposals which he, like McIntyre, believed were "wholly unAmerican."[45] He understood, however, that only a battle had been won and that hostilities would be renewed at the next legislative session. But the odds at that session would be more in Columbia's favor because the assemblymen and senators would not be debating the recommendations of the AJC but those of the politically balanced Temporary Commission on the Need for a State University. With the Austin-Mahoney battle ended, all eyes turned to the Commission and to its chairman, Owen Young.[46]

The Commission had been established in 1946 by the Legislature at the suggestion of Governor Dewey. To gain support for new facilities from upstate legislators for whom the discrimination issue was relatively unimportant, the Commission examined all the sources of insufficient educational opportunity. These included economic barriers (the difficulty of meeting tu-

ition charges imposed by the private colleges and the consequent disproportionate college attendance of students from families with higher incomes),
geographic barriers (proximity to a college seemed to be a major factor in
determining whether an individual would attend college), the shortage of
space caused by the demand for education by thousands of returning veterans, as well as racial and religious barriers. The Commission included members of all interested groups, including the Association of Colleges and Universities of the State of New York and the American Jewish Congress, as well
as representatives of both the Democratic and Republican parties.

Although the Commission instructed its staff to investigate the problem of
religious and racial discrimination, it concentrated on the problems involved
in establishing a new university, such as whether it should be centrally located or should consist of a series of local campuses and whether additional
facilities for medical education were needed. The Commission gave more
serious consideration to antidiscrimination legislation when it became apparent that its recommendations might prove decisive.

Three staff reports concerning racial and religious discrimination were
completed by the summer of 1947. Robert Leigh's report concluded that
Jewish students, both upstate and downstate, experienced greater difficulty in
gaining admission to their first-choice college than did gentile applicants.[47] E.
Franklin Frazier's study of higher education for Negroes in New York State
concluded that their greatest barrier to higher education was their generally
low economic status.[48]

David Berkowitz obtained the cooperation of the Association of Colleges
and Universities of the State of New York to compile data pertaining to the
current admissions practices of nearly all institutions of higher education
within the state. He determined that sixteen units (a unit was defined as a
separate institution or a division of a larger institution) reported the use of
restrictions or limitations in enrollment based on race or creed. Of this total,
nine units were Catholic affiliated, two were Protestant affiliated, and five
claimed to be nonsectarian. Six units limited admission of Negroes, twelve
limited admission of Jews, and eleven limited admission of Protestants. Six
units admitting to discrimination were liberal arts colleges.

After examining the application blanks used by each of the state's colleges
and universities, Berkowitz concluded that "most types of units in New York
State are well-informed about the religion, race and nationality of the applicant at the time he is being considered for admission." Berkowitz found that
many medical school candidates had been denied admission because they
could not receive the endorsement of their undergraduate colleges. Other
rejected students might have been the victims of discrimination, or of geographic barriers that limited them to applying to New York City medical
schools.[49]

In general, the Temporary Commission staff demonstrated that New York

State institutions practiced discrimination against members of various minority groups, but that the extent of such discrimination had been exaggerated by the AJC.

Release of these reports did not alter the resolve of Fackenthal and Gannon to oppose publicly any antidiscrimination legislation that would undermine the ability of the private colleges "to select their faculties and student bodies in accordance with broad and publicly announced criteria and the dictates of their own best judgment."[50] The Association told the Commission that it considered the few instances of discrimination that may have occurred "infinitesmal" in comparison with the thousands of students from minority groups educated at the state's private colleges. It resolved to undertake a voluntary effort aimed at the total elimination of discrimination.

But when the Commission's subcommittee on antidiscrimination legislation met in the fall of 1947, it was apparent that such reassurances would not sway the group's majority. When Father Gannon, who chaired the subcommittee, was asked whether he thought that McIntyre's statement the previous spring implied that the Catholic hierarchy opposed all antidiscrimination legislation, Gannon would not answer in the affirmative.[51] It then became clear that the subcommittee would recommend some form of legislation.

Finding outright opposition untenable, Gannon argued that the subcommittee's recommendations should not be modeled on the Austin-Mahoney legislation, and that the resulting legislation should contain no definitions or legal findings. This had been the fallback position of the Association since the previous spring.[52] He tried to convince the subcommittee that the agency responsible for determining violations of the law had to understand all the complexities of admissions policies. He suggested that the task be performed by a regular employee of the State Education Department, not by an independent commission in the Department as the AJC had suggested. He also insisted that complaints only be heard from students who believed themselves to be victims of discrimination, and that whoever was finally assigned to hear these complaints be denied authority to initiate investigations in the absence of such a formal complaint.

American Jewish Congress representatives told the subcommittee they hoped enforcement would be placed in the hands of an independent commission that would have the power to proceed on its own initiative. Shad Polier testified that "fair educational practices legislation, to be effective, must not place the burden of investigation and complaint on the individual who has been rejected for admission," since such an individual might fear blacklisting and would find it difficult to prove he was the victim of discrimination.[53]

The compromise unanimously arrived at within the subcommittee was later ratified without change by the entire Commission. Its final report concluded that "some non-sectarian educational institutions have criteria of selection that appear to be different for different groups. This inequality of treatment is indicated by the fact that a smaller proportion of applicants are accepted from members of certain groups than from other groups of equal academic standing from the same geographic areas."[54]

The Commission recommended that in the future public funds should be given only to institutions that admitted students on the basis of merit and not with regard to race, color, creed, or national origin. It also recommended that all state and local scholarships be similarly awarded. Most important, it recommended that the

Commissioner of Education be expressly authorized to investigate the existence of discrimination hereafter committed in the admission of students to an educational institution of the post-secondary level on account of race, color, creed or national origin whenever such discrimination is charged by an applicant for admission to such institution or whenever the Commissioner has reason to believe that any applicant has been discriminated against, except that preferential selection by religious or denominational institutions of students of their own creed shall not be considered an act of discrimination.

The Commissioner would first use the techniques of "conference, conciliation and persuasion" to correct such discriminatory conditions as existed. Only if such techniques failed was he to report the case to the Board of Regents, which would have the power to hold public hearings, to issue cease and desist orders and, if necessary, to seek orders from the State Supreme Court for their enforcement. Until proceedings were turned over to the Regents, they were to remain completely confidential.[55] Thus, according to the compromise, the Commissioner of Education would investigate charges brought by an aggrieved party, as well as initiate his own probe when he believed an applicant may have been rejected for invidious reasons.[56]

Shortly after the Temporary Commission made its recommendations public in February, 1948, Governor Dewey endorsed them. Although privately sympathetic to the position of the private colleges, he had remained publicly neutral. During the antidiscrimination subcommittee's discussion, one of his representatives promised the AJC's Shad Polier the governor's support if Polier would agree to deletion of the provision permitting investigation at the commissioner's initiative.[57] Polier rejected this offer. Dewey supported the measure only after all groups had given it their assent. The governor's presidential ambitions also dictated support of the measure, since President Truman's Commission on Higher Education and his Commission on Civil Rights had both denounced discriminatory college admissions policies in no uncertain terms and had recommended passage of fair educational practices legislation.[58]

The recommendations of the Young Commission were translated into legislation during February, 1948 and despite fears on all sides that attempts would be made to amend the proposal on the floor of the Legislature, it passed intact. Archbishop McIntyre did not oppose the compromise.[59] When Governor Dewey signed the bill on April 3, 1948 the three year battle for antidiscrimination legislation was over.

Q: WHO RUNS NEW YORK?
A: NO ONE. COLUMBIA ONCE THOUGHT IT DID
ALTHOUGH IT DOESN'T THINK SO NOW

Commissioner E. M. Spaulding of the State Education Department assigned administration of Section 313 of the Education Law, the Fair Educational Practices Act, to an Administrator under the direction of the Associate Commissioner for Higher Education. The first Administrator, Frederick W. Hoeing, devoted most of his time to working for the removal from application blanks of questions concerning the race, religion, and nationality of candidates for admission to the state's private colleges. The Administrator subsequently undertook several investigations of admissions practices, but although they revealed a lower acceptance rate of Jewish than other students to some colleges or professional schools, these results could not be positively attributed to invidious admissions policies.[60] Students rejected from private colleges filed only a handful of complaints charging unfair discrimination. The two filed against Columbia, one concerning Columbia College and another concerning the Medical School, were investigated and dismissed.

During its 1948 session, the New York Legislature also passed a bill creating the new State University of New York. The law provided for establishmant of a Board of Trustees for the new university which would have authority over all existing units of public higher education currently administered by the Regents and over two previously private medical schools located in Brooklyn and in Syracuse. The Board was instructed to submit plans for the expansion of the University.

Creation of the new institution meant that Columbia's relative importance in the politics of education in New York State would diminish. However, with Butler gone, Columbia was willing to pay this price. The University still had as its fundamental goal the education of America's leaders and the Fair Education Practices Act permitted it to retain its selective admissions policy for the choosing of those leaders, so long as the University did not employ it invidiously.

CODA:
THE COLUMBIA PLAN

Having discussed the methods by which Nicholas Murray Butler attempted to implement the selective function, we conclude by evaluating the performance of the entire Columbia Plan, which involved the selection, the liberal education, and the professional education of the leaders of the next generation. Edward J. Grant, Columbia's registrar from 1920 to 1950, provided one criterion when he wrote in 1939, "4,697 or 60 percent of the 7,846 graduates of Columbia College have within the past quarter of a century gone forward into the several graduate and professional schools of the University" (see Table 8.1). Grant provided statistics showing which divisions these students had entered (see Table 8.2).

He also indicated the percentage of each graduating class that continued in a Columbia graduate or professional school. Grant estimated that another 10% of each graduating class went elsewhere for their subsequent education. Truly, Columbia College was the vestibule for admission to the rest of the University.[61]

But did Columbia educate a large contingent of the nation's leaders? George W. Pierson's study of the education of American leaders provides an affirmative answer. Pierson concluded that Harvard, Princeton, and Yale produced a highly disproportionate share of the nation's leadership, and that Columbia ranked fourth. He found that the top ten colleges in terms of the education of leaders formed a distinctive group. Five of these institutions were private or independent, three were public, and two were of intermediate character. Two were located in New York, one each in New Jersey and

Table 8.1. Number of Columbia College Students Entering the Graduate and Professional Schools of Columbia University: 1914–1939.

	By Professional Option	Otherwise	Total
Architecture	78	22	100
Business	170	82	252
Dentistry	39	27	66
Engineering	635	107	742
Graduate		1092	1092
Journalism	58	24	82
Law	1002	346	1348
Medicine	452	327	779
Teachers College	4	223	227
Other Schools	1	8	9
Totals:	2439	2258	4697

SOURCE. Edward J. Grant, "Memorandum Regarding the Twenty-Five Year Survey of the Proportion of Columbia College Graduates Going Forward to Advanced Study at the University." October 31, 1939, CUF, G file.

Table 8.2. Percentage of Columbia College Graduating Classes Entering the Graduate and Professional Schools of Columbia University: 1915–1939.

Year	%	Year	%	Year	%
1915	65%	1924	63%	1933	52%
1916	61	1925	62	1934	46
1917	66	1926	64	1935	54
1918	67	1927	62	1936	54
1919	60	1928	65	1937	55
1920	69	1929	58	1938	52
1921	68	1930	68	1939	46
1922	66	1931	63		
1923	59	1932	61		

SOURCE. Edward J. Grant, "Memorandum Regarding the Twenty-Five Year Survey of the Proportion of Columbia College Graduates Going Forward to Advanced Study at the University." October 31, 1939, CUF, G file.

Pennsylvania, three in the Great Lakes region, and one on the West Coast—"a familiar if not universally popular distribution," according to Pierson.[62]

Butler had never intended that Columbia train all future American leaders by itself. He envisioned a regional system of universities sharing the responsibility. He made no distinction between public and private sponsorship of higher education, claiming that all universities were public in the sense that they were nonprofit institutions that served a public function. He might have been disappointed to learn that Columbia had not displaced Harvard as the prime source of leadership, but would have been glad to learn that Pierson rated Columbia's graduate and professional schools ahead of all others except Harvard. He would have been glad to learn of Pierson's conclusion that "from the point of view of society as a whole, of course, the gross totals of leadership production have been and will continue to be of the first significance."[63] He would have been euphoric to hear a historian's conclusion that Columbia's contribution to furthering higher education's control over access to the upper middle classes was of singular importance. He would have been far less happy to hear of recent attacks on the quality of American leadership, and on the system of elite recruitment which produced it.

NOTES TO CHAPTER 8
WHO RUNS NEW YORK?

1. See Richard Hofstadter. *Anti-Intellectualism in American Life* (New York, Vintage Books, 1963), pp. 197–229.
2. Schiff to Low, December 21 and December 23, 1891; Low to Schiff, December 22, 1891, CUF, Jacob H. Schiff file.

3. John B. Pine to Low, December 29, 1891, CUF, John B. Pine, 1890–1893 file.

4. Schiff to Low, December 31, 1891; Butler to Schiff, January 17, 1905; and Schiff to Butler, January 18, 1905, CUF, Jacob H. Schiff file. See also Theodore Francis Jones, ed.,*New York University 1832–1932* (New York, The New York University Press, 1933), pp. 251–255.

5. Low to Butler, January 30, 1911, CUF, and Butler to Low, January 31 and February 3, 1911; CUF, President Seth Low file. A three-way merger between Columbia, NYU, and CCNY was briefly discussed in 1914. See Joseph S. Auerbach to Butler, February 3, 1914; Butler to Auerbach, February 6, 1914; and Pine to Auerbach, February 10, 1914, CUF, AR file.

6. Low to Butler, January 3, 1907, CUF, President Seth Low file; Butler to Keppel, December 12, 1910; Keppel to Butler, December 21, 1910, CUF, Dean Frederick P. Keppel, 1910–1913 file.

7. Richard Whittemore, *Nicholas Murray Butler and Public Education* (New York, Teachers College Press, 1970), pp. 68–75. Draper to Butler, January 21, 1904, Draper Personal Letters, 1892–1913, New York State Education Department Unification, v. 1; A–MAC, pp. 53–54. Record Series 2/4/5, box 5, University of Illinois Archives; Nicholas Murray Butler, *Across the Busy Years: Recollections and Reflections,* v. 1 (New York, Charles Scribner's Sons, 1939), pp. 16–17.

8. Whittemore, *Nicholas Murray Butler,* p. 75.

9. Butler to Maxwell, May 17, 1902, CUF, MAT file; Fiske to Butler, January 17, 1905, CUF, Thomas S. Fiske file. Draper to Butler, April 10, September 26, and September 28, 1905; Butler to Draper, April 11, September 25, and September 27, 1905, CUF, Andrew S. Draper file; Augustus Downing to Butler, May 18, 1907; Butler to Downing, May 20, 1907, CUA, Butler Papers, Augustus S. Downing (4) file. See also Wilson Farrand, "Five Years of the College Entrance Examination Board," *Educational Review* (October, 1905), 30:220–221.

10. "Brooklyn Makes Plans for a Great University," *New York Times,* February 8, 1906, 8:5.

11. Butler to Howard Rogers, February 6 and March 9, 1906; Rogers to Butler, February 7, 1906, CUA, Butler Papers, Howard J. Rogers, 1903–1913 file. Butler to John Finley, March 8, 1906, CUA, Butler Papers, John H. Finley (3) file. Butler to Charles Evans Hughes, June 10, 1907, CUA, Butler Papers, Charles Evans Hughes file.

12. Butler to Downing, February 25, 1910; Downing to Butler, February 28, 1910, CUF, Downing file.

13. Keppel to Butler, October 4, 1912, CUF, Dean Frederick P. Keppel 1910–1913 file. There were 115 students from Brooklyn in Columbia College in the fall of 1910 and the number was growing. See Keppel to Butler, December 21, 1910, CUF, Dean Frederick P. Keppel, 1910–1913 file.

14. "Memorandum concerning the organization of a Junior College in Brooklyn," attached to Hawkes to Butler, January 25, 1928, CUF, Herbert E. Hawkes file.

15. Fackenthal to Butler, June 27, 1930, CUF, Frank Fackenthal, July 1, 1928–June 30, 1930 file.

16. For William Barclay Parsons's less than enthusiastic opinion about Columbia's Brooklyn maneuvers, see Parsons to Butler, December 27, 1930, CUF, William Barclay Parsons file.

17. See Thomas Evans Coulton, *A City College in Action: Struggle and Achievement at Brooklyn College 1930–1955* (New York, Harper and Brothers, 1955).

18. Regents' Inquiry into the Character and Cost of Public Education in the State of New York, Luther H. Gulick, director, *Education for American Life: A New Program for the State of New York* (New York, McGraw-Hill, 1938), pp. 59, 61. The staff reports from which Gulick

wrote the final summary were more critical of the status quo. "Most, if not all, of the non-publicly owned colleges and universities in the State of New York probably could not carry on without the tuition and fees paid by the students. The establishment of free tuition in liberal arts institutions, under State support and for youth of the State living outside of the City of New York, would be resisted by many boards, as well as by executives and professors of non-publicly-owned colleges. Their enterprises, their salaries, the modes of life of themselves, might be seriously disturbed if the State were to open more accessible opportunities for able but poor students to obtain a general college education. How far this attitude is sound is problematical since thousands of youth would not go to any college unless the existing economic hurdles of tuition and fees were overcome by the State" [Edward C. Elliott, *Summary Memorandum with Reference to Higher Education*, p. 15, in Regents Inquiry Material, New York State Education·Department Library, Albany, New York (hereafter referred to as NYSEDL), package #13].

19.   H. L. Caswell, "Comments on the Act of the New York Legislature on the State University, Community Colleges and State Aided Four Year Colleges, " attached to Caswell to Albert Jacobs, July 23, 1948, CUF, Hollis L. Caswell file; Saxe to Jacobs, September 30, 1948, CUF, John Godfrey Saxe, July 1–December 31, 1948 file.

20.   Columbia publicly contended that it practiced no invidious discrimination in its admissions policies. Privately, Fackenthal's statements were more equivocal. "While it is always exceedingly difficult to know what may have been said by somebody that is open to misconstruction, checking with our Deans and Admissions people indicates that there is no discriminatory practice here," he wrote trustee Arthur Hays Sulzberger. Note his use of the present tense (Fackenthal to Sulzberger, April 3, 1946, CUF, Su file). Fackenthal told Professor of Sociology Robert I. MacIver, "Quite regardless whether or not we consider them [the charges of discrimination] just, we will need to find some way of meeting them and establishing an understanding of what we are doing" (Fackenthal to MacIver, July 15, 1946, CUF, McD file.)

21.   Harry Carman to Frank H. Bowles, March 14, 1945; Fackenthal to Carman, March 19, 1945, CUF Harry J. Carman file; Fackenthal to Virginia Gildersleeve, July 25, 1945, CUF, Virginia C. Gildersleeve file. During the ensuing controversey, Bernard Ireland of the Columbia College admissions staff informed Fackenthal that black applicants were given preferential treatment, "This has been done in no patronizing spirit but merely in recognition of the fact that it seems to us important to society that more negroes should receive advanced education in order that the beneficial results of that education may be passed on to their race and then inevitably back into society as a whole" (Ireland to William J. O'Shea, June 4, 1947, CUF, Bernard P. Ireland file).

22.   H. L. Caswell, "Comments . . . "

23.   "In the Matter of the Application of Julius L. Goldstein, Petitioner, for an Order Under Article 78 C.P.A., against William Wirt Mills, et al., Respondents," attached to William J. O'Shea to Mr. Fackenthal, Mr. Goetze, Mr. Jackson, and Mr. Putnam, July 27, 1945, CUF, John G. Saxe, 1945–1946 file. Matter of Goldstein v Mills, Supreme Court, September, 1945, v. 185, misc. 851.

24.   City of New York, City Council, Committee on Rules, Privileges and Elections, *In the Matter of Res. 128, Resolution Urging the New York City Tax Commission to Immediately Investigate Charges of Discrimination Against Columbia University and to Take Steps to Withdraw Tax Exemptions from Columbia University if Charges Are Found to Be True, May 17, 1946*" (New York, Sills Reporting Service, 1946); College of Physicians and Surgeons, School of Medicine, Columbia University, "40 Entering Classes," CUF, John Godfrey Saxe file (May 1, 1947); *City Record*, December 26, 1946. The City Council's Committee on Rules, Privileges, and Elections recommended passage of some form of antidiscrimination legislation, of legislation estab-

lishing a state university with medical and dental schools, and denial of the use of city hospitals to medical schools with discriminatory admissions policies. The Committee did not conclude that Columbia's policies were discriminatory, but only that "too much discretion is placed in the hands of one man." However, Cornell was charged with discrimination. Its former dean had written, "Cornell Medical College admits a class of 80 each fall. It picks these 80 men from about 1,200 applicants of whom 700 or more are Jews. We limit the number of Jews admitted to each class to roughly the proportion of Jews in the population in this State, which is a higher proportion that in any other part of the country. That means that we take in from 10–15 percent Jews." A member of the Cornell admissions committee said that religion affects the personality of applicants and that personality was considered in making admissions decisions (*City Record*, December 26, 1946, p. 5598).

25. Author's interview with Dan Dodson, February 7, 1972.

26. *Ibid.*; O'Shea to Fackenthal, April 5, 1946, CUF, John G. Saxe, 1945–1946 file.

27. Mayor's Committee on Unity, *Report on Inequality of Opportunity in Higher Education* (New York, 1946), p. 2.

28. *Ibid.*, p. 19.

29. The purpose of this provision was to insure that neither individuals nor corporations denied the rights and protections of law which the federal and state governments were forbidden to deny under the fifth and fourteenth amendments, respectively. During the debate on this provision at the 1938 Constitutional Convention the phrase "in his civil rights" was added. Someone asked whether "civil rights" included "constitutional rights" and this was answered in the affirmative [*Record of the 1938 New York State Constitutional Convention* (Albany, 1939), pp. 2626–2628].

30. See Harry Carman, "Short History of New York State Legislation and Commissions on Discrimination," attached to Harry J. Carman to Roderick Stephens, May 17, 1945, CUA, Harry J. Carman Papers, Series II:1, A–B, 1940–1950: American Council on Race Relations file. Columbia's employees were not subject to the provisions of the Fair Employment Practices Act—which was fortunate for Columbia. When a black woman was refused employment in the University library system, she charged she was the victim of discrimination. Butler commented to Fackenthal, "We have never said that we do not employ negroes so far as I know, and I do not see how we can say it without getting into trouble—even though we practice it" (Butler to Fackenthal, November 19, 1942, CUF, Nicholas Murray Butler file. See also C. C. Williamson to Fackenthal, November 11, 1942, CUF, Charles C. Williamson file; and Albert Putnam to Butler, November 28, 1944, CUF, Pu file). In 1947, as a result of a complaint filed by the AJC, the State Commission Against Discrimination ruled that it had jurisdiction over the practices of Columbia's placement office and that the University would have to remove questions concerning race, religion, nationality, and place of birth from the office's registration forms (O'Shea to Fackenthal and Jackson, November 12, 1946; Edward Edwards to Saxe, Bacon, and O'Shea, February 11, 1947, attached to O'Shea to Fackenthal and Jackson, February 15, 1947, CUF, John G. Saxe, July 1, 1946– January 31, 1947 and John G. Saxe, February 1, 1947–June 30, 1947 files).

31. S. No. 2472, Int. 2187, March 6, 1946.

32. "Austin-Mahoney Bill: Preliminary Analysis for Columbia University," Proof of February 11, 1947, attached to O'Shea to Fackenthal and Jackson, February 11, 1947, CUF, John G. Saxe, February 1, 1947–June 30, 1947 file. Emphasis his.

33. See, for example, Saxe to Fackenthal, July 14, 1947, CUF, John Godfrey Saxe, July 1, 1947–January 31, 1948 file for an attempt to enlist the aid of Herbert Brownell, a prominent New York Republican and a friend of Governor Dewey.

34. Fackenthal to Sulzberger, February 27, 1947, CUF, Arthur Hays Sulzberger file.

35. MacIver to Fackenthal, June 13, June 21, and June 27, 1946; Fackenthal to MacIver, June 18 and June 24, 1946, CUF, Robert MacIver file; MacIver to Fackenthal, July 13, July 19, and July 24, 1946; Fackenthal to MacIver, July 1, July 15, July 22, and July 27, 1946, CUF, McD file; Frank D. Fackenthal notes concerning meeting with Louis Carp, July 19, 1946, CUF, Car file; Fackenthal to Sulzberger, August 6, August 9, August 14, and August 20, 1946; Sulzberger to Fackenthal, August 5, August 12, August 19, and August 22, 1946, CUF, Arthur Hays Sulzberger file.

36. *The New York Sun,* October 31, 1946.

37. *Columbia Daily Spectator,* February 19, 1947, p. 2.

38. Fackenthal to O'Shea, October 2, 1946, CUF, John G. Saxe, July 1, 1946–January 31, 1947 file.

39. O'Shea to Fackenthal, February 11, 1947, CUF, John G. Saxe, February 1, 1947–June 30, 1947 file.

40. Father Gannon, in an interview conducted by the author on February 15, 1972, stated that he did not recall the incident.

41. "Austin-Mahoney Bill: Preliminary Analysis for Columbia University," Proof of February 11, 1947, attached to O'Shea to Fackenthal, February 11, 1947, CUF, John G. Saxe, February 1, 1947–June 30, 1947 file.

42. Maslow to *New York Times,* February 27, 1947, in *New York Times,* February 28, 1947.

43. Saxe memorandum, February 27, 1947, CUF, John G. Saxe, February 1, 1947–June 30, 1947 file. Sidney Katz to "Dear Friend," March 6, 1947, NYSEDL, Edward Spaulding Papers, Box 231: Anti-Discrimination-Army Advisory Committee, anti-discrimination file.

44. At the last moment, Austin introduced a bill that specifically stated that antidiscrimination legislation was not to be "construed as to interfere in any way with the internal administration or affairs" of exempt institutions, but any possibility of passage was lost when Senator Mahoney withdrew his legislation. Austin followed shortly thereafter.

45. Fackenthal to Sulzberger, March 8, 1947, CUF, Arthur Hays Sulzberger file.

46. For a full discussion of the Commission and its work, see Oliver Carmichael, Jr., *New York Establishes a State University* (Nashville, Tenn., Vanderbilt University Press, 1955).

47. Robert D. Leigh with the assistance of Helen Roberts, "Rejection of Jewish Applicants," in David S. Berkowitz, *Inequality of Opportunity in Higher Education: A Study of Minority Group and Related Barriers to College Admission* (Albany, New York Legislative Document, 1948).

48. E. Franklin Frazier, "Post High School Education of Negroes in New York State," in David S. Berkowitz, *Inequality,* pp. 174–175.

49. David S. Berkowitz, "Preliminary Memoranda on Minority Group Barriers," received August 22, 1947, NYSEDL, E. M. Spaulding Papers, carton 250, Temporary Commission on the Need for a State University (3)–(4) box, Temporary Commission on the Need for a State University (4) file; Berkowitz, *Inequality,* p. 75.

50. "Statement of the Association of Colleges and Universities of the State of New York," October 20, 1947. Copy in CUF, "Association of Colleges and Universities of the State of New York" file.

51. Author's interview with Shad Polier, February 2, 1972. See also Carmichael, *New York Establishes,* pp. 148–158.

52. Saxe memorandum, February 27, 1947, CUF, John G. Saxe, February 1, 1947–June 30, 1947 file.

53. State of New York, Temporary Commission on the Need for a State University, *Public*

Hearing, Chancellor's Hall, State Education Building, Albany, New York, October 20, 1947 (Albany, New York, 1947), pp. 40–41. Copy in CUF, John C. Adams file.

54. State of New York, Temporary Commission on the Need for a State University, *Report* (Albany, New York, 1948), p. 35.

55. *Ibid.*, p. 34.

56. Just before ratification of the compromise by the full Commission, the Association drafted a telegram urging that it be rejected. At the last moment, it was not sent.

57. Author's interview with Shad Polier, February 2, 1972.

58. President's Commission on Higher Education, *Higher Education for American Democracy,* vol. 2, *Equalizing and Expanding Individual Opportunity* (Washington, D.C., U.S. Government Printing Office, 1947), chapter 3.

59. During a strategy meeting of groups aligned with the AJC, Judge Joseph Proskauer, Chairman of the American Jewish Committee, arranged an appointment between Polier and McIntyre. The Archbishop stated his opposition to the bill. Proskauer, who had been influential in state politics for many years, replied, "It's a good bill. I know a good bill when I see one. After all, I write enough for you, don't I?" (author's interview with Shad Polier, February 2, 1972).

60. Theodore Bienstock and Warren W. Coxe, *Decrease in College Discrimination—A Repeat Study and Comparison of High School Graduates to Colleges in New York State in 1946 and in 1949* (Albany, Division of Research, State Education Department, The University of the State of New York, 1950); Harold E. Wilson, director, *A Study of Policies, Procedures and Practices in Admission to Medical Schools in New York State* (Albany, State Education Department, The University of the State of New York, 1953). See also: American Jewish Congress, Commission on Law and Social Action, "Analysis of 'Decrease in College Discrimination—A Report of the New York State Education Department'"; and Edwin J. Lukas and Arnold Forster, "Study of Discrimination at Colleges of New York State," October 13, 1950, The American Jewish Committee and the Anti-Defamation League of B'nai Brith.

61. Edward J. Grant, "Memorandum Regarding the Twenty-Five Year Survey of the Proportion of Columbia College Graduates Going Forward to Advanced Study at the University," October 31, 1939, CUF, G file.

62. In addition to Harvard, Yale, Princeton, and Columbia, Pierson's top ten included Michigan, Pennsylvania, Chicago, Cornell, Wisconsin, and Stanford.

63. George W. Pierson, *The Education of American Leaders: Comparative Contributions of U.S. Colleges and Universities* (New York, Frederick Praeger, 1969), pp. 250–254.

PART

III

IMPLICATIONS

CHAPTER

9
─────

The University Spirit
and the University of Chicago

Columbia's assumption of the selective function after World War I marked a major change in the way that university authorities perceived and compared their institutions. During the prewar years of university emergence and expansion, all hoped that the high schools would attract increasingly large numbers of students and would send the best of those on to college. Indicators of prestige for an institution of higher education included attainment of the university ideal and successful recruitment of faculty—which in turn were expected to attract large numbers of students who had survived the secondary school sifting process.

These were appropriate criteria for institutions that during the nineteenth century had come to believe that internal self-restraint had impeded their ability to influence society. After World War I, these criteria changed most rapidly at those institutions that had experienced the greatest increases of plant, faculty, and students. For such institutions, once the house of cards built on the foundation of secondary school performance of the selective function collapsed, there existed an increased tendency to measure prestige in terms of the ability of a given institution to perform the selective function. Or, to put it another way, the more it appeared that further expansion would only lead to diminishing returns in student quality, however the word "quality" was defined, the more highly regarded became those institutions willing to forego additional enrollments (and additional tuition) in favor of maintaining standards—both academic and social.

In this part, we examine a number of markers along this new academic procession since World War I. The story of admission to the University of Chicago provides an interesting and important variation on many of the themes first raised at Columbia for an institution near the head of the academic procession. This constitutes the subject of the present chapter. Beginning in the twenties and continuing to our own day, educators, politicians, and others debated the question of who should go to college. One way of rephrasing this question is to ask what social strata higher education is supposed to sort out. Nicholas Murray Butler viewed the Columbia Plan as a mechanism of elite recruitment; during the twenties contemporaries offered more liberal answers. After World War II, even these responses seemed conservative compared with actual happenings, especially at the City University of New York. These matters are discussed in subsequent chapters.

ADMISSION TO THE UNIVERSITY
OF CHICAGO TO 1920

The successive sharp images of the University of Chicago that have come down to us—first, as the American institution at which the *wissenschaft* ideal received greatest homage, and then as an institution that undertook notable advances in general education—should not obscure the initial ambiguity about functions present at the University's incorporation in 1890. To secure support from many influential Baptists, and to avoid schism within that denomination's Education Society, University spokesmen publicly insisted that the institution's first and chief benefactor, John D. Rockefeller, and its academic guiding lights intended to establish a first-rank college, and not a university. Indeed, Rockefeller's private position did not lack ambiguity, and two of those intimately involved in establishing the University judged that Rockefeller's munificence toward graduate education would be directly tied to the willingness of William Rainey Harper to accept the presidency.[1] Harper taught Hebrew at that great nineteenth century breeding ground for college presidents, Yale University, and had a firsthand understanding of the difficulties Semitics and other *wissenschaft* studies experienced in legitimating themselves at such ongoing institutions. In fact, he accepted the Chicago presidency only after Rockefeller made a second endowment specifically for graduate and theological instruction.[2]

Harper, like Butler, envisioned that his institution might quickly take its place among America's most prestigious and influential universities. However, the emphases of the two men differed. Whereas Butler urged the parallel development of collegiate and graduate education, Harper intented "to make the work of investigation primary, the work of giving instruction secondary."[3] Although the newly opened University of Chicago contained both junior (freshman and sophomore years) colleges and senior (junior and senior years) colleges, Harper desired to eliminate at least the former to spare his faculty the need to offer elementary instruction.[4] Advanced students would be recruited from "affiliated" colleges, which would offer instruction comparable to that offered by the University's own undergraduate units.

The Chicago president believed that this arrangement permitted a more rapid growth of graduate and professional divisions than would mere dependence on its own undergraduate colleges. He also knew that this plan would appeal to Mr. Rockefeller's business sense. Let Chicago be a university, Harper wrote him, "made up of a score or more colleges with a large degree of uniformity in their management; in other words an educational trust."[5] Finally, Harper hoped that affiliation with other colleges would enable the University to uplift the standard of college (and indirectly of secondary) instruction in the Midwest and South above "its present lamentably low level." Chicago's self-proclaimed mission was "to help make every educational institution within the circuit of its possible influence stronger and more efficient than it could be without the cooperation of a great educational clearing house."[6]

Harper hoped to exploit the University's Baptist affiliations to encourage some of the better Baptist "country colleges," such as Colgate in New York to enter into affiliation agreements. He also hoped that affiliates would open in major Midwestern cities. But he soon found that the better colleges had little interest in such a relationship. Chicago's remoteness from some of the colleges it courted was certainly a factor. So were the University's stipulations that affiliates reorganize their course offerings to conform with those offered by Chicago's junior and senior colleges and that they award a University of Chicago diploma. Several country colleges expressed fear that the mastery levels they would have to require for admission under the plan would be so high that local students would not be able to meet them. Most feared loss of institutional identity—a large price to pay for some fellowships to graduates who attended the University, the privilege of undergraduate attendance at the Hyde Park campus for a semester, and some special considerations for the faculty.[7]

Although Harper managed to negotiate affiliation agreements with a few small colleges in the Chicago vicinity during the fifteen years the plan remained on the books, the University found itself largely dependent on other methods of recruitment to its advanced divisions. These included recruitment from its own junior and senior Colleges as well as individual recruitment of students from colleges without formal affiliation agreements.

By the end of the University's first decade, Harper realized that he could not divest it of the junior colleges—at least within the foreseeable future. For the first time, he and his staff gave serious consideration to their problems of admission. At first, they thought the junior colleges would be swamped with applicants who desired the training prerequisite for admission to the graduate and professional schools. Although junior college enrollment grew steadily during the University's first two decades, a massive influx never occurred, and most students did not appear interested in continuing their studies at the advanced level (see Table 9.1).

Advisors and local educators told Harper that some strong forces would have to be overcome for enrollments to increase more rapidly. The University's urban location worked against it. A headmaster wrote that "the

Table 9.1.   Enrollment at the Junior Colleges, the University of Chicago, 1892–93 through 1939–40.

1892–93	180	1916–17	1592
1893–94	274	1917–18	1431
1894–95	366	1918–19	1869
1895–96	427	1919–20	1968
1896–97	438	1920–21	1958
1897–98	446	1921–22	1852
1898–99	545	1922–23	1934
1899–00	636	1923–24	1902
1900–01	733	1924–25	1912
1901–02	772	1925–26	2043
1902–03	821	1926–27	2006
1903–04	840	1927–28	2061
1904–05	860	1928–29	1990
1905–06	974	1929–30	2017
1906–07	957	1930–31	1999
1907–08	1038	1931–32	2211
1908–09	1118	1932–33	1874
1909–10	1130	1933–34	1818
1910–11	1145	1934–35	1902
1911–12	1263	1935–36	1894
1912–13	1295	1936–37	1901
1913–14	1305	1937–38	1762
1914–15	1303	1938–39	1878
1915–16	1403	1939–40	1817

SOURCE.   "Summary of Attendance—The University of Chicago," Harold H. Swift Papers, Special Collections, University of Chicago Library, 140:4.

impression that the 'small college' is best for undergraduate work and that a large city is not a good place of residence for those who enter young" were views entertained even "by some men of conspicuous position in your own University." "A feeling of distrust" among Baptists "as to the Orthodoxy of the University" adversely affected early enrollments. Its late appearance on the educational scene meant it had to compete with institutions that had long been cultivating strong relationships with those who might direct students to them, such as local educators and alumni. Finally, its emphasis on graduate and professional education led undergraduates to complain that they had not been provided with the amenities of undergraduate life which they expected. "The *younger* men of *moderate* means, without special athletic or musical gifts, do not seem to find the satisfaction and enjoyment that come from the class, social and fraternal life of the small colleges of the East."[8]

To counteract these influences, about most of which little could be done directly, Harper and his successors undertook a number of initiatives. In 1895 they took one step in this direction when they began to negotiate "partial affiliation agreements" with many of the private secondary schools in the Chicago vicinity. These agreements provided for school inspection by University officials and for periodic examination of students in subjects required for junior college admission using examinations provided and graded by the University. A student from such an accredited school who received a subject grade in the top third "of an average class" was exempted from the regular entrance examinations in that subject. By 1905, more than two-thirds of the students admitted came on certificate from schools with some sort of agreement with the University, including schools with partial affiliation agreements, Chicago's public schools, and cooperating high schools outside the Chicago area.[9]

At the same time, the faculty gradually liberalized the entrance requirements to both the junior and senior colleges. The great variation in the quality of Midwestern secondary schools forced the junior colleges to accept students offering a relatively wide variety of subjects and to require conditions in perhaps several of them. The type of course the student intended to follow at the University determined the precise entrance requirements. Thus, future scientists might be expected to present two units of Latin while others might be required to offer four. In time, the University placed even more subjects on the list of acceptable subjects for admission. The faculty expected that students would make up all deficiencies in the junior colleges before admission to the senior colleges.

Classicists made little attempt to hold off reductions of the Greek and Latin requirements for the junior colleges. They did object to the demands of the science instructors for deemphasis of the classics in the entrance requirements to the senior colleges. Although this battle dragged on for several years, a faculty majority that viewed classical study as an impediment to an early introduction to their disciplines finally liberalized the requirements in 1902.[10]

In 1911, in response to growing criticism over conditioned admittances, the academic caliber of the student body and a leveling off in enrollment, the faculty further modified the entrance requirements for the junior colleges. Henceforth, up to five of the fifteen points required for admission could be offered from any course or courses regularly studied in the high school curriculum. Practically, this permitted a student to offer vocational work in place of the usual academic subjects. "The new scheme," said Professor of Botany Otis W. Caldwell, "recognized vocational studies as having educational and cultural value quite worthy of place in the preparation of students for college work." Only three units of English would subsequently be prescribed. The remaining seven units, including a group of three and a group of two, had to be chosen from among the ancient and modern languages, ancient and modern history, and economics, mathematics and the sciences.[11] The Chicago faculty hoped the new plan would help eliminate conditioned admittance and broaden the pool of eligible students. The University warned, however, that this liberalization did not imply a relaxation of academic standards.

By the onset of World War I, Chicago's junior colleges, though remaining in a subordinate status, had overcome the danger of abolition. Although a large number of students in the senior colleges and in the graduate and professional schools had transferred from or were graduates of other colleges, the University found the junior colleges indispensable for the recruitment of students, at least into the senior colleges, and for keeping a balanced budget.

SELECTIVE ADMISSIONS AT CHICAGO

Although a few diehards continued to fight for abolition of the junior colleges, the vast majority of faculty, administration, and trustees conceded their permanence and turned their attention to molding that division into a more acceptable model. Most disagreed with the philosophy that guided the junior colleges immediately after World War I—a utilitarian philosophy perhaps best enunciated by dean of the Colleges of Arts, Literature, and Science, David Allan Robertson. Recognizing that only a small percentage of Chicago undergraduates continued their education after receiving their bachelor's degree, Robertson stated, "The general function of the Colleges is to provide training for efficiency in labor for one's self and for society and for the enjoyment of leisure by one's self and in society. Efficiency in labor . . . is ordinarily developed for the purpose of securing the largest and easiest pecuniary reward for efforts. . . . Even courses which are not contributions to a technical skill in making a living may appeal to selfish interest in success."[12]

Those primarily concerned with graduate research and instruction denounced such reasoning and complained that the administrators in charge of the undergraduate colleges did too little to convince the students in their charge of the importance of research, and sanctioned too readily the students' concern with nonacademic pursuits. Students however, chronically complained that the University lacked many of the amenities of college life and that the faculty stressed intellectual achievement at the expense of all other kinds of accomplishment.

The assumption of Chicago's presidency by Ernest DeWitt Burton, a New Testament scholar and a faculty member since 1892, and his subsequent appointment of Ernest Hatch Wilkins as dean of the Colleges of Arts, Literature, and Science, placed in powerful positions two men sympathetic to development of strong, purposeful undergraduate divisions. They manifested this new emphasis in a variety of ways, including enlargement of the guidance staff, increased emphasis on individual students, and establishment of a freshman orientation week. Although the trustees took no action on a rather grandiose plan drafted by Dean Wilkins and others for the reorganization of undergraduate education around the concept of residential colleges, the dean had greater success in introducing several interdisciplinary survey courses modeled after similar courses at Columbia and aimed at providing undergraduates with what came to be called a general education.[13]

In 1923, just as these changes were about to take place, Chicago adopted much of the selective admissions apparatus first employed by Columbia. In the future, the University announced, it would solicit information concerning the applicant's health and "character and promise" as well as his or her scholastic record. Psychological tests were also authorized.

The new policy's framers explicitly noted that they did not necessarily expect selective admissions to result in a limitation of enrollment. "The plan proposed below," stated the Committee on Selective Admission and Selective Retention, "will produce a superior student body. . . . It may result in a temporary reduction in numbers, or it may result in replacing inferior students with others of better quality." If the faculties desired a permanent reduction in numbers, the committee recommended that they pass legislation with that end specifically in view.[14]

Similarly, the University did not adopt selective admissions to regulate the racial and religious composition of the student body. Despite considerable anti-Semitism among Chicago's undergraduate student body, no evidence exists showing that, *at this time*, the Chicago administration intended to employ selective admissions invidiously. Indeed, the fragmentary written record shows that President Burton took a relatively liberal position on racial and religious questions. Further, the percentage of Jews in the student body more than doubled between 1920 and 1932.[15]

Nor did the University contemplate changes in academic entrance requirements. "[We] are now merely seeking," said the Committee, "a more satisfactory and intelligent method of selecting students who have technically met the scholastic requirements prescribed in previous legislation."[16] The faculties did not wish to reduce the pool of students from which it could select an entering class. But neither did they wish to accept automatically all students who met their relatively liberal entrance requirements. "The intention [of selective admissions]," stated the first draft of the Committee's report, "is to place the burden of the proof upon the candidate."[17]

Considerable ambivalence pervaded the report of the Committee on Selective Admission and Selective Retention. President Burton may have applauded the report's implication that subjective judgments should be employed in the admissions process. No machinery "in the form of regulations, tests, personality measurements or estimates and the like, which will automatically yield the results" desired could be relied upon.[18] Burton probably hoped that selective admissions would produce a socially and economically heterogeneous student body. But the report also contained the definite influence of the graduate divisions. For example, the dominant faction on the Committee succeeded in defining the desirable traits of personality and character as "satisfactory evidence of adequate mentality, seriousness of purpose, intellectual interests and attainments, intellectual promise, and such personal characteristics as will make the candidate a desirable member of the college community."[19] Dissatisfaction with the current state of affairs led this faction to unite temporarily behind the concept supported by President Burton. But this unity was born of expedience, and was probably achieved because other universities, such as Columbia, with which the faculty majority wished to be associated, had already adopted apparently similar policies. The authorized psychological tests would not be employed until the early 1930s. The Admissions Office employed subjective judgment sparingly; in fact, by 1926, it became apparent that this office interpreted selective admissions to have mandated the rejection of nominally qualified students who failed to obtain a favorable recommendation from their secondary school principal.

From the point of view of the faculty majority, selective admissions provided a slight improvement in the student body's quality; however, faculty restiveness remained high.[20]

THE UNIVERSITY SPIRIT

In 1925, after the death of President Burton and the inauguration of Max Mason, his successor, Dean Wilkens requested faculty consideration of a document entitled "A Theory of Education," which proposed the establishment of a new administrative unit devoted to offering general education and having a faculty primarily devoted to teaching. With knowledge of President Mason's sympathy, those powerful faculty members committed to advanced research used the occasion to make a strong, explicit denunciation of the existing conditions of undergraduate education and to suggest a philosophy quite different from that offered by Dean Wilkens.

Their "Report on Theory of Education" concluded that all divisions should be pervaded by "The University Spirit," by which they meant "the combination of the desire and the ability to participate in the advancement of knowledge or the application of knowledge, as it advances, to the development of human welfare." This meant that room existed at the University only for faculty members who possessed this spirit, and students exhibiting it or showing promise of its development. It also implied a positive commitment by the University to maintain conditions that helped foster it.

The report asserted that the undergraduate and graduate schools were not at that time "adequately pervaded by this spirit," and claimed this was indicated by the low percentage of senior college students who continued their studies at the University graduate schools, as well as by "the notorious fact that curricular and other intellectual interests rate low in student opinion as compared with social, athletic and 'activity' interests." The framers of the report blamed for these conditions not only the presence of students and faculty members lacking this spirit, but also poorly designed curricula, the inability of students to register for the courses they desired, and poor laboratory, library, and housing facilities. However, the report repeatedly returned to the lack of the University Spirit among the students, and recommended that only students who desired a university education be accepted for admission in the future.[21]

Thus at the same time that Columbia was devising ways of making itself more attractive to students with other than intellectual and career interests, Chicago was moving in the opposite direction. The junior colleges may have provided students for the senior colleges, but the latter were not providing the graduate and professional schools with anything like the 60% to 70% of graduates of Columbia College who went to that university's advanced divisions. Even if Columbia's percentages were unusually high, it was none the less embarrassing for an institution whose strong faculty entitled it to a place in the pantheon of great American universities to send only 15% of its graduates on to advanced education. The Chicago faculty thus decried what it considered to be the unacademic life pursued by undergraduates because of status considerations. The perceived student life style challenged the primacy of the academic function at Chicago and threatened to render a faculty with a national reputation "irrelevant" on its own campus.[22]

This restiveness prompted the Chicago faculty first to stiffen academic admissions requirements and then to limit enrollments. Such measures had been adopted by those universities with which Chicago desired to associate itself. It hoped that the apparent improvement in student body quality reported by these institutions might be duplicated at the South Side university.

ATTAINING THE UNIVERSITY SPIRIT:
ACADEMIC RETRENCHMENT

The mechanical methods employed by the Chicago Admissions Office in accepting or rejecting students discouraged those who had hoped that selective admissions might yield an undergraduate student body imbued with the University Spirit. The admissions requirements in force during this period included presentation of a favorable principal's recommendation, offering of fifteen secondary school units in accordance with the liberal 1911 subject requirements, and attainment of a secondary school average at least 25% higher than the difference between the school's passing grade and 100%.[23] During the late 1920s, some faculty members attempted to impose stricter subject requirements and to increase the minimum required high school average.

"One of the most important and notorious factors in the poor results of college education the last fifteen years," wrote a signer of the Report on Theory of Education, "is that we have not asked students to prepare for college but have taken them with any kind of high school preparation and have allowed them to make good their high school deficiencies in their college years!"[24] A large proportion of the faculties had concluded that Chicago's admissions policies would be much improved if students were no longer permitted to devote as much as one-third of their secondary school program to vocational subjects. Strong high school preparation in the academic subjects would permit Chicago's students to begin advanced work that much sooner—and might even increase the percentage of undergraduates who continued their work at the University by permitting the introduction of a Columbia-style combined collegiate and professional course.

Some therefore suggested that fourteen (instead of ten) secondary units be completed in academic subjects. Others proposed that certain preparatory sequences be made mandatory for each of the University's degree programs. Still others advocated introduction of a distribution requirement in which a minimum of two units would be prescribed in each of four academic areas, in addition to the three units already prescribed in English.

The University's Committee on Admissions gave this last proposal serious consideration, especially after a sample of high school teachers assented.[25] It reluctantly concluded that such a requirement would work an undue hardship on those feeders which emphasized vocational studies to meet the needs of their many vocational students. Many of these schools would be financially unable to increase their modern language and science offerings sufficiently to meet the proposed minimums. The most the Committee could do was admonish the secondary schools that their graduates might be refused admission unless they were able to present programs containing fewer vocational courses. The Committee also proposed that admissions officers take into account "the intellectual power of applicants as shown in their choice of subjects" and "rate applications on purposeful selection of subjects as well as on grades." [26]

At the same time, the Committee reconsidered its policy concerning cutoff scores. Requests for a liberalization had come from alumni who felt that their recommendations should outweigh an unsatisfactory academic record and from some principals who thought that provisions should be made for "extenuating circumstances." [27] When the Committee investigated the performance of those students who had recently been admitted despite failure to attain the minimum average, it found that most of them had either been dismissed or had dropped out for academic reasons. A masters thesis completed at about the same time found that students with averages just above the cutoff also tended to be unsuccessful in their studies. Drawing on these conclusions, the Committee decided to *raise* the grade for automatic admission to 40% of the difference between the high school's passing grade and 100%, and to require that all students with averages between the old and the new automatic grade achieve a minimum score on an intelligence test administered by the University. [28] Although intelligence tests had not been considered reliable enough for use by themselves, the faculty was satisfied with the results they yielded when used in conjunction with the high school average. [29]

ATTAINING THE UNIVERSITY SPIRIT: LIMITATION OF ENROLLMENT

In 1928, the University of Chicago limited freshman enrollment to 750 students plus replacements for those who dropped out. Many contemporary observers could not explain why this step was taken. The authors of the 1933 study of admission and retention of students completed as part of the comprehensive University of Chicago Survey commented that it "was not based on a valid estimate of the number of qualified applicants that would present themselves." Nor was it based on a study of plant capacity, "for a study of the utilization of buildings indicates that classrooms are available for the accommodation of a much larger number of students than are now enrolled." Nor was it based on the size of the teaching staff. [30] To make matters more confusing, only 676 freshmen enrolled in the fall of the year in which the limitation of 750 was announced.

The reasons for adoption of this policy cannot be found from an examination of objective indicators. Certainly there was some truth in the official rationale that the "scientific control of registration and formation of first-year classes" permitted by limitation would bring about greater efficiency and economy.[31] But, as one trustee was informed, the decision to set a maximum class size was really taken "with the hope that we shall thereby arouse students to apply in far greater numbers."[32] Recognizing that the recent increase in the cutoff point might lead to declining enrollments unless new sources of students were tapped, the University hoped that limitation would create for the junior colleges the aura of exclusiveness which appeared to attract so many of the better Midwestern students to the Eastern colleges. In order that such students might not be lured east by the lucrative scholarships that many selective colleges reserved for geographically remote students, the University announced it would henceforth award similar scholarships to highly qualified applicants. These steps received publicity and may have contributed to the widely noted higher academic caliber of subsequent entering classes.

THE UNIVERSITY SPIRIT—DID IT
EVEN IMBUE THE JUNIOR COLLEGES?

The Report on Theory of Education, which played such an important role in determining Chicago's admissions policies during the 1920s, called for admission of a student body with high academic potential and desirous of graduate or professional, as well as undergraduate, education. According to all indicators, in the years before World War II the University succeeded in recruiting academically talented students while gradually attracting an increasing proportion of students preparing for advanced study. For these achievements, the University paid the price of uncertain enrollments during the deepening Depression; the graduate school faculty paid the additional price of control over the junior college curriculum.

Aided in 1931 by adoption of a new plan of studies distinguished especially for its reliance on comprehensive examinations instead of final course exams for measurement of student progress, the junior colleges recruited entering classes of even greater academic caliber. Almost half of the 1932 entering class, the first admitted under the new plan, consisted of students from the top tenth of their high school class; only 10% were from the bottom half. Perhaps 40 or 50 freshman had been first in their class.[33]

But, one might ask, if academic competence really did increase, why did the failure and dropout rates not decrease from their mid-1920s levels? The staff of the 1933 Chicago Survey considered this question, and reported that "year after year certain instructors and certain departments have followed about the same curve of grading, irrespective of the increased ability of the entering classes. This being the case, it has been almost impossible to reduce materially the percentage of failing students." [34] This resulted in an ever more intense competition among ever more talented students—a situation that proved costly during the Depression when the junior colleges deemphasized academic excellence to maintain enrollments.

Attainment of the second of the report's goals, eventual matriculation of a high percentage of undergraduates in the University's graduate and professional schools, came about gradually. In 1929, the situation was such that Robert Maynard Hutchins could state in his inaugural address, "The emphasis on productive scholarship that has characterized the University from the beginning and must characterize it to the end has naturally led us to repeated questions as to the place and future of our colleges. They could not be regarded as training grounds for the graduate schools, for less than 20 percent of their graduates went on." [35] Several reasons might explain why the other 80% did not. Dean Robertson's belief that the colleges should prepare students for pecuniary success probably reflected the aspirations of many students. Further, four years of Chicago-style rigor was probably enough for most students.

Soon after he assumed office, President Hutchins proposed remedies for this situation. He believed that the junior colleges should "do the work of the University in general higher education," while the graduate and professional divisions should assume responsibility for all students immediately upon completion of the general education course. He proposed that such students be permitted to enter one of four graduate divisions (Biological Sciences, Humanities, Physical Sciences, and Social Sciences) or one of the professional schools (Business, Divinity, Law, Library, Medicine, and Social Service). A student would receive a certificate (later, the Associate of Arts degree) after completion of the general education course, and receive the bachelors as well as the advanced degrees from his graduate or professional school. [36] This arrangement proved attractive to students and many more continued their education.

Adoption of these policies did involve costs, and it is to this subject that we now turn.

MAINTAINING ENROLLMENTS
DURING THE DEPRESSION

Between 1931 and 1932, enrollment at Chicago's junior colleges declined by 337 students (about a sixth of the student body)—the largest one-year decline since their founding. With the "bottoming out" of the Depression nowhere in sight, University officials became apprehensive that similar declines would continue—declines the University could ill-afford.

The financial cost to the University resulting from the loss of tuition was far from inconsiderable. But the University suffered in another, less tangible way. For the prestige of Chicago—like all American institutions of higher learning—now depended on the degree of selectivity it could exercise in choosing a student body. This in turn presupposed an adequate supply of applicants. Even one more comparable downturn in enrollment might prove calamitous on both counts—and University officials moved quickly to counter this threat.

During the 1932 academic year, Chicago effected further liberalizations in its entrance requirements, ostensibly in recognition of the growing junior high school movement. The number of units required for admission was reduced from 15 to 12, but all of those units had to be completed during the last three years of the secondary school course (the first year of the high school course was now the third and last year of the junior high school). However, the number of elective units remained five, and the list of acceptable courses for meeting entrance requirements in "social studies" and "natural sciences" was broadened to include just about anything the high schools offered in those categories. The University did, however, impose a distribution requirement for the first time. Milder than those under consideration during the mid-1920s, the requirement was further softened by provisions allowing application of some junior high school work toward meeting it.[37]

At the same time, the University no longer automatically rejected students with records below the cutoff point, nor did it require them to attain a minimum score on the intelligence test. Chicago's registrar justified this change by saying that the marking practices of the high schools varied too widely to justify imposition of an ironclad cutoff. "This being true," he concluded, "we do not wish to discourage all lower-half students from applying for admission, nor do we desire that all upper-half students shall assume that they are automatically eligible for admission."[38]

Despite these moves, enrollment for 1933 declined again, although at a slower rate. Slowly, Chicago had begun to cut its sails. Whereas in the late twenties it routinely compared its admissions policies to those of the best universities in the nation, by 1933 it realized that it would have to rely heavily on local students for whom attendance at the University might be made economically feasible by their ability to commute. At this point, the admissions policies of Northwestern, located in the North Side suburb of Evanston, loomed more important than those of Harvard or Columbia.[39]

Chicago believed it could hold its own in competition with Northwestern. Although the latter had lower entrance requirements and a number of "back doors" through which students could enter and then transfer to the regular liberal arts course, it managed to register only slightly more students than Chicago. The South Side institution did not view this situation complacently, however. In the keen competition for solvent students Northwestern, using a variety of techniques including the employment of academic recruiters, "grabbed every student they could get." The authorities at Chicago knew that they would have to get their feet wet to prevent Northwestern from gaining the upper hand.[40]

The University's records for the Depression years are replete with memoranda discussing the merits and costs of various recruitment activities. "Please observe the 87% increase in catalogue requests this summer in July and August," wrote the registrar. "This must be indicative of a quickening interest in the University, but, of course, it is difficult to predict how soon this interest will be converted into enrollments."[42]

Several administrators compiled mailing lists of students who might be interested in Chicago. The University mailed an "eight page pamphlet with business reply card" to the students on one such list. Those who returned the card were sent a copy of the 60-page booklet, "The College in the University."[43]

But the successful recruitment of solvent students, as everyone at Chicago knew, "requires more than attractive printing." As a trustee said, "It's down to personal work, and we are doing it and shall have to do more of it."[44] At Chicago, as at many universities, this meant the hiring of professional recruiters who could visit secondary schools and junior colleges, speak to groups of interested students, answer individual questions, and distribute promotional material. These techniques seemed to work, for a late 1930s survey of factors inducing students to attend Chicago indicated that personal contact had attracted many of them.[45]

It did not take long for the first charges of unethical recruiting to be heard from practitioners in that highly competitive business. There is no evidence that Chicago's recruiters ever indulged in such conduct. In fact, the University led the North Central Association's drive to define unethical practices. The list included sending unsolicited representatives to secondary schools, sending solicited representatives whose salaries depended on their success in recruitment, bidding on the part of colleges for the best students, and requesting lists of only the best graduates of a high school. Singled out as especially unethical was an attempt by a college "to try to operate when it knows it is so situated with respect to its financial condition, its faculty and its facilities that it must hand 'gold bricks' to a majority of its graduates." The Association concluded, "A bankrupt college ought to go into voluntary bankruptcy even more quickly than a bankrupt business."[46]

Most probably, resort to unethical practices by competitor colleges took only a marginal toll on Chicago's enrollment. The University's recruiters and administrators were more concerned with devising responses to the more basic complaints often voiced against the junior colleges. To the charge that the University was an excellent place "for the best high school graduates, but it is too hard for the average entering student," the recruiters responded that an average well-prepared high school senior would find no difficulty. They acknowledged the existence of a competitive atmosphere but reminded applicants that competition "is only stimulating to the ambitious student."[47]

When potential applicants claimed to have heard that little social life existed at Chicago, recruiters told tham about the available athletic and extracurricular facilities and about the existence of fraternities and sororities. Assertions that Chicago was primarily interested in graduate and professional students were met by acknowledging that such might have been the case in the past, but that "today Chicago is definitely interested in undergraduates." Chicago officials answered charges that "student-teacher contacts in a large university are minimal" by indicating that the undergraduate divisions, although part of a large university, were themselves "no larger than many midwestern high schools and much smaller than the average state university."

Finally, they replied to charges that "there are too many Jews at Chicago" by admitting existence of a discriminatory policy:

The Office of Admissions at the University of Chicago does not accept all students who apply. It attempts to see that we have a representative student body. It has attempted to keep the percentage of Jews at the University the same as the percentage of Jews in the city.

Although the greatest concern appeared to be over the number of Jews at Chicago, the Admissions Office also received complaints about the number of Blacks, Catholics, and Communists. The recruiters answered such complaints by explaining that the University desired a diverse student body, geographically and racially. "The Jews don't want to go to a Semitic school," one said. "Others won't go to one which looks like it is tending that way." In other words, too many Jews (often on scholarship) scared away the cash customers. Invidious discrimination began at Chicago sometime after 1932. It does not seem to have survived World War II.[48]

Thus, Chicago tried to change its image in an attempt to maintain enrollment levels. The ideal student of the twenties had been one with the University Spirit. The ideal student of the thirties remained above average in intellectual ability, but, in some circumstances, was allowed certain qualities of personality and character that might make up for intellectual deficiencies, "We do not want Chicago to become overpopulated with grinds, introverts and cranks who possess high I.Q.'s. We want persons who are interested in and can deal with people as well as with facts and ideas." Last, but extremely important, the ideal student "should be able to pay his own way."[49]

THE UNIVERSITY SPIRIT
AND THE HUTCHINS PLAN

If the University as a whole had to pay a price of academic selectivity during the Depression, the graduate divisions had to pay an extra price of control over the content of undergraduate education. The first series of concessions occurred in 1931, and included an emphasis on general education courses and on comprehensive examinations, and establishment of a distinct undergraduate faculty although entirely composed of instructors from the upper divisions offering undergraduate courses. In 1932, the Chicago University Senate abrogated this last requirement in the expectation that a fully autonomous undergraduate faculty would overcome the University's reputation for impersonality and for emphasis on graduate work.

The second and third sets of reforms, effected in 1937 and 1942, generated considerable national interest over the next quarter century. Arguing that the high schools from which Chicago recruited had demonstrated themselves unable to prepare students for what the University had to offer, Hutchins proposed that the undergraduate faculty devise a general education curriculum that would replace the last two years of high school and the first two years of college. In 1937 this program augmented the ongoing two-year general education course; in 1942 it replaced it. Students would be accepted into the program after their high school sophomore year (1937 reform) and would receive a bachelors degree upon completing the program (1942 reform). The curriculum devised in 1937 required all students to complete the same basic program (consisting of three-year courses in the humanities, the natural sciences including biological and physical sciences, the social sciences, and in reading, writing, and criticism, and a one-year philosophy course designed to encourage integration of previously acquired subject matter), and provided room for two departmental electives. The 1942 reforms merged the two- and four-year courses and prescribed additional work in the humanities and social sciences and in the course on the integration of knowledge. The same legislation permitted the substitution of two electives for two general courses (humanities, social sciences, or integration). Students making this substitution would be awarded the Bachelor of Philosophy degree; others would receive the Bachelor of Arts degree. The administration of comprehensive examinations remained an integral feature of the program.[50]

Hutchins viewed this brand of higher education as an end in itself—as the terminal point for the education of many students and only in the broadest sense preprofessional or preparatory to graduate work. The downward extension of the undergraduate course would in effect eliminate dependence on the high schools and would offer a coherent, meaningful experience to students who would otherwise have been stifled in an inhospitable educational institution. At the same time, the general education program offered a positive definition of the role of the undergraduate division, which had traditionally been seen as the place to make up deficiencies before entrance to advanced study, and in the twenties as tangentially offering some general education. Instead of stigmatizing undergraduate students as second-rate academic citizens, the Hutchins plan aimed at turning the terminal status of many Chicago undergraduates into a virtue.

CONCLUSION

Ironically, during the post-World War II years, the heyday of the Hutchins Plan, the professional orientation of the Chicago undergraduate student body peaked. Although not intended as such, the general education program became an intermediate step for the 80% of the student body planning further study, including many in the University's own graduate and professional schools.[51] This influx of students with the University Spirit led to renewed interest by the graduate and professional school faculties in the undergraduate curriculum, an interest further heightened when in 1950 the University announced that the four-year undergraduate program would henceforth cover the traditional four collegiate years.[52] During the 1950s and 1960s the College effected a gradual retreat from "pure" general education.

But why should students with the University Spirit seek out an institution whose undergraduate division had apparently forsaken that Spirit? The answer is that Chicago had retained its image as a selective college, and this image attracted good undergraduate students regardless of Hutchins's curricular innovations.

NOTES TO CHAPTER 9
THE UNIVERSITY SPIRIT
AND THE UNIVERSITY OF CHICAGO

1. Richard J. Storr, *Harper's University: The Beginnings—A History of the University of Chicago* (Chicago and London; The University of Chicago Press, 1966), pp. 26–27.

2. *Ibid.*, pp. 47–49.

3. Unfinished manuscript of Harper's projected "First Annual Report," The Department of Special Collections, The University of Chicago Library, p. 149, as quoted in Reuben Frodin, "'Very Simple, but Thoroughgoing,'" in Present and Former Members of the Faculty, *The Idea and Practice of General Education: An Account of the College of the University of Chicago* (Chicago, The University of Chicago Press, 1950), p. 27.

4. Storr, *Harper's University*, p. 117.

5. *Ibid.*, p. 24.

6. Draft of letter from W. R. Harper to J. C. Colgate, submitted by Albion Small, undated (early 1890s), University Presidents' Papers, 1889–1925, The Department of Special Col-

lections, The University of Chicago Library (hereafter cited as UPP), box 1, file 14.

7. Storr, *Harper's University*, pp. 211–221.

8. H. J. Vasburgh to Harper, 1899 (exact date illegible), UPP, 1889–1925, box 1, file 16 (italics his); Rev. A. A. Kenbrick to Harper, April 25, 1892, UPP, 1889–1925, box 1, file 15.

9. "Partial Affiliation," undated, UPP, 1889–1925, box 1, file 16; Report of a "conference of gentlemen interested in the affiliation work of the University," undated, UPP, 1889–1925, box 1, file 16; J. Miller to Harper, October 20, 1905, UPP, 1889–1925, box 1, file 16. See also Floyd W. Reeves and John Dale Russell, eds., *Admission and Retention of University Students* (Chicago, The University of Chicago Press, 1933), pp. 13–14.

10. Storr, *Harper's University*, pp. 118–128.

11. Otis W. Caldwell, "The New University of Chicago Plan for College Admission," *Journal of Proceedings and Addresses of the National Education Association*, 1911:574.

12. The President's Report, 1920–1921, p. 23, as quoted in Frodin, "'Very Simple,'" p. 38.

13. *Ibid.*, pp. 40–44.

14. Report of the Committee on Selective Admission and Selective Retention," (undated), UPP, 1889–1925, box 1, file 11.

15. Vincent Sheean, *Personal History* (Garden City, N. Y.; Doubleday, Doran and Co., 1936), chapter 1; E. D. Burton to Wallace Heckman, March 29, 1923, and attachments: Heckman to Burton, April 5, 1923; B. S. Hurlbut to Burton, April 2, 1923, UPP, 1889–1925, box 54, file 15: Racial Question; Theodore Soares and Harold Lasswell, "Social Survey of the Undergraduates of the University of Chicago," 1920, UPP, 1889–1925; box 61, file 14: "Social Survey for Undergraduates, University of Chicago" and tables accompanying "Chicago Plan Attracts Superior Students," attached to W. F. Cramer to E. T. Filbey, March 24, 1933, UPP, 1925–1945, box 67, file 7: Registrar's Office, 1929–1939 file.

16. "Minutes of the Commission appointed by the President to formulate requisite administrative details for carrying into effect legislation of the Faculties of the Colleges approving the principles of 'selective admission and selective retention,'" February 20, 1923, UPP, 1889–1925, box 1, file 11.

17. "Report of the Committee on Selective Admission—Draft," (undated), UPP, 1889–1925, box 1, file 11.

18. *Ibid.*

19. "Report of the Committee on Selective Admission and Selective Retention," (undated), UPP, 1889–1925, box 1, file 11.

20. Several years later, Chicago's faculties and administrators concluded that "the selection of freshmen will not accomplish the result we desire unless the same selective process is applied to those who seek admission with credits from other colleges." In 1930, the first steps were taken toward selective admission of transfer and graduate students, including submission of a detailed application blank and a college transcript. No one, however, wished the procedure to become too selective since no uniform standards existed by which to judge students from different colleges and since, at least in the case of graduate school candidates, the applicant pool was already "very highly selective by the eliminative factors of a four year college course" (President Woodward to Roy Bixler, June 3, July 2, July 5, and July 15, 1930; Bixler to Woodward, June 26 and July 19, 1930; George H. Chase to Bixler, March 22, 1930; Bixler to Harlan H. Barrows, July 8, 1930; Bixler to G. J. Laing, August 20, 1930, UPP, 1925–1945, box 110, file 3: Admissions: Graduate Schools, 1926–1930 file).

21. "Report on Theory of Education, Approved as Amended by the Joint Meeting of the

Faculties of the Graduate Schools and Colleges of Arts, Literature and Science," January 19, 1927, UPP, 1925–1945, box 3, file 8: Admissions Committee, 1927–1928 file.

22.   "A Study of University of Chicago Graduates," attached to N. Payne to E. B. Burton, February 28, 1925, UPP, 1889–1925, box 1, file 11.

23.   Thus, a student coming from a high school where the pass grade was 70% would be admitted only if his or her average exceeded 77.5%. If the pass grade was 75%, the cutoff average was 81.25%.

24.   Julius Steiglitz to T. V. Smith, April 29, 1927, UPP, 1925–1945, box 3, file 8: Admissions Committee, 1927–1928 file.

25.   The University of Chicago, "Conference on Admission to the Junior Colleges," November 19, 1927, UPP, 1925–1945, box 3, file 8: Admissions Committee, 1927–1928 file.

26.   D. H. Stevens, "Suggested changes in the methods of admission to the colleges and graduate schools," undated, (c. March, 1927), UPP, 1925–1945, box 3, file 8: Admissions Committee, 1927–1928 file. Conclusions concerning the academic capabilities of Chicago's feeders were derived from Stevens's memorandum and from "Total Number of Units of Work Added to the Curriculum and Dropped from the Curriculum during Each Five Year Period Since 1900, and the Number in the Curriculum in 1900, in the Following High Schools: Batavia, Bloom, Blue Island, East Aurora, Elgin, Geneva, Glenbard, Hammond, Highland Park, Lyons, Morton, New Trier, Oak Park, Proviso, Thornton, Waterman, Waukegan, West Aurora, Wheaton," and from "Number of Units Required in Each Year of High School in 1900; Number Added to the Required List and Dropped from the Required List in Each Five Year Period in the Following High Schools: Batavia, Bloom, Blue Island, East Aurora, Elgin, Geneva, Glenbard, Hammond, Highland Park, Lyons, Morton, New Trier, Oak Park, Proviso, Thornton, Waterman, Waukegan, West Aurora, Wheaton," in UPP, 1925–1945, box 3, file 8: Admissions Committee, 1927–1928.

27.   Harold H. Swift to D. H. Stevens, April 1, 1927, and M. R. McDaniel to Stevens, December 14, 1927, UPP, 1925–1945, box 3, file 8: Admissions Committee, 1927–1928.

28.   Thus, if the high school pass grade was 75%, a student with an average of more than 85% did not have to take an intelligence test, while a student with an average between 81.25% and 85.00% had to receive a grade of 35 or better in his intelligence test to be admitted. A student with an average of below 81.25% was still denied entrance.

29.   Stevens to Swift, January 25, 1928, UPP, 1925–1945, box 3, file 8: Admissions Committee, 1927–1928. Ethel Ester Gallup, "A Personnel Study of First Year Students in the University of Chicago" (unpublished masters thesis, University of Chicago, 1926); N. Payne to Stevens, December 22, 1927, UPP, 1925–1945, box 3, file 8: Admissions Committee, 1927–1928. See also Edward F. Potthoff, "A Statistical and Analytical Study of the Selective Admission of Chicago Students" (unpublished dissertation, University of Chicago, 1928): Douglass Scates, *Selective Admission and Selective Retention of College Students at the University of Chicago* (Chicago; The University of Chicago Press, 1926): and The University of Chicago, "Conference on Admission to the Junior Colleges," November 19, 1927, UPP, 1925–1945, box 3, file 8: Admissions Committee, 1927–1928.

30.   Reeves and Russell, eds., *Admission and Retention*, pp. 73–74.

31.   Stevens to Swift, January 25, 1928, UPP, 1925–1945, box 3, file 8: Admissions Committee, 1927–1928. See also "Advanced Draft of Plan—Suggested changes in the methods of admission to the colleges and graduate schools," UPP, 1925–1945, box 3, file 8: Admissions Committee, 1927–1928.

32.   Stevens to Swift, January 25, 1928, UPP, 1925–1945, box 3, file 8: Admissions Committee, 1927–1928.

33. Tables accompanying "Chicago Plan Attracts Superior Students," attached to W. F. Cramer to E. T. Filbey, March 24, 1933, UPP, 1925–1945, box 67, file 7: Registrar's Office, 1929–1939.

34. Reeves and Russell, eds., *Admission and Retention*, pp. 26–27.

35. "The Inauguration of President Hutchins," *University Record* (January, 1930), 16(n.s.):12–13, as quoted in Frodin, "'Very Simple,'" p. 48.

36. *Ibid.*, pp. 49–50.

37. Bixler to "The Principal," May 7, 1932, UPP, 1925–1945, box 67, file 7: Registrar's Office, 1929–1939. For an earlier consideration of this question, see "Effect of the Junior High School Upon College Entrance Requirements," (undated, c. 1927), UPP, 1925–1945, box 3, file 8: Admissions Committee, 1927–1928.

38. Bixler to "The Principal," May 7, 1932, UPP, 1925–1945, box 67, file 7: Registrar's Office, 1929–1939.

39. On Chicago's peer group during the twenties see "Admissions Requirements," undated (c. 1929–1930), UPP, 1925–1945, box 110, file 3: Admissions: Graduate School; 1926–1930.

40. James M. Stifler to Swift, January 27, 1933, Harold H. Swift Papers, The Department of Special Collections, The University of Chicago Library, box 143, file 16.

41. Bixler to Filbey, September 12, 1934, UPP, 1925–1945, box 67, file 7: Registrar's Office, 1929–1939.

42. *Ibid.*, July 24, 1934.

43. Martha B. Defebaugh, Carl A. Birdsall, and Neil F. Sammons, "Suggested Program for Attracting Students to the University of Chicago," undated (c. 1935–1936), UPP, 1925–1945, box 79, file 1: Student Recruitment, 1936–1939.

44. Stifler to Swift, January 27, 1933, University of Chicago, Harold H. Swift Papers, The Department of Special Collections, The University of Chicago Library, box 143, file 16.

45. "Summary Freshman Report, October 1938, Chief Motives Bringing Freshman to the University of Chicago," Harold H. Swift Papers, The Department of Special Collections, The University of Chicago Library, box 140, file 3.

46. L. A. Pittenger, "Ethical and Unethical Practices and Procedures in the Recruiting of Students from Secondary Schools by Institutions of Higher Education," *North Central Association Quarterly* (July, 1937), 12:13–16.

47. Also, "the desire of high school officers to protect the reputations of their respective schools for good academic work" worked against recruitment of students with less than superior ability. One administrator wrote that Chicago's failure rate worked against this: "A considerable percentage of failure among the graduates of any given high school is likely to discredit the quality of work done at that school." Another factor was "the difficulty that principals and teachers themselves had in securing their degrees from the University" (A. J. Brunburgh to Hutchins, October 14, 1937, UPP, 1925–1945, box 76, file 15: Statistics: Enrollment-Factors Affecting).

48. Martha B. Defebaugh, Carl A. Birdsall, and Neil F. Sammons, "Suggested Program for Attracting Students to the University of Chicago," 1935–1936; "Report on Student Promotions," undated (c. 1936), UPP, 1925–1945, box 79, file 1: Student Recruitment, 1936–1939; A. J. Brunburgh to Robert M. Hutchins, October 14, 1937, UPP, 1925–1945, box 76, file 15: Statistics: Enrollment-Factors Affecting; George Works (?), "Criticisms of the University Which May Tend to Explain the Declining Enrollment," undated (c. 1937), UPP, 1925–1945, box 76, file 15: Statistics: Enrollment-Factors Affecting. The percentage of Jews in the entering class remained at about 26% for most of the thirties. Just before World War

II, it declined to about 20%. (For 1932 statistics, see tables accompanying "Chicago Plan Attracts Superior Students," attached to W. F. Cramer to Filbey, March 24, 1933, UPP, 1925–1945, box 67, file 7: Registrar's Office, 1929–1939. For 1936 and 1937 statistics, see "Statistics for 1936–1937 Freshman Classes," attached to Valarie G. Wickham to Filbey, May 6, 1938, UPP, 1925–1945, box 77, file 1: Statistics: Freshmen. For 1939 and 1940 statistics, see "Statistics of Freshman Class: Fall, 1940," attached to Wickham to Filbey, April 12, 1941, UPP, 1925–1945, box 77, file 1: Statistics: Freshmen. As late as 1931, Heywood Broun and George Britt could write about Chicago, "among the more cosmopolitan universities, Chicago has probably exhibited less prejudice against Jews in recent years than any. There is no restriction on entrance and many Jews attend" [*Christians Only: A Study in Prejudice* (New York, The Vanguard Press, 1931), p. 100]. During World War II, the Chicago administration reconsidered its policy and tried to decide whether the University should conform to its perception of the prejudices of society or try to surmount them. Hutchins stated unequivocally, "a university, of all institutions, cannot talk about the limitations of social tolerance. A university is supposed to lead, not to follow." After the war, he set upon convincing a somewhat hostile faculty, including some department chairmen notorious for their racism and anti-Semitism, that "as long as we are a university, and not a club, we cannot invoke racial distinctions as a basis for the selection of our students" (Filbey to W. C. Munnecke, August 17, 1944: Munnecke to Hutchins, August 15, August 21, 1944; Hutchins to Munnecke, August 26, 1944; E. C. Colwell to Hutchins, August 18, 1944, UPP, 1925–1945, box 60, file 1: Negroes).

49. "Report on Student Promotion." undated (c. 1936), UPP, 1925–1945, box 79, file 1: Student Recruitment 1936–1939.

50. For a detailed discussion of legislation implementing the Hutchins Plan, see Frodin, "'Very Simple,'" pp. 56–73. See also Daniel Bell, *The Reforming of General Education—The Columbia College Experience in its National Setting* (Garden City, New York: Anchor Books, 1968), and Robert M. Hutchins, *The Higher Learning in America* (New Haven: Yale University Press, 1936).

51. Bell, *The Reforming of General Education . . .* , p. 29.

52. After World War II, it became apparent that few high school sophomores applied for admission and that students who completed the four year program found their Bachelors degrees were not accepted as representing four years of college work.

10

The Selective Function
and the Transition
from Elite to
Mass Higher Education

. . . the race for numbers is over, and . . . the race for quality has begun. A few years ago our colleges and universities were competing for students, and great emphasis was laid upon "healthy growth." Now we are beginning to limit our numbers, to compete only for the best students, and to point with pride to the multitude that we turn away.

FRANK AYDELOTTE, President, Swarthmore College, 1928[1]

For the present our primary task is that of taking all types of young people and discovering their powers.

ALEXANDER MEIKLEJOHN, President, University of Wisconsin, 1927[2]

On most college campuses the early 1920s were a time for taking stock. American higher education had come a long way since the beginnings of the university movement some forty years before. From their former status as peripheral institutions, the colleges and universities had taken on great social importance as the training ground for entrance into the upper middle and

upper classes. Most campuses had greatly expanded their plant to accommodate the rapid growth of faculties and student bodies. But many college presidents had come to realize that existing facilities were fast becoming saturated
and that some decision about further growth would soon have to be made.

Although the demand for higher education continued to increase during
the early twenties, many college presidents became reluctant to undertake
the expansion necessary to accommodate more students. They questioned the
economic aspects of the situation. Perhaps the consequence of failing to expand would be the loss of tuition revenue. But on the other hand, it was
becoming harder to raise funds for capital construction. They felt unsure
about the academic aspects. Would not further expansion mean a dilution of
the academic caliber of the student body? Expansion could not be justified on
status grounds. Why expand at a time when prestige was no longer measured
by numbers, but by selectivity? Finally, many presidents had ideological reservations. Was not the purpose of higher education the training of future
leaders? Would not education of all the students who met the minimum
entrance requirements produce an oversupply for the available positions?
And if the purpose of higher education was something else, what was that
something else?

These questions vexed American educators for the next several decades
and indeed still vex them.[3] The answers provided by universities such as Yale
and Columbia were straightforward. These institutions decided not to expand
and instead used their sophisticated admissions procedures to choose the best
entering class from among their enlarged applicant pools. Many other American colleges and universities for various reasons could not or would not be as
selective. It is to these institutions that we now turn.

THE DEMAND FOR HIGHER EDUCATION

*I came from China last August to get an education. I had supposed that to get an education you had
to have a place to sit down. I have had no place to sit down. Can you give me a place to sit down?*

From a young Chinese student to the president of Stanford University[4]

From the time that the United States Bureau of the Interior began to keep
statistics on high school graduates in the 1870s until World War II, their
number, expressed as a percent of the 17-year-old population, never decreased. But the years between 1910 and the mid-1930s exhibited unprecedented growth. In 1910, about 8.8% of the 17-year-old population was graduated from high school. By the early 1920s this percentage had doubled, and
by the early 1930s it had doubled again. The increase did not stop there, and
ultimately more than half the age group received high school diplomas before
World War II temporarily forced the percentage down.

Until the twentieth century, the growth rate of American colleges and universities managed to keep pace with high school expansion. But beginning in the late 1890s, and continuing with only brief interruptions until World War II, the ratio of baccalaureate degree holders to high school graduates (four years earlier) began a long decline.[5] The high schools cited this fact when they demanded liberalizations in college entrance requirements. It was impossible, they claimed, to do all the preparatory work the colleges required while offering a terminal course to the vast majority of their students.

But the colleges viewed the same phenomenon from an entirely different perspective. The high schools had grown so fast that even the smaller *percentage* of their graduates who desired to go to college represented a far greater absolute *number* of such students than ever before. And because these students came from high schools where terminal rather than preparatory education was emphasized, the colleges began to question the worth of their high school credentials.

VOCATIONAL EDUCATION
AND THE HIGH SCHOOLS'
SELECTIVE FUNCTION

What especially distressed many college officials was the increased emphasis in many high schools on vocational education. The movement to introduce such instruction, which (so its advocates said) would directly prepare students for jobs in farming, industry, or the trades, into the nation's schools gathered considerable momentum during the first years of the twentieth century.[6] As appears to be true of most modern American educational reforms, vocationalism entered the popular parlance via a commission's report, in this case the *Report of the Massachusetts Commission on Industrial and Technical Education* (1906), commonly known as the Douglas Commission after the governor who had appointed its members.[7]

Although the report showed no hostility toward the classics, nor for that matter against what we have termed the "newer disciplines," it did bemoan the lack of "industrial intelligence" in most young people. Claiming that "the State needs a wider diffusion of industrial intelligence as a foundation for the highest technical success," the Commission recommended the establishment of either independent industrial high schools or the introduction of industrial courses in existing high schools.

Significantly, the Commission's report argued that education which cultivated industrial intelligence would satisfactorily serve other purposes. Many advocates of vocational education took the term "other purposes" to include the fulfilling of college entrance requirements, and they began a campaign to make such courses as business, shop, home economics, and agriculture acceptable for college entrance. The movement culminated, inevitably, in establishment by the NEA of the Committee on the Articulation of High School and College, chaired by Clarence Kingsley, a mathematics teacher at the Brooklyn Manual Training High School. The Kingsley Commission's major recommendation called for the colleges to permit candidates for admission to offer four of a required fifteen Carnegie units in any subject offered by the high school.[8] This would permit the offering of vocational or practical subjects without requiring the colleges' affirmative acceptance of every such course. Kingsley hoped this device would permit the high schools to continue to offer the same program of studies to all students whether or not they were college bound. However, Edward A. Krug, in *The Shaping of the American High School*, argues that a provision in the Commission's supplementary report accompanying the main report had the opposite effect. Kingsley recommended that colleges no longer require for admission both mathematics and foreign language. Krug contends that, on the whole, the colleges ignored this recommendation, while the high schools accepted it in redrafting their graduation requirements, thus creating two classes of students.[9] On the other hand, Harry McKown, in his 1922 report on college entrance requirements for the United States Bureau of Education, found that many colleges had dropped their foreign language requirement and that most had reduced their mathematics requirements.[10] Whatever the reality, many college authorities began to express disenchantment with the quality of students appearing at their institutions, not only because they offered several credits of vocational courses, but also because they feared that the quality of instruction in academic subjects may have diminished as the high schools devoted more of their energy to vocational subjects. In short, the vocational movement did for many colleges, especially Midwestern institutions accepting students on certificate, what the influx of Jews had done for elite Eastern colleges such as Columbia: it led them to retreat from permitting the high schools to perform the selective function and to reassume an active role in the selection of their students.

COPING WITH THE DEMAND

In face of the increased demand for higher education, Nicholas Murray Butler remained committed to his vision of True Democracy.[11] Selective admissions would permit the discovery of the best material from among all applicants and the University would prepare them for positions of responsibility. But other colleges, especially the public ones, wondered whether true democracy implied the rejection of a large number of students—including those without the traditional preparation. Serious consideration has had to be given, wrote an official at one state university, "to the attainment of a proper balance between the democratic ideal of free higher education for all who may seek it on the one side, and the legitimate protection of the tax-paying population against useless, wasteful expenditures of public money on the other."[12] The debate over exactly where to strike this balance raged both inside and around many campuses.

At the University of Minnesota during the 1920s, two groups offered differing views concerning the University's educational mission. One faction, led by the dean of the University's undergraduate liberal arts college, John Black Johnston, emphasized the training of an intellectual elite for leadership.[13] Earlier in the century, Johnston had advocated the liberalization of the University's admissions policies, and had denounced the straightjacketing to which the University had subjected the state's secondary schools. He took this stance because he expected more liberal policies to attract high quality students who might otherwise have been dissuaded from going to college. By the 1920s, Johnston had concluded that the University had been too lenient in granting admission to students who did not belong there.

The other faction, led by President Lotus D. Coffman, agreed that education of an elite was an important function for a university, but argued that a publicly supported institution must instruct all minimally qualified students. Coffman's own research and observation led him to conclude that any decline in the academic caliber of Minnesota's students was mainly due to the poor preparation of primary and secondary school teachers, and to the emphasis in the secondary schools on nonacademic subjects.[14] He argued that a student should not be penalized for this. Many with poor qualifications on paper might bloom once exposed to good instruction. As for the others, Coffman believed that democracy needed more than good leaders—it also needed "intelligent followership." If the University could help make more residents of the state good citizens, it was performing a valuable function.

The difference between the two positions was one of emphasis. Johnston admitted that students of less than first-rate ability had a place on campus just as readily as Coffman admitted that elite training should not be neglected. During the 1920s, Coffman argued against any arbitrary limitations of enrollment to keep the University from growing too large. Instead, he constantly urged that more money be appropriated by the state for higher education. More money meant more ways to expand the University's offerings, and more ways to "salvage abilities."

During the early 1930s, each of these viewpoints became the guiding philosophy for a new undergraduate division. Superior students were permitted to enroll in the University College and could thereby take courses anywhere in the University without having to conform to specific sequences or distributions. Although the General College was open to any student with a high school diploma, it mainly attracted students of moderate ability, usually unqualified to enter any of the University's other undergraduate divisions. The College offered "overview" courses designed to give students an understanding of their world and the ability to confront problems upon which, Coffman said, "students must exercise judgment later on."[15]

The University of Minnesota consciously attempted to "educate for democracy." It implemented this goal in a way that both factions could live with. Public authorities permitted the University to treat this discussion internally and merely ratified proposed solutions. Universities in other states did not have similar luck.

In Missouri, a law on the books since the turn of the century required the University to give full credit toward admission for all work completed in an accredited Missouri public high school.[16] The law gave the University leeway by leaving to the faculty the final say as to which subjects could be offered for entrance. In the late twenties, the faculty exercised this freedom and increased from six to nine the number of prescribed units from among the fifteen required entrance units.[17] This was a serious change since it also dropped a provision exempting graduates of University accredited high schools from the old requirement.[18] Deciding to head off possible legislative objections or a possible court fight, the faculty backtracked somewhat and permitted students to enter without offering a foreign language, but it required additional study in foreign language by deficient students once matriculated.[19]

In Michigan, a controversy arose during the early 1920s over the admission of out-of-state students. Some lawmakers questioned the University's policy of accepting students from other states while rejecting local candidates. When President Angell had been confronted with such criticism in the late nineteenth century, he had replied that the tuition of out-of-state students actually subsidized the education of state residents, especially in the professional schools, and that the number of Michigan students attending colleges in other states was roughly equal to the number of out-of-state students at the University. Regulation of out-of-state admissions would invite retaliatory legislation against Michigan students by other states. Finally, he had argued that a heterogeneous student body was educationally desirable.

After World War I, the return of many members of the armed forces to the campus overtaxed existing facilities. University authorities requested additional funds for dormitory construction from the Legislature. Some local groups used the occasion to renew the attack on the University's admissions policies concerning out-of-state students. They argued that these policies were responsible for much of the overcrowding and for the highly inflated prices charged for most goods and services in Ann Arbor. It was noted that more students came to the University from neighboring Ohio than from 48 Michigan counties. Everyone knew that few of those counties produced many high school graduates, but this type of documentation did have some weight with a legislature apportioned by county. Last, it was asserted that local students were as able to do work at the University as out-of-state students, but that many could not afford an education there. Some urged that the University devote additional resources to extension work to help the youth from rural counties.

Michigan officials contended that most of these charges were incorrect; the rest misleading. Although numerical restrictions on out-of-state students were not imposed, a differential scale of tuition based on residence was maintained. Other state universities established residential quotas, and accepted only out-of-state students of significantly superior academic caliber.[20]

During the twenties, all colleges, but especially public ones, had to reexamine many traditional assumptions about their constituencies and their missions. It became apparent that education for democracy no longer meant education for leadership. But no universally acceptable definition of education for democracy emerged at this time, and each college groped for its own, often with the aid of interested outside parties.

IMPLICATIONS FOR ADMISSIONS POLICIES:
SELECTIVE ADMISSIONS
AND LIMITATION OF ENROLLMENT

Schools like the University of Minnesota's General College which opted for a relatively broad definition of their constituencies continued to accept the traditional certificate signifying completion of a four-year course at an approved high school. But schools that perhaps for financial reasons or perhaps for ideological or status reasons decided to stop short of such a broad definition found that procedure inadequate. If a student came from a high school that emphasized terminal education, his or her ability to do college work might be questionable even if the student's certificate indicated that he or she met the college's stated entrance requirements. Some further discrimination had to be made between high school graduates applying for admission.

Many private colleges did adopt policies of selective admissions, and these institutions admitted on a variety of criteria. Swarthmore gave preference "to candidates who are children of Friends or of alumni of the College," and laid great stress on personal interviews conducted by college officers or alumni.[21] Goucher College required, in addition to a good high school record, submission of personality reports from the principal, two teachers, and two others.[22] Lawrence College in Appleton, Wisconsin, expected students to be in the upper half of their high school classes and asked them to file preliminary application forms after their junior year. It inquired about the student's family environment, and assured itself that accepted candidates were "emotionally adapted to take what we have to give."[23]

Many colleges required candidates to fill out Cumulative Record Forms published by the American Council on Education. Max McConn described these questionnaires as providing

> an instrument for organizing and presenting, compactly and in part graphically, on a time projection, all the significant facts, both scholastic and personal, in regard to a student's career from the time he enters the junior high school until he is graduated from college. These significant facts include not only school marks and the results of objective tests, but also such items as health, physical and mental, family background, financial situation, study conditions and programs, extra-curricular activities, summer experiences, vocational experiences, unusual accomplishments, reported interests, educational and vocational plans, and the like, all carried forward from year to year to exhibit both permanent and changing conditions and tendencies.

McConn exclaimed that "for personnel purposes these forms and the local adaptions of them which many institutions are making compare with ordinary high school and college record cards as an automobile compares with an oxcart."[24]

Although many public colleges and universities announced limitations on their enrollments, few had the luxury of implementing full-fledged selective admissions policies. The essence of selective admissions was the subjective judgment of the admissions officer. State law usually prohibited invidious discrimination, while public opinion prohibited just about any method not completely based on "merit."

The University of Michigan was one public institution that inquired of high school principals about candidates' personal qualifications. Ira Smith, the University's Registrar, announced the new policy in 1926, justifying the step by emphasizing the difficulty of transition from high school to college. The application form would stimulate students to think carefully about their college plans, would acquaint parents and teachers with the difficulties of transition, and would enable the University to advise students on how to cope with university studies. Smith concluded, "we are convinced that it is essential for us to become as well acquainted as possible with the individual applicant for admission and learn more of his personal and school record and background than it is possible to obtain from the report of his grades alone."[25]

Given a limited number of seats in each entering class, admissions policies aimed to find those students who would make the best use of available facilities. Many colleges had become concerned about the high number of failures among students already admitted. At the University of Washington, for example, of 581 students admitted one year, 290 failed to complete their work.[26]

At the University of Minnesota, freshmen comprised 60% of the student body. President Coffman asserted that most dropouts did not leave for academic reasons but for lack of finances or poor health. Studies at other campuses seemed to indicate the reverse. But whatever the reason, high attrition rates and increased demand for higher education prompted adoption of admissions policies designed to assure that those admitted were the ones most likely to succeed in their chosen course.

IMPLICATIONS FOR ADMISSIONS POLICIES: THE ECLIPSE OF COLLEGE ENTRANCE EXAMINATIONS AND COLLEGE ENTRANCE REQUIREMENTS

One possible method of coping with the perceived inadequacies of the traditional certificate system might have been a return to the traditional entrance examinations. However, contemporaries believed that such a step would not find general acceptance. In the first quarter of the century, all the major examining colleges (notably Harvard, Yale, and Princeton simultaneously in 1916) gave up their entrance examinations in favor of the CEEB's. The Board's ranks were further increased by the decision by Vassar, Smith, Mount Holyoke, and Wellesley in 1919 to end their policies of admission on certificate in favor of CEEB examinations.[27] Other institutions, however, did not imitate this example. By 1925, the CEEB administered 72,418 examinations to 19,775 candidates. Since most college applicants took their exams in two parts, the 10,000 different students the Board examined represented only 5% of the 200,000 freshmen who entered college in that year. Only ten colleges admitted all of their students on the basis of CEEB exams in that year. Clearly, dissatisfaction with certificates had not produced a corresponding stampede back to the College Board.[28]

One CEEB official believed it virtually impossible for a community accustomed to the certificate system to return to the use of written examinations. He related the story of a former CEEB examiner who accepted the principalship of a high school whose graduates went to college on certificate. When the school's PTA learned that he had unobtrusively introduced written tests as a supplement to daily classroom recitations, it interpreted the innovation as a personal affront and aroused the community against the reform. The principal soon ended the innovation. The CEEB official lamented, "It has been said that he was charged with violating a provision of the Constitution of the United States dealing with unusual forms of punishment and cruelty. That the Board's operations do not have the cordial support of that community, and that it is difficult to secure intelligent and effective supervision of the Board examinations there, will surprise no one."[29]

More than habit made a return to traditional entrance examinations so undesirable. There had been a change in the philosophy of college admission which made these tests appear passé. As early as 1900, President Arthur Hadley of Yale adumbrated the general tenor of remarks of the following generation: "most don't see entrance examinations as tests of ability to go on with college studies. They have become examinations of past work, rather than on the power for subsequent work."[30] E. L. Thorndike, who virtually founded the science of educational measurement, concluded that success in college could not be predicted from entrance examinations with enough accuracy to make such tests worth taking or to prevent gross injustice to many students. His research revealed a low correlation between standing in entrance examinations and standing in junior and senior classes, enormous discrepancies between grades on repeated examinations, and internal differences between scores on various parts of an examination in a single subject.[31]

A. D. Whitman criticized the examinations offered by the CEEB during the late teens and the twenties for denying admission to students "who would, if admitted, succeed in the scholastic work required of them rather better than do some of those who gain admission." He examined the records of nearly 4000 high school graduates tested by the CEEB between 1918 and 1921, admitted to one of seven Eastern colleges requiring entrance examinations, and remaining in college for at least a year. He found that the correlation coefficients between success in the entrance examinations and success in the same or related subjects in college ranged from $+.73$ to $-.02$ with an average of $+.29$, a relatively low coefficient.[32]

Carl Campbell Brigham, another specialist in educational measurement who had been associated with the War Department's intelligence testing program in World War I, cited many similar studies in attempting to convince the CEEB to modify its policies. He said that the Board had been successful in regulating entrance requirements and in maintaining school standards, but claimed that with the maturation of the secondary school the aim of its tests should henceforth be the qualitative differentiation of individual students. That is, the tests should attempt to reveal the broad expanse of a student's knowledge, not the minute details of his preparation.

At his urging, the CEEB introduced a number of modifications in its examinations. Increased reliability in evaluation of exams would be attained by giving each reader only one or two questions to grade so that the readers could become experts on a small section of the exam. The work of each reader was subject to careful cross-checking. The Board retired old readers and hired specially trained replacements in their stead. The grading system was changed so that scores of the current year would better conform to scores of previous years. But despite all these changes, Brigham had doubts about whether such tests would ever be the best predictors of success in college. He continually urged the CEEB to consider adoption of intelligence tests either as replacements or supplements.[33]

The written entrance examination, which directly descended from the entrance examinations given since the seventeenth century, gave way to other methods of admission by World War II. During the 1930s, the American Council on Education developed objective achievement tests that claimed to test general knowledge of a subject without mandating a specific curriculum on the high schools, the way that traditional entrance exams had done. Shortly thereafter, the College Board began to offer similar exams along with the older types, and it found that most colleges preferred their candidates to take the objective tests. During the war, the traditional exams were suspended because of the impracticality of grading the exams administered in June in time for the beginning of wartime summer sessions, or of offering the tests earlier in the year, since they took a week to administer. The CEEB did not reinstitute the tests after the war.[34]

At the same time that educators discounted traditional entrance *examinations* as predictors of success in college, entrance *requirements* became increasingly liberalized. The colleges' emphasis on future ability meant that the deemphasis on past mastery could continue. The reports issued decennially by the United States Bureau of Education charted this trend in great detail. For example, the report for the years 1913 to 1922 concluded that during this period most colleges required fewer prescribed units for admission and that the permitted number of unrestricted electives had increased. In 1922 the median number of free electives allowed by colleges permitting any latitude at all was four units, the number recommended by the Kingsley Report. In fact, the 1922 report found that most colleges closely followed Kingsley's suggested subject distributions. Generally, they required three units of English, two units of mathematics (a decrease of one-half unit since 1913), one unit of social studies, two units of languages (if required at all), and one unit in science (required by about half the colleges). The remaining units could be offered from any subjects credited toward the high school diploma, including vocational subjects.[35]

Thus, colleges looking to limit their enrollment, but unwilling or unable to employ selective admissions, had to find new predictors of success in college. Although traditional entrance examinations proved to be poor predictors, several other indicators fared better.

IMPLICATIONS FOR COLLEGE ADMISSIONS POLICIES: PREDICTING SUCCESS IN COLLEGE

The period after World War I was the heyday of the correlation coefficient. An endless debate persisted over whether intelligence test scores, high school average, or some other indicator best predicted success in college.

Supporters of intelligence tests were not at all modest in their claims for this instrument. "The most inexorable basis for admission to college is native general intelligence," wrote a believer. He argued that "no amount of health, character, ambition or preparation can make a moron a successful and responsible college citizen."[36] Some advocates of intelligence testing (perhaps recalling some of the rhetoric expounded at Columbia on the just use of the tests) believed their use could expand educational opportunity by unearthing students with ability to do college work, but lacking the specific preparation required by the colleges. But the testers did not make admissions policies and those colleges employing the instruments used them to choose students from among the existing applicant pool—not to expand that pool.

During the 1920s, some of the claims for intelligence tests began to be seriously questioned. The correlation between race and "intelligence" was explained by reference to such interfering variables as knowledge of English. Even the concept of "native intelligence" was called into question. By 1930, Brigham had completely rejected his own earlier positions, calling the belief that "*native intelligence* purely and simply without regard to training or schooling" was measured by these tests "one of the most serious fallacies in the history of science." Brigham came around to the conclusion that the test scores measured many variables "including schooling, family background, familiarity with English, and everything else, relevant and irrelevant." "The *'native intelligence'* hypothesis," he concluded, "is dead."[37]

But the tests were not. "Just what mental tests measure," wrote Dean Hawkes of Columbia College, as belief in the native intelligence hypothesis waned, "I do not know . . . But I do know that it indicates more definitely and accurately than anything we are familiar with whether the boy will succeed in Columbia College."[38] The mere utility of the device satisfied most admissions officers and few made serious attempts to determine exactly what was being measured, or why significant correlations between test scores and college performance were obtained. In 1926, the CEEB finally offered the tests to member colleges under the name that has been employed ever since—the Scholastic Aptitude Test. After World War II, many of the colleges that previously refrained from CEEB membership availed themselves of the services of the American College Testing Service, which has had its greatest strength west of the Alleghenies.

Rivaling the intelligence test as a predictive device was the student's high school average. The earliest certificates required the listing of all courses taken to assure that each applicant had met the specified entrance requirements. Early in the twentieth century, some institutions required the high schools to include the actual grades received along with the list of courses.

During the twenties, admissions officers found that the average of these grades correlated highly with success in college.

Another indicator with some predictive ability was the student's rank in his or her high school graduating class. Caution had to be employed in using the secondary school average or the rank in class since the variance in quality of high schools feeding the same college might act as an interfering variable. At Northwestern during the twenties the correlation between high school rank and first semester college rank was +.70, while the correlation between intelligence test score and first semester rank in class was +.60, two relatively high correlations.[39] Whitman's study of 4000 students discovered a higher correlation between high school grade and college record than between performance on the traditional entrance examinations and college record. But the correlation between intelligence test score and college record was highest of all.[40] Brigham found a slightly *lower* correlation between the rechristened "aptitude" tests and first term freshman grade than between high school grades and first term freshman scores.[41]

Brigham proceeded to experiment with combinations of the various criteria. By combining the entrance examination score, high school average, and aptitude test results of applicants to Princeton into a multiple regression equation, he produced a grade (called the Princeton bogie grade) that had a correlation of +.75 with the student's actual freshman grade. Officers of admission widely adopted such equations by the late twenties, and many colleges still employ them.

THE COLLEGES AND THE EIGHT YEAR STUDY

By the early 1930s, most college admissions officers believed they had made a large number of concessions to the nation's high schools. Various methods had been employed to remove the selective function from the secondary school. The better colleges used selective admissions; others used indicators of future success such as high school average or intelligence test score. College entrance requirements did not hinder secondary education as much as they had earlier in the century.

But just at this time a new outcry was raised against the "repressive" admissions policies of most colleges. The proponents of progressive education—or at least the movement's institutional form, the Progressive Education Association—voiced this complaint. Fully aware of the fast approach of the age of universal secondary education, the Association sided with the advocates of vocational education in opposing efforts by the colleges to use entrance requirements in a way which would distort the high schools' function. The educational terminal point for the vast majority of students would be high school graduation—and most college entrance requirements seemed to have little place in a curriculum intended to prepare students for life.

The PEA believed that for progressive education to succeed in the secondary schools, progressive school graduates intending to go to college needed assurances that the colleges would not discriminate against their applications because they lacked the traditional entrance subjects. During the early thirties, the PEA asked the nation's major colleges and universities for a chance to prove that students having a progressive secondary education had the potential to do college work and that credentials from progressive secondary schools should be accepted on a par with those of traditional schools. The plan devised to demonstrate these assertions was called the Eight Year Study and the results of the experiment have been published in five volumes collectively entitled *Adventure in American Education*.[42]

Implementation of the study began after the major American colleges agreed not to discriminate in judging the applications of graduates of the participating thirty schools on the grounds that they had not met the usual entrance requirements. Most colleges probably had few serious reservations about the experiment. The colleges were not obliged to accept any student. They would make their decision on the basis of a report on secondary school performance and on a principal's recommendation. The proposal came at a time when most colleges were interested in potential, not preparation, despite the PEA's belief to the contrary. It also came at a time of concern about enrollments—during the Depression many colleges had further liberalized their admissions policies in the hopes of attracting more students. Endorsement and funding of the experiment by the General Education Board and by the Carnegie Foundation for the Advancement of Teaching gave it added legitimacy. Finally, the existence of successful experiments in general education on the college level made college officials less hesitant about a similar secondary school course of studies.

Once freed of the "restrictive" college preparatory curricula, each of the thirty schools introduced its own unique innovations. As they developed, however, the various programs appeared to gravitate toward a central theme of "the democratic ideal." "The high school in the United States," wrote the author of the summary report of the study, "should be a demonstration, in all phases of its activity, of the kind of life in which we as a people believe." The ultimate goal of the Eight Year Study was a broadly social one, "the chief concern of every school now is to maintain and promote the American way of life."[43]

This democratic ideal was a conscious rejection of that held by men like Butler. The difference, according to the progressives, was between benevolent autocracy on one hand and democratic leadership on the other. Education for the former implied the training of some individuals to make intelligent judgments on behalf of all the citizenry, and the training of all the rest to acquiesce in the judgment of those chosen as leaders. Education for the latter implied cooperation between leaders and followers not only to achieve immediate tangible ends, but to perpetuate the democratic form. The activist citizenry envisioned by the progressives perhaps was slightly to the left of Coffman's "intelligent followership" on a scale of egalitarianism. The real difference was that Coffman believed secondary education had shown itself incapable of accomplishing this purpose and hoped that higher education could salvage as many students as possible. The progressives believed that the vast majority of Americans were not college bound and that secondary education, which was rapidly becoming universal, had to educate for democracy, if it were to be done at all.

Studies of the 2000 graduates of the thirty schools who entered college each year showed that they did about as well as students from similar social and economic backgrounds from traditional secondary schools. This conclusion is not surprising: the colleges increasingly looked for students with potential—not for specific preparation. After World War II, many partisans of the Eight Year Study lamented that the war had thwarted any chance for the wide adoption of the study's innovative features. The real reason for the failure of the Eight Year Study to revolutionize secondary education, however, was probably the postwar upturn in the percentage of high school graduates intending to continue their education. The American college—not the high school—was destined to educate for democracy.[44]

EDUCATION FOR DEMOCRACY: THE PRESIDENT'S COMMISSION ON HIGHER EDUCATION

When thousands of World War II veterans armed with benefits enacted under the GI Bill knocked at the doors of the nation's colleges, a new era began in the history of American higher education. Schools that had only a few years earlier contemplated closing their doors because of their inability to meet expenses during the Depression found their capacities taxed to the limits. A similar phenomenon had occurred on a smaller scale after World War I. The influx was larger this time not only because the federal government was willing to underwrite the cost of the veterans' higher education and because a much longer war had created a larger backlog of students, but also because a larger percentage of the returning veterans were high school graduates and therefore met the minimum criterion of eligibility for college admission. Many contemporaries witnessing this unprecedented demand began to ask if it would continue. Others asked if it should continue. It was to these questions that the President's Commission on Higher Education, appointed by Harry S. Truman in 1946, addressed itself.

The Commission's staff, under the direction of Francis J. Brown, had been impressed with the conclusions contained in the 1943 National Resources Development Report that 90% of the proper age group had the capacity to do secondary school work and that 80% had the ability to graduate. These percentages were greater than the retention rates of even the best secondary schools in the country. Intelligence tests administered to all army personnel during World War II (except to illiterates on one end of the spectrum and officers on the other) were also examined. On the basis of that evidence, the Commission ratified the suggestion made by some intelligence testers years earlier that there was considerable talent in the country going untapped. It was estimated that conservatively "at least 49% of our population has the mental ability to complete the 14th year of education which includes some general education and offers a variety of vocational, social and liberal arts studies which lead either to employment or to continued study in a liberal arts or terminal college." The Commission further concluded that this group represented "the same people as those with the ability to continue formal education leading to advanced degress in graduate or professional schools."[45] It predicted large increases in college enrollment because of the increase in the birthrate during and after World War II, and because historically an increasing proportion of the college age population had been enrolling in college.

After concluding that a far greater proportion of American youth could and would enroll in college, the Commission turned to the question of whether this trend should be applauded or condemned. The Commission took the former attitude, saying that "the educational attainments of the American people are still substantially below what is necessary either for effective individual living or for the welfare of society."[46]

This conclusion flew in the face of much conventional wisdom concerning the appropriateness of college for American youth. The consensus of opinion between the two world wars had been that any further increases in enrollment could only come at the expense of the academic and social quality of the student body, and that in any case only a minority of students required any postsecondary education. The Commission confronted this view directly.

American colleges must envision a much larger role for higher education in the national life. They can no longer consider themselves merely the instrument for producing an intellectual elite; they must become the means by which every citizen, youth, and adult, is enabled and encouraged to carry his education, formal and informal, as far as his native capacities permit.[47]

The Commission cited rapidly changing conditions in the American economy as well as the contemporary political climate to justify its stand. The major economic change, resulting from the rapid advancement of American technology, was a shift in the economy's occupational center from the major producing industries to the distributive and service trades. One result of this, the Commission said, "is a new and rapidly growing need for trained semi-professional workers in these distributive and service occupations."[48] Increased technological complexity would call forth a variety of talents, including "social sensitivity and versatility, artistic ability, motor skill and dexterity, and mechanical aptitude and ingenuity."[49] If the colleges were to meet the demand for these talents, they could no longer single out as their exclusive clientele students "possessing verbal aptitudes and a capacity for grasping abstractions." Or in other words, they cannot "continue to concentrate on students with one type of intelligence to the neglect of youth with other talents."[50]

But why did such training have to take place in postsecondary institutions? One answer was that greater maturity was necessary to master subject matter of increased complexity. But a more basic answer was that the preservation of American democracy required "a combination of social understanding and technical competence" in its citizens. And it was in a collegiate setting that a student could receive education "for personal and social development" and technical education "that is intensive, accurate, and comprehensive enough to give the student command of marketable abilities."[51]

The Commission believed that the emergence of a major totalitarian threat so soon after the defeat of another posed an urgent challenge for American education. A century earlier, both its friends and foes accepted democracy as the wave of the future, but "today," the Commission stated, "we cannot be so sure that the future of the democratic way of life is secure." Although America had the responsibility of supporting democratic forces around the world, the best way to preserve and extend the democratic ideal was "by increasing the vigor and effectiveness of our achievement at home. Only to the extent that we can make our own democracy function to improve the mental and physical well-being of our citizens can we hope to see freedom grow, not vanish, from the earth." The Commission concluded that the improvement of American democracy was "one of today's urgent objectives for higher education."[52]

Just as higher education was expected to prepare American youth to function in the American economy, it would have to teach it to function in the American democracy. This specifically meant "the development of self-discipline and self-reliance, of ethical principles as a guide for conduct, of sensitivity to injustice and inequality, of insight into human motives and aspirations, of discriminating appreciation of a wide range of human values, of the spirit of democratic compromise and cooperation."[53]

This task could not be accomplished by leaving it to a few courses in scattered departments; it had to be a part of every phase of college life. The well-designed college course would provide learning experiences leading to certain basic results including development of an ethical system consistent with democratic ideals, active participation in public activities, recognition of mutual interdependence of people and nations, appreciation of the role of science in the modern world, comprehension and communication of ideas, satisfactory emotional and social adjustments, maintenance of health, enjoyment of cultural activities, acquisition of knowledge and attitudes basic to a satisfying family life, choice of satisfying vocation, and acquisition of skills involved in critical and constructive thinking.[54]

The Commission called the educational experience that would produce these results "general education." The liberal education offered in the past by American colleges had provided similar results for their elite constituency. General education, said the Commission, "is liberal education with its matter and method shifted from its original aristocratic intent to the service of democracy. General education seeks to extend to all men the benefits of an education that liberates."[55]

The Commission called for the removal of economic, curricular, racial, and religious barriers to higher education; the establishment of community colleges with an emphasis on terminal vocational education, but including exposure to general education; the strengthening of the four-year liberal arts college; and the expansion of opportunities for graduate and professional training. It envisioned that federal funds would be made available toward these ends. Last, it called for the acceleration of the trend toward more education at every level.

The Report elicited an onslaught of criticism from those who thought that higher education either could not or should not expand.[56] But time was on the side of the Commission—in fact, the percentage of American youth now attending college approximates the Commission's predictions.

CONCLUSION:
DEMOCRACY AND THE SELECTIVE FUNCTION

Despite all the disagreements in the political and educational philosophies of Butler, Coffman, and the President's Commission, certain themes reappear in the ideas of each. All believed that higher education was vital for the perpetuation of democracy, but they differed in their conceptions of democracy.

For Butler, True Democracy required the training of future leaders to whom deference could be legitimately accorded. For Coffman, leadership training was to be supplemented by education of an "intelligent followership." The Commission's vision of democracy provided for the least amount of social distance between leaders and led. All three shared an apprehension at the many divisive forces that they believed permeated American society, and hoped that education might act as a counteracting and unifying force. Finally, all believed in a society stratified by ability. For Butler, ability to lead men had a social component not emphasized in the thought of Coffman or the Commission. But all believed that individuals having ability should be given every opportunity to develop it.

By the late 1890s, American society had developed to the point where the recruitment of leaders could no longer be accomplished by informal methods. Butler envisioned that the rapidly growing secondary school would unearth talent and send it to the colleges and professional schools for the necessary training. By the end of World War I, he concluded that the high schools did not perform this function properly, and he urged the colleges themselves to perform this role. Even institutions that did not employ all the criteria of selection used by Columbia and other prestigious colleges assumed a more active role in student selection.

Colleges still employ the admissions apparatus developed after World War I, although the actual instruments now in use are supposedly more sophisticated. Today's institution of higher education has final say about whom it shall admit, although in a number of states public institutions must operate within certain parameters specified by the state. However, this situation may be changing again, as we see in Chapter 12.

It is perhaps not altogether coincidental that the debate over the role of higher education in a democracy was most potent during the adult lifetime of John Dewey (roughly 1890 to 1950), the man who permanently juxtaposed the terms "democracy" and "education" in American educational thought. Dewey's notion that the school should be a continuation of society fits well with the socialization function that educators such as Butler hoped the undergraduate college (including its extracurriculum) would perform. Although the colleges still carry out this task and although most Americans understand this implicitly, the recent debate over the role of higher education in American society has concentrated on its economic payoff. The Report of the President's Commission was in a sense Janus-faced, since it concerned itself with both sets of issues. In the current debate over the worth of a college education, it might do educators well to recall the complexity of the college experience, and not reduce the debate to the question of rate of return on investment.

NOTES TO CHAPTER 10
THE SELECTIVE FUNCTION
AND THE TRANSITION
FROM ELITE TO
MASS HIGHER EDUCATION

1. Frank Aydelotte, "The American College of the Twentieth Century," in Robert Lincoln Kelly, ed., *The Effective College* (New York, The Association of American Colleges, 1928), p. 6.

2. Alexander Meiklejohn, "Wisconsin's Experimental College," *The Survey* (June 1, 1927), 58:269.

3. For an important discussion emphasizing the difference between elitists and democrats, see R. Freeman Butts, *The College Charts Its Course* (New York, McGraw-Hill, 1939), pp. 345–357.

4. As quoted in "The Superior Student," *New York Times*, September 27, 1925, II 6:5.

5. Abbott L. Ferriss, *Indicators of Trends in American Education* (New York, Russell Sage Foundation, 1969), pp. 105, 110.

6. This discussion is largely based on Edward A. Krug, *The Shaping of the American High School 1880–1920* (Madison, Milwaukee, and London, The University of Wisconsin Press, 1969), chapters 10, 11, and 12.

7. *Report of the Massachusetts Commission on Industrial and Technical Education* (Boston, The Commission, 1906), pp. 18–19, as quoted in Krug, *The Shaping*, pp. 220–221.

8. Clarence D. Kingsley, "Report of the Committee of Nine on Articulation of High School and College," National Education Association, *Journal of Proceedings and Addresses*, 1911:561.

9. Krug, *The Shaping*, pp. 302–303.

10. Harry Charles McKown, "The Trend of College Entrance Requirements," *United States Bureau of Education Bulletin*, 1924, no. 35.

11. For his separation from the NEA as that organization became dominated by opposing ideological forces, see Richard Whittemore, *Nicholas Murray Butler and Public Education* (New York, Teachers College Press, 1970), pp. 101–108. For his denunciations of vocationalism, see [Nicholas Murray Butler], "Notes and News," *Educational Review* (November, 1911), 42:431, and Krug, *The Shaping*, pp. 293–294.

12. Alexander G. Roberts, "A Program of Admission to and Elimination from a Tax-Supported State Institution," *School and Society* (October 20, 1923), 18:457.

13. See John B. Johnston, *The Liberal College in a Changing Society* (New York, D. Appleton-Century Company, Inc., 1930).

14. See Lotus D. Coffman, *The Social Composition of the Teaching Population* (New York, Teachers College, 1911).

15. James Gray, *The University of Minnesota: 1851–1951* (Minneapolis, The University of Minnesota Press, 1951), pp. 220–221, 282–285, 308–322. See also his *Open Wide the Door. The Story of the University of Minnesota* (New York, G. P. Putnam's Sons, 1958), pp. 138–139.

16. Laws of Missouri, 1903, p. 264.

17. The old requirement was three units of English, one in mathematics, and two in foreign language. The new requirement was three units in English, two in mathematics, two in foreign language, one in social science, and one in laboratory science.

18.   Frank Stephens, *A History of the University of Missouri* (Columbia, University of Missouri Press, 1962), p. 527n.

19.   Stephens, *A History*, pp. 503–504.

20.   Marion Burton to Arthur G. Hall, October 12, 1920; Hall to Burton, October 27, 1920; A. N. Farmer, "Comments, Questions and Suggestions Regarding Student Registration, Michigan State University," (undated), MHC, Arthur G. Hall Papers, Office of the Registrar, Arthur G. Hall, Statistics, Burton Letters box. See also James E. Pollard, *History of Ohio State University. The Story of Its First Seventy-Five Years 1873–1948* (Columbus, The Ohio State University Press, 1952), p. 244.

21.   Robert L. Duffus, *Democracy Enters College—A Study of the Rise and Fall of the Academic Lockstep* (New York; Charles Scribner's Sons, 1936), p. 157.

22.   *Ibid.*, p. 162.

23.   *Ibid.*, p. 170.

24.   Max McConn, "The Co-operative Test Service," *The Journal of Higher Education* (May, 1931), 2:227.

25.   [Ira Smith] "The Admission of High School Graduates to the University of Michigan," *School and Society* (March 27, 1926), 23:396–397.

26.   Roberts, "A Program," p. 457.

27.   Wilson Farrand, "A Brief History of the College Entrance Examination Board," in College Entrance Examination Board, *The Work of the College Entrance Examination Board* (Boston, etc., Ginn and Company, 1926), p. 27.

28.   Henry S. Pritchett, "Has the College Entrance Examination Board Justified Its Quarter-Century of Life?" in College Entrance Examination Board, *The Work*, p. 13.

29.   *Ibid.*, pp. 163–164.

30.   Arthur T. Hadley, "Conflicting Views Regarding Entrance Examinations," *School Review* (December, 1900), 8:583–593.

31.   E. L. Thorndike, "The Future of the College Entrance Examinations Board," *Educational Review* (May, 1906), 31:470–483. For a rebuttal see Adam Leroy Jones, "Entrance Examinations and College Records: A Study in Correlation," *Educational Review* (September, 1914), 48:109–122.

32.   A. D. Whitman, "The Selective Value of the Examinations of the College Entrance Examination Board," *School and Society* (April 30, 1927), 25:524–525.

33.   Mathew T. Downey, *Carl Campbell Brigham: Scientist and Educator* (Princeton, Educational Testing Service, 1961), pp. 32–36. Brigham sat on the CEEB's Subcommittee on Questions of Policy which advised the Board "to adopt a less restrictive definition of requirements, to analyze all of the Board's examinations with the object of making them more reliable and valid, to rescale the examination papers to compensate for fluctuations in the level of difficulty from year to year," and to modify the examinations in language, history, and science.

34.   College Entrance Examination Board, *Report of the Commission on Tests: Righting the Balance* (New York, College Entrance Examination Board, 1970), pp. 19–20.

35.   McKown, "The Trend," pp. 99–100, 133.

36.   Ben D. Wood, "Functions and Methods of Admissions Offices," *School and Society* (May 17, 1924), 19:575.

37.   Downey, *Carl Campbell Brigham*, p. 27, italics his.

38. Herbert E. Hawkes, "Examinations and Mental Tests," *Educational Record* (1924), 5:28–29.

39. E. L. Clark, "Selection of Freshmen at Northwestern University College of Liberal Arts," *Educational Record* (April, 1927), 8:122–128.

40. Whitman, "The Selective Value," p. 525.

41. Downey, *Carl Campbell Brigham*, pp. 20–21.

42. The five volumes are Wilford M. Aikin, *The Story of the Eight Year Study* (New York and London, Harper, 1942); Hermann H. Giles et al., *Exploring the Curriculum: The Work of the Thirty Schools from the Viewpoint of Curriculum Consultants* (New York and London, Harper, 1942); Eugene R. Smith et al., *Appraising and Recording Student Progress* (New York, Harper, 1942); Charles Dean Chamberlin et al., *Did They Succeed in College?—The Follow-Up Study of the Graduates of the Thirty Schools* (New York, Harper, 1942), and *Thirty Schools Tell Their Story: Each School Writes of Its Participation in the Eight Year Study* (New York and London, Harper, 1943).

43. Aikin, *The Story of the Eight Year Study*, p. 30.

44. See Agnes E. Benedict, *Dare the Secondary Schools Face the Atomic Age?* (New York; Hinds, Hayden and Eldridge, 1947); and James Hemming, *Teach Them to Live*, 2nd ed. (London, Longmans, Green and Co., 1957). See also Lawrence Cremin, *The Transformation of the School* (New York, Knopf, 1961), pp. 251–256.

45. Francis J. Brown to Commission Members, August 6, 1947, Harold H. Swift Papers, Department of Special Collections, The University of Chicago Library, box 180, file 2; and President's Commission on Higher Education, *Higher Education for American Democracy*, vol. 1, "Establishing the Goals" (Washington; D. C., U. S. Government Printing Office, 1947), p. 41.

46. President's Commission, *Higher Education*, 1:25.

47. *Ibid.*, 1:101.

48. *Ibid.*, 1:68.

49. *Ibid.*, 1:32.

50. *Ibid.*, 1:32.

51. *Ibid.*, 1:69.

52. *Ibid.*, 1:9.

53. *Ibid.*, 1:10.

54. *Ibid.*, 1:50–58.

55. *Ibid.*, 1:49.

56. See Gail Kennedy, ed., *Education for Democracy: The Debate Over the Report of the President's Commission on Higher Education* (Boston; D. C. Heath and Company, 1952). Shortly after issuance of the President's Commission report, the Association of American Universities sponsored a Commission on Financing Higher Education. Its final report is usually considered a conservative rejoinder to *Higher Education for American Democracy*. [see Commission on Financing Higher Education, *Final Report: Nature and Needs of Higher Education* (New York, Columbia University Press, 1952) and David D. Henry, *Challenges Past, Challenges Present: An Analysis of American Higher Education Since 1930* (San Francisco, Jossey-Bass, 1975), pp. 79–84.]

11

Higher Education for All:
The Mission of the
City University of New York

After World War II, the United States witnessed social and economic changes on a scale rivaling, if not exceeding, those of the late nineteenth century. The rapid growth of the economy's tertiary or service sector created a large demand for white-collar workers—a demand that America's colleges and universities hastened to fill. In the postwar era, American higher education monopolized upward social mobility not only by regulating access to graduate and professional school, but now also by controlling access to at least the white-collar portion of the middle class. "There is a growing link between educational attainment and occupational advancement," commented Seymour Martin Lipset and Reinhard Bendix in the late 1950s. "With over half of the gainfully employed working in tertiary industries, and with the increasing growth of industrial and governmental bureaucracies," they stated, "nonmanual skills are requisite for a large proportion of the available jobs each year." "And," they concluded, "nonmanual skills are increasingly acquired through formal education."[1]

Higher education's growth rate between World War II and the early 1970s exceeded even the most optimistic immediate postwar predictions. In the

1970s, despite recent reverses, almost half of the college-age population actually attended college, and the more than eight million students represented by this fraction constituted more students than the number attending high school just thirty years earlier.

Most of this growth took place in the public sector. Expansion by America's private colleges and universities was thwarted by the lack of either capital funds and/or motivation. The growth of many state university systems followed similar patterns. A central campus would be reserved for those most qualified academically; regional and local campuses would serve students with less impressive qualifications. This pattern developed most fully in California with its three-tiered system of universities, four-year regional liberal arts colleges, and two-year community colleges.[2]

During the 1960s, educational progressives began to speak of universal higher education as a desirable national goal.[3] Just as universal secondary education had been accepted by a once dubious public, universal higher education would one day be accepted, its supporters reasoned. Access to higher education would bring about fulfillment of one of the great tenets of the nation's credo: true equality of opportunity. The rapid growth of higher education facilities roughly paralleled the growth in available positions during the postwar years, and during the prosperous sixties it appeared that this trend would continue. Coming at a time of heightened social concern for groups that had been the victims of past discrimination, the prospect of rectifying past injustice simply by providing an opportunity for a college education seemed highly attractive.

Events at the City University of New York during the late 1960s led it to undertake a program of expansion based on the most advanced embodiment of the theory of universal higher education. Beginning in the fall of 1970, the University guaranteed admission to one of its undergraduate divisions and to the desired program of studies to all New York City high school graduates. Although CUNY admissions officers assigned them to a given division based on students' "ability," they simultaneously employed several different measures of this quality to assure that each student body would reflect the heterogeneity of this most heterogeneous of all American cities. City University authorities acknowledged that the achievement of this social goal implied the presence on each campus of students with a fairly wide range of abilities, but they intended to take concrete steps to permit the maximum development of each student.

Broad political, rather than narrow academic reasons, underlay adoption of this "Open Admissions" program. These reasons reflected an awareness of the social implications of admissions policies.

BACKGROUND: DEMAND AND RESPONSE

The College of the City of New York, the city's first municipal college, had not been New York's foremost institution of higher education at any time in this century. Always in Columbia's shadow, the College took its subordinate position into account in determining its course and paths of growth. Given the middle and working class background of most of its students, the College's emphasis on the rapid acquisition of usable skills comes as no surprise. Many CCNY students in the years before World War II could not afford to remove themselves from the work force for the nine or ten years required by the Columbia Plan (that is, 4 years of high school, 3 of college, and 2 or 3 more of professional school). Typically, they would complete a three-year program at Townsend Harris Hall, CCNY's preparatory division, study at CCNY for perhaps the two years necessary to complete a preprofessional course, and then attend one of the professional schools in the city—perhaps one of Columbia's.[4] Alternately, a student might enter one of City College's under-graduate professional schools such as the School of Business and Civic Administration, the School of Technology, or the School of Education, all operational divisions by the 1920s. Students were not charged for attending any of these divisions; City College maintained a free tuition policy from the day it opened its doors in 1847.

Limitation of enrollment by Columbia, and later by other colleges attractive to New York City students, increased pressure on CCNY to accept students who could not gain admission elsewhere. The continued growth of New York's population, especially in the outlying boroughs remote from the College's upper Manhattan campus, forced the College to consider establishment of additional facilities. The demands for further growth led the New York State Legislature in 1926 to abolish the City College Board of Trustees and replace it with a Board of Higher Education of the City of New York. The new body was responsible not only for the affairs of City College and Hunter College (the municipal college for women), but also for any additional public colleges to be subsequently opened. The same year, a Brooklyn branch of CCNY was opened in downtown Brooklyn. Continued overcrowding forced the Board of Higher Education to establish an independent municipal college in Brooklyn, which opened its doors in 1930. Construction of a Bronx branch of Hunter College began in 1929. A fourth independent municipal college, Queens College, opened in 1937.[5] Despite the increased taxing of facilities in the years just after World War II, the Board of Higher Education undertook no additional expansion at that time.

Admission to the municipal colleges was never determined by any "subjective" factor such as personality. Originally, City College admitted students by examination. Like most other colleges, it shifted to the certificate system, and then to the use of "objective" criteria to predict success in college. During the immediate post-World War II years, each municipal college granted admission to all graduates of any New York City high school whose high school average exceeded the annually determined cutoff for that college. At that time, cutoff scores hovered in the high 70% range. In the late 1940s, a modification in policy allowed admission of the bottom third of each entering class on the basis of an average of high school record and aptitude test score.[6]

Complaints that the municipal colleges, despite several expansions, had not met the legitimate demand for higher education in New York City continued as in the past. After World War II, Donald Cottrell, who had been asked by the Board of Higher Education to prepare a master plan for future growth of the municipal college system, renewed the charge. A long-time advocate of the democratization of education, he had been influenced by the Report of the President's Commission on Higher Education and impressed with the successful growth of the California system of higher education. Cottrell argued that in 1950 there would be more than 48,000 New York City students "capable and desirous" of completing either a two- or a four-year college program which the municipal system was not accommodating. He further demonstrated that "occupational shifts involving the expansion of certain fields, the rise of new industries, and the relative decline of other industries and occupations" created in New York City a considerable demand for workers with at least some college education. For example, in 1950, New York City needed an additional 7500 men and 2350 women college graduates to fill professional and semiprofessional positions. Overall, he estimated that the city needed about 25,000 additional college graduates and an additional 32,000 workers with some college education to fill professional, semiprofessional, managerial, clerical, sales, and miscellaneous positions. He projected that the demand for workers in these categories would decline by only 10% during the following decade.[8]

The BHE discussed Cottrell's recommendations for increased higher educational facilities, but decided to take no action. Cottrell's own figures indicated that the number of unaccommodated students capable and desirous of completing four years of college would slacken off in the mid-1950s and not reach appreciable levels again until the end of the decade, when the war and postwar babies would begin to come of college age. The Board took no heed of Cottrell's figures concerning the ongoing need for two-year college programs. Thus, it ignored the admonition that his figures constituted minimum projections, and that "to base long-term planning on either a temporary valley or a temporary peak" was unreasonable.[9]

Little growth occurred in the municipal college system during the next dozen years. Between 1950 and 1962, total annual admissions to the four-year colleges increased from 10,337 to 11,945, but admission of bachelor's degree candidates decreased from 8859 to 8563. Three community colleges were founded during the mid- and late 1950s (Staten Island Community College in 1955, Bronx Community College in 1957, and Queensborough Community College in 1958), but in 1961 these colleges together only enrolled 3% of the city's high school graduates. During the 1950s, the ratio of those enrolled in the four-year colleges to public and private high school graduates declined considerably. This resulted from an increase in the cutoff points required for admission—a conscious attempt to keep the size of the entering classes constant.[10]

In 1962, the BHE established a subcommittee to draft another master plan, and again received a report that was an indictment. The Committee to Look to the Future criticized the Board's current admissions policies as "restrictive" and charged that they eliminated "a large group of New York City high school graduates who may have a legitimate claim to free public higher education." It attributed recent increases in the cutoff point to limited plant capacity, not to inflated high school grades, as some had claimed. The Committee's staff concluded that a policy of increasing academic exclusiveness was not "in keeping with the functions of a publicly supported university," and would no longer be feasible once the postwar babies attained college age. A reasonable goal, suggested the staff, would be the establishment of cutoffs making 30% of the city's academic high school graduates eligible for admission to the four-year colleges and a third of the city's academic *and vocational* high school graduates eligible for admission to the community colleges. Of course, not all of these students would attend, but establishment of such an eligibility pool would allow City University "to provide high quality instruction suitable to the various levels of ability of those persons who have a reasonable expectation of success in their education beyond the high school."[11]

Thus, two master plans issued twelve years apart came to the same general conclusions. If the Cottrell Report could be ignored because the crisis it predicted would take place a decade later, the Report of the Committee to Look to the Future made it clear that increased academic selectivity should no longer be opted for at the expense of expansion.

By 1962, the question of exclusiveness was not the BHE's only problem in the area of admissions policies. Major racial and ethnic changes were taking place in the city's population, and these changes were not reflected in the student bodies of the municipal colleges. In a period of increased concern with civil rights and equality of opportunity, this growing imbalance could not be ignored.

ETHNICITY, RACE, AND PUBLIC HIGHER EDUCATION IN NEW YORK CITY

"The student population [of CCNY] has always reflected the tendencies of the population of the city at large," wrote the author of a history of City

College. Almost from the time of its founding, New Yorkers perceived CCNY
as an important vehicle for upward mobility. Until the beginning of the
twentieth century, the majority of CCNY students had been middle class,
native born Protestants. A sizable number of Jews of German descent began
to appear in the last decades of the nineteenth century, and, after the lifting
of a prohibition on admission of private and parochial school graduates in the
1880s, they were joined by many Catholic students.[12]

A substantial shift in the City College student body occurred at the turn of
the century with the admission of large numbers of East European and Russian Jews. As early as 1903, they constituted perhaps 75% of all students. If
anything, this percentage increased over the next three decades. In the thirties and forties, as the percentage of Italian-Americans, blacks, and Latin
Americans in the city's high schools increased, their representation in the
CCNY student body also increased.[13]

During the years after World War II, the general concern over barriers to
higher education led some to perceive that the municipal colleges might not
be absorbing students from new ethnic and racial groups as quickly as before.
"It is interesting to observe," wrote Donald Cottrell, "that so-called 'problem
neighborhoods'—those which have a high proportion of crime, juvenile delin-
quency, truancy and other undesirable characteristics—are much below the
average of the City in percentage of population who have had some post-high
school education."[14] The BHE's concern for exclusiveness, rather than a purposefully discriminatory policy, probably created the problem. Cottrell believed that his proposed expansion of the municipal colleges would lead to
attendance of students from these neighborhoods in substantial numbers. He
based this belief on past performance. Students from similar neighborhoods
had been accommodated by CCNY in the past and, most probably, many
"capable and desirous" members of these newer groups were among those
denied admission by the failure of the municipal colleges to expand.

This belief in "automatic incorporation" would be strongly challenged in
the coming years. During the 1950s, a major demographic revolution took
place within New York City. While the city's population remained constant
during that decade, about a million blacks and Puerto Ricans replaced the
same number of whites who moved to the suburbs or out of the area completely. The social profiles of the city's high school graduates and its municipal college students did not reflect this change. Throughout the fifties, the
percentage of nonwhites among the city's high school graduates remained
constant at 13%; nonwhite enrollment at the municipal colleges remained at
5%. Further, although these colleges admitted roughly 20% of New York
City's high school graduates, nonwhites constituted only 1% of the high
school graduates admitted.[15]

The Committee to Look to the Future gave scant attention to the under-representation of blacks and Puerto Ricans at the municipal colleges. Not only did the Committee envision no positive steps to remedy this situation, it actually modified its enrollment projections *downward* since the increasing proportion of the high school population composed of nonwhites did not appear to attend college at the same rate as whites. No one suggested the modification of admissions policies to increase the percentage of nonwhites; such a suggestion would have been dismissed immediately as reintroducing discriminatory mechanisms that had been outlawed by the state fifteen years before. But in the New York City of the mid-1960s, the problem of race and education proved volatile. Leaders of the civil rights movement perceived that education could provide a major route out of the ghetto, but that admission of representative numbers of nonwhites to the municipal colleges would not be automatic.

The two problems of numbers and race, although distinct, became increasingly related. Even if New York's population had been all white, the city's economy would have required additional college-trained workers. Both the Cottrell Report and the Report of the Committee to Look to the Future assumed there existed a sufficient supply of capable individuals to meet the demand if the municipal colleges would only undertake to educate them. But the presence of an increasing proportion of nonwhites who were not making their way through the educational system placed this assumption in doubt. Albert Bowker, who became Chancellor of the City University of New York shortly after issuance of the Report of the Committee to Look to the Future, took alarm at this trend, and resolved that positive steps would have to be taken to avoid both an economic and a social disaster in New York City. But Bowker knew that such steps would be difficult to implement, given the conservative nature of the BHE and its Chairman, Gustave Rosenberg.

BOARD OF HIGHER EDUCATION, ROSENBERG, AND BOWKER

Although the legislation creating the Board of Higher Education had given it authority to coordinate the activities of the municipal colleges, the Board preferred to allow them to develop autonomously. It conceived its own principal task to be the consideration of those routine matters which happened to concern more than one college. Criticism of the BHE's inattention to major policy considerations led it to establish in 1946 an Administrative Council, composed of the presidents of each of the municipal colleges.[16] The Council successfully coped with the many short-run problems that emerged just after World War II, but it did not succeed in removing many routine items from the BHE's agenda.

The Board's lack of attention to broad policy questions can be attributed to a pragmatic conservatism. "[The] College Trustees Board is a sort of Preparation School for Supreme Court Judgeships and other high salaried offices," wrote an early twentieth century observer.[17] The BHE had its share of judicial aspirants when it replaced the CCNY Board. As a result, it hesitated to undertake projects that might alienate the city's major political factions. Expansion would be implemented only in response to a demonstrable, immediate need, and then only when it could be accomplished without harm to the city's capital budget.

The social and economic backgrounds of the Board members reinforced this conservative thrust. As late as 1963, the year of Albert Bowker's appointment as Chancellor, the average age of the twenty men and four women to serve on the Board at some time during the year was 68; their average tenure on the Board was 13 years. Racially, the BHE included twenty-two whites and two blacks. (the first Puerto Rican would be appointed the following year). The three major religions were represented in roughly equal numbers. Democrats comprised a majority, reflecting the political affiliation of the mayors who had appointed most of them. The Board's 1963 membership included eight lawyers; other members came from such professions as banking, medicine, business, and public relations. Two academicians and three "volunteer-housewives" also served. Significantly, very few BHE members had attended the municipal colleges; most had studied at private institutions. Their upper middle class career patterns plus their elitist educations led them to provide a narrow answer to the question of who should go to college.

In many ways, Gustave Rosenberg, the Chairman of the Board of Higher Education from the mid-1950s to the mid-1960s, personified these general characteristics. Born in New York in 1900, Rosenberg was an attorney and a lifelong Democrat active in local politics. Appointed to the Board by Mayor Impelliteri in 1952, he became its chairman five years later. Like some other Board members, Rosenberg aspired to a judgeship. In 1961 he was defeated in an elective judicial contest when a split within the Democratic Party forced him to run on the Liberal Party line. After suffering a second defeat in 1965, he finally achieved his goal two years later with his appointment to fill a vacancy on the State Supreme Court. Later he would be appointed to the Court of Claims.

Rosenberg found the BHE a useful device for the furthering of his political career since it gave him considerable visibility as well as access to important public officials. He continued the Board's tradition of undertaking no long-range planning—even the report issued by the Committee to Look to the Future had been produced only in response to the requirements of a recently passed state law. Rosenberg personally attended to the day-to-day administration of systemwide problems, a practice that created considerable friction after the appointment of the system's first chancellor in 1960.

In 1955, after a decade of haggling, the BHE and the Administrative Council finally agreed to the creation of the administrative entity to be known as the City University of New York, and to the creation of the office of Chancellor of the University. The resolution creating the office stated that its occupant would be the chief *educational* officer of the municipal college system, the presiding officer of the Administrative Council, the officer responsible for preparation of the University's operating and capital budgets, a representative to outside agencies, administrator of overall *Board* policies, and the supervisor of a staff to prepare reports on policy matters.[18]

After the city government ratified creation of the chancellor's office in 1957, the BHE permitted the Administrative Council to nominate its first occupant, probably in the expectation that it would choose one of its own members. Two years later, the Council had still to be heard from. The Board, wishing no further delay, proceeded to conduct its own search. In June, 1960, a Committee on the Chancellor recommended the appointment of John Rutherford Everett as CUNY's first Chancellor, effective September, 1960.

Everett served a short and unhappy tenure as chancellor. Some critics charged that he did not have the temperament to deal with his assigned duties, nor to cope with the sometimes conflicting demands of the BHE and the Administrative Council. Most important, Everett found himself unable to function as the University's chief *administrative* officer, a function retained by Rosenberg. In 1962, Everett resigned to assume the position of Director of the New School for Social Research.

Before a new chancellor was chosen, the Administrative Council expressed its concern to the Board that any person it might appoint would soon find himself as frustrated as Everett unless the BHE recognized the new appointee as "a professional administrator," with his professional responsibility not "qualified or limited through the exercise of administrative prerogatives by any person or agency outside the Administrative Council." Although the Council expressed concern that an "iron chancellor" might "stultify our undergraduate institutions to a point of mediocrity and reduce their presidents to the status of geographically assigned deans," the Everett affair made it more concerned that another weak chancellor would reduce the University to the status of a "legal fiction with a figurehead chancellor."

The Council also hinted that Rosenberg had usurped the legitimate powers of the Board as well as the legitimate powers of the Chancellor. "The powers of the Board," it said, "are by law vested in the Board of Higher Education as a corporate entity and not as individual members." This implied that each member of the Board had an equal right to information and an equal say on any matter worthy of the Board's attention. It reminded the members that "no single member can act for the Board except as the Board may authorize."

The Council chided the Board for its preoccupation with detail. "The present agenda of the Board might be compared to that of a board of directors of a bank whose officers insisted on passing in review every cancelled check as proof of the integrity of the bank's operations." "The full concern of the Board," the Council concluded, "is with the establishment of policies; and after that with being assured that the policies are rightly and effectively administered."[19] After issuing this set of warnings, the Administrative Council eagerly awaited the appointment of the City University's next chancellor.

Its choice, Stanford's graduate school Dean Albert Hosmer Bowker, had gained exposure as a BHE consultant on current trends in graduate education during planning for a CUNY graduate division intended primarily to alleviate the city's serious teacher shortage. Bowker, said Rosenberg, "gave promise that he grasped our problems and purposes." Since it was widely assumed that the chancellor would be devoting most of his time to graduate education Bowker had been thought of as a possible successor to Everett all along. All sides applauded Bowker's acceptance of the Board's formal offer in 1963. "Dr. Bowker as a scholar and organizer stood out as best suited to building the great university which the board envisions," commented the BHE chairman. The Administrative Council noted that "really fine advanced graduate programs offered in the name of the university as a single entity, and leading to university doctoral degrees, require at least a limited type of central direction operating from a base of real authority." Privately, its members resolved to see that Bowker would get this authority.[20]

BOWKER VS ROSENBERG

Although hired because of his expertise in graduate education, Chancellor Bowker soon became deeply involved with the two major problems confronting CUNY's undergraduate divisions—numbers and race. His liberal answer to the question "Who should go to college?" led him to a confrontation with Chairman Rosenberg in 1965. His determination to take special steps to equalize opportunity for black and Puerto Rican New Yorkers made the City University the scene of a much greater confrontation in 1969.

Bowker's first exposure to the effects of the BHE's chronic shortsightedness came in 1964 when the Board failed to anticipate the additional demands on facilities created by the first influx of postwar babies. At the last moment it met the crisis by implementing "Operation Shoehorn," which squeezed into each college a number of students significantly in excess of each plant's intended capacity. Bowker and the Administrative Council resolved that planning for the next major increase in student enrollments, due in the late sixties, would be begun far in advance.

Bowker's plans for this new wave of students included increasing the proportion of the city's high school graduates who would be eligible for admission to at least one senior college. During the early sixties, the percentage of students so eligible hovered at about 23%. The City University's 1964 Master Plan envisioned an ultimate increase in this proportion to 33%.[21] But given increasingly larger high school graduating classes, Bowker concluded that a more realistic percentage for the immediate future would be 25%. The BHE's approval of the Master Plan committed it to such an expansion, but again Bowker became convinced of its unwillingness to implement that commitment.

Bowker's frustration with the Board's shortsightedness matched his frustration with the limitations Chairman Rosenberg had imposed on his authority. In April of 1965, the Chancellor decided that in this deteriorated situation he had no choice but to present a bill of particulars to the entire Board. Bowker accused Rosenberg of restricting his access to government officials and agencies, citing specifically his refusal to allow the chancellor to consult with the budget director of the city administration. He accused Rosenberg of monopolizing communications with the media. Last, he complained of inadequate access to the various committees of the Board as well as to its individual members.[22] It is not clear what action the Board took in response to Bowker's complaint, but judging from subsequent events, any steps taken were insufficient.[23]

During the summer of 1965, Bowker and his aides considered various alternative methods of raising the capital funds necessary to undertake a major expansion of City University. They concluded that the most likely source of such funding would be the state government. State support for the municipal colleges had been negligible until 1961, when it began to provide increased funding for the State University system as well as for CUNY. By 1965, state support for CUNY exceeded city support for the first time.[24]

In September, Bowker submitted a memorandum concerning long-range planning to all members of the Board. Cautioning that construction lead times required rapid decisions concerning financing to avoid a repetition of the "Shoehorn" fiasco, Bowker suggested that the BHE lobby for additional state aid. He proposed two specific plans. Under the more "modest" proposal, the Board would request complete state financing for CUNY's doctoral programs, a revision in CUNY's favor of the formula for funding of teacher training, and the equal sharing of the costs of operating the four-year colleges by New York State and New York City. He also submitted "A Somewhat Bolder Proposal."

This would have the State assume the total operating budget of the components of the City University other than the community colleges. By nominally imposing tuition (but in actuality retaining the substance of our present free tuition policy by a combination of Mayoral Scholarships and State Scholar Incentive Plan), we would reduce the operational costs to the City of the units affected to less than $10 million; the sums collected as tuition, applied to the State Dormitory Authority Program, would finance a $400 million capital budget for the senior colleges and divisions without any significant outlay by the City.[25]

Rosenberg's treatment of Bowker's proposals at the Board's October 25, 1965 meeting proved the ultimate frustration. Bowker later recounted his version of what took place.

At the Board meeting of October 25, 1965, the Chancellor displayed charts showing in graphic form some of the problems which the City University faces as it approaches the critical years ahead. The Chancellor presented his preliminary discussion; instead of allowing and encouraging Board members to discuss this vital problem freely, to ask questions, and to get the advice of the Chancellor and the presidents present, the Chairman sent up to his office for a chart which had been prepared for his personal use. This chart lauded the achievements of the Board under his leadership for the past eight years. With this display of past action, devoid of any reference to future needs, he closed the discussion and called for the next item of the agenda.[26]

At this point, Bowker decided that further efforts to prod the Board to address the questions of planning and of the relationship of the chairman to the chancellor would be pointless. Within a few days, the public received the first inkling that something was amiss at City University.

GOING PUBLIC

In deciding to air the dispute in public, Bowker had the support of the members of the Administrative Council.[27] On November 6, three days after the election of John V. Lindsay as mayor of New York, President Meng of Hunter College publicly suggested imposition of tuition fees on CUNY students as a method of avoiding increased budgetary dependence on the state. Shortly thereafter, President Gallagher of CCNY publicly spelled out the details of the planning problem and suggested imposition of a "theoretical" $400 per semester tuition fee—the same suggestion made in Bowker's "Somewhat Bolder Proposal."

Both men later claimed their tuition proposals were taken out of context and that the real point of their remarks was to call attention to the need for expansion. However, the presidents had struck a deep nerve. In reality, "student fees" already comprised perhaps a fifth of CUNY's income, but most New Yorkers believed the *principle* of free tuition at the municipal colleges was an important guarantor of opportunity. A number of interested groups denounced the presidents' remarks, including alumni and politicians. Students threatened a permanent strike upon the imposition of tuition and made plans for a six-hour teach-in on the virtues of free tuition. Rosenberg expressed "shock" at the presidents' statements and commented, "I think that a matter such as this which involved a fundamental change in policy should come from the Board."[28] Of course, he had the benefit of Bowker's proposals and of his elaboration at the October 25 Board meeting. His shock probably came from Bowker's willingness to make his proposal public.

By the time that Bowker released the full text of his proposals on November 11, the furor created by the tuition issue led him and the Administrative Council to conclude that the public's attention had been deflected from the real issue—the need "to hasten the completion of our desperately needed construction program."[29] Bowker told the Council that he would recommend to the BHE "as part of any financing plan adopted, the maintenance of free tuition in all of the colleges of the University." The Council decided to adopt an alternate proposal that would have involved increased city funding of the CUNY capital budget.

A few days later, the BHE held an emergency meeting, not to discuss the question of capital construction, but to rebuke the chancellor and the presidents for taking their grievances to the public. At the meeting, the Board reaffirmed its commitment to free tuition at the City University, and expressed regret that recent unauthorized public statements led some to believe that the Board had changed its policy. Finally, it warned that it "has a right to expect undivided fealty on the part of all its officers of administration to the policies and by-laws of the Board, irrespective of any other position they may hold."[30]

Bowker decided that in light of this last resolution he had no recourse but to offer his resignation. "When the chief administrative officer of a university finds," he wrote in his letter of resignation, "that, however unjustifiably, his board of trustees has manifested a lack of confidence in him, it is my judgment that his real usefulness to the university is at an end, and he should resign."[31] Several presidents immediately supported Bowker's decision. Gideonese of Brooklyn College and Meng announced their retirements, while Harry Levy, Bowker's dean of Studies, resigned from that position. In his letter of resignation, Gideonese wrote, "Fealty is a medieval concept and it describes the position of a medieval lord in his relation to his feudal serfs. Members of the Board of Higher Education are not medieval lords—and I am not inclined to become a serf."[32]

The majority of the Board did not expect its November 17 actions to precipitate these resignations and retirements. At the Board's regular monthly meeting of November 22, it extended an olive branch to the chancellor and his supporters. The Board explained that the only "fealty" asked of CUNY's educational officers was loyal cooperation in support of the Board's policies, and it regretted any misunderstanding of this sentiment. It reaffirmed its

desire to maintain open lines of communication between itself and the Administrative Council, and stated that Board decisions should be taken only
after "free and open" discussion with its educational officers. Finally it asked
the chancellor and the others to reconsider their decisions. In taking these
steps, the Board had done something virtually unprecedented: it invoked its
authority to overrule its chairman. Rosenberg and three close associates voted
no on the peace feeler.[33]

In the public's eye, the issue still appeared to be free tuition. Rosenberg
was not disposed to alter the public's perception. Just after public announcement of Bowker's resignation, Rosenberg told the *New York Times*, "President
Meng . . . made an address . . . which went to the press and was widely
interpreted as immediately calling into serious question the continuation of
the free tuition policy of this board and of the municipal colleges. . . . Beyond this, I am aware of no difference between President Meng and the
Board."[34] He would later state, "Some educators have begun to say that 'the
free tuition issue is a sham.' The only sham I see is in the semantics used in
pretending that the establishment of the principle of a tuition charge is not
the disestablishment of the principle of no tuition charge."[35]

The public learned the other side to the story when State Senator Manfred
Ohrenstein, chairman of the State Legislature's Joint Legislative Committee
for Higher Education, conducted a series of hearings to ascertain the facts of
the dispute. During the hearings, Mary Ingraham, a long-time member of
the Board, testified, "We have a lot to thank Mr. Rosenberg for," but added,
"there is a serious need to clarify the relations between the board and the
administrators." Ruth Shoup, the only Board member to oppose the "fealty"
resolutions, was more blunt. She charged that the chairman had made decisions for the Board on his own or with a small group of members and that the
Board had been placed in a position of being "an assenting audience."[36]

The *New York Times* editorialized that by his testimony to the Ohrenstein
Committee, Rosenberg exhibited "a depressing failure to comprehend the
basic issue of the crisis. That issue is the precarious financial condition of the
City University. Instead of admitting the dilemma, Mr. Rosenberg stressed
his Board's past achievements and implied that there was no reason for alarm
about the future." Although the *Times* had been critical of Bowker's stance
during November, it admitted that his actions "can now be more readily
understood in light of Mr. Rosenberg's testimony. The frustrations which the
Board permitted to build are largely responsible for the administrators' des-
perate and injudicious actions."[37]

Sensing that both the Board and the chancellor wished to pull back from
the brink, Mayor Robert Wagner dispatched his aide Julius Edelstein to
mediate a final settlement.[38] Bowker and Levy offered to withdraw their
resignations if certain immediate steps were taken, including access by the

chancellor to all government officials short of the mayor and the governor, transfer of the public relations staff from the chairman's to the chancellor's control, and permission for the chancellor to attend all subsequent BHE meetings. Pending revision of the BHE's by-laws, mediation of all jurisdictional disputes would be undertaken by a five-member commission appointed by the Board.[39] Mutually acceptable interim procedures (including establishment of a Committee to Devise Remedies Against Future Misunderstandings) were implemented and Bowker withdrew his resignation.[40] Bowker considered early drafts of the Board's proposed by-law revisions unacceptable, mainly because they did not incorporate his insistence that the chancellor be henceforth described as "the chief educational *and administrative* officer of the City University of New York *and the chief administrative officer for the Board of Higher Education.*" When the Board finally offered to revise its draft to describe the chancellor's role in precisely those terms, Bowker agreed and the immediate crisis ended.[41]

Shortly after completion of his hearings, Senator Ohrenstein proposed that the state increase its contribution to the City University's operating costs and that the necessary funds for capital construction be raised by the issuance of bonds by the New York State Dormitory Authority. Despite the endorsement of the legislative form of Ohrenstein's plan by Assembly Speaker Anthony Travia, the bill languished for several months. Bowker believed that immediate passage was essential if needed facilities were to be ready in time for the enrollment bulge predicted for the late sixties. In April, 1966, when passage of the legislation still did not appear imminent, Bowker announced that 2300 high school graduates who would normally have been admitted to the four-year colleges (based on the standards of the previous year) would have to be rejected unless the construction legislation were passed. Even if emergency space could be found for these students during their freshman year, the chancellor reasoned that current facilities were inadequate to accommodate them during their junior and senior years.[42] Bowker's announcement had the intended effect, and heightened public concern was translated into legislative progress. The Assembly finally passed the bill on June 22, 1966; the Senate followed on July 1. The City University ultimately admitted all students qualified for admission under the previously existing criteria.[43]

That fall, Bowker recommended the accelerated development of previously proposed new units of the University and provision for additional students in four-year colleges through the rental of space and the construction of new facilities. On October 24, 1966, almost exactly a year after the Board meeting that precipitated the crisis, the BHE approved Bowker's specific suggestions for the opening of a new four-year college (subsequently known as York College) a year ahead of schedule, the establishment of an experimental freshman program under the auspices of the CUNY Graduate Center, and the enrollment of an additional 3000 students in the four-year colleges according to an allocation formula to be devised.[44]

During the months of delicate negotiations with the Board, Bowker convinced it to redefine its goals for the University in broader terms. At its meeting of February 28, 1966, the BHE announced that the goal of City University would henceforth be "to offer the benefits of post-high school education to all residents of New York City who are able and eager to avail themselves of such benefits." This general statement was backed with a proposal aimed at offering admission to some unit of the University to all the city's high school graduates by 1975. This would be accomplished by the planned expansion of the senior colleges so that they would continue to offer admission to the top 25% of all high school graduates, and by the expansion of the community colleges so that they would provide "post high school education for all young people of college age whose qualifications are not such as to admit them under present arrangements."[45] Specifically, the next 50% of high school graduates would be offered admission to the community colleges. The remaining 25% would be accepted by Educational Skills Centers, which would offer "a number of different but integrated programs to answer the needs of many New Yorkers who seek occupational skills."[46] This 100% Admissions Plan was fairly well received by the New York press. The *Times* commented that California appeared to be successful in a similar effort and that the plan would not threaten the standards of the City University: "The excellence of the senior colleges would be preserved but without barricades against extending educational opportunities at every level."[47]

Given the nature of the changes taking place at City University, changes in the BHE's composition did not come unexpectedly. Soon after Bowker's resumption of his duties as chancellor, Abraham Feinberg, an ally of Rosenberg, submitted his resignation. Calling Bowker a "heartless and ruthless and power-hungry Chancellor," he charged that "all that has been built in over one hundred years is in jeopardy." The hands-off attitude expressed by Mayor Lindsay in the two months since he replaced Wagner indicated to Feinberg that "he will continue to allow a rabid group, led by the Chancellor, further to deteriorate the status of the City University and further to endanger its existence as an independent entity granting free tuition to all who qualify."[48]

Rosenberg's own days were numbered. It had been apparent all along that either he or Bowker had to go. When the Board decided to ask Bowker to return, it became only a matter of permitting Rosenberg to save face. After passage of legislation creating the City University Construction Fund, Rosenberg was appointed to head it. Bowker protested until informed that in exchange for the appointment Rosenberg promised to resign from the Board. Upon his appointment to the State Supreme Court in January, 1967, Rosenberg completely severed his relationship to City University.

BOWKER AND THE PROBLEM
OF RACIAL INCLUSION

By 1966, City University had committed itself to offer in 1975 some form of postsecondary education to all graduates of New York City high schools. But as Bowker became better acquainted with the status of public education in New York City, he realized that even such a commitment would be insufficient. "If we look at areas of poverty in New York City," he wrote in 1964, "we find major erosion of the schools. We find high schools with only twenty or thirty graduates with academic diplomas, and other factors which could lead us to say that higher education is an unrealizable aspiration for many." Bowker considered such an attitude "destructive for the City of New York and for the individuals involved." The faster the white middle class fled the city, the more it became dependent on the increasing proportion of nonwhites who remained. But precisely these citizens derived the least benefit from the schools. Bowker concluded that a massive upgrading of the public schools was necessary, and that the City University could be of direct service. "But most of all," he said, "the school and college must say to these youngsters that they are expected to succeed and there will be opportunities for them beyond high school. The places for freshmen must be there."[49]

Bowker conceived the mission of City University to be the provision of higher education for all those who knocked at its door, and also the seeking out of those who refrained from knocking, but who might profit from higher education. Like any good missionary, Bowker asked students in the latter category for an act of faith—faith in themselves that they could succeed, and faith in the City University that such success would be meaningful. During his tenure as chancellor, Bowker took a number of initiatives designed to reward that faith.

In 1963, Bowker returned from his first pilgrimage to Albany with a promise of $500,000 for a small experimental admissions program. Under the terms of the College Discovery Program, disadvantaged students would be admitted to various units of the City University on the basis of their principal's recommendation instead of on their high school averages or their composite scores. On learning of Bowker's intention of circumventing the regular admissions process, some BHE members voiced bitter objections. Bowker called justifiable the use of nontraditional methods of admission, since the traditional criteria did not unearth nonwhite students with college abilities. "There are . . . young men and women," he said, "who because of economic deprivation and lack of expectation of opportunity which surround them in their home environment, do not rank high in academic achievement despite their native abilities; in large measure, these are adolescents in what have been called 'pockets of poverty.'" When objections persisted, Bowker informed Rosenberg that he would resign unless the Board sanctioned his program. After some discussion, the Board gave Bowker the approval he sought.[50]

The program permitted each high school in the city to make two nominations, and allotted extra nominations to ghetto high schools. Besides the recommendation of the principal or guidance counselor, an applicant had to have completed at least twelve units of secondary school work (with exceptions) and had to come from a family with an income below $1700 per family member. A final screening limited the number of admitted students to the number of places provided for in the budget.[51]

CDP did not have a special curriculum. Instead, various community colleges received the students and assigned them a limited program from the regular curriculum until they felt more at ease in the college environment. More than 40% of those who entered CDP were blacks, about 25% Puerto Ricans, and less than 20% were whites. Almost 27% of the 760 students who began the program in either 1964 or 1965 received their Associate of Arts degree by the spring of 1968. Among those who left the program, some entered a regular college program and a considerable number continued to attend the community college to which they had been assigned on a part-time nonmatriculated basis. Personal difficulties, responsibilities at home, job demands, and financial pressures were the most frequently cited reasons for leaving the program.[52]

A second "prong" of CDP was initiated in 1965. Guidance counselors or others in community action or social welfare programs nominated ninth-grade students showing potential for enrollment in high school development centers. At these centers, students followed intensive college preparatory courses, featuring small classes, double periods in basic subjects, tutors, guidance, and a small stipend for incidental expenses. More than three-quarters of those who entered the program during its first years completed the course and were admitted to either a community or a senior college.[53]

Later in 1966, the same Legislature that established CUNY's $400 million construction fund established and funded, at the behest of black legislators and with the covert sponsorship of the chancellor, the SEEK program. Search for Education, Elevation, and Knowledge was designed to place high school graduates from officially designated poverty areas into special programs at the senior colleges. Most SEEK students did not meet the normal criteria for admission to the senior colleges, and many had not even taken an academic course in high school. The program featured a special curriculum that integrated remedial work with regular college offerings. Most SEEK courses featured more contact hours per week than did regular courses covering the same subject matter. In addition, individual tutoring was available. Well over half the full-time students in SEEK achieved passing grades during its first two years. About 10% had averages of B or better.[54]

Several aspects of SEEK and CDP disturbed various groups at CUNY. Many faculty members resented imposition of the SEEK program on the University by the State Legislature. Once established, SEEK students and faculty began to press for full autonomy over their program, while many thought the program already too autonomous. Some white students resented admission of nonwhites who did not have to meet the admissions criteria in force for everyone else. As these programs expanded, and as new programs were established to supplement them, this resentment increased dangerously.

PRELUDE TO CONFRONTATION:
THE 1968 ADMISSIONS CONTROVERSY

The 1967–68 academic year began quietly. The CUNY construction program had gone beyond the planning stage and there was general optimism that new facilities could be opened in time to meet the increases in enrollments expected in each of the next several years. In the fall of 1967, the media gave City University's plans considerable publicity. After several years of discomfort, the general theme ran, greater numbers of CUNY students would be accommodated in expanded facilities. "The chances that these students will get into schools of their choice next September are held to be the best in years." said *U.S. News and World Report*. "If anything, City University will try to drive down admissions requirements despite an expected increase in applications of more than 5000," reported the *New York Post*.[55]

Thus when several months later chancellor Bowker announced that budgetary considerations had forced the University to establish a series of cutoff points *higher* than those of 1967, considerable protest ensued. A student newspaper quoted a Brooklyn College registrar as calling it "irresponsible" to raise the requirements for admission after applications had been filed: "The students couldn't make a value judgment about which branch of CUNY to apply to since they were given erroneous information about what the cut-off points would be." Specific reference was made to an information booklet for applicants which implied that the 1968 cutoff points would be the same as those of 1967.[56]

The Chancellor's Office, which for the previous several years had tried to emphasize the eligibility of anyone with an 82% average for admission to a senior college, made known the fine print: "We do not decide each year what high school averages shall be required. Rather, we rank all applicants and admit them until all available places are filled, with students with higher grades and test scores considered first. While the grades and test scores of the last student admitted to each program can therefore be considered to be the 'admissions requirement' for that program, they are determined *after* matching the number of applicants to the number of seats available rather than before." Between 1967 and 1968, the secondary school averages of applicants had increased, and thus the cutoff scores for most, but not all divisions, had increased. The argument that Baruch College had accepted all applicants with an 82% average did not appease the many students with averages over 82% who had not applied to Baruch and who had been rejected from those divisions to which they did apply.[57]

The common knowledge that special efforts were being made to accommodate additional students into CDP and SEEK exacerbated resentment over CUNY's handling of the situation. The BHE purposefully gave no publicity to impending admission of students into these special programs but, when word of this practice got out, its representatives reassured concerned citizens that such admittance came in addition to regular student acceptances.[58] Those students, mainly white, who saw themselves as victims of unmerited favoritism to nonwhites, remained unconvinced.

Bowker knew he was treading on thin political ice by emphasizing minority enrollments at just this time, but he felt he had little choice. The assassination of Martin Luther King in early April had increased racial tension, which manifested itself at CUNY in demonstrations and sit-ins at several campuses. Although numerically small, the black and Puerto Rican students on the various campuses often molded themselves into a forceful political unit, and sometimes enlisted the support of key faculty members.

Bowker's responsiveness to these students' demands stemmed from his conviction that the City University's efforts in the area of nonwhite student recruitment were still insufficient. CUNY's Ethnic Census revealed that such students still did not gain admission in proportion to their representation in the city's high school graduating class.[59] Further, if it had not been for the SEEK Program, the percentage of nonwhite enrollment in the senior colleges would have *declined* from 6.1% to 4.7% between 1967 and 1968, and the total nonwhite enrollment at CUNY would have declined from 8.9% to 8.0%.[60]

Bowker concluded that the traditional methods of admission could not be counted on to insure additional minority student enrollment, and therefore undertook an intensive effort to convince the BHE to create yet more special programs. By midsummer, 1968, his effort had paid off. The Board concluded that social inequities, injustices, and frustrations had resulted in heightened intergroup tension, and specifically that the need for college education for high school graduates from deprived neighborhoods was "a social danger requiring our immediate attention." It proclaimed "the historic mission of the public college system of New York City . . . to provide expanding educational opportunities, particularly for those whose backgrounds of social, educational and economic disadvantage clearly identify them as most needful of the special concern and assistance of the City University." Finally, it resolved that "the maximum use of the resources, capabilities and creative capacities of the City University be mobilized and focused on this mission which must be given one of the highest priorities among all the undergraduate missions of the City University."[61]   It approved two specific steps to take effect when classes resumed the following month. First, it offered admission to some unit of the City University to any student among the top 100 graduates of each city high school not already admitted by some other mechanism. Second, it upgraded the SEEK program by raising SEEK students from part-time to full-time matriculated status and by identifying it as a five-year program, thus permitting remedial work to be counted toward full-time status. The BHE also recommended that units of the City University directly administer five New York City public high schools (one in each borough) to obviate the need for remedial work at college by assuring adequate secondary training. This last recommendation elicited little enthusiasm among the city's educational establishment and was never implemented.[62]

Immediately after the Board took these actions, CUNY's admissions office set to work to recruit students into the Top 100 Scholars Program in time for the fall semester. It offered each eligible student admission to a senior college and offered most students admission to a SEEK program. Since many eligible students had already been admitted to CUNY or to some other college and since a number of high schools did not have 100 graduates, the actual pool of students who might be affected by the program was about 800. One hundred and fifty-four students were actually recruited and assigned to various units of the City University. Most of these had been graduated from the city's ghetto high schools. About 40% of those admitted were Puerto Rican (or students with Spanish surnames), 32% were black, and 29% were whites or others. At a time when the cutoff points for admission to the senior colleges had risen from 82%, more than three-quarters of those students admitted under the Top 100 Scholars Program had averages between 70% and 80%.[63]

Adoption of this program so soon after the problems of the previous spring brought a barrage of criticism on Bowker and the BHE. Some did not read the fine print and interpreted the Board's action as admitting the Top 100 Blacks and Puerto Ricans. Others charged that the Board had established a quota system and cited in evidence the Board's request that the chancellor report on the progress toward "the end that minority groups shall be represented in the units of the University in the same proportion as they are represented among all high school graduates of the City."[64] Many argued that if additional places had been available at CUNY's senior colleges, they should have been filled by students next on the list of rankings under the normal criteria for admission.

Procedural criticism also came from the City University Senate, which had just been established during the 1967–68 academic year, on the grounds that it should have been consulted in advance of adoption of any resolutions. That fall, the Senate gave consideration to CUNY's admissions policy and concluded, "the present admissions criteria coupled with the inadequacies of most ghetto high schools, have been keeping out of the University many black and Puerto Rican young men and women who have the ability to absorb and build upon a college education." It ratified the BHE's recent initiatives, called for additional experimental programs, for expansion of SEEK and CDP, and for greater university influence over the city's high schools. Finally, the Senate criticized the Board for not carrying its reforms far enough. The problem with those reforms, said its report, "is not that they would admit large numbers of students with severe educational deficiencies, but rather that they largely ignore the necessity for concomitant changes in the colleges, to meet the needs of these students." In the long run, however, the Senate's stance was not significant for its criticisms, but for its support of policies that many other faculties would have steadfastly opposed.[65]

THE SOUTH CAMPUS SEIZURE

The assassination of Martin Luther King in April of 1968 began a year of heightened racial tension in New York City. The next fall, the United Federation of Teachers, which represented the city's public school teachers, struck against the policies in hiring and dismissal in effect at the Ocean Hill-Brownsville "demonstration school district." The charges of racism and anti-Semitism that had been made by the various sides in the dispute had barely disappeared from New York's newspapers when another crisis emerged at City University and raised racial tensions even further.

The reaction of New York's white majority to the BHE's announcement of the Top 100 Scholars Program had led Bowker to conclude that adoption of further policies that appeared to favor one group over another would place himself and the Board in a politically untenable situation. Thus, when it became apparent that both the city and the state governments would sharply reduce CUNY's proposed budget, Bowker had to develop a strategy to assure that any cutbacks would not disproportionately affect any group. Perhaps the only way City University could effect significant savings was by a cut in the size of its entering class. But cuts in the regular programs would further increase white student resentment of blacks and Puerto Ricans admitted under special programs. If CDP and SEEK were cut, black and Puerto Rican students would be equally resentful at a system that seemed to favor whites. Bowker therefore announced in March, 1969 that no freshman class would be admitted to the City University unless the state and the city provided funds that would permit the continuance of all CUNY programs.

This announcement stunned the present CUNY student population as well as those who had been momentarily expecting to receive their letters of acceptance to the University. The students responded as Bowker had hoped. Instead of infighting, they conducted massive demonstrations against the city and state governments in Harlem, at Governor Nelson Rockefeller's office in Manhattan, and in Albany.[66] This pressure brought first fruit on the state level. The enacted state budget provided $90 million for the City University, an increase of $9 million over 1968, although $20 million less than the University's request. Later that spring, the city also came up with adequate funding. But by that time Bowker's efforts to maintain internal unity had been doomed by the seizure by more than 150 black and Puerto Rican students of eight buildings on the South Campus of City College.[67]

Although it was not the first demonstration by black and Puerto Rican students during the spring, 1969 semester, the South Campus seizure was by far the largest. The newspapers first reported that the demonstrators demanded a "much larger percentage of Negroes and Puerto Ricans be admitted to the college."[68] Subsequently the demonstrators issued a list of five demands. The most important called for adoption of admissions criteria to assure that in the future the entering class at City College would reflect the racial composition of the city's high schools. The other demands included a separate black and Puerto Rican studies program, a separate freshman orientation for minority students, a greater student voice in the SEEK program, and a requirement that students preparing to become elementary schoolteachers at the City University take courses in black and Puerto Rican history and culture.

After consulting with members of his faculty, CCNY president Gallagher responded to the seizure by ordering the entire College closed and by assigning a faculty team to commence negotiations with the demonstrating students. After eleven days, three of the five demands seemed to have been settled. During this period the BHE approved Gallagher's handling of the situation, despite growing public criticism. In early May, Mario Procaccino, a candidate for the Democratic Party nomination for Mayor, obtained an order for the Board to show cause why the courts should not direct that CCNY be reopened. Although the order was not returnable for several days, Supreme Court Justice Edward McCaffery ordered the College opened in the interim.

Just before its required appearance in court, the BHE ordered CCNY's reopening and conditioned any further negotiations between demonstrators and official representatives on the vacating of the areas of the South Campus held by the students. The demonstrators vacated those areas on the next day, but attempted to reclose the campus several days later by conducting a series of "hit and run" disruptions. Violence between opposing factions of students occurred during these disruptions, just as Bowker feared. Gallagher ordered the campus closed again, but this time the Board's Executive Committee, after considerable debate, announced, "The majority of the Executive Committee, based on the action of the Board of Higher Education of May 4 [which reopened the campus], concluded that the Executive Committee could not close the college."[69]

At this point, President Gallagher, who had submitted his resignation during the recent budgetary crisis, made that resignation immediately effective. His statement made clear his sympathies with the demonstrators, his anger that politicians had exploited the confrontation for partisan advantage, and his distress that the Executive Committee's majority had overruled him.[70] Professor Joseph J. Copeland, who had been a member of Gallagher's faculty negotiating team, replaced him.

Police patrolled the CCNY campus as Copeland began his first day as president. Leaders of the student demonstrators conditioned any resumption of negotiations upon the removal of those police, a stipulation Copeland agreed to. Discussions began again on Saturday afternoon, May 17, and lasted until 3:00 A.M. on the morning of May 23. At that time, agreement was announced on a new mechanism of admission to CCNY by which half of each entering class would be admitted under the traditional criteria, while the other half would be admitted from poverty areas "without regard to grades." As a first step toward implementation of this dual admissions plan, 300 additional freshmen would be admitted in both of the following two semesters.

The terms of this agreement set off a political uproar. In an attempt to steal some headlines from Procaccino, former Mayor Robert Wagner and Congressman James Scheuer, both candidates for the Democratic mayoral nomination, denounced the plan. Herman Badillo, a Puerto Rican and yet another candidate for the Democratic nomination, stated that "implementation of such a policy would lead to two separate and unequal colleges of uncertain quality and would merely continue an extension of the educational disaster of the New York City public schools into the system of higher education, with no benefit to the children involved whether they be white, black, or Puerto Rican."[71] Mayor Lindsay at first issued a noncommittal statement in which he expressed support for efforts to provide additional opportunities for students from disadvantaged neighborhoods "provided they do not set up a quota system or violate the Board's pledge to admit all students with averages of 82 or higher." Two days later he announced that further study led him to conclude that the dual admissions plan was a "quota system" and that if necessary he would use the prerogatives of his office to thwart its implementation.[72] Of all the candidates for the mayoral nomination of the city's major parties, only the author, Norman Mailer, supported the proposal. The

CCNY Faculty Senate rejected the dual admissions proposal in favor of a more modest plan that would have admitted 300 additional freshmen in the fall, and another 100 the following spring. The 400 would have been admitted without regard to their academic performance in high school, and would have been chosen on the basis of "motivation, determination to undertake college work and other subjective evaluations of their suitability for higher education."[73] The Faculty Senate referred its plan to the Board of Higher Education which, as everyone knew, would have the final say.

OPEN ADMISSIONS:
THE ACCEPTABLE ALTERNATIVE

On the first evening of the South Campus seizure, Chancellor Bowker concluded that CUNY could not remain an arena for racial confrontations. For City University to continue to perform its mission, it would have to adopt an admissions policy that eliminated the competition between various groups for a limited number of places. He decided that immediate implementation of a 100% Admissions Plan was the only way to achieve significant minority inclusion, especially at the senior colleges, while assuring that such gains would come at minimal expense to the (mostly white) constituency already present.

Advocacy of such a plan by blacks and Puerto Ricans, the groups most adversely affected by the current admission system, came as no surprise to Bowker.[74] And it may not have come as much of a surprise to learn that such a proposal would have the support of many influential whites. Harry Van Arsdale, the powerful chairman of the city's Central Labor Council, opposed dual admissions at CCNY, but believed that the City University should be admitting more students. Not only blacks and Puerto Ricans, but many whites desirous of going to college achieved high school averages below the current cutoff points. Van Arsdale argued that in the working class homes of many such students the family income, although not much above the poverty level, was too high to meet SEEK and CDP criteria.[75] A lawyer for the Central Labor Council commented, "the people who are just a little bit more fortunate, those among us also need a lot of help and also need a lot of attention and also are crying out for the aid that you are responsible to give them."[76] Another member of the Central Labor Council made the same complaint and then asked, "Maybe there could be an open enrollment for all the kids in the City of New York?"[77] Other groups such as the City College Alumni Association, which opposed dual admissions, advocated adoption of open enrollment.[78] Bowker knew that such a plan meant pressuring City Hall and Albany for the necessary funding, but he also knew that a united City University had just been successful in resisting severe cuts on its budget.

The Board of Higher Education, which Bowker had to convince of the need for open admissions, was in the midst of a rapid turnover. By the fall of 1970, the implementation date of the new admissions plan, a majority of the Board had been appointed by Mayor Lindsay; in other words, they had not been on the Board at the time of the Bowker-Rosenberg confrontation. The average tenure of Board members had declined to four years, and the average age declined by almost 16 years. Members of the Board represented a broader spectrum of occupations. In 1970 it included two social workers, two clergymen, two public administrators, an artist, a student, and five academicians. More Board members, including some of the youngest, had been graduated from CUNY. Fewer could be identified by traditional political affiliations. Last, the Board included several black and Puerto Rican members who had been active in community affairs. Bowker believed that the Board's prior receptivity to his presentations on the problem of racial inclusion bode well for its acceptance of his new proposal.

At a meeting conducted during the South Campus seizure, the BHE had reaffirmed its commitment to implementation of the 1966 100% Admissions Policy "as a first priority." [79] In early July, after taking testimony from all interested parties, and after extensive discussions with Bowker and his staff, the Board committed itself to implementation of an Open Admissions Plan by the fall of 1970. The Board spelled out the specific objectives of the plan. Admission to some City University program would be offered to all New York City high school graduates. Remedial and supportive services would be supplied to all who needed them. Standards of academic excellence would be maintained. Ethnic integration of each unit would be achieved. Mobility between divisions would be provided for. Admission to a specific program and college would be guaranteed to those who would have been admitted to them under the old admissions criteria.

The Board charged the Commission on Admissions, which it had created during the spring, with recommending "a specific system of admissions criteria which will implement the preceding provisions, and which will also insure that each unit of the University is given significant responsibilities for preparing the academically less prepared student to engage in collegiate study." [80]

The commission understood that the stated goals of Open Admissions were potentially contradictory, but intended to gain the broadest support possible. It took its real task to be to devise a plan politically acceptable to all external groups and yet with enough educational rationale to gain acceptance by internal constituencies. It first decided that all applicants should be accepted either by the community colleges or by the senior colleges. Separate Skills Centers, envisioned in the 1966 100% Admissions Plan, would most likely be attended exclusively by blacks and Puerto Ricans—a violation of the Board's requirement of ethnic integration. The Committee recommended that long-run planning be undertaken for establishment of comprehensive colleges offering a diversity of programs of various lengths as a replacement or a supplement for the community colleges.

Admission to the senior colleges posed the commission's most important problem. The Board's mandate that all units share in the education of "the less prepared student" implied a change in their current admissions criteria. The Committee offered three alternative plans for admission based on the principles that "the primary determinant of student allocation should be student choice; that allocation to a college should reflect in some way the academic achievement of the applicants, and that 'integration' should be defined primarily in terms of attempting to equalize the ethnic distribution in the senior college freshman class and the community college freshman class."

The first of the three proposed options would have admitted most students on the basis of rank in the student's own high school; the remainder would have been admitted under SEEK criteria. The second would have admitted 60% of the freshman class on the basis of high school rank, 15% on the basis of SEEK criteria, and the remaining 25% on the basis of student choice, with a lottery to allocate places in cases of excessive demand. The third option would have admitted students by high school rank and SEEK criteria, but would have specifically assured that students previously admitted to specific senior and community colleges would still be so admitted. The Committee recommended that all students be guaranteed admission to the *program* they wanted, regardless of the unit to which they were assigned. Thus, a student admitted to a community college would be guaranteed access to a liberal arts program, if that was his wish.[81]

The first and second proposals largely aimed at achievement of ethnic integration of the senior colleges. Studies of the Top 100 Scholars Program indicated that the group deriving the greatest benefit from the use of rank in class were students with relatively low averages who were enrolled in high schools with very few graduates, or where most students who obtained diplomas did so with barely passing averages. Although some high schools fitting this description were located in working class white neighborhoods, most were in black and Puerto Rican ghettos. Most black and Puerto Rican spokesmen stated their preference for one of the first two options.

Opponents charged that the first and second proposals violated the Board's mandate to insure that all students who would have been guaranteed admission to a given college under the old admissions criteria would still have the same option. They argued that some form of the old criteria would therefore have to be retained. The white and especially the Jewish groups that commented on the Committee's proposals favored the third, or an alternative offered by CCNY Professor Harry Lustig that would have first admitted all students qualified under the traditional criteria, and then have admitted students on the basis of their high school ranking with 10% of the seats in each college set aside for "students to be selected by admissions counselors on the basis of their potential, motivation, professional objectives and the goal of ethnic integration," who did not qualify under any of the other criteria.[82]

Since the City University would be dependent for funding of Open Admissions on the city (and on the state), the Board decided to await the results of the city's mayoral election before adopting a final plan. Incumbent Mayor John Lindsay had been the first of the three major candidates to endorse the principle of Open Admissions. His opponents, Democratic nominee Mario Procaccino and Republican candidate John Marchi, followed suit later in the campaign. All three had urged that careful consideration be given to the method of implementation. When the Commission on Admissions announced its proposals, Procaccino and Marchi denounced all three. When Lindsay indicated that he supported the Lustig proposal over any of those in the Commission report, it became apparent to Bowker that to some extent at least the traditional admissions criteria would have to be preserved.

Once the Board knew that Lindsay had defeated his opponents, it set to work with the chancellor on a compromise plan that retained some use of class rank—something that would not have been possible if either Marchi or Procaccino had been victorious. "The use of rank in class," the Board argued, "evaluates the performance of students in competition with peers in their own high school, and provides college going motivation for students in each high school in the City. Data indicating the performance of students in the secondary schools in our City show that rank in class is an effective means of minimizing the differences in college opportunity now caused by great variances in the grading patterns of the different high schools." Under the Board's compromise plan, all applicants would be placed in one of ten admissions groupings. Each group contained all students with a given range of high school averages or with a certain high school rank. Each student would be assigned to the lowest numbered group to which he qualified.

Under the Board's plan, students in all groups would be admitted to the City University and students in Groups 1 through 5 would be guaranteed admission to a senior college. No student would be denied admission to a unit to which he or she would have been admitted before the implementation of Open Admissions. Preference for admission to a specific unit within the City University would be given to students in lower number groupings.[83]

Thus, the Board attempted to gain at least partial acceptance of the use of high school ranks by retaining academic average as an alternative criterion and by lowering the cutoff point for admission to some senior college from 82% to 80%. All concerned groups expressed approval of the plan at the time of its implementation.

Subsequently, various city departments and the New York State Board of

Regents approved the program, and the city agreed to match the state's contribution toward its funding. Final implementation turned on 'he agreement of Governor Rockefeller. The governor agreed to provide the state's share of funding for the program without making any demands in return, such as the imposition of tuition. His reasons were compelling. During his reelection campaign the following fall he would be asking for the votes of a city whose major interest groups had united behind the open admissions plan. His own State University had adopted a policy of gradual expansion and it would have been politically foolish to cut off funds for a similar, though more ambitious, downstate proposal. In short, Governor Rockefeller would have been marked as the political villain if Open Admissions had failed at that stage.

CONCLUSION

To a significant degree, the deficits of the black and Puerto Rican students are the result of inadequate preparation in the elementary and high schools. The New York City high schools stand in the same functional relationship to the University as the elite prep schools once did in relationship to the Ivy League colleges. In other words, the organization of the college work has been based on the premise that the students were adequately prepared by the public high schools. But if the colleges can no longer rely upon that preparation, then any educational process based on the traditional premise is bound to be ineffective.

The inadequacies of the high schools are not peculiar to New York. They occur, with varying seriousness, across the country. But a private university is largely free to select students from the population of all American high schools and the most prestigious colleges do just that. The City University, however, is tied to one set of high schools; it is not free to sample the secondary school universe . . . [84]

At the turn of the century, when Nicholas Murray Butler proposed that Columbia University encourage closer relations with the newly opened New York City high schools, he intended to recruit their best graduates. As time passed Butler concluded that the high schools were not sufficiently selective in sending students to Columbia, and he reassigned the selective function to his own admissions office, which began to recruit from a wider constituency.

New York's municipal colleges had no similar option. By law, they were dependent on the New York City high schools for their student bodies. Although the municipal colleges never practiced invidious discrimination, many charged the Board of Higher Education during its fifty year history with maintaining unnecessarily exclusive admissions policies.

When Albert Bowker arrived on the scene in 1963, an immediate surge in demand for places at the colleges confronted him. Passage of the construction fund legislation went far to solve this problem. But at the same time, Bowker perceived a serious long-run problem. The demand for higher education came mainly from the residents of the city's white, middle class neighborhoods, precisely the group that had been fleeing from New York in large numbers for more than a decade. The black and Puerto Rican groups that replaced them did not perform as well in school as the white students, and therefore at some distant but real point City University would begin to face an enrollment decline.

Bowker attributed the blame for this to environmental factors, and singled out the New York City public educational bureaucracy for special condemnation. He concluded that the failure of elementary and secondary education to be responsive to the needs of these new groups meant that their success, on which turned the survival of New York City, depended on the responsiveness of City University. The chancellor walked a tightrope as he tried to strike a balance between the claims for places put forward by the various groups. The South Campus seizure of spring, 1969 convinced him that immediate implementation of Open Admissions was the only acceptable solution.

At this point it is appropriate to ask a hypothetical question. What would have happened to the City University if Bowker had not succeeded in getting his way each time he brought its problems to the attention of city and state governments, the media, and the public? The political consequences of following through on one of his threats, for example his threat not to admit a freshman class, might have seriously jeopardized attainment of his long-run goals. The costs to the students affected, many of whom would have become immediately subject to the draft, could not have been measured. Perhaps Bowker adhered to what Max Weber called an ethic of ultimate ends, that is, an ethic which places responsibility for the consequences of one's acts upon others.[85] Although muted by Bowker's success, it is a real question that all groups—politicians, trustees, students, faculty, administrators—failed to give adequate consideration during the turbulent late 1960s.

NOTES TO CHAPTER 11
HIGHER EDUCATION FOR ALL
THE MISSION OF THE CITY UNIVERSITY OF NEW YORK

1. Seymour Martin Lipset and Reinhard Bendix, *Social Mobility in Industrial Society* (Berkeley and Los Angeles, University of California Press, 1959), p. 189.

2. See Neil J. Smelser and Gabriel Almond, *Public Higher Education in California* (Berkeley, University of California Press, 1974).

3. See Earl J. McGrath, ed., *Universal Higher Education* (New York, McGraw-Hill, 1966).

4. S. Willis Rudy, *The College of the City of New York: A History 1847–1947* (New York, The City College Press, 1949), pp. 308–312. See also Nathan Glazer, "City College," in David Riesman and Verne A. Stadtman, *Academic Transformations* (New York, etc., McGraw-Hill, 1973), pp. 71–98.

5. Rudy, *The College*, pp. 382–389.

6. In the early 1960s each college was permitted to accept its entire student body on the basis of the composite score. See Louis M. Heil, Louis Long, Marjorie Smiley, and Emma Spaney, *An Investigation of Criteria for Admission to the City University of New York* (New York, City University of New York, 1961); *Minutes of the Administrative Council*, November 28, 1961, p. 22: January 11, 1962, p. 30; May 7, 1963, p. 30.

7. Donald P. Cottrell, "The Liberal Arts College Problem," *Teachers College Record* (February, 1932), 32: 457–462; Donald P. Cottrell, Adrian Rondileau, and Leo S. Schumer, *Public Higher Education in the City of New York: Report of the Master Plan Study* (New York, 1950), p. 22; *Minutes of the Board of Higher Education*, February 20, 1950, p. 56.

8. Cottrell et al., *Public Higher Education*, pp. 12, 44.

9. *Ibid.*, p. 13.

10. Thomas C. Holy, *A Long-Range Plan for the City University of New York 1961–1975* (New York, The Board of Higher Education, 1962), p. 91; *Minutes of the Board of Higher Education*, November 18, 1957, p. 472; November 17, 1958, p. 518; November 16, 1959, p. 536; November 21, 1960, p. 562; November 21, 1961, p. 634; November 19, 1962, p. 663; December 16, 1963, p. 337; and December 21, 1964, p. 519.

11. Holy, *A Long-Range Plan*, pp. 73, 127–128, 68–69.

12. Rudy, *The College*, pp. 124–126, 173–174.

13. *Ibid.*, pp. 292–294, 396–397.

14. Cottrell et al., *Public Higher Education*, p. 17.

15. Holy, *A Long-Range Plan*, pp. 82–83, 99 (Table 12).

16. Joint Legislative Committee on the State Education System, *Report of the New York City Sub-committee Concerning Administration and Financing of the Public Education System of the City of New York Under the Control of that City's Board of Higher Education* (Albany, Williams, 1944).

17. H. G. Schneider to John H. Finley, May 3, 1922, John H. Finley Papers, New York Public Library, box C-4, CCNY through '26 file.

18. *Minutes of the Board of Higher Education*, April 18, 1955, p. 210.

19. The Administrative Council to the Board of Higher Education, *The Chancellorship and Its Implications for the City University*, October 11, 1962, pp. 5–6. Office of Vice Chancellor Timothy Healy, CUNY, Miscellaneous Material on BHE's and Chancellor's Functions Prior to Administrative Reorganization (1965–66) file (hereafter referred to as Healy, Miscellaneous Material file).

20. The Administrative Council, *The Chancellorship*, p. 11, Healy, Miscellaneous Material file; *New York Times*, July 26, 1963, p. 1.

21. Board of Higher Education of the City of New York, *1964 Master Plan* (New York, 1964), p. 113.

22. Bowker to the Members of the Board of Higher Education of the City of New York, April 15, 1965, Healy, Miscellaneous Material file.

23. At its next meeting the BHE adopted certain measures designed to streamline the Board's agenda. *Minutes of the Board of Higher Education,* April 26, 1965, p. 114.

24. See Committee on Higher Education, Henry T. Heald, Chairman, *Meeting the Increasing Demand for Higher Education in New York State* (Albany, 1960).

25. Office of the Chancellor, "New York State Appropriations to the City University," September, 1965, revised September 29, 1965, Healy, Miscellaneous Material file. The state's share of community college support had been fixed at one-third of operating costs.

26. Bowker et al. to James Allen, December 6, 1965, Healy, Miscellaneous Material file. *Minutes of the Board of Higher Education,* October 25, 1965, p. 447.

27. In Bowker's last communication with the City University Committee before going public, he asked it to consider the recommendations in his "Somewhat Bolder Proposal." He stated that Presidents Gallagher (CCNY), Meng (Hunter), Gideonese (Brooklyn), and McMurray (Queens) enthusiastically concurred in those recommendations (Bowker to Rosenberg, November 3, 1965, Healy, Miscellaneous Material file).

28. *New York Times,* November 8, 1965.

29. Administrative Council Statement—draft, November 14, 1965, Healy, Miscellaneous Material file.

30. *Minutes of the Board of Higher Education*, November 17, 1965, p. 472.

31. Bowker to Rosenberg, November 19, 1965, Healy, Miscellaneous Material file.

32. Gideonese to Rosenberg, November 19, 1965, Healy, Miscellaneous Material file.

33. *Minutes of the Board of Higher Education*, November 22, 1965, p. 476.

34. *New York Times,* November 21, 1965.

35. Rosenberg to Allen, November 29, 1965, Healy, Miscellaneous Material file.

36. *New York Times*, December 10, 1965.

37. *Ibid.*, p. 40:1.

38. Edelstein to Bowker, November 27, 1965; Levy to Edelstein, December 16, 1965, Healy, Miscellaneous Material file.

39. Bowker et al., "Memorandum," December 14, 1965, attached to Bowker to the Board of Higher Education of the City of New York, December 14, 1965, Healy, Miscellaneous Material file.

40. Bowker to the Board of Higher Education of the City of New York, December 14, 1965, Healy, Miscellaneous Material file.

41. "Report of the Special Committee for the Study of Administrative Relationships and Functions," March 3, 1966, p. 12, Healy, Miscellaneous Material file. Italics mine.

42. This was partly because of an expected increase in the number of community college students who would be transferring into the senior colleges after receipt of the Associate of Arts degree.

43. The City University of New York, *The Administration of the City University of New York* (New York, The City University of New York, 1967), pp. 82–83; Board of Higher Education,

Master Plan of the Board of Higher Education for the City University of New York 1968 (New York, BHE, 1968), pp. 171–172.

44. The City University of New York, *The Administration*, pp. 93–94.

45. *Minutes of the Board of Higher Education*, February 28, 1966, pp. 60–63.

46. Board of Higher Education, *2nd Interim Revision—1964 Master Plan*, p. 30. The Skills Centers would also accept high school dropouts who needed training in educational fundamentals, who showed promise of academic achievement, or who desired occupational preparation.

47. *New York Times*, May 2, 1966, p. 36.

48. Feinberg to Rosenberg, June 7, 1966, Healy, Miscellaneous Material file.

49. Board of Higher Education of the City of New York, *1964 Master Plan for the City University of New York* (New York, BHE, 1964), p. 7. See Rosenberg's statement, p. 3.

50. Board of Higher Education, *Minutes of the Board of Higher Education*, February 17, 1964, p. 39.

51. Angelo Dispenzieri and Seymour Giniger, *The College Discovery Program: A Synthesis of Research* (New York, The City University of New York Research and Evaluation Unit, 1969), pp. 2–6.

52. Dispenzieri and Giniger, *The College Discovery Program*, pp. 11, 21, 26–27.

53. Board of Higher Education, *Master Plan . . . 1968*, pp. 197–198. When the 100% Admissions Plan was adopted in 1966, CUNY officials envisioned that the community colleges would employ traditional criteria to offer admission to about 40% of the city's high school graduates.

54. Board of Higher Education, *Master Plan . . . 1968*, pp. 198–199.

55. *U.S. News and World Report*, January 8, 1968, pp. 56–57; *New York Post*, December 10, 1967.

56. Press release, April 5, 1968, Office of University Relations, City University of New York; *Kingsman*, April 26, 1968, p. 3.

57. Form letter, undated (draft written by Robert Birnbaum), Vice Chancellor T. E. Hollander files (hereafter referred to as Hollander), Form letters sent re 1968 admissions policies of CUNY file.

58. Chandler to Frederick W. Richmond, May 9, 1968, Hollander, Admissions 1967–68, 1968–69 file.

59. The City University of New York, "Report of the Fall 1970 Undergraduate Ethnic Census," p. 5.

60. Calculation based on the City University of New York, "Report of the Fall 1970 Undergraduate Ethnic Census," p. 11.

61. *Minutes of the Board of Higher Education*, May 27, 1968, p. 117; June 21, 1968, p. 121; August 1, 1968, pp. 180–181.

62. Lester Brailey to Dr. Birnbaum, Mr. Palmer, Mr. Rosner, December 19, 1968, Hollander, New Admissions Policy (approved by BHE 8/1/68) file.

63. Robert Birnbaum to Bowker, September 24, 1968, May 27, 1969, Hollander, Top 100 Scholars 2 file.

64. Bowker to Dr. Mortimer I. Bloom, September 17, 1968, Hollander, New Admissions Policy (approved by BHE 8/1/69) file. *Minutes of the Board of Higher Education*, August 1, 1968, pp. 180–182.

65. Minutes of the Meeting of the Faculty Senate of the City University of New York, Wednesday, September 25, 1968, p. 2; Senate Resolution No. 1 (Proposed by the Temporary Executive Committee); Resolution on Faculty Participation on the Formulation of University Policy; The City University of New York, The University Senate, "Report on Special

Admissions Policy," adopted by the Senate on February 12, 1969, pp. 1.10, 1.9.

66. *New York Times,* March 13, 1969, p. 41:2; March 14, 1969, p. 34:1; March 16, 1969, p. 69:4.

67. *New York Times,* March 31, 1969, p. 48:8; *Minutes of the Board of Higher Education,* March 24, 1969, p. 48; April 28, 1969, p. 59.

68. *New York Times,* April 23, 1969, p. 1.

69. *Minutes of the Executive Committee of the Board of Higher Education,* May 9, 1969, p. 79.

70. Statement of Buell Gallagher, May 9, 1969, Office of University Relations, City University of New York.

71. *New York Times,* May 26, 1969, p. 1.

72. *New York Times,* May 26, 1969; May 28, 1969.

73. *New York Times,* June 3, 1969. See also *New York Daily News,* May 27, 1969.

74. Statement by Simeon Golar, Chairman, City Commission on Human Rights Regarding CCNY Crisis, Office of the City Commission on Human Rights.

75. *New York Times,* June 3, 1969. Murray Kempton, a columnist for the *New York Post,* argued that if the dual admissions system had been implemented, many of the students admitted without regard to the traditional admissions criteria would have been white. His estimate was 35% (*New York Post,* June 26, 1969).

76. *Minutes of the Special Meeting of the Board of Higher Education,* June 16, 1969, p. 11.

77. *Ibid.,* p. 6.

78. Statement of Charles Ohrenstein, June 16, 1969, Office of the Secretary of the City University of New York. See also "Summary of Statement for Board of Higher Education Hearing of June 16, 1969," Council for Public Higher Education, Office of the Secretary of the City University of New York.

79. *Minutes of the Board of Higher Education,* May 4, 1969, p. 71.

80. *Ibid.,* July 9, 1969, pp. 188–189.

81. University Commission on Admissions, *Report and Recommendations to the Board of Higher Education of the City of New York, October 7, 1969* (New York, The City University of New York, 1969), pp. 19–20.

82. Harry Lustig, "Commission on Admissions, Minority Report," October 16, 1969, p. 14, Office of the Secretary of the Board of Higher Education.

83. "Statement of Admissions Policy Adopted by the Board of Higher Education, November 12, 1969," p. 3, Office of the Secretary of the Board of Higher Education.

84. The City University of New York, The University Senate, "Report on Special Admissions Policy," adopted by the Senate on February 12, 1969, pp. 1.6–1.7.

85. Max Weber, "Politics as a Vocation," in Hans Gerth and C. Wright Mills, eds., *From Max Weber: Essays in Sociology* (New York; Oxford University Press, 1958), pp. 125–127.

CHAPTER

12

The Future of
the Selective Function

Exactly one hundred years after the University of Michigan announced that it would begin to admit students on diploma, the City University of New York announced that it would admit all graduates of New York City high schools. Many partisans of open admissions have cited historical precedent to show that the innovation was not all that radical. In a way they are right, since as the certificate system spread it did come' to resemble the current practice. But Michigan had different intentions. Although both universities admitted all who met their "entrance requirements," Michigan published a precise list of necessary subjects. CUNY accepted the diploma of any New York City high school graduate, no matter what subjects he or she completed and no matter what type of diploma the student held.[1] Further, whereas the University of Michigan initiated the certificate system in order to foster good relations with the state's high schools, City University resorted to open admissions to compensate for the deteriorating relations between the University and its feeders.

Enrollment considerations entered into the decisions at both institutions, but whereas Michigan expected gradual growth concomitant with high school expansion, CUNY expected extremely rapid growth. And, whereas at Michigan most conceded that students admitted on diploma were well pre-

pared (and in fact better prepared than students admitted by entrance examination), at City University all agreed that open admissions students were
more poorly prepared than were students admitted under the old admissions
criteria. Thus, while Frieze and Angell at Michigan hoped that certificates
would enable them to raise the University's academic standards while remaining competitive, Bowker and others at the City University understood
(even if they would not admit) that open admissions might come at the cost
of lowered institutional standards.

Whatever the actual merits of the parallels, the controversy surrounding
adoption of open admissions led proponents to seek out historic legitimation
for their initiative. Open admissions supporters did not point out (although
most probably understood) the fundamental difference between the
Michigan and City University situations: in the last hundred years, the academic degree had become more central to determination of the life chances of
more Americans. The debate over open admissions at City University stemmed from a concern that rapid growth and lowered standards would lead to
a "cheapened" degree. And in a city where all believed that a degree from
Brooklyn, City, Hunter, or Queens College had heretofore facilitated social
mobility and provided some economic security, a "cheap" degree rendered it
too easy for newer racial and ethnic groups to "make it," and also placed in
jeopardy the worth of "hard-earned" degrees previously acquired by members of the older ethnic groups. If City University's four-year colleges had not
previously admitted from (at most) the top quarter of New York City's high
school graduates, and if racial and ethnic considerations had been absent,
open admissions would not have been very controversial.[2]

Throughout the twentieth century, both New York City and State had
been in the rear guard of the movement for public higher education expansion. Perhaps Chancellor Bowker decided that so long as a major period of
catching-up was inevitable, City University should place itself in the forefront
of a national movement. Certainly this reasoning was not inconsistent with
the rhetoric of mission employed in many CUNY official publications. In a
nation where about 80% of the 18 to 21 age cohort graduated from high
school and almost 50% of that cohort continued their education past that
point, many would deem adults with no higher education as having a liability. Bowker believed that the urban environment and the poor quality of
elementary and secondary preparation had already done harm to many students, and wished to assure that no student would be denied the opportunity
to obtain a college degree for reasons beyond his or her control. He attempted
to accomplish this by admitting to each CUNY unit a student body of wider
abilities than is usually the case.[3] The cost of educating the thousands of new
students admitted, and the dominance of conservative ideologies in the 1970s
provided significant deterrents to other reformers convinced of the worth of

Bowker's innovation. However, the convergence of several factors may compel other colleges to look beyond SAT scores and high school average in recruiting future freshman classes.[4]

The existence of a limited (and perhaps decreasing) number of students with good SAT scores and the ability to pay for their college education will prompt this, and so will the honest perception by many colleges that students with other assets may profit from and succeeed in their curriculum.[5] The corollary to this proposition is that the mechanism of selective admissions, heretofore employed to select a subgroup of those meeting the college's stated entrance requirements, will be used in the future for inclusionary purposes: to seek out those who may not meet the traditional criteria but who have the ability to profit from a college's offerings. The reasons for and implications of these assertions are the subject of the remainder of this chapter.

THE BENIGN USE OF SELECTIVE ADMISSIONS

Since college admissions offices began to employ them in the 1920s, selective admissions policies have been associated with a desire for restrictions on admission. However, when Nicholas Murray Butler urged late in the nineteenth century that the high schools should perform the selective function he did not at all intend to limit the number of students going to college. Quite the contrary, he expected that high school principals and teachers would identify, using objective indicators of achievement and their own judgment, college material and then urge such students to continue their education. Certainly he favored such a system over the more "objective" entrance examinations still widely employed at the turn of the century.

Even when Butler ended his flirtation with certificates and urged establishment of the College Entrance Examination Board, he shifted his ground largely in recognition of the academic realities of the East Coast, and in the hope that the uniformity brought about by the College Board would measurably facilitate the work of the high schools. Only when Butler's prejudices overcame his educational vision did he urge retrenchment. The selective admissions mechanisms he and his staff devised were neutral instruments. They could just as easily have been used to identify talent among those who did not perform consistently well on the entrance examinations as to limit admission to a proportion of socially qualified students who had done well.[6]

Although fifty years have passed, there is still no theoretical reason why selective admissions must be universally employed in an exclusionary manner. Certainly colleges such as Harvard, Stanford, and Columbia still receive applications from a greater number of "qualified" students than they can accept, but even some elite colleges facing financial problems have begun to enlarge their entering classes. For other colleges that do not have the luxury of a surplus of students qualified for admission under traditional criteria, the only alternative to declining enrollments will be the gathering of detailed information concerning each applicant and the judging of his or her capability to profit from the course offerings and college experience.

Neither the City University open admissions experiment nor the coming of academic "hard times," alone or in combination, provides a sufficient explanation for this projected increased diversity in the entering class and a concomitant reliance on selective admissions apparatus. Four other causes will be identified and discussed briefly. They are the attacks on the use of the traditional predictors of academic performance, criticism of the quality of high school preparation, the need for new devices to measure the capacities of the adult learner, and the implications of recent court cases involving charges of invidious discrimination in college admissions decisions.

Although most authorities agree that high school grades and SAT scores are the best predictors of collegiate academic performance, this fact has been subjected to two major types of criticism when employed as the rationale for an "objective" college admissions policy. First, while such measures of ability account for between 35% and 45% of the variance in academic performance, this leaves much of the variance unaccounted for. Also, most studies have compared high school grades and SAT scores to performance in college during the freshman year, which, at least from the point of view of grades may be the least typical of any of the four years in the usual college program. Others have voiced more fundamental criticism. "Researchers," writes David McClelland, "have in fact had great difficulty demonstrating that grades in school are related to any other behaviors of importance—other than doing well on aptitude tests . . . It seems so self-evident to educators that those who do well in their classes *must* go on to do better in life that they systematically have disregarded evidence to the contrary that has been accumulating for some time."[10]

Of course, there is no general consensus on what "better in life" means; however, if this term implies adult occupational status, McClelland could marshall considerable evidence to support his point of view.[11] It does seem to be true, however, that graduation from college and especially from a selective college improves one's life's chances.[12] If Alexander Astin is correct in his assertion that "evidence on the interaction between student ability and institutional selectivity does not show that students persist better if they attend colleges with students of similar ability," then colleges may admit students with average grades and SAT scores who might be desirable on other grounds and find, first, that persistence rates have not worsened and, second, that the life chances of their students have not changed.[13]

The deficiencies in college preparation, evident not only in open admissions students but even in students with above average high school records, will induce colleges to place less reliance on high school records. Although college teachers who believe their students have received the best possible college preparation have always been rare, the recent crescendo of complaints, backed by some impressive data, indicates that this chronic student ailment may have taken a turn for the worse. Blame for the decline in fundamental skills, especially those involving use of the English language, has been laid on "the simplistic spoken style of television," poorly qualified teachers, overcrowded classes that induce teachers to administer short-answer examinations and exercises, and even on structural linguistics, which urges the superiority of spoken to written language forms.

The contemporary secondary school curriculum cannot go blameless; in the 1950s the United States Commissioner of Education commented that the teaching of English was so poor that it threatened the nation's entire educational system. Since then the reforms that have been undertaken have been largely in the area of literature. In 1973, the National Commission on the Reform of Secondary Education commented, "the most distressing finding in the National Assessment [of Educational Progress] reports is the low level of competency in the mechanics of writing at every age level. The evidence mandates increased emphasis on these skills, even at some cost from reduced emphasis on the teaching of literature."[15] Many college authorities have cast a critical eye on recent high school reforms, which they viewed as pale carbon copies of college level instruction, while at the same time noting that the National Assessment has indicated serious deficiencies in the achievement of minimal skills and understandings in the traditional secondary curriculum. Colleges are less likely to accept the grades awarded by secondary schools at face value when the preparation those grades measure appears to be inadequate. It is appropriate to record here that the National Commission on the Reform of Secondary Education also recommended that college and secondary school authorities cooperate to "develop alternatives to grade-point average and rank in class for assessing the scope and quality of the education received by students at the secondary level."[16]

The shift in the 1920s from an emphasis on preparation to an emphasis on prediction came about in part as the colleges and universities concluded that secondary school standards had risen to the point where most schools offered at least a minimally acceptable level of instruction and hence differences in ability *within* each school could take precedence over differences in instruction quality *between* schools. In the last decade many college authorities concluded that this assumption, even if formerly true, could be seriously questioned in the present and for the future. Colleges dissatisfied with the preparation of their incoming freshman class have two options. They can require remedial work (which many of them do), or they can use their entrance requirements as they did seventy years ago to influence the high school offerings and to raise mastery levels. At City University, a strong case could be made for widespread remediation, given the quality of the New York City high schools as reflected on the National Assessment. However, it should be recalled that most colleges spent the latter part of the nineteenth century attempting to abolish their preparatory departments; general acceptance of remedial work, especially in the four-year colleges, would be a considerable retrogression.

Likewise, the current emphasis on adult, recurrent, and lifelong learning will force many admissions offices to abandon the traditional predictors of college success in favor of more sophisticated methods. Students long out of high school cannot be evaluated by the traditional predictors. Further, the growing practice of awarding credit for life experience implies that a detailed assessment will be made of each applicant at some point soon after admission.[17] Finally, the need for individual counseling for such students will probably be greater than for students entering college directly out of high school. All of these factors will lead colleges wishing to recruit from this group to employ selective admissions apparatus benignly.

Although at this moment one can merely speculate, it is possible that an adverse Supreme Court ruling against a college or university admitting a proportion of its freshman class by race (the "benign quota") will lead many colleges to employ a more sophisticated selective admissions policy to the same end. An institution so enjoined, yet committed to a policy of racial inclusion, may simply give preference to students from poverty areas, a practice thus far held as constitutional on the elementary and secondary levels. However, other institutions may decide to conduct their own inquiry for evidence of *educational disadvantage* (as opposed to race). For such institutions the traditional freedom the courts have granted colleges in the area of admissions would probably be continued.[18]

IMPLICATIONS

In the future, colleges and universities will resort to more sophisticated mechanisms of college admission out of necessity. Traditional predictors and traditional preparation are questioned and applicant pools must be widened to cope with financial exigency and social demands. Although most evaluation procedures may not be so complex as that currently employed by Harvard, that university's thoroughness is instructive. After Harvard solicits a thick application folder for each candidate, its admissions committee assigns two or more members to read the files of a specified number of students and to estimate how students of given characteristics would fare in the Harvard admission process. Their evaluations are reported in the form of a summary profile which includes about twenty-five evaluations, including assessments of academic performance, participation in extracurricular activities, participation in athletics, personality, strength of letters of recommendation, father's occupation, and fields of interest for future study. In addition, the profile contains SAT and achievement test scores, rank in class, and the student's minority status if any. Finally, the profile indicates whether the student was the son of a Harvard alumnus (about 200 of the 500 sons of alumni who applied were accepted in 1975; the overall ratio of acceptances to applications was about one to six). After a thorough screening of students from each major geographical region (the regional subcommittees might take half an hour to discuss an applicant), the entire admissions committee meets to evaluate the work of the regional subcommittees and to make final decisions on admission and rejection. This is also a time-comsuming task. The entire process requires considerable personal knowledge of and personal attention to each case and obviously benefits from the expertise admissions committee members have gained over the years.[19]

Whether or not one believes that the entering class finally chosen by this procedure is that which can best benefit from what Harvard has to offer,[20] the procedure does permit Harvard to maximize its options. Colleges not having the luxury of several qualified applicants for each place in their freshman class can, by investing some resources on their admissions office, employ these measures in an inclusionary rather than an exclusionary manner. In fact, if Alexander Astin is correct in his assertion that other indicators besides high school performance and SAT scores have value for predicting persistence in college, this type of apparatus may become a competitive necessity. Among other factors, Astin lists in order of predictiveness "student degree plans at the time of college entrance, religious background, and religious preference, followed by concern about college finances, study habits, and educational attainment of parents."[21] Certainly this is not an all-inclusive list, nor is it necessarily a legal or the best admissions policy for a college simply to select the students most likely to complete its course.[22] However, colleges desirous of having academic success in college as one goal of their admissions policy should find a policy of inclusionary selective admissions to their benefit.

In this final section we examine the implications of not only the most recent changes but also of the century long trend toward turning the college admissions office into a social sorter. After examining the implications for the constituencies directly concerned with the colleges, this section explores the broader implications.

Perhaps the place to begin our survey of the implications for internal constituencies is in the admissions office itself. Typically, this office is presented each year with a pile of applications and a general mandate, perhaps from a multicampus governing body that can allocate enrollments among the campuses under its jurisdiction, or perhaps from the faculty which then collectively withdraws from the admissions process, leaving behind one or more representatives to serve on the admissions committee. In such a situation, an admissions office can acquire considerable latitude and can easily cross the line dividing policy implementation from policy design.

As earlier chapters have indicated, the bureaucratization of the admissions process slowly evolved partly because of the overwork of faculty members, partly because of the introduction of subjective judgment into admissions decisions, and partly in resonance with the general growth and rationalization of the university. As more students applied for admission to college in the late nineteenth century, the burden on individual faculty members became overwhelming. To alleviate the strain, written examinations replaced oral tests; the administration and evaluation of exams were centralized on the campus and then among campuses (CEEB). The faculty at certificating colleges rapidly became overburdened with inspections and, after implementation of some stopgap measures, most authorized centralization of inspections perhaps under the authority of a full-time inspector supplemented by accreditation work undertaken by a regional association. As institutions began to employ subjective admissions criteria, common judgmental standards had to be established and the hiring of a permanent admissions officer, well-acquainted with the desires of the faculty and other interested groups, achieved at least some degree of consistency. It is sometimes lamented that college faculties have abandoned so much of their authority over admissions, especially since they must live with admissions office "mistakes" for up to four years. And yet, is the judgment of faculty members concerning the nonacademic matters that make up an important part of the admissions officer's job any less fallible than the judgment of specialists? If anything, the trend toward the professionalization of the admissions office will accelerate in the future.

Nevertheless, there is still an important role for college faculty in this area. It does not necessarily involve the ongoing process of individual student selection but the evaluation and revision of the general criteria for admission, especially the academic criteria. Although at this stage specification of specific subject matter that a student must master for admission would constitute a retrogression, perhaps colleges might require mastery of certain competencies. A college faculty concerned about the writing ability of its entering class could require applicants to take a composition test that could be graded for the complexity of thought a student correctly expressed in a given time.[23] In the past, high schools willy-nilly altered their curricula when presented with similar demands by the colleges. Although colleges recruiting primarily from inner city high schools may decide to admit and offer remedial instruction rather than to require specified competencies at the time of admission, colleges recruiting from high schools where a significant proportion of the student body desires to enter postsecondary education might profitably introduce such requirements.[24]

Certainly the typical college and university president in the last third of the twentieth century has been less concerned with academic considerations in admissions than were his or her predecessors. But then again college presidents are less involved with academic questions in general. Most are, however, concerned with enrollments and their effects on the institution's budget. At a time when national college attendance rates are declining, administrators wishing to maintain enrollment levels and the tuition income they represent may find themselves pitted against a faculty desirous of continued selectivity. Certainly, most presidents are aware that considerations other than financial ones are relevant to the admissions process (the institution's long-run survival may depend on its maintenance of a selective image), but confronted with red ink, a president's inclination toward financial reductionism may be overwhelming.[25]

Intervention by college or university trustees into the admissions process is rare in practice, although most college charters assign them the task of defining those policies. In the cases considered in this book, trustee intervention usually occurred when admissions involved broad social issues, usually the appearance of new populations desirous of access to higher education. Perhaps in this period of academic hard times, when the student contribution to the college budget can mean life or death to some institutions, governing boards will take increased interest in the institution's mechanisms of admission. This trend may be accelerated by attempts by external agencies (mainly governmental) to mandate certain criteria of admission in return for the continuance of financial aid or for the institution to be in compliance with state and federal law (e.g., Title IX of the 1972 Education Amendments).

It is not out of place in this survey of constituent stakes in admissions policies to comment on the "public" concern about the various criteria of admission as manifested in governmental interventions and rulings. Attempts to employ the government's "power of the purse" to regulate admissions can be traced back at least to the 1940s, when the American Jewish Congress sued the New York Tax Commission to force it to remove Columbia from the rolls of tax-exempt institutions on the grounds that it discriminated on the basis of religion in its admissions policies. But it has only been in the last decade that the federal government has flexed its financial muscles in this area. Title VI of the Civil Rights Act of 1964 prohibited discrimination on the basis of race, color, or national origin under any program or activity receiving federal financial assistance.[26] Although the Nixon administration had notified ten states in 1969 and 1970 that they were not in compliance with Title VI and were required to submit plans for the desegregation of their public colleges and universities, it never followed up on the directives either by forcing compliance or by cutting off federal funds. The NAACP Legal Defense Fund sued the Department of Health, Education, and Welfare to compel the law's enforcement. In 1972 a Federal District Court found for the plaintiffs and the United States Court of Appeals for the District of Columbia upheld the ruling. Faced with the alternatives of compliance or cutoff of federal funds, eight states submitted rather weak compliance plans, another (Mississippi) submitted a partial plan, and the last (Louisiana) refused to comply and was sued by the Department of Justice. The greatest impact of Title VI and of this case, *Adams* v. *Richardson*, will be felt in the South where a dual system of higher education has left a legacy of black exclusion from the better institutions.[27]

Title IX of the Education Amendments of 1972 provided that "no person in the United States shall, on the basis of sex, be excluded from participation in, be denied the benefits of, or be subjected to discrimination under any educational program or activity receiving Federal financial assistance."[28] The regulation implementing Title IX restricted its scope to "institutions of vocational education, professional education, graduate higher education, and public institutions of undergraduate higher education."[29] Such institutions were enjoined from discriminating on the basis of sex either in admission or recruitment of students.[30] The impact of Title IX will probably be felt most strongly by those graduate and professional divisions that have traditionally held down the percentage of women admitted.

Similarly, resort to the federal courts for redress of discriminatory or "reverse discriminatory" practices has been largely confined to questions of admission to professional schools. The major cases concerning racial discrimination coming before the Supreme Court before the Brown decision mostly concerned admission to state supported law schools,[31] as did the DeFunis case rendered moot by the Supreme Court in 1974.[32]

Despite the controversy surrounding the DeFunis case, it seems unlikely that the Supreme Court will greatly truncate the discretion traditionally accorded public institutions, especially undergraduate colleges, in the area of admissions so long as the criteria are reasonable and are not employed invidiously. This implies that public institutions are not confined to use of "objective" criteria such as SAT scores in choosing an entering class, and the long tradition of selective admissions in the United States should provide the colleges enough latitude to select demonstrably disadvantaged students even if inclusionary racial quotas are prohibited.[33]

Finally, of course, students have the last word concerning a college's admissions policy. In the late 1960s students on some campuses made admissions policies the focal point of their demonstrations; however, student influence in this area is perpetual. Their decisions as to whether to go to college and where to apply determine how selective an institution can be. There has been considerable controversy over enrollment projections for the next fifteen years,[34] but Lyman A. Glenny has at least defined the parameters of the debate. Glenny pointed out that the absolute number of college-age youth will continue to increase throughout the seventies, but that the proportion of the age group attending college has already leveled off, thus producing what he calls "the illusions of steady-state." In the 1980s, college enrollments may be adversely affected by a sharp drop in the live birth rate during the late 1960s and early 1970s, which will reduce the number of young people (defined as 18–21) from 16.8 million in 1980 to 15.6 in 1984, and to about 13 million in the early 1990s. Thus, unless the colleges and universities can reverse the recent dropoff in college attendance rates among American youth, only recruitment from other age groups can forestall a rather severe decline in college attendance.[35]

Under these circumstances, students who decide to go to college will be in a buyer's market. As predicted above, even the more selective colleges will choose students from a wider range of abilities than ever before. Since American students have traditionally taken into account probably social and economic as well as educational benefits in choosing colleges, and since students have perceived that the more selective colleges have more successfully provided these, colleges able to maintain their reputations as selective will probably more than hold their own in the competition for students. The balance here suggested between admitting students with a wider range of abilities while maintaining a selective image will not be easy to achieve, and it is probable that a number of institutions will fail at the attempt. Yet such tightrope walks have always been performed in the admissions process, and the "grace period" given American higher education by the Census Bureau should be seized as an opportunity for advance planning.

Today's undergraduate college continues the sorting mechanism role it acquired early in this century. In fact, one result of open admissions may be that this sorting, until recently confined to the middle through upper classes, will now be extended to lower strata that previously were sorted by other mechanisms. In her two major books, K. Patricia Cross argued that the education received by open admissions students should not be simply a pale carbon copy of the instruction given to more traditional types of students; that all students, but especially open admissions students, would profit from a curriculum that would teach not only specific knowledge, but also interpersonal skills and the ability to work with objects and materials.[36] The general credentialization of interpersonal and mechanical skills might very well have the effect of increasing college enrollments since, for example, if a credential in interpersonal relationships existed many employers would require that anyone they hired in an "out-front" capacity possess it. Such a credential might, however, exact real hardships on those unwilling or unable until now to attend college. It certainly would place even more stamps of failure on those who opt not to attend in the future.

In any case, college and university authorities will have to do some serious thinking about their instructional goals. Students with diverse backgrounds may very well require new forms of instruction. College curricula have changed in the past to meet the needs of new clienteles, and today the optimism that appears to surround the implementation of innovations such as mastery learning contrasts with the pessimism prevalent in much of the world of higher education.

Having now discussed the past, present, and future of the selective function of college admissions policies, it is appropriate to ask a philosophical question. Higher education acquired the selective function in part because the public acquiesced in the assertions made by educational authorities that they could perform that function well. But is it legitimate that education perform this function? And if so, what are "legitimate" criteria of selection? The material presented in this book does not fit neatly into the schemes of either meritocrats or egalitarians. It is consistent with the view that the educational system has a prime role to play in stratification. The public's increased consciousness of this function, and its concern over the criteria the colleges and universities have employed accounts for the many controversies over admissions in recent years. Just as higher education gave up considerable autonomy in the area of research when it began to accept funding from outside sources, it could not expect the public to remain indifferent while its admissions policies had important social consequences. Early in this century, Max Weber noted that democracies are ambivalent on the legitimacy of education as a stratifying mechanism. On the one hand it means, or appears to mean, "a 'selection' of those who qualify from all social strata rather than a rule by notables. On the other hand, democracy fears that a merit system and educational certificates will result in a privileged 'caste.'"[37] Perhaps this explains why American society has tolerated the selective function of education, yet has never truly accepted it.

NOTES TO CHAPTER 12
THE FUTURE OF
THE SELECTIVE FUNCTION

1. Students who took and passed Regents examinations obtained academic diplomas; students who took academic courses, often watered down, which did not culminate in Regents examinations received general diplomas. Other students obtained commercial diplomas. New York State and City did prescribe that all students obtaining a diploma study certain subjects including English, social studies, mathematics, and science.

2. Community colleges and four-year colleges, academically inferior to the main state university, had opened all over America during the 1960s. Most have fairly liberal if not "open" admissions policies, yet few elicited much negative reaction. Generally they permitted expansion of higher education while permitting the continued exclusiveness of each state's central campus. In such academically stratified systems, the "worth" of a degree was more easily identifiable than at CUNY, which admitted students from a wide range of ability groups.

3. See Alexander Astin, *Preventing Students from Dropping Out* (San Francisco, Jossey-Bass, 1975), p. 136.

4. See C. W. Wing and M. A. Wallach, *College Admissions and the Psychology of Talent* (New York, Holt, Rinehart and Winston, 1971) for evidence that at most colleges these are the main criteria relied upon in admissions decisions.

5. See Humphrey Doermann, *Crosscurrents in College Admissions*, rev. ed. (New York, Teachers College Press, 1970).

6. Butler himself made this point when he berated Director of Admissions Adam Leroy Jones in 1912 for relying too heavily on entrance examination results at a time when he should have been introducing the "human element" into the admissions procedure (see pp. 125–127).

7. The CEEB's official policy has been that scores on its tests are supplementary to the information collected directly by the colleges.

8. David E. Lavin, *The Prediction of Academic Performance: A Theoretical Analysis and Review of Research* (New York, Science Editions, John Wiley & Sons, 1967), p. 59.

9. *Ibid.*, p. 58.

10. David C. McClelland, "Testing for Competence Rather Than for Intelligence," *American Psychologist* (January, 1973), 28:2. He also commented, "The games people are required to play on aptitude tests are similar to the games teachers require in the classroom. In fact, many of Binet's original tests were taken from exercises that teachers used in French schools. So it is scarcely surprising that aptitude test scores are correlated highly with grades in school" (*ibid.*, p. 1).

11. Donald P. Hoyt, *The Relationship Between College Grades and Adult Achievement: A Review of the Literature* (Iowa City, American College Testing Program, 1965); Lavin, "Introduction to the Paperback Edition," in *The Prediction*. See also E. E. Ghiselli, *The Validity of Occupational Aptitude Tests* (New York, John Wiley & Sons, 1966), but see McClelland, "Testing," pp. 3–4.

12. McClelland says, "while grade level attained seems related to future measures of success in life, performance within grade was related only slightly" (McClelland, "Testing," p. 2).

13. Astin, *Preventing*, p. 145.

14. See Merrill Sheils, "Why Johnny Can't Write," *Newsweek* (December 8, 1975), 86, 23:58–65.

15. The National Commission on the Reform of Secondary Education. B. Frank Brown, Chairman, *The Reform of Secondary Education: A Report to the Public and the Profession* (New York, McGraw-Hill, 1973), p. 44. See also Daniel Bell, *The Reforming of General Education: The Columbia College Experience in Its National Setting* (Garden City, N.Y., Anchor Books, 1968), pp. 124–126.

16. National Commission, *The Reform*, pp. 18–19.

17. See Peter Meyer, *Awarding Credit for Non College Learning* (San Francisco, Jossey-Bass, 1975).

18. Suggestive on this point is Richard A. Posner, "The DeFunis Case and the Constitutionality

of Preferential Treatment of Racial Minorities," in Philip H. Kurland, ed., *1974 Supreme Court Review* (Chicago and London, The University of Chicago Press, 1975), pp. 1–32. On the courts' traditional reluctance to rule on admissions policies, see William T. O'Hara and John G. Hill, Jr., *The Student, The College, The Law* (New York, Teachers College Press, 1972), chapter 1.

19. Francis D. Fisher, "A Day and a Half in the Harvard Admissions Office," *Harvard Today* (Winter, 1975), 18, 2:11–12.

20. See the intriguing discussion in Christopher Jencks and David Riesman, *The Academic Revolution* (Garden City, N.Y., Anchor Books, 1969), pp. 148–150.

21. Astin, *Preventing*, p. 45.

22. See Astin's caveats in *ibid.*, pp. 150–152.

23. McClelland, "Testing," p. 10.

24. Daniel Bell stated this idea in rather stern terms in his 1966 book, *The Reforming of General Education:* "one has the right to assume that by the time a student enters college, he can write clearly enough to make a special course in freshman composition unnecessary . . . Given the general upgrading that is taking place in the secondary schools, it is entirely the responsibility of these schools to assure the proficiency of their students in English composition." Although admitting that one college could not enforce such a regulation by itself, he suggested that the Ivy League colleges collectively adopt a rule that "any student seeking admission to these colleges must meet a standard of composition set forth in a common college-board type entrance examination." Bell would allow for admission with a deficiency in composition (conditioned admittance), but noted that it would be the student's obligation to make up the deficiency (p. 239).

25. See Lyman A. Glenny, John R. Shea, Janet H. Ruyle, and Kathryn H. Freschi, *Presidents Confront Reality: From Edifice Complex to University Without Walls* (San Francisco, Jossey-Bass, 1976), chapter 8. Interestingly, a minority of presidents surveyed by Glenny et al. believed that "steady-state" conditions might improve the quality of students because those who do enter college would be more motivated (p. 91).

26. Public Law 88–352, July 2, 1964. A convenient summary of all federal antidiscrimination legislation relevant to higher education may be found in The Carnegie Council on Policy Studies in Higher Education, *Making Affirmative Action Work in Higher Education* (San Francisco, Jossey-Bass, 1975), chapter 4.

27. See John Egerton, "*Adams* v. *Richardson*: Can Separate Be Equal?" *Change* (December–January, 1974–1975), 6, 10:29–36.

28. Public Law 92–318, June 23, 1972.

29. *Code of Federal Regulations*, Title 45, Part 86.15(d). Regulation 86.15(e) further exempted "any public institution of undergraduate higher education which traditionally and continually from its establishment has had a policy of admitting students of one sex."

30. *Ibid.*, Parts 86.15(c), 86.21–86.23.

31. *Missouri ex rel. Gaines* v. *Canada*, 305 U. S. 337 (1938); *Sweatt* v. *Painter*, 339 U. S. 629 (1950); and *McLaurin* v. *Oklahoma State Regents*, 339 U. S. 637 (1950).

32. *DeFunis* v. *Odegaard*, 94 S. Ct. 1704 (1974).

33. For an interesting discussion of the implications of the DeFunis case see David L. Kirp and Mark G. Yudof, "DeFunis and Beyond," *Change* (November, 1974), 6, 9:22–26.

34. The Carnegie Foundation for the Advancement of Teaching, *More Than Survival* (San Francisco, Jossey-Bass, 1975), chapter 4 provides a convenient summary.

35. Lyman A. Glenny, "Nine Myths, Nine Realities: The Illusions of Steady State," *Change* (December–January, 1974–1975, 6, 10:24, 26.

36. K. Patricia Cross, *Beyond the Open Door: New Students to Higher Education* (San Francisco, Jossey-Bass, 1974), chapter 10; and *Accent on Learning: Improving Instruction and Reshaping the Curriculum* (San Francisco, Jossey-Bass, 1976), chapter 1. See also K. Patricia Cross, "New Forms for New Functions," in Dyckman W. Vermilye, ed., *Lifelong Learners—A New Clientele for Higher Education* (San Francisco, Jossey-Bass, 1974).

37. Max Weber, "Bureaucracy," in Hans Gerth and C. Wright Mills, eds., *From Max Weber: Essays in Sociology* (New York, Oxford University Press, 1958, p. 240.

BIBLIOGRAPHY

GENERAL

Public Documents

Cowen, Philip, *College Admissions in New York State 1958–1961* (Albany, The University of the State of New York, 1962).

Cowen, Philip, *College Entrance Inquiry* (Albany, The University of the State of New York Press, 1932).

Cowen, Philip, *Factors Related to the College Plans of High School Seniors* (Albany, The University of the State of New York, 1960).

Cowen, Philip, *Trends in Requirements for Admission to Liberal Arts Colleges 1931–41* (Albany, The University of the State of New York Press, 1945).

Coxe, Warren W., and Philip A. Cowen, *Applicants Refused Admission by Colleges and Professional Schools of New York State* (Albany, The University of the State of New York Press, 1934).

Davis, Calvin O., *The Accredited Secondary Schools of the North Central Association* (Washington, D.C., U.S. Government Printing Office, 1920).

Fryer, John, "Admission of Chinese Students to American Colleges," *United States Bureau of Education Bulletin*, 1909, no. 2.

Kingsley, Clarence D. "College Entrance Requirements," *United States Bureau of Education Bulletin*, 1913, no. 7.

MacLean, George E., "Present Standards of Higher Education in the United States," *United States Bureau of Education Bulletin*, 1913, no. 4.

McKown, Harry C., "The Trend of College Entrance Requirements," *United States Bureau of Education Bulletin*, 1924, no. 35.

President's Commission on Higher Education, *Higher Education for American Democracy* (Washington, D.C., U.S. Government Printing Office, 1947), 6 vols.

Reports, Documents, Proceedings, etc.

Association of Colleges and Preparatory Schools of the Middle States and Maryland, *Proceedings of the Thirteenth Annual Convention,* 1899.

The Carnegie Foundation for the Advancement of Teaching, *Annual Report of the President and Treasurer,* 1906–1908.

College Entrance Examination Board, *Report of the Secretary,* 1901–1910.

National Education Association, "Report of Committee on College-Entrance Requirements," *Journal of Proceedings and Addresses of the National Education Association,* 1913:561–67.

National Educational Association, "Report of the Committee on College Entrance Requirements," in *Journal of Proceedings and Addresses of the National Educational Association,* 1899:632–817.

National Educational Association, *Report of the Committee on Secondary School Studies Appointed at the Meeting of the National Educational Association, July 9, 1892* (Washington, D.C., U.S. Government Printing Office, 1893).

Books and Monographs

Abbott, Frank C., *Government Policy and Higher Education: A Study of the Regents of the University of the State of New York 1784-1949* (Ithaca, Cornell University Press, 1958).

Aikin, Wilford M., *The Story of the Eight-Year Study* (New York and London, Harper & Brothers, 1942).

Allmendinger, David F., *Paupers and Scholars: The Transformation of Student Life in Nineteenth Century New England* (New York, St. Martin's Press, 1965).

Astin, Alexander W., *Predicting Academic Performance in College: Selectivity Data for 2300 American Colleges* (New York, Free Press, 1971).

Astin, Alexander W., *Preventing Students from Dropping Out* (San Francisco, Jossey-Bass, 1975).

Baltzell, E. Digby, *The Protestant Establishment: Aristocracy and Caste in America* (New York, Random House, 1964).

Bath, Joseph R., "A Historical Survey of College Admission Practices in Baccalaureate Degree Granting Colleges in America 1609–1876" (unpublished dissertation, Boston College, 1965).

Bell, Daniel, *The Coming of Post-Industrial Society: A Venture in Social Forecasting* (New York, Basic Books, 1973).

Bell, Daniel, *The Reforming of General Education, The Columbia College Experience in Its National Setting* (New York, Columbia University Press, 1966).

Benedict, Agnes E., *Dare the Secondary Schools Face the Atomic Age?* (New York, Hinds, Hayden and Eldridge, 1947).

Bishop, Morris, *A History of Cornell* (Ithaca, Cornell University Press, 1962).

Bloom, Benjamin S., and Frank R. Peters, *The Use of Academic Prediction Scales for Counseling and Selecting College Entrants* (New York, Free Press, 1961).

Boone, Richard, *A History of Education in Indiana* (New York, D. Appleton and Company, 1892).

Bowles, Frank H., *How to Get into College* (New York, Dutton, 1959).

Bowles, Frank H., *The Refounding of the College Board, 1948-1963, An Informal Commentary and Selected Papers.* (New York, College Entrance Examination Board, 1967).

Brigham, Carl Campbell, *A Study of American Intelligence* (Princeton, Princeton University Press, 1923).

Bronson, Walter C., *The History of Brown University* (Providence, Published by the University, 1914).

Broome, Edwin C., *A Historical and Critical Discussion of College Admission Requirements* (New York, Macmillan, 1903).

Brown, Edwin J., *A Study of the Facts and Conditions Involved in the Problem of College Admissions* (Topeka, Printed by the Kansas State Printing Plant, 1931).

Brown, Elmer Ellsworth, *The Making of Our Middle Schools, An Account of the Development of Secondary Education in the United States* (New York, Longmans, Green and Co., 1902).

Bryce, James, *The American Commonwealth*, L. M. Hacker, ed. (New York, Capricorn Books, 1959).

Butts, R. Freeman, *The College Charts Its Course: Historical Conceptions and Current Proposals* (New York, McGraw-Hill, 1939).

Butts, R. Freeman, and Lawrence A. Cremin, *A History of Education in American Culture* (New York, Henry Holt and Co., 1953).

Carnegie Council on Policy Studies in Higher Education, *Making Affirmative Action Work in Higher Education* (San Francisco, Jossey-Bass, 1975).

Carnegie Foundation for the Advancement of Teaching, *More than Survival* (San Francisco, Jossey-Bass, 1975).

Catholic University of America, *Workshop on Philosophy and Problems of College Admissions*, 1962 (Washington, D.C., Catholic University of America Press, 1963).

Chamberlin, Charles D., et al., *Did They Succeed in College?—The Follow-Up Study of the Graduates of the Thirty Schools* (New York, Harper, 1942).

Chandler, Alfred D., "The Beginnings of 'Big Business' in American Industry," *Business History Review* (Spring, 1959), 33:1–30.

Chandler, Alfred D., *Strategy and Structure: Chapters in the History of the Industrial Enterprise* (Cambridge, Mass., MIT Press, 1962).

Cicourel, Aaron V., and John I. Kituse, *The Educational Decision-Makers* (Indianapolis, Bobbs-Merrill, 1963).

Coffman, Lotus D., *The Social Composition of the Teaching Profession* (New York, Teachers College, 1911).

College Entrance Examination Board, *The Work of the College Entrance Examination Board 1901–25* (Boston, Ginn and Co., 1926).

Colloquium on College Admissions Policies, Interlochen, Mich., 1967, *College Admissions Policies for the 1970s* (New York, College Entrance Examination Board, 1968).

Conference on College Admission and Guidance, New York, 1932, *College Admission and Guidance* (Washington, D.C., American Council on Education, 1933).

Conference on Discrimination in College Admissions, Chicago, 1949, *Discrimination in College Admissions* (Washington, D.C., American Council on Education, 1950).

Connecticut Commission on Civil Rights, *College Admissions Practices with Respect to Race, Religion and National Origin* (Hartford, The Commission, 1949).

Connecticut Commission on Civil Rights, *A New Study of College Admissions Practices with Respect to Race, Religion and National Origin* (Hartford, The Commission, 1953).

Cooper, Sam R., "A Study of the College Admission Guidance Practices in the High Schools in the Northeast Section of the United States" (unpublished dissertation, Teachers College, Columbia University, 1962).

Coulton, Thomas Evans, *A City College in Action: Struggle and Achievement at Brooklyn College 1930–1955* (New York, Harper, 1955).

Counts, George S., *The Selective Character of American Secondary Education* (Chicago, The University of Chicago, 1922).

Crane, Theodore Rawson, ed., *The Colleges and the Public 1787–1862* (New York, Bureau of Publications, Teachers College, 1963).

Cremin, Lawrence A., *The American Common School: An Historic Conception* (New York, Bureau of Publications, Teachers College, 1963).

Cremin, Lawrence A., *The Transformation of the School: Progressivism in American Education 1876–1957* (New York, Knopf, 1961).

Cross, K. Patricia, *Accent on Learning: Improving Instruction and Reshaping the Curriculum* (San Francisco, Jossey-Bass, 1976).

Cross, K. Patricia, *Beyond the Open Door: New Students to Higher Education* (San Francisco, Jossey-Bass, 1971).

Curti, Merle, *The Social Ideas of American Educators: Report of the Commission on Social Studies,* part 10 (New York, Charles Scribner's Sons, 1935).

Davis, Calvin O., *A History of the North Central Association of Colleges and Secondary Schools 1895–1945* (Ann Arbor, The North Central Association of Colleges and Secondary Schools, 1945).

Davis, Charles M., *A Survey of Transfer Admissions in Colleges and Universities* (Ann Arbor, University of Michigan Press, 1948).

Doermann, Humphrey, *Crosscurrents in College Admissions: Institutional Response to Student Ability and Family Income,* rev. ed. (New York, Teachers College Press, 1970).

Downey, Mathew T., *Carl Campbell Brigham, Scientist and Educator* (Princeton, Educational Testing Service, 1961).

Duffus, Robert L., *Democracy Enters College—A Study of the Rise and Decline of the Academic Lockstep* (New York, Charles Scribner's Sons, 1936).

Educational Records Bureau, Committee on School and College Relations, *Improving Transition from School to College: How Can School and College Best Cooperate* (New York, Harper and Brothers, 1953).

Eschenbacher, Harry F., *The University of Rhode Island: A History of Land Grant Education in Rhode Island* (New York, Appleton-Century-Crofts, 1967).

Fenner, Mildred, *NEA History: The National Education Association—Its Development and Program* (Washington, D.C., National Education Association, 1945).

Ferriss, Abbott L., *Indicators of Trends in American Education* (New York, Russell Sage Foundation, 1969).

Fine, Benjamin, *Admission to American Colleges—A Study of Current Policy and Practice* (New York and London, Harper and Brothers, 1946).

Fine, Benjamin, *How to be Accepted by the College of Your Choice* (Great Neck, N.Y., Channel Press, 1957).

First Annual Report of the New England College Entrance Certificate Board 1902–1903 (Providence, Snow and Farnham, 1904).

Flexner, Abraham, *Henry S. Pritchett: A Biography* (New York, Columbia University Press, 1943).

Flexner, Abraham, *I Remember* (New York, Simon & Schuster, 1940).

Flexner, Abraham, *Universities: American, English, German* (New York, Oxford University Press, 1930).

Fuess, Claude M., *The College Board: Its First Fifty Years* (New York, Columbia University Press, 1950).

Fund for the Advancement of Education, *They Went to College Early* (New York, Fund for the Advancement of Education, 1957).

The General Education Board, *The General Education Board: An Account of its Activities 1902–1914* (New York, General Education Board, 1915).

Gerth, Hans, and C. Wright Mills, eds., *From Max Weber: Essays in Sociology* (New York, Oxford University Press, 1958).

Ghiselli, E. E., *The Validity of Occupational Aptitude Tests* (New York, John Wiley & Sons, 1966).

Brother Giles, *Latin and Greek in College Entrance and College Graduation Requirements* (Washington, D.C., Catholic University of America, 1926).

Giles, Herman H., et al., *Exploring the Curriculum: The Work of the Thirty Schools from the Viewpoint of Curriculum Consultants* (New York and London, Harper and Brothers, 1942).

Glenny, Lyman, John R. Shea, Janet H. Ruyle, and Katheryn H. Freschi, *Presidents Confront Reality: From Edifice Complex to University Without Walls* (San Francisco, Jossey-Bass, 1976).

Gray, James, *Open Wide the Door: The Story of the University of Minnesota* (New York, G. P. Putnam's Sons, 1958).

Gray, James, *The University of Minnesota 1851–1951* (Minneapolis, University of Minnesota Press, 1951).

Hauser, Jane Z., and Paul Lazersfeld, *The Admissions Officer in the American College—An Occupation Under Change* (New York, Bureau of Applied Social Research, 1964).

Hays, Edna, *College Entrance Requirements in English: Their Effects on the High Schools, an Historical Survey* (New York, Teachers College, Columbia University, 1936).

Hemming, James, *Teach Them to Live,* 2nd ed. (London, Longmans, Green and Co., 1957).

Henderson, Joseph L., *Admission to College by Certificate* (New York, Teachers College, Columbia University, 1912).

Higham, John, *Strangers in the Land: Patterns of American Nativism,* 2nd ed. (New York, Atheneum, 1969).

Hofstadter, Richard, *Anti-Intellectualism in American Life* (New York, Vintage Books, 1963).

Hofstadter, Richard, and C. DeWitt Hardy, *The Development and Scope of Higher Education in the United States* (New York, Columbia University Press, 1952).

Hofstadter, Richard, and Walter P. Metzger, *The Development of Academic Freedom in the United States* (New York, Columbia University Press, 1955).

Hofstadter, Richard, and Wilson Smith, eds., *American Higher Education: A Documentary History.* 2 vols. (Chicago and London, The University of Chicago Press, 1961).

Hollinshead, Bryon S., *Who Should Go to College?* (New York, Columbia University Press, 1952).

Horner, Harlan H., *The Life and Work of Andrew Sloan Draper* (Urbana, University of Illinois Press, 1934).

Hoyt, Donald P., *The Relationship Between College Grades and Adult Achievement: A Review of the Literature* (Iowa City, American College Testing Program, 1965).

Ivy, Andrew C., and Irwin Ross, *Religion and Race: Barriers to College?* (New York, Public Affairs Committee, 1949).

Jencks, Christopher and David Riesman, *The Academic Revolution* (Garden City, N.Y., Doubleday, 1968).

Johnston, John B., *The Liberal College in a Changing Society* (New York, D. Appleton-Century Co., 1930).

Joint UNESCO–IAU Research Programme in Higher Education, *Access to Higher Education,* 2 vols. (Paris, UNESCO, 1963, 1965).

Jones, Theodore Francis, *New York University 1832–1932* (New York, The New York University Press, 1933).

Kandel, Isaac L., *American Education in the Twentieth Century* (Cambridge, Harvard University Press, 1957).

Katz, Michael B., *The Irony of Early School Reform: Educational Innovation in Mid-Nineteenth Century Massachusetts* (Boston, Beacon Press, 1968).

Kelly, Robert Lincoln, ed., *The Effective College* (New York, The Association of American Colleges, 1928).

Kennedy, Gail, ed., *Education for Democracy: The Debate Over the Report of the President's Commission on Higher Education* (Boston, D. C. Heath, 1952).

Kolesnik, Walter B., *Mental Discipline in Modern Education* (Madison, The University of Wisconsin Press, 1962).

Krug, Edward A., *The Shaping of the American High School,* 2 vols. (Madison, Milwaukee, and London, The University of Wisconsin Press, 1964–1972).

Kurani, Habib Amin, *Selecting the College Student in America—A Study of Theory and Practice* (New York, Teachers College, Columbia University, 1931).

Lavin, David E., *The Prediction of Academic Performance: A Theoretical Analysis and Review of Research* (New York, Science Editions, John Wiley & Sons, 1967).

Lipset, Seymour Martin, and Reinhard Bendix, *Social Mobility in Industrial Society* (Berkeley and Los Angeles, University of California Press, 1959).

Lord, John King, *A History of Dartmouth College,* 2 vols. (Concord. The Rumford Press, 1913).

Machlup, Fritz, *The Production and Distribution of Knowledge in the United States* (Princeton, Princeton University Press, 1962).

Malik, Herbert, "A Historical Study of Admissions Practices in Four Year Undergraduate Colleges of the United States 1870–1915" (unpublished dissertation, Boston College, 1966).

McCarthy, Charles, *The Wisconsin Idea* (New York, Macmillan, 1912).

McCormick, Richard, *Rutgers: A Bicentennial History* (New Brunswick, Rutgers University Press, 1966).

McGrath, Earl J., ed., *Universal Higher Education* (New York, McGraw-Hill, 1966).

Mehl, Bernard, "The High School at the Turn of the Century: A Study of the Changes in the Aims and Programs of Public Secondary Education in the United States, 1890–1900" (unpublished dissertation, The University of Illinois, 1954).

Midwest Educator's Conference on Discriminations in Higher Education, Chicago, 1950, *Discriminations in Higher Education* (Washington, D.C., American Council on Education, 1951).

Monroe, Paul, ed., *Cyclopedia of Education,* 5 vols. (New York, Macmillan, 1911–1919).

Morrison, Wilma, *The School Record: Its Use and Abuse in College Admissions* (Princeton, College Entrance Examination Board, 1961).

National Commission on the Reform of Secondary Education, B. Frank Brown, Chairman, *The Reform of Secondary Education: A Report to the Public and the Profession* (New York, McGraw-Hill, 1973).

Nightengale, Augustus, *Hand-book of Requirements for Admission to the Colleges of the United States* (New York, 1879).

O'Hara, William T., and John G. Hill, Jr., *The Student, The College, The Law* (New York, Teachers College Press, 1972).

Orr, Charles W., *Admissions Policies and Practices in Negro Land-Grant Colleges* (New York, Teachers College, Columbia University, 1954).

Perkinson, Henry J., *The Imperfect Panacea: American Faith in Education 1865–1965* (New York, Random House, 1968).

Perry, Bliss, *The Amateur Spirit* (Boston and New York, Houghton Mifflin, 1904).

Pierson, George W., *The Eduation of American Leaders: Comparative Contributions of U.S. Colleges and Universities* (New York, Frederick Praeger, 1969).

Pollard, James E., *History of Ohio State University: The Story of Its First Seventy-Five Years 1873–1948* (Columbus, The Ohio State University Press, 1952).

Probst, Carrie Mae, *A Study of College Entrance Requirements* (Washington, American Association of University Women, 1930).

Riesman, David, and Verne A. Stadtman, *Academic Transformation* (New York, McGraw-Hill, 1973).

Ringer, Fritz K., *The Decline of the German Mandarins: The German Academic Community 1890–1933* (Cambridge, Harvard University Press, 1969).

Rischin, Moses, *The Promised City* (Cambridge, Harvard University Press, 1962).

Roper, Elmo, *Factors Affecting the Admission of High School Seniors to College* (Washington, D.C., American Council on Education, 1949).

Rudolph, Frederick, *The American College and University: A History* (New York, Vintage, 1962).

Sizer, Theodore, ed., *The Age of the Academies* (New York, Bureau of Publications, Teachers College, 1964).

Sizer, Theodore, *Secondary Schools at the Turn of the Century* (New Haven, Yale University Press, 1964).

Slosson, Edwin E., *Great American Universities* (New York, Macmillan, 1910).

Smelser, Neil, and Gabriel Almond, *Public Higher Education in California* (Berkeley, University of California Press, 1974).

Smith, Eugene R., et al., *Appraising and Recording Student Progress* (New York and London, Harper and Brothers, 1942).

Smith, George Baxter, *Who Would Be Eliminated—A Study of Selective Admission to College* (Lawrence, University of Kansas, School of Education, 1956).

Stephens, Frank F., *A History of the University of Missouri* (Columbia, University of Missouri Press, 1962).

Ten Brook, Andrew, *American State Universities: Their Origin and Progress* (Cincinnati, R. Clarke and Co., 1875).

Tewksbury, Donald C., *The Founding of American Colleges and Universities Before the Civil War* (New York, Teachers College, 1932).

Thirty Schools Tell Their Story: Each School Writes of Its Participation in the Eight Year Study (New York and London, Harper and Brothers, 1943).

Thresher, Brainerd A., *College Admissions and the Public Interest* (New York, College Entrance Examination Board, 1966).

Tomlinson, Lawrence Elliott, *College Entrance Requirements: A Study of Ideals, Trends, and Institutions in the United States as Related to Secondary Education* (Portland, Ore., Educational Studies, 1945).

Tyack, David B., *The One Best System: A History of American Urban Education* (Cambridge, Harvard University Press, 1974).

Veblen, Thorstein, *The Higher Learning in America: A Memorandum on the Conduct of Universities by Businessmen* (New York, Sagamore Press, 1957 [1918]).

Veysey, Laurence, *The Emergence of the American University* (Chicago, The University of Chicago Press, 1965).

Warner, William L., Robert Havighurst, and Martin B. Loeb, *Who Shall Be Educated? The Challenge of Unequal Opportunities* (New York and London, Harper and Brothers, 1944).

Wayne State University, College of Education, *Research Studies in Selective Admission and Placement* (Detroit, Wayne State University, 1939).

Wesley, Edgar B., *The NEA: The First Hundred Years—The Building of the Teaching Profession* (New York, Harper and Brothers, 1957).

Western Interstate Commission for Higher Education, *Selecting Students for Western Colleges and Universities* (Boulder, Colo., 1959).

White, Morton, and Lucia White, *The Intellectual Versus the City: From Thomas Jefferson to Frank Lloyd Wright* (New York and Toronto, Mentor Books, 1964).

Wiebe, Robert H., *The Search for Order: 1877–1920* (New York, Hill & Wang, 1967).

Wing, Cliff W., and Michael A. Wallach, *College Admissions and the Psychology of Talent* (New York, Chicago, etc., Holt, Rinehart and Winston, 1971).

Woodburn, James Albert, *History of the Indiana University*, 2 vols. (Bloomington, Indiana University Press, 1940).

Articles

Abbott, Allan, " 'Entrance English' from the Boy's Point of View," *Education* (October, 1901), 22:78–88.

Allen, William O., "College Admissions," *School and Society* (October 1, 1921), 14:235–240.

Allen, William O., "Who Shall Go to College?" *School and Society* (February 23, 1924), 19:230–232.

Allmendinger, David, "Strong Men of the Academic Revolution," *History of Education Quarterly* (Winter, 1973), 13:415–425.

Amen, Harlan P., "Is the Curriculum Crowded?" *Educational Review* (May, 1900), 19:417–436.

American Society of Zoologists, "College Entrance Option in Zoology," *Science,* n.s. (December 16, 1904), 20:850–853.

Anderson, Robert V. V., "The Selective University," *Education* (February, 1924), 337–347.

Angell, James R., "The Combination of Certificate and Examination Systems," *School Review* (March, 1912), 20:145–160.

Angell, James R., "The Over-Population of the College," *Harper's Magazine* (October, 1927), 155:529–538.

Anibal, E. W., "College Entrance as an Administrative Problem," *School and Society* (March 11, 1922), 15:274–277.

Atwood, Albert, "Who Should Go to College?" *Saturday Evening Post* (September 10, 1927), 200:24–25, 76, 81–2, 84.

Bagley, William C., "Entrance Requirements and 'College Domination' as Sources of Motivation in High-School Work," *School Review* (February, 1911), 19:73–84.

Bancroft, Cecil F. P., "Report of the Committee of Ten: From the Point of View of the Academy," *Educational Review* (March, 1894), 7:280–285.

Barnes, Harry Elmer, "The Education Factory for Mass Production," *Current History* (January, 1928), 27:478–488.

Beatley, Bancroft, "The Relative Standing of Students in Secondary School, on Comprehensive Entrance Examinations, and in College," *School Review* (February, 1922), 30:141–147.

Bergen, J. Y., "College Entrance Examinations," *Science,* n.s. (June 29, 1906), 23:981–982.

Bishop, Remsin, "College Entrance Requirements in Greek," *School Review* (June, 1896), 4:437–447.

Blaisdell, Thomas C., "Should Colleges Admit High-School Graduates Without Regard to Subjects Studied in the High School?" *School and Society* (March 11, 1916), 3:366–370.

Bolenbaugh, Lawrence, and William M. Proctor, "Relation of Subjects Taken in High School to Success in College," *Journal of Educational Research* (February, 1927), 15:87–92.

Bowman, John G., "College Entrance Requirements in Theory and Practice," *Independent* (January 21, 1909), 66:133–136.

Bradley, John E., "The Report of the Committee of Ten: From the Point of View of the Smaller Colleges," *Educational Review* (April, 1894), 7:370–374.

Briggs, L. B. R., "College Preparation," *Nation* (December 17, 1908), 87:599.

Briggs, L. B. R., "Transition from School to College," *Current Literature* (September, 1900), 29:320–321.

Brooks, Wendell, "Who Can Succeed in College?" *School nrd Society* (April 12, 1924), 19:423–427.

Bruce, Mary S., "College Entrance Requirements in French," *Educational Review* (April, 1907), 33:406–413.

Butts, R. Freeman, "Public Education and Political Community," *History of Education Quarterly* (Summer, 1974), 14:165–183.

Caldwell, Otis W., "Should High-School Botany and Zoology Be Taught with Reference to College Entrance Requirements?" *School Review* (January, 1907), 15:27–31.

Cary, C. P., "Proposed Changes in the Accrediting of High Schools," *School Review* (April, 1909), 17:223–229.

Chadsey, Charles E. "The Relation of the High School to the Community and to the College," *Journal of Proceedings and Addresses of the National Education Association,* 1909:203–207.

Churchman, Philip H., "Certification or Examinations for College Entrance," *Nation* (February 25, 1909), 88:194.

Clark, E. L., "Selection of Freshmen at Northwestern University College of Liberal Arts," *Educational Record* (April, 1927), 8:122–128.

Clark, John S., "The Report of the Committee of Ten: Art in Secondary Education—An Omission by the Committee of Ten," *Educational Review* (April, 1894), 7:374–381.

Cleary, T. Anne, "Test Bias: Validity of the S.A.T. for Negro and White Students in Integrated Colleges," *E.T.S. Research Bulletin,* 66–31 (1966).

Cleary, T. Anne, and T. L. Hilton, "An Investigation of Item Bias," *E.T.S. Research Bulletin,* 66–17 (1966).

Collar, W. C., "College Entrance Requirements in French and German," *School Review* (December, 1906), 14:758–759.

"College Entrance Requirements in English," *Educational Review* (April, 1909), 37:426–429.

"The Cost of a College Education," *The World's Work* (August, 1903), 6:3722–3723.

Cottrell, Donald P., "The Liberal Arts College Problem," *Teachers College Record* (February, 1932), 32:457–462.

Counts, George S., "Selection as a Function of a Secondary Education," *Journal of Proceedings and Addresses of the National Education Association,* 1929:596–603.

Cousens, John A., "Who Should Go to College?" *School and Society* (May 28, 1927), 25:613–617.

Cowley, William, "Historical and Statistical Analysis of College Admissions Criteria," *Association of American Colleges Bulletin* (December, 1940), 26:554–557.

Cremin, Lawrence, "The Revolution in American Secondary Education, 1893–1918" *Teachers College Record* (March, 1955), 56:295–308.

Cross, K. Patricia, "New Forms for New Functions," in Dyckman W. Vermilye, ed., *Lifelong Learners—A New Clientele for Higher Education* (San Francisco, Jossey-Bass, 1974).

Davis, Calvin O., "Reorganization of Secondary Education," *Educational Review* (October, 1911), 42:270–301.

Davis, Nathaniel F., "Is the Present Mode of Granting Certificate Rights to Preparatory Schools Satisfactory?" *School Review* (February, 1907), 15:145–152.

DeForest, Frederick M., "College Requirements in Latin and the School Curriculum," *Educational Review* (September, 1909), 38:109–121.

De Garmo, Charles, "Report of the Committee of Ten: From the Point of View of Educational Theory," *Educational Review* (March, 1894), 7:275–280.

Denny, Joseph V., "English Requirements," *School Review* (May, 1898), 6:339–343.

Deutsch, B., "The Social Aspect of College Entrance Restriction" *Education* (January, 1927), 47:272–279.

Distler, Theodore A., "The High-School Problem in Regard to College Entrance," *School and Society* (May 15, 1926), 23:629–630.

Egerton, John *"Adams* v. *Richardson:* Can Separate Be Equal?" *Change* (December–January, 1974–1975), 6, 10:29–36.

Eliot, Charles W., "The Gap between the Elementary Schools and the Colleges," *Journal of Proceedings and Addresses of the National Educational Association,* 1890:522–533.

Eliot, Charles W., "The Report of the Committee of Ten," *Educational Review* (February, 1894), 7:105–110.

Eliot, Charles W., "The Unity of Educational Reform," *Educational Review* (October, 1894), 8:209–226.

Eliot, Charles W., "What Has Been Gained in Uniformity of College Admissions Requirements in the Past Twenty Years?" *School Review* (December, 1904), 12:757–769.

"Entrance Requirements in English," *School Review* (March, 1898), 6:222–223.

Farrand, Wilson, "Are College Entrance Requirements Excessive?" *School Review* (January, 1908), 16:12–41.

Farrand, Wilson, "Are College Entrance Requirements Excessive—The Reasonable Solution," *Education* (May, 1909), 29:567–575.

Farrand, Wilson, "The Determination of Fitness for College" *School and Society* (May 21, 1927), 25:592–596.

Farrand, Wilson, "The Existing Relations Between School and College," *Educational Review* (February, 1903), 25:182–199.

Farrand, Wilson, "Five Years of the College Entrance Examination Board," *Educational Review* (October, 1905), 30:217–230.

Farrand, Wilson, "The Quantity of College Entrance Requirements," *School Review* (May, 1908), 16:341–343.

Fisher, Francis, D., "A Day and a Half in the Harvard Admissions Office," *Harvard Today* (Winter, 1975), 18, 2:11–12.

Forbes, Charles H., "Entrance Requirements and the College Degree," *Education* (January, 1913), 33:263–268.

Foster, William T., "The Movement for Uniformity in College Requirements," *Nation* (December 10, 1908), 87:571–572.

Foster, William T., "Our Democratic American Colleges," *Nation* (April 1, 1909), 88:324–326.

Foster, William T., "Should the High School Diploma Admit to College?" *Education* (December, 1905), 26:203–208.

Fowler, Henry T., "Entrance Requirements and the College Degree," *Education* (January, 1913), 33:269–275.

French, C. W., "Special Report of the Joint Committee on English Requirements," *School Review* (May, 1898), 6:344–349.

Furst, Clyde, "College Entrance Requirements," *Educational Record* (October, 1927), 8:295–309.

Ganong, W. A., "Suggestions for an Attempt to Secure a Standard College Entrance Option in Botany," *Science*, n.s (April 19, 1901), 13:611–616.

Gauss, Christian, "Should Johnny Go to College?" *Scribner's* (October, 1927), 82:411–416.

Glenny, Lyman A., "Nine Myths, Nine Realities: The Illusions of Steady State," *Change* December–January, 1974–1975), 6, 10:24–28.

Goodwin, Edward J., "A Comparison of College Entrance Examinations," *Educational Review* (December, 1903), 26:440–456.

Gosling, Thomas W., "The Relationship Between a University and the Public Schools," *School and Society* (March 27, 1926), 23:383–388.

Hadley, Arthur T., "Conflicting Views Regarding Entrance Examinations," *School Review* (December, 1900), 8:583–593.

Hanson, Charles L., "Recommendations of the Committee on College Entrance Requirements in English," *School Review* (May, 1904), 12:339–347.

Hanus, Paul H., "College Admissions Requirements in Mathematics," *School Review* (September, 1896), 4:535–538.

Harris, William T., "The Committee of Ten on Secondary Schools," *Educational Review* (January, 1894), 7:1–10.

Hart, Albert B., "College Entrance Requirements in History," *Educational Review* (December, 1895), 10:417–429.

Hargreaves, R. T., "To What Extent Should the High School Course Be Modified to Prepare Students for College?" *School and Society* (October 29, 1921), 14:358–363.

Hawkes, Herbert E., "Examinations and Mental Tests," *Educational Record* (1924), 5:28–39.

Herbst, Jurgen, "The Eighteenth Century Origins of the Split Between Private and Public Higher Education in the United States," *History of Education Quarterly* (Fall, 1975), 15:273–280.

Hinsdale, Burke A., "Discussion of Entrance Requirements in History," *School Review* (June, 1896), 4:438–442.

Hollister, H. A., "Some Results from the Accrediting of High Schools by State Universities," *Education* (November, 1908), 29:133–139.

Johnson, Elizabeth F., "A Proposed Plan of College Entrance Examinations," *Nation* (February 4, 1909), 88:111.

Johnston, J. B., "Predicting College Success for the High School Senior," *Educational Record* (January, 1928), 9:17–25.

Jones, Adam L., "Entrance Examinations and College Records: A Study in Correlation," *Educational Review* (September, 1914), 48:109–122.

Jones, Adam L., "Some New Methods of Admission to College," *Educational Review* (November, 1913), 46:351–360.

Jones, R. W., "Our Proposed New Requirements for Admission to College," *School Review* (February, 1901), 9:105–114.

Jordan, Mary A., "Report of the Delegates to the Conference on Uniform Entrance Requirements in English," *School Review* (December, 1905), 13:795–800.

Kelsey, Francis W., "Entrance Requirements in Latin," *School Review* (June, 1896), 4:443–451.

Kent, R. A., "Articulation of Colleges and Secondary Schools with Respect to College Admissions," *School and Society,* (June 14, 1924), 19:686–690.

Keyes, Charles H., "College Admissions Requirements," *Educational Review* (January, 1900), 19:59–67.

Kingsley, Clarence D., "Report of the Committee of Nine on the Articularion of High School and College," *Journal of Proceedings and Addresses of the National Education Association,* 1911:559–567.

Kirp, David L., and Mark G. Yudof, "DeFunis and Beyond," *Change* (November, 1974), 6, 9:22–26.

Kirtland, John C., "The College Requirements and the Secondary-School Work," *School Review* (December, 1905), 13:818–827.

Kirtland, John C., "Defects of College Entrance Requirements," *Nation* (October 24, 1907), 85:372.

Krug, Edward, "Charles W. Eliot and the Secondary School," *History of Education Quarterly* (September, 1961), 1:4–21.

Lewis, Grace T., "Is My Child To Be Debarred from College?" *Educational Review* (June, 1925), 70:26–31.

Lewis, W. D., "College Domination of High Schools," *Outlook* (December 11, 1909), 93:820–825.

Lisberger, Carolyn, "Living on the Quota," *North American Review* (1932), 234:117–123.

Lowell, A. L., "The College Student," *School and Society* (May 28, 1927), 25:617–621.

Lowell, D. O. S., "A New Method of Admission to College," *Educational Review* (November, 1902), 24:338–345.

Lowell, D. O. S., "The Setting of a College Admission Paper in English," *School Review* (December, 1902), 10:755–777.

MacLean, George, "Which Is Better: The Western Plan of Admitting Students to Colleges and Universities by Certificates from Duly Inspected Secondary Schools, or the Eastern Method of Admitting Only by Examinations Conducted by Representative Boards or Otherwise?" *Journal of Proceedings and Addresses of the National Educational Association,* 1905:501–512.

Main, John H. T., "Greek or Latin for Admission to College," *School Review* (September, 1908), 16:453–462.

Mann, C. R., "Industrial and Technical Training in the Secondary Schools and Its Bearing on College-Entrance Requirements," *School Review* (September, 1908), 16:425–438.

Mann, C. R., "The Interpretation of the College Entrance Examination Board's New Definition of the Requirement in Physics," *Educational Review* (September, 1909), 38:150–159.

Manny, Frank A., "The Background of the Certificate System," *Education* (December, 1909), 30:199–206.

McClelland, David C., "Testing for Competence Rather than for Intelligence," *American Psychologist* (January, 1973), 28:1–14.

McConn, Max, "The Co-operative Test Service," *The Journal of Higher Education* (May, 1931), 2:225–232.

McCrea, Nelson G., "The Latin Papers of the College Entrance Examination Board," *Educational Review* (June, 1904), 28:28–37.

McVey, Frank L., "Who Should Go to College?" *School and Society* (October 1, 1927), 26:410–414.

"Medical Schools Fair to Jews," *Literary Digest* (September 13, 1930), 106:20.

Meiklejohn, Alexander, "Are College Entrance Requirements Excessive?—The College Point of View," *Education* (May, 1909), 29:561–566.

Meiklejohn, Alexander, "Wisconsin's Experimental College," *The Survey* (June 1, 1927), 58:268–270.

Metzger, Walter P., "What Is a Profession?" in Program of General and Continuing Education in the Humanities, Columbia University, *Seminar Reports*, vol. 3, no. 1. (September 18, 1975).

Mooney, W. D., "Substitutes for Latin and Greek in Admission Requirements," *School Review* (March, 1902), 10:224–227.

Moore, F. W., "The Equalization of the Requirements for Admission into the Different Courses Leading to the First Collegiate Degree," *School Review* (March, 1902), 10:217–223.

Naylor, Natalie A., "The Ante-Bellum College Movement: A Reappraisal of Tewksbury's Founding of American Colleges and Universities," *History of Education Quarterly* (Fall, 1973), 13:261–274.

New England Association of Colleges and Preparatory Schools, "Report of the Conference on Entrance Requirements in History," *School Review* (October, 1895), 3:469–485.

New England Association of Teachers of English, "Report of the Standing Committee on Entrance Requirements: Historical Sketch of the Joint or National Conference on Entrance Requirements in English, With Especial Reference to the Conference of 1908," *School Review* (December, 1908), 16:646–659.

"The New English Requirements for College," *Nation* (April 1, 1909), 88:323–324.

Nicolson, Frank W., "The Certificate System in New England," *Educational Review* (December, 1911), 42:486–503.

Norlin, George, "The Liberal College," *School and Society* (January 22, 1927), 25:85–91.

Odell, Charles W., "Predicting the Scholastic Success of College Freshmen," *University of Illinois Bulletin* (September 13, 1927), 25, 2.

Orr, William, "Are College Entrance Requirements Excessive?—The Point of View of the Preparatory School," *Education* (May, 1909), 29:551–560.

O'Shea, M. V., "Shall We Keep the Doors Wide Open?" *Nation's Schools* (January, 1928), 1:33–36.

Owen, J. M., "Some Student Opinions on Entrance Requirements in English," *Education* (June, 1905), 25:619–626.

Palmer, Charles S., "Resumé and Critique of the Tabulated College Requirements in Natural Sciences," *School Review* (June, 1896), 4:452–460.

Parker, Francis W., "The Report of the Committee of Ten—Its Use for the Improvement of Teachers Now at Work in the Schools," *Educational Review* (May, 1894), 7:479–491.

Parmenter, Charles W., "Entrance Requirements and the College Degree," *Education* (January, 1913), 33:276–280.

Posner, Richard A., "The DeFunis Case and the Constitutionality of Preferential Treatment of Racial Minorities," in Philip A. Kurland, ed., *1974 Supreme Court Review* (Chicago and London, The University of Chicago Press, 1975), pp. 1–32.

Potts, David B., "American Colleges in the Nineteenth Century: From Localism to Denominationalism," *History of Education Quarterly* (Winter, 1971), 11:369–373.

Potts, David B., "Students and the Social History of American Higher Education," *History of Education Quarterly* (Fall, 1975), 15:317–327.

"Preparatory Course in English," *School Review* (September, 1897), 5:445–455.

Prettyman, Virgil, "The Lack of Uniformity in the History Requirements for Admission to College," *Educational Review* (December, 1911), 42:516–518.

Pritchett, Henry S., "Are Our Universities Overpopulated?" *Scribner's* (1923), 73:556–560.

Proctor, William M., "The High-School's Interest in Methods of Selecting Students for College Admission," *School and Society* (October 10, 1925), 22:441–448.

Ramaley, Francis, "Some Thoughts on College Entrance Requirements," *Education* (January, 1904), 24:277–280.

Ramsay, Charles C., "Report on Admission to College on Certificate and by Examination," *School Review* (December, 1900), 8:593–604.

Roberts, Alexander G., "A Program of Admission to and Elimination from a Tax-Supported State Institution," *School and Society* (October 20, 1923), 18:456–460.

"Round Table in English," *Journal of Proceedings and Addresses of the National Educational Association,* 1897:684–694.

Russell, James E., "The Educational Value of Examinations for Admission to College," *School Review* (January, 1903), 11:42–54.

Ryan, William Carson, "Selection as a Function of American Secondary Education," *Journal of Proceedings and Addresses of the National Education Association,* 1929:592–596.

Sachs, Julius, "The Report of the Committee of Ten: From the Point of View of the College Preparatory School," *Educational Review* (June, 1894), 8:75–83.

Sandison, Helen, "What Shall Be Determining Factors in Requirements for Admission to College Examinations?" *Journal of Proceedings and Addresses of the National Education Association,* 1926:427–430.

Sanford, Edmund C., "Entrance Requirements and the College Degree," *Education* (January, 1913), 33:281–288.

Scott, Walter D., "Intelligence Tests for Prospective Freshmen," *School and Society* (April 8, 1922), 15:384–388.

Seashore, Carl E., "Progressive Adjustment versus Entrance Elimination in a State University," *School and Society* (January 13, 1923), 17:29–35.

Secor, W. B., "Credit for Quality in the Secondary School," *Educational Review* (May, 1908), 35:486–490.

Seeyle, L. C., "College Entrance Requirements," *Educational Review* (April, 1908), 35:428–431.

Shackford, Martha H., "The College Entrance Examination Board's Questions in English," *Education* (December, 1906), 27:231–239.

Shiels, Merrill, "Why Johnny Can't Write," *Newsweek* (December 8, 1975), 86, 23:58–65.

[Smith, Ira], "The Admission of High School Graduates to the University of Michigan," *School and Society* (March 27, 1926), 23:396–397.

Smith, Ira, "From High School to College," *University of Michigan Bulletin* (June, 1927).

Snyder, Morton, "Selecting College Freshmen," *Progressive Education* (October-December, 1927), 4:253–259.

Steffens, Lincoln, "Sending a State to College," *American Magazine* (February, 1909), 350–363.

Story, Ronald, "Harvard Students, the Boston Elite, and the New England Preparatory System, 1800–1876," *History of Education Quarterly* (Fall, 1975), 11:281–298.

Stuart, M. H., "The Cosmopolitan High School in Its Relation to College Entrance," *Journal of Proceedings and Addresses of the National Education Association,* 1913:471–478.

Tanner, George W., "Report of the Committee Appointed by the English Conference to Inquire into the Teaching of English in the High Schools of the Middle West," *School Review* (January, 1907), 15:32–45.

Taylor, Charles K., "The College Entrance Problem—And a Solution," *Outlook* (April 27, 1927), 145:523–524.

Thomas, Isaac, "The New England Entrance Certificate Board from the Standpoint of Schools," *School Review* (November, 1904), 12:696–705.

Thorndike, E. L., "An Empirical Study of College Entrance Examinations," *Science,* n.s. (June 1, 1906), 23:839–845.

Thorndike, E. L., "The Future of the College Entrance Examination Board," *Educational Review* (May, 1906), 31:470–483.

Toops, Herbert A., "The Prediction of Scholastic Success in College," *School and Society* (February 26, 1927), 25:265–268.

"Uniform Entrance Examinations in English Language and Literature," *School Review* (November, 1894), 2:562–567.

Wheeler, Benjamin I., "College Requirements in Greek," *School Review* (February, 1893), 1:73–83.

Whitman, A. D., "The Selective Value of the Examinations of the College Entrance Examination Board," *School and Society* (April 30, 1927), 25:522–525.

Whitney, A. S., "Methods in Use of Accrediting Schools," *School Review* (February, 1903), 11:138–148.

Wilkinson, John W., "Problems in High School Curricula," *Education* (December, 1903), 24:193–208.

Wood, Ben D., "Functions and Methods of Admissions Offices," *School and Society* (May 17, 1924), 19:575–576.

Young, Walter H., "The High Schools of New England as Judged by the Standard of the College Certificate Board," *School Review* (February, 1907), 15:134–144.

THE UNIVERSITY OF MICHIGAN

Archival

Michigan Historical Collections, Bentley Historical Library, The University of Michigan, Ann Arbor, Michigan

James Burrill Angell Papers

Thomas M. Cooley Papers

Faculty Committee Reports, Petitions, Resolutions, etc.

Henry Simmons Frieze Papers

Arthur Hall Papers

Policy and Organization of the Literature School Papers

Records, 1874, of Kalamazoo Case, or *Stuart et al.* v. *School District No. 1*

Records of the Dean of the College of Literature, Arts and Science

Records of High School Accreditation, Bureau of School Services of the University of Michigan

Alexander Winchill Papers

Public Documents

Annual Report of the Superintendent of Public Instruction of the State of Michigan with Accompanying Documents

Demmon, Isaac N., ed., *University of Michigan Regents' Proceedings, 1837–1864* (Ann Arbor, 1915). *Proceedings of the Board of Regents, 1864–1930*

Newspapers

Ann Arbor Courier and Visitant
Detroit Evening News
Kalamazoo Gazette
Michigan Alumnus
Michigan Argus
Michigan Chronicle

University Records, Proceedings, Reports, etc.

University of Michigan, *The President's Report to the Board of Regents,* 1853–1909, 1920–1930.
University of Michigan, College of Science, Literature and Arts, Faculty Record

Books and Monographs

Adams, Charles K., *Historical Sketch of the University of Michigan* (Ann Arbor, The University of Michigan, 1876).

Angell, James Burrill, *The Reminiscences of James Burrill Angell* (New York, Longmans, Green and Co., 1912).

Angell, James Burrill, *Selected Addresses* (New York, Longmans, Green and Co., 1912).

Butler, Leslie A., *The Michigan Schoolmasters' Club: A Story of the First Seven Decades, 1886–1957* (Ann Arbor, The University of Michigan, 1958).

Davis, Calvin O., *Public Secondary Education* (New York, Rand McNally, 1917).

Dunbar, Willis F., "The Influence of the Protestant Denominations on Higher Education in Michigan," (unpublished dissertation, The University of Michigan, 1939).

Dunbar, Willis F., *The Michigan Record in Higher Education* (Detroit, Wayne State University Press, 1963).

Eggertsen, Claude, ed., *Studies in the History of Higher Education in Michigan* (Ann Arbor, School of Education, The University of Michigan, 1950).

Farrand, Elizabeth M., *History of the University of Michigan* (Ann Arbor, The University of Michigan, 1885).

Goodsell, Charles True, and Willis F. Dunbar, *Centennial History of Kalamazoo College* (Kalamazoo, Kalamazoo College, 1933).

Haven, Erastus O., *Autobiography of Erastus O. Haven* (New York, Phillips and Hunt, 1883).

Hinsdale, Burke A., *History of the University of Michigan* (Ann Arbor, The University of Michigan, 1906).

Huber, John Parker, *Toward Camelot—The Admission of Women to the University of Michigan* (Ann Arbor, Michigan Historical Collections, 1970).

McCracken, S. B., *Religion in the University—A Review of the Agitation of the Subject Before the Legislature of Michigan During the Session of 1873* (Detroit, Detroit Free Press, 1873).

McGuigan, Dorothy Gies, *A Dangerous Experiment: 100 Years of Women at the University of Michigan* (Ann Arbor, Center for Continuing Education of Women, 1970).

Peckham, Howard H., *The Making of the University of Michigan 1817–1967* (Ann Arbor, The University of Michigan Press, 1967).

Perry, Charles M., *Henry Philip Tappan, Philosopher and University President* (Ann Arbor, The University of Michigan Press, 1933).

Putnam, Daniel, *The Development of Primary and Secondary Public Education in Michigan* (Ann Arbor, George Wahr, 1904).

Shaw, Wilfred B., *A Short History of the University of Michigan* (Ann Arbor, George Wahr, 1934).

Shaw, Wilfred B., ed., *The University of Michigan: An Encyclopedic Survey,* 9 vols. (Ann Arbor, The University of Michigan, 1941–58).

Smith, Shirley W., *James Burrill Angell: An American Influence* (Ann Arbor, The University of Michigan Press, 1954).

Stout, John Elbert, *The Development of High-School Curricula in the North Central States from 1860 to 1918* (Chicago, The University of Chicago Press, 1921).

Article

Brown, Elizabeth Gaspar, "The Initial Admission of Negro Students at the University of Michigan," *Michigan Quarterly Review* (Winter, 1963).

COLUMBIA UNIVERSITY
Archival

American Jewish Congress, New York City
   Records of the American Jewish Congress

American Jewish Historical Society, Waltham, Mass.
   Richard J. H. Gotthiel Collection
   Stephen Wise Papers

Columbia University Archives, Butler Library, New York City
   John Burgess Papers
   Nicholas Murray Butler Papers
   Harry J. Carman Papers
   Columbia College Papers
   Melvil Dewey Papers
   Thomas Scott Fiske Papers
   Frederick P. Keppel Papers
   Seth Low Papers
   Nelson G. McCrea Papers
   John B. Pine Papers
   Lillian Wald Papers

Columbia University Files, Low Library, New York City
   Records of the University, 1890–1950

Michigan Historical Collections
   Albert B. Jacobs Papers

New York Public Library
   William Barclay Parsons Papers

New York State Education Department Library, Albany, N.Y.
   F. Spaulding Papers
   New York State Department of Public Instruction Papers

New York State Regents Inquiry into the Character and Cost of Education in New York State Papers

New York State Temporary Commission on the Need for a State University Papers

University of Illinois
Andrew Sloan Draper Personal Papers

Public Documents

Berkowitz, David S., *Inequality of Opportunity in Higher Education: A Study of Minority Group and Related Barriers to College Admission* (Albany, New York Legislative Document no. 3, 1948).

Bienstock, Theodore, and Warren W. Coxe, *Decrease in College Discrimination—A Repeat Study and Comparison of High School Graduates to Colleges in New York State in 1946 and in 1949* (Albany, Division of Research, State Education Department, The University of the State of New York, 1950).

City of New York, City Council, Committee on Rules, Privileges and Elections, *In the Matter of Res. 128, Resolution Urging the New York City Tax Commission to Immediately Investigate Charges of Discrimination Against Columbia University and to Take Steps to Withdraw Tax Exemptions from Columbia University If Charges Are Found To Be True, May 17, 1946* (New York, Sills Reporting Service, 1946).

New York City Mayor's Committee on Unity, *Report on Inequality of Opportunity in Higher Education* (New York, 1946).

New York City Record, December 26, 1946.

Record of the 1938 New York State Constitutional Convention (Albany, 1939).

Regents' Inquiry into the Character and Cost of Public Education in the State of New York, Luther H. Gulick, director, *Education for American Life: A New Program for the State of New York* (New York, McGraw-Hill, 1938).

State of New York, Temporary Commission on the Need for a State University, *Public Hearing, Chancellor's Hall, State Education Department Building, Albany, New York, October 20, 1947* (Albany, 1947).

State of New York, Temporary Commission on the Need for a State University, *Report* (Albany, New York, 1948).

Wilson, Harold E., director, *A Study of Policies, Procedures and Practices in Admission to Medical Schools in New York State* (Albany, State Education Department, The University of the State of New York, 1953).

Newspapers

Columbia Daily Spectator
New York Sun
New York Times

University Records, Proceedings, Reports, etc.

Columbia College, *Minutes of the Faculty of Columbia College,* 1892–1950

Columbia University Council, *Minutes of the Columbia University Council,* 1890–1920

Columbia University Council, *Minutes of the Executive Committee of the Columbia University Council,* 1910–1920

Columbia University, *Annual Reports of the President and Treasurer to the Trustees,* 1889–1947

Pine, John B., ed., *Charters, Acts of the Legislature, Official Documents and Records,* 3 vols. (New York, Columbia University, 1920–1952).

The Trustees of Columbia University, *Minutes of the Committee on Education*, 1905–1923.

The Trustees of Columbia University, *Minutes of the Trustees of Columbia University*, 1889–1950

Books and Monographs

Barnard, Frederick, *Causes Affecting the Attendance of Undergraduates in the Incorporated Colleges of the City of New York* (New York, D. Van Nostrand, 1872).

Broun, Heywood, and George Britt, *Christians Only: A Study in Prejudice* (New York, The Vanguard Press, 1931).

Burge, Howard G., *Our Boys: A study of 245,000 Sixteen, Seventeen and Eighteen Year Old Employed Boys of the State of New York* (State of New York, Military Training Commission, Bureau of Vocational Training, 1921).

Burgess, John W., *Reminiscences of an American Scholar: The Beginnings of Columbia University* (New York, Columbia University Press, 1934).

Butler, Nicholas Murray, *Across the Busy Years: Recollections and Reflections*, 2 vols. (New York, Charles Scribner's Sons, 1939–1940).

Carmichael, Oliver, *New York Establishes a State University* (Nashville, Vanderbilt University Press, 1955).

Coon, Horace, *Columbia: Colossus on the Hudson* (New York, Dutton, 1947).

Cremin, Lawrence, David A. Shannon, and Mary E. Townsend, *A History of Teachers College, Columbia University* (New York, Columbia University Press, 1954).

Elliott, Edward C., ed., *The Rise of a University*, vol. 2, *The University in Action, from the Annual Reports, 1902–1935, of Nicholas Murray Butler* (New York, Columbia University Press, 1937).

Fulton, John, ed., *Memoirs of Frederick A. P. Barnard* (New York and London, Macmillan, 1896).

Gifford, Walter J., *Historical Development of the New York State High School System* (Albany, J. B. Lyon Co., 1922).

Goebel, Julius, *A History of the School of Law, Columbia University* (New York, Columbia University Press, 1955).

Hammack, David C., "The Centralization of New York City's School System, 1896: A Social Analysis of a Decision" (unpublished masters essay, Columbia University, 1969).

Howe, Irving, *The World of Our Fathers: The Journey of the East European Jews and the Life They Found and Made* (New York, Harcourt Brace Jovanovich, 1976).

Keating, James Martin, "Seth Low and the Development of Columbia University" (unpublished dissertation, Teachers College, 1973).

Keppel, Frederick P., *Columbia* (New York, Oxford University Press, 1914).

Keppel, Frederick P., *The Undergraduate and His College* (Boston and New York, Houghton Mifflin, 1917).

Lerner, Max, ed., *The Portable Veblen* (New York, The Viking Press, 1948).

Mathews, Brander, ed., *A History of Columbia University* (New York, Columbia University Press, 1904).

Miner, Dwight C., ed., *A History of Columbia College on Morningside* (New York, Columbia University Press, 1954).

Pupin, Michael, *From Immigrant to Inventor* (New York, Charles Scribner's Sons, 1960 [1922]).

Russell, James Earl, *Founding Teachers College, Reminiscences of the Dean Emeritus* (New York, Teachers College, 1937).

Russell, William F., ed., *The Rise of a University*, vol. 1, *The Later Days of Old Columbia College from the Annual Reports of Frederick A. P. Barnard, President of Columbia College, 1864–1889* (New York, Columbia University Press, 1937).

Summerscales, William, *Affirmation and Dissent: Columbia's Response to the Crisis of World War I* (New York, Teachers College Press, 1970).

Talese, Gay, *The Kingdom and the Power* (New York and Cleveland, The World Publishing Co., 1969).

Thomas, M. Halsey, *Bibliography of Nicholas Murray Butler 1872–1932* (New York, Columbia University Press, 1934).

Van Denburg, Joseph King, *Causes of the Elimination of Students in Public Secondary Schools of New York City* (New York, Teachers College, Columbia University, 1911).

Whittemore, Richard, *Nicholas Murray Butler and Public Education 1862–1911* (New York, Teachers College Press, 1970).

Wood, Ben D., *Measurement in Higher Education* (Yonkers-on-Hudson, World Book Publishing Co., 1923).

Articles

Bowles, Frank H., and Harry Schwartz, "The Pulitzer Scholars: A Record of Thirty Years," *Columbia University Quarterly* (1939), 3:263–271.

[Butler, Nicholas Murray], "Democracy, True and False," *Educational Review* (April, 1904), 27: 431–432.

[Butler, Nicholas Murray], "The Dual System of State Educational Control in New York," *Educational Review* (March, 1903), 25:322–324.

Butler, Nicholas Murray, "A New Method of Admission to College," *Educational Review* (September, 1909), 38:160–172.

Butler, Nicholas Murray, "The Reform of Secondary Education," *Century* (June, 1894), 48:314–316.

Butler, Nicholas Murray, "Regulation of Secondary Education," *The Nation* (January 18, 1894), 58:44–45.

Butler, Nicholas Murray, "Relation of Colleges to the Preparatory Schools," *Science*, n.s. (November 26, 1886), 8:467–468.

Butler, Nicholas Murray, "The Scope and Function of Secondary Education," *Educational Review* (June, 1898), 16:15–27.

Butler, Nicholas Murray, "True and False Democracy," *Educational Review* (April, 1907), 33:325–343.

Butler, Nicholas Murray, "Uniform College Admissions Requirements with a Joint Board of Examiners," *Educational Review* (January, 1900), 19:68–74.

Chadwick, Harold King, "Why the Columbia College Student Body Is Becoming More National in Character," *Columbia Alumni News* (April, 1922), 13:366.

Hawkes, Herbert E., "Intelligence Tests as One Basis of College Admission," *Journal of Proceedings and Addresses of the National Education Association*, 1926:438.

Hawkes, Herbert E., "The Limitation of Numbers Entering College," *Columbia Alumni News* (November, 1923), 15:79–80.

Howe, Irving, "Immigrant Jewish Families in New York: The End of the World of Our Fathers," *New York* (October 13, 1975), 81, 4:51–77.

[Jones, Adam Leroy], "Annual Report of the Director of Admissions," *Columbia Alumni News* (December 7, 1917), 9:259.

Russell, William F., "Nicholas Murray Butler, 1862–1947," *Teachers College Record* (January, 1948), 49:229–231.

Torch, M. G., pseud., "The Spirit of Morningside: Some Notes on Columbia University," *Menorah Journal* (March, 1930), 18:253–261.

Whittemore, Richard, "Nicholas Murray Butler and the Teaching Profession," *History of Education Quarterly* (September, 1961), 1:22–37.

Whittemore, Richard, "Sovereignty in the University: Teachers College and Columbia," *Teachers College Record* (March, 1965), 66:509–518.

THE UNIVERSITY OF CHICAGO

Archival

University of Chicago Library
     Presidents' Papers, 1890–1925, 1925–1945
     Harold H. Swift Papers

Books and Monographs

Gallup, Ethel Esther, "A Personnel Study of First Year Students in the University of Chicago," (unpublished masters essay, The University of Chicago, 1926).

Goodspeed, Thomas W., *The Story of the University of Chicago 1890–1925* (Chicago, The University of Chicago Press, 1925).

Hutchins, Robert, *The Higher Learning in America* (New Haven, Yale University Press, 1936).

Potthoff, Edward F., "A Statistical and Analytical Study of the Selective Admission of Chicago Students" (unpublished dissertation, The University of Chicago, 1928).

Present and Former Members of the Faculty, *The Idea and Practice of General Education: An Account of the College of the University of Chicago* (Chicago, The University of Chicago Press, 1950).

Reeves, Floyd W., and John Dale Russell, eds., *Admission and Retention of University Students* (Chicago, The University of Chicago Press, 1933).

Scates, Douglass, *Selective Admission and Selective Retention at the University of Chicago* (Chicago, The University of Chicago Press, 1926).

Sheean, Vincent, *Personal History* (Garden City, N.Y., Doubleday, Doran and Co., 1936).

Storr, Richard J., *Harper's University: The Beginnings—A History of The University of Chicago* (Chicago and London, The University of Chicago Press, 1966).

Articles

Caldwell, Otis W., "The New University of Chicago Plan for College Admission," *Journal of Proceedings and Addresses of the National Education Association,* 1911:572–575.

Mann, C. R., "Changes in Entrance Requirements at the University of Chicago," *Educational Review* (September, 1911), 42:186–191.

Pittenger, L. A., "Ethical and Unethical Practices and Procedures in the Recruiting of Students from Secondary Schools by Institutions of Higher Education," *The North Central Association Quarterly* (July, 1937), 12:13–16.

THE CITY UNIVERSITY OF NEW YORK

Archival

City University of New York
     Records of the Office of University Relations
     Records of the Secretary of the Board of Higher Education
     Records of Vice Chancellor Timothy Healy
     Records of Vice Chancellor T. E. Hollander

New York Public Library

John H. Finlay Papers

New York State Education Department Library

James Allen Papers

Public Documents

Joint Legislative Committee on the State Education System, *Report of the New York City Sub-committee Concerning Administration and Financing of the Public Education System of the City of New York Under the Control of That City's Board of Education and the Board of Higher Education* (Albany, Williams, 1944).

Newspapers

Kingsman
New York Daily News
New York Post
New York Times

University Records, Proceedings, Reports, etc.

Administrative Council, *Minutes of the Administrative Council,* 1946–71

Board of Higher Education, *Minutes of the Board of Higher Education,* 1945–71

Board of Higher Education, "Statement of Administrative Policy Adopted by the Board of Higher Education, November 12, 1969," Office of the Secretary of the Board of Higher Education.

City University of New York, *The Administration of the City University of New York* (New York, The City University of New York, 1967).

City University of New York, *Master Plan,* 1964–1971

City University of New York, "Report of the Fall Undergraduate Ethnic Census," 1967–70

City University Senate, *Minutes of the City University Senate* 1968–70

City University Senate, "Report on Special Admissions Policy," adopted by the Senate on February 12, 1969.

Committee on Higher Education, Henry T. Heald, Chairman, *Meeting the Increased Demand for Higher Education in New York State* (Albany, 1960).

Cottrell, Donald P., Adrian Rondileau, and Leo S. Schumer, *Public Higher Education in the City of New York: Report of the Master Plan Study* (New York, 1950).

Dispenzieri, Angelo, and Seymour Giniger, *The College Discovery Program: A Synthesis of Research* (New York, The City University Research and Evaluation Unit, 1969).

Executive Committee, Board of Higher Education, *Minutes of the Executive Committee of the Board of Higher Education,* 1969.

Heil, Louis, Louis Long, Marjorie Smiley, and Emma Spaney, *An Investigation of Criteria for Admission to the City University of New York* (New York, City University of New York, 1961).

Holy, Thomas C., *A Long Range Plan for the City University of New York 1961–1975* (New York, The Board of Higher Education, 1962).

Lustig, Harry, "Minority Report: Committee on Admissions," October 16, 1969, Office of the Secretary of the Board of Higher Education.

University Commission on Admissions, *Report and Recommendations to the Board of Higher Education of the City of New York, October 7, 1969* (New York, The City University of New York, 1969).

330   The Qualified Student

Books and Monographs

Birnbaum, Robert, and Joseph Goldman, *The Graduates: A Follow-Up Study of New York City High School Graduates of 1970* (New York, Center for Social Research and Office for Research in Higher Education, CUNY, 1971).

Gordon, Sheila, "The Transformation of the City University of New York 1945–1970" (unpublished dissertation, Teachers College, Columbia University, 1975).

Rudy, S. Willis, *The College of the City of New York: A History 1847–1947* (New York, The City College Press, 1949).

THE UNIVERSITY OF ILLINOIS

Archival

University of Illinois
    Andrew Sloan Draper Faculty Correspondence
    Andrew Sloan Draper Personal Correspondence
    Selim H. Peabody, Speeches and Sermons, 1881–1891, 1894

Books and Monographs

Johnson, Ronald, "Captain of Education: An Intellectual Biography of Andrew Sloan Draper 1848–1910" (unpublished dissertation, University of Illinois, 1970).

Nevins, Allan, *Illinois* (New York, Oxford University Press, 1917).

Solberg, Winton V., *The University of Illinois 1867–1894: An Intellectual and Cultural History* (Urbana, Chicago, and London, The University of Illinois Press, 1968).

HARVARD UNIVERSITY

Archival

Harvard University Archives, Widener Library, Cambridge, Mass.
    Charles W. Eliot Papers
    Abbott Lawrence Lowell Papers
    David Gordon Lyon Papers
Boston Public Library
    Hugo Munsterberg Papers

University Records, Proceedings, Reports, etc.

The Harvard Graduates Magazine
President's Annual Report, Harvard University, 1870–1925

Books and Monographs

Cotton, Edward H., *The Life of Charles W. Eliot* (Boston, Small Maynard and Co., 1926).

Hawkins, Hugh, *Between Harvard and America—The Educational Leadership of Charles W. Eliot* (New York, Oxford University Press, 1972).

James, Henry, *Charles W. Eliot: President of Harvard University 1869–1909* (Boston and New York, Houghton Mifflin Co., 1930).

Krug, Edward A., ed., *Charles W. Eliot and Popular Education* (New York, Teachers College, Columbia University, 1961).

Morison, Samuel Eliot, ed., *The Development of Harvard University Since the Inauguration of President Eliot 1869–1929* (Cambridge, Harvard University Press, 1930).

Yeomans, Henry Aaron, *Abbott Lawrence Lowell 1856–1943* (Cambridge, Harvard University Press, 1948).

Articles

"Admission to Harvard College," *Science*, n.s. (July 7, 1911), 34:23.

Davis, Harvey N., "The New Harvard Plan for College Admission," *Journal of Proceedings and Addresses of the National Education Association*, 1911:567–571.

Flexner, Abraham, "An Innovation in Harvard Entrance Requirements," *Nation* (March 8, 1906), 82:199.

"Harvard's New Entrance Tests," *Nation* (January 26, 1911), 92:80–81.

"Harvard 'Talk' About Jews," *The Literary Digest* (June 24, 1922), 73:28.

Johnson, Franklin W., "The New Harvard Entrance Requirements," *School Review* (June, 1911), 19:412–413.

Moore, Clifford H., "A New Plan of Admission to Harvard College," *Educational Review* (June, 1911), 42:71–78.

Ropes, J. H., "New Harvard Entrance Requirements," *Science*, n.s. (May 26, 1911), 33:793–801.

Starr, Harry, "The Affair at Harvard—What the Students Did," *Menorah Journal* (October, 1922), 8:263–276.

Index